THE PARTY PERIOD
AND PUBLIC POLICY

THE PARTY PERIOD AND PUBLIC POLICY

American Politics from the Age of Jackson to the Progressive Era

Richard L. McCormick

OXFORD UNIVERSITY PRESS
New York   Oxford

Oxford University Press

Oxford   New York   Toronto
Delhi   Bombay   Calcutta   Madras   Karachi
Petaling Jaya   Singapore   Hong Kong   Tokyo
Nairobi   Dar es Salaam   Cape Town
Melbourne   Auckland

and associated companies in
Berlin   Ibadan

First published by Oxford University Press, Inc., 1986

200 Madison Avenue, New York, New York 10016

First issued as an Oxford University Press paperback, 1989

Oxford is the registered trademark of Oxford University Press

Library of Congress Cataloging-in-Publication Data
McCormick, Richard L.
The party period and public policy.
Includes index.
1. Progressivism (United States politics)—Addresses, essays, lectures.
2. United States—Politics and government—1865-1933—Addresses, essays, lectures.
3. Political parties—United States—History—Addresses, essays, lectures.
I. Title. E743.M33   1986   322.4'4'0973   85-30976
ISBN 0-19-503860-6
ISBN 0-19-504784-2 pbk.

2   4   6   8   10   9   7   5   3   1
Printed in the United States of America

For Warren I. Susman
In memory

Preface

This book is about some of the dominant characteristics of American politics and government in the nineteenth and early twentieth century. It is also a study of recent scholarship on these subjects and an effort to identify fruitful directions for future research. Originally written as separate articles, the chapters that follow do not provide a comprehensive narrative of American politics from the Jackson period to the Progressive era. But they do have common themes, and they present aspects of a single argument. Each of these essays is concerned, in one way or another, with the mass political parties—from their emergence in the 1820s and 1830s, through their heyday in the mid- and late-1800s, to their transformation in the early 1900s. Each deals, as well, with governance during that same century, especially with the economic policies of promotion and distribution—and later regulation—that formed the most characteristic functions of American government at every level. Above all, each of these essays tries to contribute to sorting out the complicated relationships between politics and policy during the long era that I have labeled the "party period" in American history.

Although these articles share the same themes, they vary in scope and focus. First comes an introduction laying out the leading concerns of the chapters to follow. Next are three historiographic essays that summarize and critique several of the most important recent trends in the writing of American political history. The first of these scrutinizes the ethnocultural voting studies, the second looks at the studies of realignments and critical elections, and the third analyzes some more recent efforts to do a "social analysis" of political history. If I have occasionally been a tough critic of these "schools," I hope that I have not failed to recognize their very considerable contributions to our understanding of American political history. The next three essays all treat the political parties, but they do so in diverse ways. The first is an encyclopedia article synthesizing the history of American parties and relating it to changing patterns of governance. This is the only essay in the book that strays significantly beyond the party period, and it differs from most of the others, as well, in having been written originally for a general rather than a scholarly audience. In its major argument, however, this article anticipates the more specialized piece that follows, the theme essay for the entire volume on the party period and its policies. The last article in this section also carries forward a subject introduced in the general essay on parties, in this case the anti-partyism that always formed a major element in American political culture. The final three articles all concern the political changes of the early 1900s when the party period's distinctive patterns of politics and governance were disrupted. The first of these essays, which like the encyclopedia article was intended for general readers, assesses contemporary interpretations of progressivism and suggests some directions for study. The second traces the course of political and governmental change in a single state, New York, while the last essay offers a theory about how progressivism brought similar changes to the nation at large.

Seven of these articles have previously appeared in print, and I have largely resisted the temptation to try to improve them here. I have, however, corrected a number of errors and made certain stylistic changes for the sake of consistency from one article to the next. In a few instances, I have rewritten brief passages either for the sake of clarity or to eliminate the direct repetition of an occasional sentence that appeared in more than one essay. In no case have I altered the substance of the articles. They stand essentially unchanged.

Most historical studies depend on the work of others, and this book does so to an unusual degree. It is the product of extended dialogues that I have carried on (usually in private but sometimes in public) with scholars in the field of American political history ever since I began graduate school a decade and a half ago. Inspired partly by reactions against the work of others but more frequently by the desire to understand and extend their labors, these articles were written to help me come to terms with what I considered to be some of the most important developments in nineteenth- and early twentieth-century American political history. All of these essays thus rely heavily on the existing scholarship, although a number of them also reflect my own original research. My fondest hope for this book is that fellow historians will regard the ideas it expresses as sufficiently interesting to warrant the continuation of our dialogues.

A great number of historians have already given me their reactions to one or more of these articles, usually prior to my completion of the final draft. Whatever strengths these essays may possess is due in significant part to the comments and suggestions they provided. In listing these men and women here I wish to thank them warmly for their help—but not to implicate any of them in notions they may still consider wrongheaded: Paula Baker, Rudolph M. Bell, Paul G. E. Clemens, Mary O. Furner, Lloyd C. Gardner, Gerald N. Grob, William H. Harbaugh, Michael F. Holt, Paul Kleppner, Marc W. Kruman, Suzanne Lebsock, Arthur S. Link, William A. Link, Katheryne C. McCormick, Richard P. McCormick, Peyton McCrary, Samuel T. McSeveney, William L. O'Neill, Gerald Pomper, James Reed, John F. Reynolds, Daniel T. Rodgers, Herbert H. Rowen, Joel H. Silbey, Thomas P. Slaughter, Warren I. Susman, David P. Thelen, Barbara M. Tucker, Harry L. Watson, Robert F. Wesser, R. Hal Williams, and C. Vann Woodward.

Among the historians listed above, fully a dozen are my colleagues at Rutgers University. Seeing their names reminds me what an imaginative and lively history department we inhabit together. Several of these articles were completed during two leaves of absence from teaching when I was in residence at the Shelby Cullom Davis Center for Historical Studies at Princeton University (1981–82) and at the Woodrow Wilson International Center for Scholars at the Smithsonian Institution (1985). I am very grateful to the directors of these two centers, Lawrence Stone and James H. Billington, respectively, for the stimulating scholarly environments they afforded me and, even more, to the other Davis and Wilson Fellows who shared with me their thoughts and their camaraderie during our time together. The Rutgers University Research Council has always been generous in providing grants to assist my research, and most of the articles in this book have benefited from that help. Sheldon Meyer of Oxford University Press encouraged me to publish these essays and gave me in full measure the personal and editorial support for which he is justly famous among American historians. I thank him very sincerely for making this book possible.

Finally, all books depend upon some special people without whom neither scholarship nor anything else would mean very much. These people have helped me in different ways to write this book, some simply by being my friends: Harvey Sudzin, John Reinus, Marc W. Kruman, Paul G. E. Clemens, David M. Oshinsky, Dorothy Boulia, Katheryne C. McCormick, and Richard P. McCormick. Each of them knows what I mean. Elizabeth Wells McCormick was born too recently even to slow this book down, but I trust she will make up for that by the time I complete another. I certainly hope so. Her mother, Suzanne Lebsock, greatly assisted me in writing a number of these essays, but Suzanne helps far more every day by sharing my life and letting me share hers. Warren I. Susman died as I was finishing this book. I have placed his name at the beginning because I want everyone who knew this extraordinary man to know how much his scholarship and friendship meant to me.

New Brunswick   R. L. M.
January 1986

Acknowledgments

The essays in this book that have been published before appear here with the kind permission of the journals and publications in which they first appeared: "Ethno-Cultural Interpretations of Nineteenth-Century American Voting Behavior," *Political Science Quarterly* 89 (June 1974): 351–77; "The Realignment Synthesis in American History," *Journal of Interdisciplinary History* 13 (Summer 1982): 85–105, Copyright © 1982 by the Massachusetts Institute of Technology and the editors of *The Journal of Interdisciplinary History*; "Political Parties," in Jack P. Greene, ed., *Encyclopedia of American Political History* (New York, 1984), pp. 939–63; "The Party Period and Public Policy: An Exploratory Hypothesis," *Journal of American History* 66 (September 1979): 279–98; "Progressivism: A Modern Reassessment," in Woodrow Wilson International Center for Scholars, *Woodrow Wilson: A Commemorative Celebration* (Washington, D. C., 1982), pp. 3–12; "Prelude to Progressivism: The Transformation of New York State Politics, 1890–1910," *New York History* 59 (July 1978): 253–76; "The Discovery that Business Corrupts Politics: A Reappraisal of the Origins of Progressivism," *American Historical Review* 86 (April 1981): 247–74.

Contents

THE PARTY PERIOD
AND PUBLIC POLICY

Introduction

During the 1820s and 1830s, the world's first mass parties
emerged in the United States. Organized by skillful leaders in
nearly every state by 1840, the Democrats and Whigs soon perfected a spectacular style of campaigning to arouse the voters,
and in presidential elections the parties regularly drew to the
polls three-quarters of the eligible electorate. Even in the off-
years, the great majority of the nation's adult white males loyally
voted the party tickets and relished the masculine camaraderie
found in torchlight parades, campaign rallies, and victory celebrations. When the ballots were counted, almost every man
elected—from town supervisor to president—was a representative
of one of the major parties. Fortunately for partisan officeholders, only limited public policies were expected of the nineteenth-century State, and the parties usually proved able to man-
age the everyday tasks of government. Especially in allocating the
economic resources and privileges whose distribution formed the
State's most characteristic activity, partisan legislators genuinely
excelled. Although the party system of Democrats and Whigs
lasted for only two decades, the types of parties formed in the
1830s and the patterns of partisan voting and partisan policymaking that stabilized by the 1840s endured for the rest of the
century. This was the party period in American history.

The nineteenth-century parties thrived for good reasons. Their leaders understood and cultivated the popular passions for liberty and independence that had been born of the Revolution and kept alive among succeeding generations of Americans. Addressing voters in versions of the republican language that was the common medium of American political discourse, Democratic, Whig, and Republican leaders all portrayed their own party as the instrument of republican liberty and the opposing party as its enemy. Voters found these appeals believable because party rhetoric was so often accurate in identifying the dangers to liberty felt by ordinary people—a monster bank, a Popish conspiracy, a grasping slavocracy, or an evil trust. The precise nature of these perceived threats varied from one place to another, and in that geographic variation lay the parties' second great strength: their rootedness in local communities. Party leaders knew their constituents well—their dreams for the future, their fears, their prejudices. And they spoke to these sentiments in terms carefully chosen to appeal to the ethnic, religious, and sectional identities of local voters. In a culturally heterogeneous society that was still highly decentralized, party principles could be explained one way in one place and another way elsewhere—using whatever words and symbols meant the most in each locale.

Just as party rhetoric could be tailored to individual communities, so could public policies. Indeed nineteenth-century American governance was ideally suited to the parties' needs. In allocating governmental largess to individuals, corporations, and towns, the party organizations cemented the support of diverse constituencies. Within an expanding economy and a growing nation, almost every white man could plausibly hope for his share of the resources, and every community could dream of its bank or railroad connection. Bestowing one corporation charter seldom precluded granting another, nor did policies of allocation seem to divide the nation into irreconcilably antagonistic classes. The parties thrived on making these discrete, particularistic policy decisions, just as they did on distributing patronage. So many basic features of the nineteenth-century political setting thus encouraged the political parties: a republican ideology that enabled them to present themselves as defenders of liberty, a community-based political system that permitted the parties to fashion distinctive local appeals with little regard for nationwide consistency, and a policy structure that gave precedence to the very sort of governmental decisions that the parties were best equipped to make.

Even in such a propitious environment, however, the party organizations did not always find it easy to keep control of the voters and the government. Many citizens remained deeply suspicious of political parties. The Anglo-American political tradition taught that parties tended to divide an otherwise harmonious community and that their appearance meant that some men were putting their own selfish interests above the common good of the whole people. The experience of the Revolution and its aftermath had reinforced this antipartyism, and most citizens of the early republic probably shared it. Despite the best efforts of Democratic, Whig, and, later, Republican leaders, the suspicion of parties never entirely disappeared from American political culture. Parties were always required to operate within an ideological environment that was in some ways hostile to their existence.

The party organizations also had to struggle to contain the very same cultural and sectional animosities upon which their own appeals were often based. At the local level, party leaders championed their constituents' ethnic and religious values and sought to preserve them through favorable governmental actions. Beyond the local community, however, antagonistic cultural groups clashed repeatedly over such subjects as education, liquor, leisure, and social behavior, and their struggles inevitably endangered the party coalitions. With the rise of European immigration in the 1840s, ethnic and religious conflict became a permanent—and threatening—fact of party life. The sectional crisis over slavery presented even greater dangers to the political parties. Antebellum politicians in both the North and the South capitalized on sectional differences by portraying their party as best able to defend their section's rights. But when territorial expansion forced the slavery issue into the national political arena, neither party was able to contain the resulting emotions, much less to resolve the controversy.

Despite the strength of nineteenth-century partisan attachments, these cultural and sectional quarrels constantly threatened—and frequently disrupted—party unity. Twice during the party period electoral lines were substantially reshuffled—in the 1850s and again in the 1890s. During the first of these realignments, the Whig party disappeared and the Republican party emerged. During the second, an era of intense party competition gave way to a generation of Republican dominance. For many voters, the realignments brought the dissolution of existing loyalties and their replacement by new partisan attachments; for others, realignment meant departure from the active electorate. In the aftermath of the electoral upheavals of the 1850s and the 1890s, the party organizations continued to dominate American politics, but they could never rest easy amidst the tensions generated by differences of culture and section.

Perhaps the greatest danger to the parties lay in the dissatisfaction many people felt with existing governmental policies. Some Americans, especially petty producers on the outskirts of the market economy, had never favored the public promotion of economic development—the very endeavor which the party organizations found so rewarding. Entrepreneurs and their political allies usually managed to keep developmental policies at the top of the governmental agenda, but they rarely did so without a struggle. As time passed, moreover, it became increasingly evident to many people that monumental social inequalities resulted when the government aided particular economic enterprises but gave little attention to regulating them. Unlike particularistic policies of distribution, regulatory measures explicitly grouped one social class in opposition to others and therefore were not easy for the parties to enact. But the pressure for such policies grew—not only from weaker elements in the society but also from big business interests—and by the early

1900s American governance was on the verge of a transition that would assist in creating a far less hospitable environment for the political parties.

Soon after 1900, in fact, the party period came to a close. Antiparty sentiments, which had been kept in check since the Jacksonian era, now burst forth amidst an outbreak of progressive idealism and an upsurge of interest-group organizing. Partisan loyalties weakened and party voting declined, encouraged in some cases by enactment of election laws that seemed to strike at the very bases of the party organizations' power. Governments at every level took on new tasks of managing and ordering an industrial society, and the parties' control over governance declined. The parties by no means disappeared (in some respects they may even have gained from the changes of the early 1900s), but their place in the polity was altered—and diminished—compared to what it had been for most of the previous century.

The foregoing sketch of the political parties of nineteenth-century America is in large part a product of the "new political history" of the 1960s, 1970s, and 1980s.[1] To an equally great degree, however, it is the product of my reaction against certain elements of that history. Because each of the first three essays in this book analyzes and critiques an important segment of the recent writing on nineteenth-century politics, it may be useful to summarize the findings of that literature and to locate those findings in relation to the interpretation of the party period offered here.

It is scarcely an exaggeration to say that American political historians rediscovered parties within the past quarter century. To the first generation of professional historians and political scientists in the United States (those who wrote between approxi-

1. Allan G. Bogue, "United States: The 'New' Political History," in Bogue, *Clio & the Bitch Goddess: Quantification in American Political History* (Beverly Hills, 1983), pp. 57–78.

mately 1880 and 1915), political parties were crucial institutions
in the establishment of American democracy. Scarcely uncritical
of the parties, these scholars nonetheless lavished impressive
attention on the party organizations, their nominating practices,
electoral techniques, legislative methods, and their role in government. Then, somewhat inexplicably, these topics faded from
the scholarly agenda. From the 1920s through the 1940s, political
historians were preoccupied with elaborating and testing the
seminal theses of Beard and Turner, with explaining the sectional crises of the mid-nineteenth century, and with the writing
of biographies. All of these valuable endeavors, to be sure, bore
some relationship to the study of party politics. But parties were
seldom central in this literature, and, by and large, its authors
tended to take for granted existing understandings of what parties were and how they operated. Guided by a progressive mentality that was deeply suspicious of parties, historians generally
associated parties with spoils and corruption, with subservience
to business interests, and with the thwarting of reform. The
minority of partisans who were treated with scholarly sympathy
tended to come from the ranks of third parties or of dissident
factions within the major parties. It was these dissenters, moreover,
rather than the major party leaders, who usually received credit
for the periodic upheavals—commonly termed eras of reform—
that marked American political history.[2]

Then in the 1960s and 1970s the scholarly tides turned. Taking
parties seriously as agents of political mobilization, as bearers of
ideology, and (to a lesser extent) as instruments of governmental
policymaking, historians began to produce a vast literature documenting nearly every aspect of party life. Especially in the early
years of the new political history, much of the research on parties

2. Richard P. McCormick, "The 'New American Political History': 1890–
1915," a paper presented at the Annual Meeting of the Organization of American
Historians, April 1985; Austin Ranney, *The Doctrine of Responsible Party Government: Its Origins and Present State* (Urbana, 1954); John Higham, *History:
Professional Scholarship in America*, Johns Hopkins Paperbacks Edition (Baltimore, 1983), pp. 171–211.

was quantitative in nature and directed toward uncovering general patterns over time in voter turnout, in the social bases of party politics, and in legislative roll-call votes. Together this new work significantly enlarged what was known about the political parties—their origins and development, their methods of organization, the backgrounds of their leaders, the policies for which their legislators voted, the nature of their electoral coalitions, and the belief systems of their supporters. Overall the new research tended to improve the historical image of the nineteenth-century parties. At the risk of some over-generalization, the heightened appreciation of the parties may be said to have had two basic elements, each multi-faceted and complex. First was the notion that the political parties were reasonably democratic institutions that expressed meaningful beliefs and values and sought to use the government to enact—at least in general terms—the policies they promised.[3] Second was the contention that the major political parties were important instruments of the most significant transformations in the structure of American politics—usually associated with electoral realignments and the creation of new party systems.[4]

Among the studies suggesting that nineteenth-century parties were democratic bodies filling real needs, none were more important—especially in the early years of the new political history—than the works on popular voting behavior discussed in the first article below. Published during the 1960s and early 1970s, these studies employed quantitative methods (together with more traditional historical sources) to uncover the social origins of partisan behavior and to document the values and beliefs which guided the mass of ordinary male citizens in making their voting

3. Many of the studies of popular voting behavior, of legislative roll-call votes, and of party ideologies written during the 1960s and 1970s illustrate these trends in interpretation; for prominent examples see the essays reprinted in Joel H. Silbey, *The Partisan Imperative: The Dynamics of American Politics Before the Civil War* (New York, 1985).
4. On this literature see the essay below entitled "The Realignment Synthesis in American History."

choices. By now, the findings of these works are familiar to most American historians. Party loyalties were strong and voting behavior was generally stable in nineteenth-century America because partisan attachments—like religious affiliations—had deep roots in family and community life. Party leaders voiced the same values that voters learned in their homes and churches, and when leaders discussed national issues they related them to the cultural and communal concerns of greatest importance to most people. Not surprisingly in this light, ethnicity and religion were the most important determinants of party choice, although (as observed below) ethnocultural factors could become politically salient in distinct—and sometimes contradictory—ways. These conclusions have dramatically enhanced our understanding of nineteenth-century party politics.

Influential as they have been, however, the ethnocultural voting studies have not escaped searching examination. Some quantitatively oriented observers have called their methodologies into question.[5] Other critics, emanating from the ranks of social historians, have rejected what they see as an ahistorical dichotomy between "cultural" and "economic" factors.[6] Still other researchers have carried out voting studies that appear to refute an ethnocultural interpretation, at least for particular times and places.[7] The article on the ethnocultural "school" which is reprinted here does not, for the most part, take a highly critical position. Published first in 1974, soon after the appearance of the most important works of this genre, it highlights their contribu-

5. J. Morgan Kousser, "The 'New Political History': A Methodological Critique," *Reviews in American History* 4 (March 1976): 1–14.

6. Sean Wilentz, "On Class and Politics in Jacksonian America," *Reviews in American History* 10 (December 1982): 45–63; Leon Fink, *Workingmen's Democracy: The Knights of Labor in American Politics* (Urbana, 1983).

7. Dale Baum, *The Civil War Party System: The Case of Massachusetts, 1848–1876* (Chapel Hill, 1984); Stephen E. Maizlish, *The Triumph of Sectionalism: The Transformation of Ohio Politics, 1844–1856* (Kent, Ohio, 1983). For a vigorous defense of the ethnocultural studies, see Paul Kleppner, *The Third Electoral System, 1853–1892: Parties, Voters, and Political Cultures* (Chapel Hill, 1979), pp. 357–82.

tions and observes some distinctions between the various ways in which ethnocultural factors were held to influence voting.[8] Perhaps the most pointed questions raised in this article concern the relationship between voting and policymaking. Although they are not entirely consistent on the matter, the ethnocultural historians seem to suggest that most voters were unconcerned with economic policy questions, and their studies imply that voting and governance had little to do with one another. I was dissatisfied with this implication, although (as the reader will discover) I did not entirely know what to make of it or what to put in its place. Ever since, I have continued to try to understand the relationships between politics and government—an effort that is reflected in all the succeeding essays in this book.

Where the ethnocultural studies probed the social sources of party voting, a corresponding literature on realignments and critical elections argued that periodic transformations in voting behavior were the "mainsprings" of American political history. The work of historians and political scientists alike, the realignment studies were quantitatively sophisticated and analytically bold. To some, their findings offered a comprehensive interpretation of the course of American politics and government. Occurring in the 1850s, 1890s, and 1930s, the major realignments were said to have brought dramatic and long-lasting changes in the parties' electoral support and to have decisively shaped patterns of politics and policy in the eras that followed. A number of researchers stressed the chronological regularity with which realignments took place and emphasized the fundamental similarities of each realignment to the next. Others found that the timing of critical elections varied from place to place and denied that all realignments were analytically identical. Despite such qualifica-

8. Allan G. Bogue has properly chided me for implying that Lee Benson played a less important role than Samuel P. Hays in originating ethnocultural electoral analysis. As Bogue correctly observes, Benson had privately circulated manuscripts contending for the importance of cultural factors some years before either he or Hays published their respective works on this subject. See Bogue, *Clio & the Bitch Goddess*, pp. 50n, 109n, 135n.

tions, electoral realignments were commonly held to have marked the major turning points in American political and governmental history—and perhaps even to be America's surrogate for revolution.[9]

As the second essay in this book indicates, not everyone was satisfied with what came to be called realignment theory. To some, the great variations in the nature and timing of critical elections called into doubt what realignments actually were and raised questions about whether they really constituted a common class of historical events.[10] Others were more willing to acknowledge that realignments had occurred but wondered if they had, in fact, been the all-transforming political and governmental watersheds they were often said to have been. The article below raises questions of this second sort. My own research on New York State had convinced me that an important electoral transition had indeed taken place in the mid-1890s but that political practices and governmental policies were not decisively altered as a result.[11] The changes of the early 1900s seemed far more important, and their connection to the realignment of the 1890s was tenuous and complex. Most striking to me, the critical elections of the 1890s were not immediately followed by the adoption of new and important governmental policies. Those changes came later—amidst the regulatory revolution of 1905 to 1915—for reasons having little directly to do with the preceding electoral changes. Where the ethnocultural historians had implied that voting and governance were unrelated, the realignment studies seemed to suggest a false relationship between them: that govern-

9. The most important single work in drawing out the larger implications of realignment theory is Walter Dean Burnham, *Critical Elections and the Mainsprings of American Politics* (New York, 1970).

10. Allan J. Lichtman, "Critical Election Theory and the Reality of American Presidential Politics, 1916–1940," *American Historical Review* 81 (April 1976): 317–51; Allan J. Lichtman, "The End of Realignment Theory? Toward a New Research Program for American Political History," *Historical Methods* 15 (Fall 1982): 170–88.

11. Richard L. McCormick, *From Realignment to Reform: Political Change in New York State, 1893–1910* (Ithaca, 1981).

mental turning points could be explained as the product of major electoral upheavals.

Intriguing as the connections between politics and government were to me, most political historians writing during the 1970s and 1980s contributed only indirectly to working out that puzzling relationship.[12] Many of the most creative scholars devoted their attention to other problems—especially the ideological and social bases of political behavior. Some traced the persistence of Revolutionary republicanism into the nineteenth century and sought to distinguish between those Americans who retained the old ideals and those whose republicanism metamorphosed into liberalism. Working in a related vein, other historians probed the "political culture" of mass party politics and explored the values and expectations men brought to their political experiences. A great many researchers continued to study the social origins of party alignments, although there was increasing dissatisfaction with ethnocultural analysis and a renewed interest in the economic bases of party choice. Some historians accordingly drew on Marxist insights to explain the nature and development of American politics. Although no new conceptual picture comparable to the ethnocultural interpretation or realignment theory has yet emerged from these newer works, they illustrate some of the most important directions now being taken in the study of nineteenth-century political history. Their contributions are analyzed below in an article entitled "The Social Analysis of American Political History—After Twenty Years."

Yet while they do not explicitly probe the linkages between party politics and governmental policy, some of these recent works contribute a good deal by indirection to that subject. Far from unconcerned with governmental policies, nineteenth-cen-

12. Much of the most interesting recent work on nineteenth-century American governance has come not from political historians but from legal historians and political scientists; see, for example, William E. Nelson, *The Roots of American Bureaucracy, 1830–1900* (Cambridge, Mass., 1982); and Stephen Skowronek, *Building a New American State: The Expansion of National Administrative Capacities, 1877–1920* (Cambridge, England, 1982).

tury Americans are portrayed in these studies as intensely involved in the quest to shape the government's decisions, especially those of an economic nature. Some men opposed economic
"progress" while others favored it; some wanted the government
to steer clear of entrepreneurial activity, but many others sought
their share of the goods. These issues concerning the public
promotion—and later regulation—of economic enterprise were
the stuff of everyday politics and had important effects on party
choice. Several of these recent studies add still another piece to
the politics-policy puzzle by suggesting that the appearance of
promotional questions on the governmental agenda early in the
nineteenth century was vitally important in bringing about the
subsequent emergence of mass party politics. They imply, in
other words, that changing expectations for government may
have helped call forth the transformation of politics.[13] These are
fertile insights—clues to the linkages between party politics and
governmental policy and clues to the nature and distinctiveness
of the party period in American history.

Until relatively recently, the historical relationship between politics and policy was not considered to be a very difficult problem.
If they thought about the question at all, most historians probably held to something like the notion of responsible party government: voters chose representatives on the basis of their party's
policy positions and those elected enacted (or at least tried to
enact) the promised policies. The older elitist focus in the writing
of American political history, particularly the emphasis on presidential administrations, encouraged the assumption that politics
and governance were directly tied together. Presidential candi-

13. Harry L. Watson, *Jacksonian Politics and Community Conflict: The
Emergence of the Second American Party System in Cumberland County, North
Carolina* (Baton Rouge, 1981); Robert H. Wiebe, *The Opening of American
Society: From the Adoption of the Constitution to the Eve of Disunion* (New
York, 1984). Both of these works are discussed below in "The Social Analysis of
American Political History—After Twenty Years."

dates were portrayed as campaigning for election on the basis of their party's platform pronouncements and, if they were victorious, devoting their terms of office to carrying through the announced programs.[14] These assumptions no longer command wide support among American historians. The responsible-party-government model may be useful in accounting for particular historical outcomes, but its widespread applicability seems doubtful. Elections in the United States seldom offered referenda on clear policy choices, and rarely did officials enter office and put through comprehensive programs based on preelection pledges.

The demise of the old assumptions has been encouraged by recent research suggesting that electoral behavior and policy formation were primarily shaped not by one another but by social and economic conditions. As noted above, the ethnocultural studies of the 1960s and 1970s tended to treat voting decisions as expressions of cultural, communal, and sectional values, rather than as responses to policy choices. While one ethnocultural historian has claimed that electoral cleavages can explain "the general outlines of policy," most of these historians gave little attention to governmental decision-making and regarded voting chiefly as a form of social behavior.[15] A corresponding literature, produced first by political scientists and then emulated by some historians, suggests that election results and other political factors do not make much difference in the formation of public policy. Instead, environmental circumstances—especially levels of economic growth—determine the course and development of governmental decisions. "There is," according to two historians, "an inner logic to the industrialization process which shapes the parameters and direction of public policy."[16]

14. Thomas C. Cochran, "The 'Presidential Synthesis' in American History," *American Historical Review* 53 (July 1948): 748–59.

15. Kleppner, *The Third Electoral System*, p. 382.

16. J. Rogers Hollingsworth and Ellen Jane Hollingsworth, *Dimensions in Urban History: Historical and Social Science Perspectives on Middle-Sized American Cities* (Madison, Wis., 1979), p. 157. For summaries of the relevant political

These findings have not gone unchallenged, but they do make clear that the historical linkages between elections and policy were far more complex than once thought.[17] They suggest, as well, that any comprehensive understanding of the relationship between politics and governance will have to make room for social and economic forces exogenous to politics. The problem cannot be avoided. If political history has a core subject, that subject is the political system as whole, including the methods and patterns of political participation and the decisions and actions of government. And if political history has a core purpose, that purpose is to explain the course of politics and government by relating each to the larger environment and each in turn to the other.

Within recent years, historians and political scientists have employed several strategies to restore their grasp of what once seemed simple but now seems much more complex: the connections between politics and policy in American history. The realignment studies represent one approach to the problem, although (as indicated above) much more work remains to be done to establish precisely what effects critical elections had upon subsequent shifts in governmental policy. Another research tack focuses on the relationship between legislators and their constituents. By analyzing legislative roll-call decisions and linking them up with the characteristics of the lawmakers' local districts, some historians have been able to chart the extent and nature of

science literature see Richard I. Hofferbert, "State and Community Policy Studies: A Review of Comparative Input-Output Analyses," *Political Science Annual* 3 (1972): 3–72; and Thomas R. Dye, "Politics versus Economics: The Development of the Literature on Policy Determination," *Policy Studies Journal* 7 (Summer 1979): 652–62.

17. For a critique of the policy outputs literature, see J. Morgan Kousser, "Restoring Politics to Political History," *Journal of Interdisciplinary History* 12 (Spring 1982): 569–95. My article on "The Party Period and Public Policy" (reprinted below) too readily accepts the notion that socioeconomic factors alone can largely explain the course of politics and policy. See my comments later in this introduction on how I might revise this article now.

legislative responsiveness to the electorate.[18] A third approach involves tracing the impact of political rules and institutional arrangements upon governmental decisions. Suffrage restrictions, ballot laws, party competition, and bureaucratic arrangements all have been shown to affect governmental outcomes.[19]

The articles in this book have been influenced by these endeavors, but my own approach to the politics-policy puzzle is somewhat different. I assume that because political behavior is always directed toward obtaining governmental power the conditions and expectations surrounding the exercise of that power will fundamentally determine the kind of politics in which people engage. Under many circumstances, in fact, the nature of governance may exert more influence upon politics than politics does upon government. What people expect the government to do, the actual policies and structures of government, and the rules for filling public office all will shape political behavior *whether or not* that behavior is successful in gaining for its practitioners control of the government. Men and women strive through political means to get power in the State. Sometimes they succeed, sometimes they fail. Either way, the State—by which I mean the visions people hold for the government as well as its institutions and actions—structures the political efforts of those who would control it.

These abstractions can be made concrete by returning specifically to American politics. The article below entitled "Political Parties in American History" argues that parties always shaped themselves around perceived opportunities for gaining and exercising governmental power. Successful in filling the offices, parties nonetheless experienced great difficulty in exercising the

18. Ballard C. Campbell, *Representative Democracy: Public Policy and Midwestern Legislatures in the Late Nineteenth Century* (Cambridge, Mass., 1980).

19. J. Morgan Kousser, "Progressivism—For Middle-Class Whites Only: North Carolina Education, 1880-1910," *Journal of Southern History* 46 (May 1980): 169-94; Skowronek, *Building a New American State*; Theda Skocpol, "Political Response to Capitalist Crisis: Neo-Marxist Theories of the State and the Case of the New Deal," *Politics & Society* 10 (1980): 155-201.

authority they won. As V. O. Key observed, parties are "bound together at least by the ambition to control the machinery of government."[20] Certainly this has been true of the American parties, ever since the colonial period when they were more commonly termed factions. In every era, the kind of party politics that people practiced depended primarily upon the rules for obtaining office, the accepted functions of government, and the actual State structures. When governance changed, the parties changed, although the reverse was not always the case. All the major turning points in American party history—including the creation of the first national parties, the later emergence of mass politics, the transformation and decline of parties in the early 1900s, the creation of the New Deal coalition, and the contemporary withering of party loyalties—may be traced to governmental changes. Or, to rephrase and reverse Walter Dean Burnham's formulation, it is not *elections* (critical or otherwise) that have been the "mainsprings" of American politics, it is *government*, including popular expectations for governmental actions and the rules and opportunities for getting and using the power of the State.

"The Party Period and Public Policy," the fifth article below, illustrates these propositions by relating nineteenth-century party politics to the most important governmental policies of the era. Drawing heavily on the new political history, this essay describes the intense partisanship of American voters, the cultural basis of party politics, and the persistence of these patterns from the Jacksonian period to the early 1900s. Relying equally heavily upon a somewhat older literature in economic and legal history, the article next gives an account of the distributive economic policies undertaken by nineteenth-century governments at every level. What, it then asks, was the relationship between these chronologically corresponding patterns of politics and policy-making? The answer is complicated, for partisanship and distrib-

20. V. O. Key, Jr., *Southern Politics: In State and Nation* (New York, 1949), p. 15.

utive policies affected and supported each other in many ways. Both, however, fundamentally derived not from one another but from social conditions and economic opportunities. When those conditions and opportunities changed, the nineteenth century's distinctive patterns of party politics and governmental policies were transformed.

If I were to rewrite this article now, I would lay less stress upon the autonomy of politics and governance from one another and give more emphasis to the role of distributive policies in calling forth and fueling party competition. In a nutshell, my argument would go as follows: During the first decades of the nineteenth century, economic and social conditions encouraged entrepreneurial-minded Americans to ask for governmental policies promoting capitalist development. The policies themselves were not new—they may be traced back at least to Alexander Hamilton—but now they were demanded not by national authorities possessing an all-embracing vision for the republic but by local elites dispersed throughout the states, none of whom had a grand plan, only personal hopes and schemes. By and large, these men succeeded in placing their demands at the head of the governmental agenda and keeping them there for the rest of the century. Foreseen by no one, the new policies had an enormous potential for stimulating and sustaining party conflict. These economic questions could be contested both at an ideological level (what were the republican implications of commercial growth?) and much more practically (who should get which resources?). Both ways, there was grist for partisan mills. Despite the objections of some Americans to promotional policies and, more important, the intrusion of sectional differences that party politics could not resolve, entrepreneurial elites and their political allies kept distributive issues to the fore. The parties thrived accordingly and enjoyed a heyday of mass popularity and governmental hegemony. Not until the early 1900s, when social and economic changes necessitated the adoption of a new structure of governmental policies, did the basic patterns of American politics change.

Both versions of the argument suggest a close "fit" between distributive policymaking and partisan politics.[21] Both imply, as well, that the world of politics and government was decisively influenced by the socioeconomic environment but not entirely determined by it. Once the party period's unique patterns of politics and policy came into being, political leaders, party organizations, and government officials worked diligently and successfully to maintain them, despite the countervailing pressures emanating from the sectional controversy and, later, from demands for policies of economic regulation. Eventually those patterns succumbed to the economic and social forces generated by industrialization and urbanization, but even then party leaders played a major role in the transition to new types of politics and government.

The political and governmental changes of the early twentieth century are not easy to explain, although the difficulty is hardly traceable to a want of effort on the part of historians. Few periods in American history have received closer scrutiny than the Progressive era, especially the political reforms of those years, the adoption of new governmental policies, and the assault on political bosses and machines.[22] Only infrequently, however, have historians systematically related the political changes of the Progressive era to the political and governmental arrangements of the nineteenth-century United States, that is, to the party period whose politics and policies were now transformed. Each in different ways, the last four articles in this book represent attempts to remedy that deficiency by tracing the transition from one system of politics and government to another.

21. Theodore J. Lowi, "American Business, Public Policy, Case-Studies, and Political Theory," *World Politics* 16 (July 1964): 677–715.

22. For discussions of the historical writings on progressivism see Arthur S. Link and Richard L. McCormick, *Progressivism* (Arlington Heights, Ill., 1983); and Daniel T. Rodgers, "In Search of Progressivism," *Reviews in American History* 10 (December 1982): 113–32.

In some key respects, the political changes of the early 1900s were a mirror image of those of the 1820s and 1830s when the party period's distinctive characteristics took shape. Where party voting had burgeoned in the Jackson period and become the main means of political participation for ordinary white, male Americans, the percentage of eligible voters who cast ballots declined in every section of the country during the years after 1900. Often the decline was encouraged by restrictive election laws reversing the Jacksonian trend toward expanding the electorate. For some people, political participation now became impossible, while for others new means of expression and involvement supplanted party-oriented voting. Especially for those in the best organized sectors of the economy and for many educated, articulate members of the middle class, interest groups replaced parties as the most effective vehicles for influencing the government. At the same time, government itself was transformed. Economic policies of distribution and allocation scarcely ceased, but they were supplemented by policies of regulation and administration that continually involved local, state, and national governments in the operation of society. Although the analogy should not be pressed too far, these policy changes in some respects restored and updated an older "commonwealth" ideal that had been largely abandoned during the first decades of the nineteenth century when American governments had ceased to take significant responsibility for insuring the "common good" of the whole people.[23] Now, at least in theory, public authorities tried to reassume that historic task.

To explain these political and governmental changes is to trace the lengthy, twisted pathways leading from social and economic developments to the diverse political responses made by innumerable individuals and groups. In the most general terms, industrialization, urbanization, and immigration brought forth

23. Oscar Handlin and Mary Flug Handlin, *Commonwealth: A Study of the Role of Government in the American Economy: Massachusetts, 1774–1861* (New York, 1947); Louis Hartz, *Economic Policy and Democratic Thought: Pennsylvania, 1776–1860* (Cambridge, Mass., 1948).

new needs for political expression not satisfied by party-oriented voting and encouraged expectations for government not met through existing policies. Pushing beyond these broad generalizations means asking how the new needs and expectations were felt by ordinary people under particular social circumstances and, perhaps more important, how political elites and their organizations responded to the demands now thrust upon them. Party leaders did not give in to the new political order without a struggle. The decline of confidence in parties and in voting threatened their power, just as interest-group demands for policies of regulation and administration imperiled their control over government. At the same time, however, many of the party leaders were shrewd enough to recognize what was happening and skillful enough to take a hand in shaping the new forms of politics and government that were being created.

The dissatisfaction with political parties felt by early twentieth-century Americans was not a new phenomenon. Antipartyism had deep roots in American political culture, and its restoration to prominence in the Progressive era reflected the historic republican suspicion that parties were selfish bodies oblivious to the general good. But the antipartyism of the early 1900s was also rooted in specific grievances against late nineteenth-century party practices and party government. The article below entitled "Antiparty Thought in the Gilded Age" explores these grievances by examining the writings of four men whose attacks on the political parties of the late 1800s significantly anticipated the views of many Americans a generation later. Surprisingly, perhaps, the antiparty writers' strongest objections related to the kind of government the parties gave. Party government, they believed, was conducted by ignorant, untrained men; it was haphazard and irresponsible; and, perhaps above all, it made unwise policies. If the parties were eliminated (via the complex schemes these writers proposed), talented, responsible men would fill the public offices, and governments could be trusted to take on tasks and duties never performed before. Impractical and biased though they were, the antiparty treatises contain important insights into the late nineteenth-century system of politics and government. And by the early 1900s, thousands of Americans had reached the same conclusion: if political parties were weakened, government could be improved and enlarged.

The spread of that conviction from a small elite to the general population was one sign of the advent of progressivism, a nation-wide reform movement whose complexities and ironies are the subject of the next of the articles below. For a number of reasons, progressivism is not in good repute among many historians today, and this essay, in part, tries to defend the movement against its critics. Doing that, however, requires acknowledging that there were often significant gaps between the progressives rhetoric, their actual intentions, and the results they achieved. Nowhere was this more true than in the area of political reform. New election laws, for example, were commonly said to offer remedies for the ills of party politics, but in practice some proved highly useful to party leaders. Measures of economic regulation similarly failed to live up to the anti-business expectations held by some of their supporters. Often the results of a reform pro-foundly surprised the men and women who favored it. The explanation for these ironies is complicated and cannot be laid simply to an alleged conspiracy by political and economic elites. Neither the progressives nor their enemies could have foreseen the course of political and governmental change in the early twentieth century.

Yet unpredictable as it may have been to contemporaries, the political transformation of the Progressive era need not defy comprehension by historians. Deeply rooted as they were in long-term social and economic developments, the most important po-litical changes nonetheless occurred rather quickly, in response to dramatic events and perceived crises. The careful analysis of what went on during and after those critical moments can do much to reveal how the early twentieth-century political order was established. The article below entitled "Prelude to Progres-sivism" takes this approach to New York State politics during the 1890s and early 1900s. Following a brief sketch of the Repub-lican party organization that came to dominate the state begin-ning in 1893, the article then recounts how the party's leaders responded to two unexpected developments: the desertion of the Republicans by urban independents in the city elections of 1897 and the revelations of politico-business corruption generated by a legislative investigation of the life insurance industry in 1905. In the aftermath of each crisis, party leaders took crucial steps to contain the damage and regain support. Other men and women, outside the Republican organization, also reacted to what had occurred and tried to control the subsequent course of developments. Out of these divergent attempts to order events and make sense of what had happened came significant—and unexpected— political and governmental changes marking New York's passage from the party period to a new political order.

The last article in the book, entitled "The Discovery That Business Corrupts Politics," carries these same themes to the nation at large. By the early 1900s, it argues, the United States was on the verge of a major political transition. Industrialization and its consequences had brought about the need for new governmental policies, but the will to enact them—and, indeed, even the imagination to know what they should be—were largely absent. At this juncture came dramatic events all across the country disclosing that business interests in quest of economic benefits were corrupting the government. In just two years, 1905 and 1906, the political temper of the nation was transformed. In New York the stimulus came from the life insurance investigation, in San Francisco from graft trials, and in Colorado from revelations that Denver's utility companies had bought an election. Everywhere, it appeared, the leaders of the dominant political party were in a corrupt alliance with greedy corporations, and, to judge from the resulting outcry, Americans were genuinely shocked by what they learned about their system of politics and government. In the aftermath of the disclosures of 1905–06, pent-up proposals for political reform and economic regulation were enacted in virtually every state and in the nation, too. The parties' nominating methods came under strict regulation for the first time, and the parties' business allies now found governmental boards and commissions carefully supervising their activities. The results of these reforms were many-faceted and ironical, and they scarcely ever satisfied the most radical critics of the machines and the corporations. But the effects were significant nonetheless. It is probably not too much to say that in 1905 and 1906 the party period in American history came effectively to an end.

It seems fitting and logical that disclosures of politico-business corruption should have catalyzed the transition to a new political order. For what Americans really "discovered" in 1905 and 1906 was that they no longer wanted a political system in which untamed parties dominated governments whose main function was the distribution of economic resources. Such a system had worked reasonably well for most of a century, and few could deny that it had encouraged both democracy and economic progress— at least as nineteenth-century Americans had defined those terms. But by 1905 the old practices and the old definitions no longer seemed adequate for an urban, industrial nation. In fact, they seemed to produce not democracy and progress—but corruption.

In place of the old system came a new one in which public officials took responsibility for regulating and adjusting the clashing interests of an industrial society. Frequently, of course, they did not do the job very well, and people inevitably disagreed about the scope and functions of government. But the governmental order had been transformed. And so, too, had the parties. Well suited to carry on the old tasks of government, party organizations found the new policies deeply troubling and, in a real sense, beyond their capacity. Nonpartisan agencies and commissions took over large areas of governmental decision-making, and interest-group organizations proved better suited to influencing the new boards than did the parties. To be sure, party leaders often found ways of using the new policies to benefit their organizations, and on election days the parties were still preeminent (even if relatively fewer people voted). But they never again dominated the citizenry or the government as effectively as they had in the nineteenth century. Under a simpler form of government the parties had enjoyed their golden age; under the new regime they filled a more limited place in the polity.

PART ONE

TRENDS IN HISTORIOGRAPHY

1

Ethnocultural Interpretations of Nineteenth-Century American Voting Behavior

Beginning in the early 1960s, and especially within the past half-dozen years, historians have offered strong evidence that the most important determinants of voting behavior in the American past have been the ethnic and religious identifications of citizens. Indeed, an ethnocultural "school" of American political history has emerged, and its members have produced an impressive body of historical research and writing.[1] In search of a grass-roots understanding of past politics, the ethnoculturalists have applied

---

1. The term "ethnocultural" is used here—often interchangeably with "ethnoreligious"—to denote the feelings and habits, the likes and dislikes, which were associated with the national origins and religious affiliations of nineteenth-century American voters. The precise specification of which cultural attributes were "ethnocultural" and the definition of the exact relationship between ethnocultural factors and political ones are two problems with which much of the present essay is concerned.

The major works considered in the present essay are: Lee Benson, *The Concept of Jacksonian Democracy: New York as a Test Case* (Princeton, 1961); Ronald P. Formisano, *The Birth of Mass Political Parties: Michigan, 1827-1861* (Princeton, 1971); Michael F. Holt, *Forging a Majority: The Formation of the Republican Party in Pittsburgh, 1848-1860* (New Haven, 1969); Richard Jensen, *The Winning of the Midwest: Social and Political Conflict, 1888-1896* (Chicago, 1971); Paul Kleppner, *The Cross of Culture: A Social Analysis of Midwestern Politics, 1850-1900* (New York, 1970); Frederick C. Luebke, *Immigrants and Politics: The Germans of Nebraska, 1880-1900* (Lincoln, Neb., 1969); Samuel T. McSeveney, *The Politics of Depression: Political Behavior in the Northeast, 1893-1896* (New York, 1972).

quantitative methods and behavioral theory to the political history of the United States. They have studied the complex relations between local and national orientations in politics, between leaders and masses, and between economic and cultural issues. More broadly, they have asked and answered questions about political salience: What are the sources of voter motivation? How do issues become politicized?

While ethnoculturalists share a common commitment to the study of the social and cultural bases of mass behavior, they are not in full agreement on the relationship between ethnic and religious identifications and political affiliations. A close reading of their works suggests that these historians have put forward three distinct, though not necessarily incompatible, theories to explain how cultural impulses become political ones: (1) negative reference group antagonisms, (2) conflicts of custom and life-style, and (3) differences in religious values and world views. Moreover, ethnoculturalists do not agree completely on such political concerns as the linkage between voter mobilization and policymaking. While no general appraisal of ethnocultural history is yet possible, it is time for at least an interim evaluation of the contribution made by these historians to our understanding of past political behavior.[2]

All of these titles focus on the nineteenth century. For ethnocultural works on twentieth-century politics, see the bibliography in Joel H. Silbey and Samuel T McSeveney (eds.), *Voters, Parties and Elections* (Lexington, Mass., 1972).

2. Previous evaluations of ethnocultural history include: Robert P. Swierenga, "Ethnocultural Political Analysis: A New Approach to American Ethnic Studies," *Journal of American Studies*, Vol. 5 (April 1971), 59–79; Walter Dean Burnham, "Quantitative History: Beyond the Correlation Coefficient: A Review Essay," *Historical Methods Newsletter*, Vol. 4 (March 1971), 62–66; Paul Kleppner, "Beyond the 'New Political History': A Review Essay," *Historical Methods Newsletter*, Vol. 6 (December 1972), 17–26; Robert P. Swierenga, "Clio and Computers: A Survey of Computerized Research in History," *Computers and the Humanities*, Vol. 5 (September 1970), 1–22; Joel H. Silbey, "Clio and Computers: Moving into Phase II, 1970–1972," *Computers and the Humanities*, Vol. 7 (November 1972), 67–79; Samuel T. McSeveney, "Ethnic Groups, Ethnic Conflicts, and Recent Quantitative Research in American Political History," *The International Migration Review*, Vol. 7 (Spring 1973), 14–33.

Ethnocultural history represents, in part, a response to earlier schools of historiography. An interpretation of political behavior based upon ethnic and religious antagonisms is an explicit alternative to the "progressive" view that conflict in American history has been predominantly socioeconomic. By the same token, ethnoculturalists concur with "consensus" historians who deemphasized ideological and economic divisions between Americans.[3] Despite the reliance on the consensus tradition, there is nothing "homogenizing" about ethnocultural history. These historians have argued that there were real differences between the major political parties and that voters responded to issues and images that had deep meaning for them. Indeed, in some respects, the ethnoculturalists have gone the progressives one better in the search for conflict in the American past. So long as the emphasis was on economic issues and on class as a determinant of voting behavior, it appeared that for long periods in United States history there were no significant differences between the major parties. But if cultural concerns are brought front and

3. For the best brief account of the contributions of the "progressive" historians, see John Higham, *History* (Englewood Cliffs, N. J., 1965), especially pp. 171–212. This group of historians, including preeminently Frederick Jackson Turner, Charles A. Beard, and Carl Becker perceived, in Higham's words, a nation "constantly in flux, full of real and vital conflicts between contending groups" (p. 173). Beginning in the late 1940s, with the publication of Richard Hofstadter's *The American Political Tradition* (New York, 1948), American historians became increasingly sensitive to continuity and consensus in the past. Daniel J. Boorstin and Louis Hartz have been among the most important in this group of historians, and in the 1950s and 1960s the notion of consensus permeated a great deal of writing in American history.

Among the ethnocultural historians, Lee Benson most clearly articulates both the break with a socioeconomic conflict interpretation and the application of consensus concepts; see pp. 123–164 and 270–287. Also see Formisano, pp. 31–34; and Kleppner, *The Cross*, pp. 17–19. For the clearest statement of the view that class and ethnoreligious factors jointly affected voting, see Richard Jensen, "The Religious and Occupational Roots of Party Identification: Illinois and Indiana in the 1870s," *Civil War History*, Vol. 16 (December 1970), 325–343. Michael F. Holt contends that in the late 1840s and early 1850s, economic, ethnic, and religious factors all helped to shape Pittsburgh voting but that by the late 1850s party lines were determined by religion only: pp. 74–79, 215–218, and 303.

center in an explanation of partisan allegiance, then real distinctions between the parties appear, regardless of whether differences on economic issues were significant.

Fundamentally, ethnocultural political analysis begins not with an attack on earlier patterns of historical writing, but with a particular view of what political history ought to be. Samuel P. Hays, the first of the recent ethnoculturalists, has most successfully articulated and spread the new viewpoint. In four major articles between 1960 and 1967, Hays called for political history as a kind of social history and illustrated it by the example of his own work on the 1880 to 1920 period.[4] Historians of past politics, he contends, "should focus on patterns of human relationships in the political system rather than on the succession of outcomes of political decisions."[5] The titles of two of Hays's articles indicate the new perspective: "History as Human Behavior" and "The Social Analysis of American Political History." Virtually all of the ethnocultural historians, many citing Hays, have adopted his opinion that political history ought to have a social orientation.[6]

Although "the social analysis of political history" could mean many things, in conjunction with the ethnoculturalists' determination to study grass-roots behavior, it has come to mean exploring how national origins and religion shaped voters' perceptions of issues and their party loyalties. While political historians have traditionally studied party coalitions by focusing on leaders, the ethnocultural historians have approached the problem from the perspective of the voters and their motives. Of course, Hays's

---

4. "History as Human Behavior," *Iowa Journal of History*, Vol. 58 (July 1960), 193–206; "The Politics of Reform in Municipal Government in the Progressive Era," *Pacific Northwest Quarterly*, Vol. 55 (October 1964), 157–169; "Political Parties and the Community-Society Continuum," in William Nisbet Chambers and Walter Dean Burnham (eds.), *The American Party Systems: Stages of Political Development* (New York, 1967), pp. 152–181; "The Social Analysis of American Political History, 1880–1920," *Political Science Quarterly*, Vol. 80 (September 1965), 373–394.

5. Hays, "Community-Society Continuum," p. 152.

6. Holt, p. 2; Luebke, pp. 5–6; Kleppner, *The Cross*, pp. 1–4; Formisano, p. 4.

label "the social analysis of political history" may be too broad for this subject. Certainly, ethnic and religious identifications were not the only social factors relevant to party loyalties. Moreover, social forces impinged upon political processes other than coalition-making. Finally, there is more to political history than the study of the sources of popular voting behavior. But these cautions aside, there are sound reasons to approve the particular subject to which the ethnoculturalists have directed their attention.[7]

What distinguishes the ethnocultural historians from others who have long sought to decipher the riddle of partisan choice is their concurrence with the proposition, advanced in 1960 by Hays, that "Party differences in voting patterns were cultural, not economic." "Ethnocultural issues," he says, "were far more important to voters than were tariffs, trusts, and railroads. They touched lives directly and moved people deeply." Thus issues like prohibition, nativism, and English language instruction in the public schools affected voters and voting alignments more profoundly than economic and class issues. "In fact," Hays suggests, "one can argue that the only violent shifts in voting behavior came when such issues were present."[8] In 1961, Lee Benson generalized Hays's hypothesis: "at least since the 1820's . . . ethnic and religious differences have tended to be *relatively* the most important sources of political differences."[9] Benson's *The Concept of Jacksonian Democracy* was the first full-scale ethnocultural study, and Benson stands with Hays as an originator of the

7. A justification for the coalitional perspective is offered in Samuel Lubell's *The Future of American Politics*, 3rd ed. (New York, 1965), especially, p. 196. Critiques of the traditional emphasis in American political history on leaders and on national issues and forces include Hays, "The Social Analysis"; Thomas C. Cochran, "The 'Presidential Synthesis' in American History," *American Historical Review*, Vol. 53 (July 1948), 748–759; and Joel H. Silbey, "The Civil War Synthesis in American Political History," *Civil War History*, Vol. 10 (June 1964), 130–140.

8. Hays, "History," p. 196; "Community-Society Continuum," p. 158; "History," p. 197.

9. Benson, p. 165.

school and a vigorous proponent of new methods and concepts for studying the political past.

For several years after the appearance of *The Concept*, the progress of ethnocultural history was slow. Benson had rebutted an economic interpretation of party coalitions, and while others echoed his attack on using a class perspective to interpret political behavior, only a few scholars took up the ethnocultural alternative which Hays and Benson had proposed. In 1962, George H. Daniels's study of Iowa immigrants in 1860 concluded that, contrary to the traditional view, Germans opposed the party of Lincoln and voted instead for "the [Democratic] party which consistently promised them liberty from prohibition and native-American legislation."[10] The next year, Stanley B. Parsons argued that religion was a crucial determinant of Populist voting patterns in Nebraska, though the distinction between immigrants and native-born voters was not significant.[11] Robert P. Swierenga's 1965 account of Dutch politics in Iowa confirmed Daniels's earlier finding that immigrants cast their ballots for the Democrats to oppose liquor regulation and nativism.[12] And in 1966, Paul Kleppner's study of the foreign vote in Pittsburgh in 1860 offered support both to the Swierenga-Daniels view that cultural issues influenced party choice and to Parsons's contention that in the nineteenth century religion was a more important political determinant than ethnicity.[13] The next year Joel Silbey's synthesis of political change from 1840 to 1860 combined an ethnocultural explanation of party realignment with an account of economic and sectional cleavages, thereby integrating

10. "Immigrant Vote in the 1860 Election: The Case of Iowa," *Mid-America*, Vol. 44 (July 1962), 142–162. Quoted in Silbey and McSeveney (eds.), p. 149.
11. "Who Were the Nebraska Populists?" *Nebraska History*, Vol. 44 (June 1963), 97.
12. "The Ethnic Voter and the First Lincoln Election," *Civil War History*, Vol. 11 (March 1965), 41.
13. "Lincoln and the Immigrant Vote: A Case of Religious Polarization," *Mid-America*, Vol. 48 (July 1966), 176–195.

the Hays-Benson perspective with traditional factors in a widely studied period of American political change.[14]

By the late 1960s, ethnocultural explanations became almost commonplace. In 1968, Roger E. Wyman's study of the 1890 election in Wisconsin claimed "solid evidence in support of the contention that ethnicity was a primary determinant of voting behavior in the late nineteenth century."[15] Michael F. Holt's book on the formation of the Republican party in Pittsburgh appeared in 1969 and represented the first full-length study in support of Silbey's assertion regarding ethnocultural factors in the pre-Civil War decades. That same year, an analysis of German voting in late nineteenth-century Nebraska by Frederick C. Luebke assigned to cultural issues and ethnic identifications a strong role in determining party loyalties. In 1970, Paul Kleppner's account of midwestern politics traced the persistence of ethnoreligious voting alignments from the 1850s to the 1890s; Richard Jensen's 1971 book told a similar story. Ronald P. Formisano's study of Michigan from the 1820s until 1861 and Samuel T. McSeveney's account of Middle Atlantic state politics in the 1890s appeared in 1971 and 1972, respectively, and joined the now-impressive shelf of ethnocultural histories.[16]

Most of these works concentrate on northeastern and midwestern politics in the 1850s and 1890s—those regions and eras in which European immigration and burgeoning cultural heterogeneity had decisive demographic, social, and economic consequences. Further research is needed to establish whether theories of political behavior applicable to the relatively highly urbanized northeastern quadrant of the United States are generalizable to other geographic areas. Despite the chronological limitations, it

14. *The Transformation of American Politics, 1840–1860* (Englewood Cliffs, N. J., 1967), pp. 1–34.

15. "Wisconsin Ethnic Groups and the Election of 1890," *Wisconsin Magazine of History*, Vol. 51 (Summer 1968), 283.

16. Citations to the works by Holt, Luebke, Kleppner, Jensen, Formisano, and McSeveney appear in note 1.

is not surprising that the 1850s and 1890s should attract attention from historians concerned with problems of coalition-making. These decades were not only peak eras of immigration but were also the great periods of partisan realignment in the nineteenth century. Both periods, however, witnessed unusual economic and sectional crises. Ethnocultural interpretations of realignment depend on successful efforts to demonstrate that local cultural concerns had at least as much impact upon the regrouping of voters as national economic and sectional issues.

Calling explicit attention to the divisions between politics at the national and local levels and between economic and cultural issues, ethnocultural historians make what is perhaps their most important contribution to the study of American political behavior: they explain how those divisions are bridged. They believe that the economic programs of state and national leaders are related to the aspirations of culturally oriented voters at the grassroots level with the image, aura, or character a political party projects.

The implication of "party character" is that voters respond most basically to party symbolism, not policies. According to Hays, party "ideologies are frequently instruments of mass communication which mobilize local impulses for national, cosmopolitan objectives."[17] While most ethnoculturalists have shied away from the word "ideology," they have pursued Hays's suggestion that parties employ specialized strategies to activate voters on national issues. The linkages, however, are not policy positions, but the images which party leaders project. In Benson's words, "Aside from the principles and policies it adopts and advocates, a party radiates an aura that influences the way the electorate appraises and responds to its principles and policies. A useful distinction can be made, therefore, between a party's *program* and its aura, or *character*."[18] Kleppner similarly suggests that "It is the mode of treatment, the 'style' component

17. "Community-Society Continuum," p. 161.
18. Benson, p. 216.

of the issue, that provides the link between public policies and leadership activities on one hand, and grass-roots voter concerns on the other."[19]

Formisano suggests that "The actions of leaders and parties . . . probably came to have symbolic meaning for many voters."[20] Even party rhetoric on particular economic issues could convey to voters a message about where the party stood on cultural issues close to their daily lives. Thus, according to Kleppner, in the 1890s midwestern Democrats pressed the tariff reduction issue with "the argument that the tariff was simply another example of Republican paternalism and, as such, was equivalent to the usual kinds of sumptuary [i.e., temperance] legislation that Republicans advocated."[21] Jensen similarly points to the way in which Republicans used the currency issue in 1896: "Sound money thus became the symbol of the economic and cultural pluralism that . . . [McKinley] knew would sweep the cities and the immigrants into an invincible coalition."[22] In analogous ways, almost all the ethnocultural historians have examined party propaganda for its stylistic and symbolic appeals to voters' cultural impulses. Central to the ethnocultural historians' view of American politics is the idea that partisan appeals are carefully constructed bridges between leadership goals and grass-roots aspirations. It is a party's character and image, and not its formal policy proposals, which attract voters and maintain their loyalty.[23]

Assuming party loyalties are fashioned in response to the images which parties project, and not in response to policy pro-

19. Kleppner, *The Cross*, p. 150.
20. Formisano, p. 97.
21. Kleppner, *The Cross*, p. 154.
22. Jensen, *The Winning*, p. 305.
23. Some of the ethnocultural historians have explicitly adopted the concept of party character, while others have only implied it. Formisano explores the idea at some length: pp. 56–80. Luebke strongly suggests that it was the character of the Democratic party, rather than its policy proposals, that attracted Nebraska Germans (pp. 61 and 115) and that Germans rejected Populism in response to that party's perceived nativist character: pp. 58–59 and 144–145. Holt does not

grams on national issues, two essential questions arise. First, what kinds of ethnic and religious impulses do political leaders exploit in the creation of partisan affiliations? Put another way, *how* do ethnocultural identifications become political ones? Second, if voters are primarily motivated by cultural concerns, then from where do economic policies come? And what do the processes of coalition-making and policy formation have to do with one another? To the first question, ethnoculturalists have offered strikingly diverse answers; on the second question, they are surprisingly ambivalent.

So long as explanations of party affiliation were based on socioeconomic class differences, they were of limited complexity. Most people voted to advance the material interests of their own class, though a few (like Arthur Schlesinger, Jr.'s George Bancroft)[24] were moved by sympathy for economically oppressed groups other than their own. A theory of the motivations underlying partisan allegiance is self-evidently part and parcel of an economic interpretation of politics. An ethnocultural theory, by contrast, embodies no intrinsic or obvious explanation of motives for party voting. Lacking formal church or nationality parties in the United States, an almost limitless range of factors could, in theory, transform ethnic or religious identities into political ones. Whatever the objective truth of recent historians' assertions that ethnocultural identities were the principal determinants of party affiliation, a wide range of motivations could account for that determination. The connections between culture and politics, however firm, are not simple.

---

explicitly adopt the notion of party character, but like Kleppner and Jensen, he holds that economic issues could be politicized in a culturally symbolic manner: pp. 243 and 258. McSeveney in *Politics of Depression* develops the perception that a party's image could differ at the national and local levels: pp. 186 and 210.

24. Arthur M. Schlesinger, Jr., *The Age of Jackson* (New York, 1945), chapter 13, especially pp. 161–162.

Although there is no theoretical limit to the ways in which ethnocultural identifications could be conceived to have political significance, close attention to the recent work of ethnocultural-ists reveals that they rely on three sorts of hypotheses to account for the translation of cultural differences into political ones. One explanation is that negative reference group feelings are the determinants of party affiliation. Voters cast their ballots princi-pally to oppose those ethnic and religious groups whom they dislike. A second hypothesis is that ethnocultural groups often seek political means of extending the dominion of their own cultural practices, or of protecting those practices from attack. Issues like temperance, English language instruction in the schools, and Sunday observance stimulate partisan divisions. A third explanation is that political affiliations reflect differences in religious beliefs and world views. Each major party directs its appeals to devotees of one of two clusters of religious values, usually described as evangelical, pietistic, or puritan on one hand, and nonevangelical, liturgical, or ritualistic on the other. The evangelical or pietistic religious orientation emphasizes an intense personal faith in God and stresses moral standards of individual behavior. The liturgical or ritualistic religious per-spective emphasizes belief in traditional doctrine and adherence to historic religious customs and practices.[25]

Samuel P. Hays's explanation of party realignment before the Civil War embodies all three theories of how cultural differences become political differences. He writes, "In the form of Prohibi-tion, nativism, and antislavery . . . [evangelical Protestantism] produced both a sharp realignment of voting behavior and a cultural unity for the Republican party. The Democratic party, in turn, combined Catholics and German Lutherans and non-evangelical Protestant native-born Americans in a common hos-tility to evangelical imperialism and the negative reference

25. The best concise definition of the two contrasting groups of religious values is given by Kleppner; see *The Cross*, p. 73. See below for discussion of how different ethnocultural historians have used these terms to denote politically salient religious values.

groups espousing it."[26] These sentences contain several easily distinguishable theories about the role of culture as a source of voting behavior. First, at the level of religious belief, Hays finds conflict between evangelicals and nonevangelicals. Second, at the level of life-style, Hays suggests that the efforts of one group to promote its own cultural practices, especially in regard to liquor, met resistance and that the conflict found expression in opposing political affiliations. Finally, at the level of group perceptions, Hays says that groups voted against each other because they took one another as negative referents. These impulses are theoretically compatible with one another if, indeed, they operate jointly as Hays implies. But they represent fundamentally different conceptions of the motivation for voting behavior. Religious beliefs, conflicts of custom and habit, and group hatreds may be intertwined, and yet they are distinct ways of specifying the relationship between culture and party affiliation.

Lee Benson's account of native-American voting patterns in New York's Rockland County during the Jackson period bears close comparison to Hays's analysis of the bases of realignment before the Civil War.[27] While all groups of native voters "tended to be relatively evenly divided" between the Whig and Democratic parties in New York State as a whole, Benson discovers that Rockland Yankees (descendants of New Englanders) and Yorkers (natives whose ancestors settled first in New York) sharply polarized against one another.[28] He writes, "In areas where the Dutch [a principal Yorker group] and Yankees came into more or less direct contact, we can reasonably infer from the voting statistics that social and cultural antagonisms found political expression." The Dutch in such a situation tended to be disproportionately Democratic, while their Yankee antagonists were heavily Whig. Each group took the other as a negative referent and "shape[d] their voting behavior accordingly."[29]

26. "Community-Society Continuum," pp. 158–159.
27. Benson, pp. 293–304.
28. Ibid., pp. 184 and 301.
29. Ibid., pp. 301 and 303.

Group traditions and beliefs reinforced these reference group antagonisms, according to Benson. The Rockland Dutch "tilled their ancestral fields much as their ancestors had tilled them and they abided by their fathers' faith in state rights and negative government." While the Dutch were thus "likely to respond to the [Democratic] party that preached the doctrines of the negative liberal state and state rights," Yankees traditionally demanded "precisely the kind of activist, collectivist state most repugnant to those 'Dutchmen,'" and so voted for the Whigs.[30] Just as Dutch and Yankee voters responded to party images on matters of government activism, they also reacted to perceived moral differences between the parties. According to Benson, "pious Yankees tended to respond to . . . Whig appeals for state-guided and state-enforced 'moral reformation.'" By contrast, "though the Dutch did not lack piety or respect for ecclesiastical authority, their conception of the church 'was by no means as vivid and embracing as that held in New England.'"[31]

Reference group perceptions, tradition, and religious values all work in harmony in Benson's account. While these impulses may have been jointly operative in Rockland County, producing heavily Democratic voting by the Dutch and strong Whig allegiance among Yankees, Benson's explanation is too good and too airtight to account for his own estimate that in New York State both Yankees and Yorkers divided pretty evenly between the parties.[32] By selecting for close observation a county where so many ethnocultural factors worked together, Benson has obscured our perception of any of them. Benson's technique of building one explanation upon the next undercuts his own capacity to account for the diverse political affiliations formed by native American voters of similar background throughout the state.

30. Ibid., pp. 298, 299, and 303. For Benson's concept of the "negative liberal state," see ibid., pp. 86–109.

31. Ibid., p. 300.

32. For evidence that Benson is aware of this problem to some degree, see ibid., p. 293.

Most ethnocultural historians do not, like Hays and Benson, combine so many explanations of ethnic and religious voting patterns. Though reference group hostilities, clashes of cultural tradition, and conflicts of religious values are neither contradictory to one another nor mutually exclusive, there are two compelling reasons for distinguishing among them. First, these impulses may not always function jointly as in the Hays and Benson accounts. Other ethnocultural historians have detailed instances in which voters were cross-pressured between reference group antagonisms and the urge to protect their own cultural practices, or between group hatreds and religious beliefs. Second, ethnoculturalists have opened up the complex question of the sources of voter motivation, and that problem cannot be easily disposed of by the simple assertion that on different, but harmonious, levels, ethnocultural identifications promoted party differences. There is no obvious reason why cultural differences should become political ones, and to pile one explanation upon the next is to obscure the problem of salience as quickly as it was uncovered in the first place.

Most recent ethnocultural historians assume that nineteenth-century ethnic and religious voting groups took one another as referents, often as negative referents, and that that orientation was a determinant of voting behavior. Drawn from sociologist Robert K. Merton's observation that "men frequently orient themselves to groups *other than their own* in shaping their behavior and evaluations,"[33] the negative reference group concept has been applied by historians both as an independent explanation of voting patterns and in conjunction with interpretations based on religious values and cultural practices.[34]

Michael F. Holt is the most insistent proponent of the view that simple group antagonism explains political alignments in

33. Robert K. Merton, *Social Theory and Social Structure*, Enlarged Ed. (New York, 1968), p. 288.

34. For explicit discussions of the reference group concept, see Benson, pp. 27, 284–285, 301–304, and 315–317; Luebke, p. 8; Silbey, *The Transformation*, pp. 8–11; and Swierenga, "Ethnic Voter," p. 32.

the nineteenth century. Writing of Pittsburgh politics in the 1840s, Holt says "some . . . native-born workers and shopkeepers . . . voted Whig to express their resentment against and disassociation from the immigrants and Catholics whom they considered Democrats." Similarly he contends that the growth of the Republican coalition was shaped as much by "the mutual dislike by the members of one party for those of the other" as by national questions.[35] While Holt occasionally slips into a quasi-ideological account of voting patterns (some Whigs "took a different moral view on issues than did those who belonged to the Democratic party"),[36] his basic analysis is exclusively in reference group terms. Responding directly to the view that Protestant moral zeal for temperance, antislavery, and Sabbatarian reform promoted the growth of the Republican party, Holt insists that "a large number of Protestants voted Republican out of a negative reflex response to the Catholics in the Democratic party. Simply because Catholics were Democrats, and not necessarily for any positive reasons, many Protestants voted Republican."[37]

More typically, ethnocultural analysis connects group political antagonism to conflicts of custom or belief. In general, those ethnoculturalists who have focused on foreign-born voters offer an explanation of political behavior based upon cultural defense. By contrast, those who have explored the politics of both native Americans and foreigners find that differences in religious values were the source of political divisions. Both groups of historians hold that Whigs and, later, Republicans supported temperance, Sunday observance, and English language education to attract the votes of native Americans and some Protestant ethnic groups. Democrats, they contend, fought these efforts to impinge upon ways of living to which their party's constituency was devoted. Though these historians agree on the basic scenario for the conflict, they differ in their accounts of the kinds of human motives at stake.

35. Holt, pp. 81 and 8.
36. Ibid., p. 82.
37. Ibid., p. 218n.

Emphasizing differences in custom, not belief, several ethno-cultural historians have entered the long-standing debate about the immigrant vote in 1860. Robert P. Swierenga and George H. Daniels contend, respectively, that Dutch and German voters in Iowa supported the Democrats that year in reaction against the Republican party's nativist and prohibitionist image.[38] Specifically denying that Germans were unusually attracted by the Republican ideology of liberty, Daniels says that "Like masses everywhere, the rank and file Germans . . . considered their own liberty to be of paramount importance. Apparently ignoring the advice of their leaders, they cast their ballots for the party which consistently promised them liberty from prohibition and native-American legislation."[39]

At the end of the century, too, immigrants voted to defend themselves against the imposition of native-American ways of living. Roger E. Wyman's study of the election of 1890 in Wisconsin concludes that German Lutherans, traditionally in the Republican camp, voted Democratic that year to express their opposition to the Bennett Law, a GOP measure requiring English language instruction in the schools.[40] Only once before had the Republicans lost an election in Wisconsin (in 1873, when the party pushed through the Graham liquor law setting high license fees for liquor establishments), and Wyman accounts for their defeat by reference to German determination to protect *Deutschtum*. "Throughout much of eastern Wisconsin," he says, "German immigrants jealously guarded what they regarded as their right to preserve many of the customs they brought with them from Europe."[41]

38. Swierenga, "Ethnic Voter," p. 41; Daniels in Silbey and McSeveney (eds.), p. 149.

39. Daniels in ibid., p. 149. Kleppner's study of the immigrant vote in Pittsburgh in 1860 supports the Swierenga-Daniels view of the importance of the prohibition issue that year, but Kleppner finds a religious division more important than an ethnic one ("Lincoln," p. 187).

40. Wyman, "Wisconsin Ethnic Groups." Other ethnocultural historians also deal with the political consequences of the Bennett Law: Jensen, *The Winning*, pp. 123–140; and Kleppner, *The Cross*, pp. 158–159 and 165–167.

41. "Wisconsin Ethnic Groups," p. 273.

Like the Wyman study, Frederick C. Luebke's analysis of Nebraska Germans in the 1880s and 1890s explains voting patterns in terms of cultural defense. "As the 1880s passed," he writes, "the identification of the German voters with the Democratic party was strengthened under the pressure of continued agitation for woman suffrage, prohibition, and Sabbatarianism. By 1890 . . . a remarkable consensus had been achieved among a diverse people as they embraced the Democratic party as the champion of personal liberty."[42] As in Wyman's Wisconsin, Germans in Nebraska switched to the Democrats in response to a perceived threat to *Deutschtum*. "Prohibition," in Luebke's words, "was in reality not a simple political issue. It was the political symbol of a general conflict of cultures that confronted the immigrant." German Democratic votes represented a "defense of their cultural heritage" against the bigotry of both Republicans and Populists.[43]

Several ethnocultural historians demonstrate that ethnic voters were not always able to reconcile their reference group perceptions and life-style interests. Samuel T. McSeveney's account of New York City voting patterns in the middle 1890s is illustrative.[44] German Lutherans, McSeveney says, "voted Democratic despite their antipathy toward Irish Catholics because of Republican involvement with [i.e., implicit support for] Prohibitionism." In 1894, however, Germans joined Republicans in an anti-Tammany coalition that downplayed cultural issues and elected William Strong mayor of New York. Within a year, the fusion organization was deeply divided over the liquor and Sunday-

42. Luebke, p. 115.
43. Ibid., pp. 124 and 151.
44. McSeveney, *Politics of Depression*, pp. 99–106, 108–113, 142–148, 151–155. McSeveney is something of an exception to the generalization offered concerning the division between ethnoculturalists who focus on ethnic voters and those who explore the political behavior of all groups. His study of northeastern politics in the 1890s covers native-born members of the electorate as well as immigrants, but McSeveney's account generally relies on reference group perceptions and cultural defense to account for party identifications. At least twice, however, he uses religious values to explain native-American voting behavior; see pp. 47 and 205–206.

closing questions; when Republican Police Commissioner Theodore Roosevelt demanded strict enforcement of the Sunday laws, Germans returned to the Democratic party.[45] As McSeveney's analysis makes plain, both Tammany and the GOP represented groups and practices which German Lutherans abhorred. Tammany stood for Irish Catholic power and political corruption. The Republicans symbolized native-American domination and a threat to Sundays and beer. German voting behavior in the mid-1890s signifies the impossibility of keeping all reference group and life-style impulses in harmony. Each election day posed a choice in which a range of ethnocultural voting determinants were by no means easily reconciled.

Wyman's analysis also suggests that politically salient cultural feelings cannot be assumed always to be jointly operative. The elections of 1873 and 1890 in Wisconsin ran counter to the overall drift of German Protestants into the Republican party as a result of the "subtle exploitation of the inherent religious antagonisms between Catholic and Protestant Germans by Republican party leaders."[46] Reference group antagonisms helped solidify Republican domination in Wisconsin, but there was always the possibility that a life-style issue like English language instruction or temperance would override those religious hatreds and swing crucial votes to the Democratic party. Republicans lost the election in the Bennett Law year of 1890 because their efforts to overcome cultural protection with cultural dislike were unsuccessful.

While at least one ethnocultural historian, Frederick C. Luebke, asserts that a theory of cultural defense or cultural protection can explain native-American voting as well as immigrant political behavior,[47] most ethnocultural historians suggest that native activity on life-style issues is more logically regarded as aggressive rather than defensive. The line between cultural pro-

45. Ibid., pp. 102–103, 142–144, and 153.
46. "Wisconsin Ethnic Groups," p. 270.
47. Luebke, p. 130.

tection and cultural imperialism is a thin one. The drive of native Americans to impose their styles of Sunday behavior, education, and beverage consumption upon immigrants (cultural imperialism) could easily be conceived of and expressed as a desire to protect American moral standards from the corruption of alien ways. Similarly, immigrant defense of ethnic habits could be regarded and denounced as an effort to transmit those ways of living to all Americans. In spite of their rhetorical similarities, the urge to protect one's customs and habits and the effort to impose cultural practices upon others represent quite different kinds of links between ethnocultural identifications and politics. The simple desire to go on living a certain way can explain the ethnic response without recourse to ideological or psychological factors. The desire to extend one's own cultural mores, by contrast, is not so simple. Religious beliefs, or perhaps an inbred cultural paranoia, might better account for the behavior of native Americans. Consequently, it is understandable why ethnocultural historians who try to explain the political affiliations of voters other than immigrants find the source of conflict not simply in different ways of living but also in different ways of believing.

Benson and Hays were the first historians to suggest that partisan political differences reflect primarily the division between devotees of two identifiable strains of religious values. More recently, Kleppner, Jensen, and Formisano have treated this subject.[48] Despite differences in terminology and willingness to identify the politically salient values with particular theological creeds,[49] all five ethnoculturalists agree that in the nineteenth century voters

48. Benson, pp. 198–205; Hays, "History," pp. 196–197; Kleppner, *The Cross*, pp. 69–91; Jensen, *The Winning*, pp. 58–88; Formisano, pp. 137–164.

49. Benson's terms are "puritan" and "nonpuritan"; Hays uses the word "Pietism" but it has no opposite; Kleppner distinguishes between "pietists" and "ritualists"; Jensen calls them "pietists" and "liturgicals"; Formisano's phrases are "evangelical" and "nonevangelical."

whose religious heritage was pietistic or evangelical were prone to support the Whigs and, later, the Republicans, while those whose religion was nonevangelical or ritualistic normally voted Democratic. Expressed as a generalization by Kleppner: "The more ritualistic the religious orientation of the group, the more likely it was to support the Democracy; conversely, the more pietistic the group's outlook the more intensely Republican its partisan affiliation."[50]

These historians find the link between religious values and politics in the urge of evangelicals and pietists to "reach out and purge the world of sin." In Jensen's words, "The bridge linking theology and politics was the demand by pietists that the government remove the major obstacle to the purification of society through revivalistic Christianity, institutionalized immorality." Formisano agrees: "The feature of evangelical Calvinism holding most salience for political behavior was concern for the moral and social welfare of the community."[51] Pietists favored Sabbatarian legislation, temperance, and, before the Civil War, abolition. Ritualists opposed all three. Differences in religious values became political when the Whig and Republican parties gave at least tacit approval to the moral reform wanted by pietists, while the Democrats supported the liturgical demand for state neutrality regarding personal behavior.[52]

Kleppner, Jensen, and Formisano are all quite explicit in crediting religious values and world views based on those values

Benson and Formisano are reluctant to associate the two clusters of values with theology; see *The Concept*, p. 200, and *The Birth*, pp. 137–138. For Hays, Kleppner, and Jensen the distinction is more closely tied to religious practices and theology: see Hays, "History," p. 196; Kleppner, *The Cross*, p. 73; Jensen, *The Winning*, pp. 62–68.

50. Kleppner, *The Cross*, p. 71. See also Jensen, *The Winning*, p. 69; Hays, "History," pp. 196–197; Benson, pp. 198–207; Formisano, pp. 138, 324, and 330.

51. Kleppner, *The Cross*, p. 73; Jensen, *The Winning*, p. 67; Formisano, p. 141; see also Benson, pp. 205–207; Hays, "History," p. 196.

52. Benson, pp. 205–207; Hays, "History," p. 197, and "Community-Society Continuum," pp. 158–159 and 174; Kleppner, *The Cross*, pp. 71–79; Formisano, pp. 102–127.

with the creation of party differences. According to Kleppner, "Partisan affiliations . . . were political expressions of shared values derived from the voter's membership in, and commitment to, ethnic and religious groups." Elsewhere he says "The conflict was literally one of divergent value systems, and of value systems which had been *sanctified*." Jensen asserts directly that "theology, rather than language, customs, or heritage, was the foundation of cultural and political subgroups in America." Of the political situation in the Midwest in 1889, he writes, "The issue was the tension between the pietistic and liturgical world views." Formisano refers to the "value conflicts imbedded in party cleavages," and he asserts that "Whigs and Democrats did possess diverging ideologies which must be seen in the broader context of their antipathetic world views of man and society."[53]

The very same issues which other ethnocultural historians regard as clashes of custom and habit are treated by Kleppner, Jensen, and Formisano as conflicts of value and belief. Thus, for Kleppner, the debate over education was a "question of *whose* value system was to be transmitted to future generations." According to Jensen, "the prohibition issue tapped a deeper layer of values and beliefs" than a simple old-stock versus immigrant cleavage. To the drys, "opposition to the evils of alcohol was a tenet of religious belief."[54]

The point is not that if Wyman and Luebke are right about these issues, then Kleppner, Jensen, and Formisano must be wrong, or vice versa. It is easily imaginable that the conflict over liquor, for example, represented a clash of beliefs as well as ways of living. As already noted, to explain the aggressive behavior of native Americans, it may be necessary to treat cultural issues as reflections of deep-seated values and beliefs. Nevertheless, crediting world views with the determination of partisan loyalties is quite a different explanation than citing cultural defense or

53. Kleppner, *The Cross*, pp. 35 and 75; Jensen, *The Winning*, pp. 82 and 89; Formisano, pp. 102 and 55.

54. Kleppner, *The Cross*, p. 78; Jensen, *The Winning*, pp. 70 and 72.

simple group hatreds. These represent strikingly divergent theories about the kinds of human motives which are the source of political activity.

Strong support for the proposition that different kinds of ethnocultural political impulses must explicitly be differentiated from one another is provided by close examination of the "world view" interpretations of Kleppner and Jensen. Though these historians are reluctant to admit it, the link between religious beliefs and political behavior is quite different for the liturgicals (or ritualists) than for the pietists. Like Benson, Hays, and Formisano, Kleppner and Jensen establish the initial connection between politics and religion by pointing to the pietistic urge to regulate social morality by legal means. There is no analogous linkage between the liturgical world view and political action. "The *ritualistic* perspective," according to Kleppner, "views the world as a sinful one, but one that has to be accepted as such." Jensen agrees that liturgicals believed "the state had no right to assert a role in delineating public morality."[55] It is not that liturgicals lack values, but that these values have no political significance until they are assaulted by pietists. Kleppner fleetingly admits that "the pietistic orientation obviously has greater social relevance than that stressing intellectual assent to doctrine," but he immediately obscures the assertion with the irrelevant observation that "neither perspective is *inherently* radical nor *inherently* conservative."[56] The question is not one of radicalism versus conservatism, but of "social relevance." Pietism (as defined by Kleppner and Jensen) is intrinsically political; liturgicalism is political only when its adherents are on the defensive.

Though religious values are the source of political action in different ways, Kleppner and Jensen are consistent in upholding a "world view" explanation of ethnocultural voting. Formisano, by contrast, slips back and forth between interpretations based upon reference group antagonisms and interpretations based on

55. Kleppner, *The Cross*, p. 73; Jensen, *The Winning*, p. 64.
56. Kleppner, *The Cross*, p. 74.

religious beliefs. Indeed, it is doubtful that Formisano intends to ground his account simply on value clashes between evangelicals and nonevangelicals. The opening sentence of his chapter on religion and political parties asserts that "Religion as a group experience and source of values profoundly influenced political behavior in nineteenth-century America."[57] The problem is that Formisano never indicates that religion "as a group experience" may not be politically significant in the same manner as religion as a "source of values." Sometimes Formisano explains voting in terms of values only: "to promote their values evangelicals voted anti-Democratic."[58] In other passages, he appears to equate a conflict of values with group hatreds: "Patterns of negative reaction between evangelicals and other groups explain much voting behavior in Michigan from 1835 to 1852."[59] The point is not that group hatreds and clashes of values are incompatible explanations of political behavior, but that by running them together Formisano is imprecise about how ethnocultural impulses become political. Precision is necessary because group feelings and religious beliefs do not always operate together.

Formisano's account of the social and cultural sources of realignment in the 1850s suffers because he cannot fully explain the movement to the "evangelical" Republican party by groups he has previously identified as "nonevangelical," particularly Methodists and German Lutherans.[60] By the logic of Formisano's own analysis, members of these religious groups should have felt torn between their nonevangelical religious values and their dislike

57. Formisano, p. 137.
58. Ibid., p. 143. See also p. 160.
59. Ibid., p. 194. See also p. 167. In his discussion of individual religious groups, Formisano often moves back and forth between comments on religious values and on group antagonism. See, for instance, his account of Baptist behavior, pp. 142–143.
60. For discussion of the Methodists and German Lutherans as "nonevangelicals," see ibid., pp. 152–155 and 184. For the account of the movement by members of these groups to the Republican party, see ibid., pp. 277, 298–304, and 312–314. Formisano is careful to note that many Methodists and German Protestants remained in the Democratic party.

for Catholics. The Republican party represented a version of Protestant beliefs which Methodists and Lutherans rejected, while the Democrats were the party of Popery. But Formisano neglects to differentiate the contradictory effects on voting of religion as a "group experience" and as a "source of values." Religion should have worked in two ways for nonevangelicals who moved in the anti-Democratic direction, and the full development of ethnocultural analysis ought to make the distinction.

Aside from the need for distinctions between different ethnocultural impulses, there are special reasons for caution regarding the linkages between religious values and political behavior which Kleppner, Jensen, and Formisano describe. They explain the relationship between religious world views and politics by referring to the pietistic urge to enforce communal adherence to specific moral standards. But American religious scholars have pointed to ambiguities and divisions in the pietistic tradition, particularly on the question of coercing morality by legal means, such as through prohibition laws. William G. McLoughlin cites an "inherent tension within pietism" between traditions of coercion and voluntarism.[61] Other historians have described an ongoing conflict in nineteenth-century evangelical religion between proponents of moral suasion as a means of social reform and those who urged the legal regulation of personal behavior.[62] The

61. William G. McLoughlin, "Pietism and the American Character," *American Quarterly*, Vol. 17 (Summer 1965), 165.

62. Clifford S. Griffin, *Their Brothers' Keepers: Moral Stewardship in the United States, 1800–1865* (New Brunswick, N. J., 1960), especially pp. 99–151. Joseph R. Gusfield in *Symbolic Crusade: Status Politics and the American Temperance Movement* (Urbana, Ill., 1963) argues that the nineteenth-century temperance movement embodied both "assimilative and coercive traditions" and that the commitment to coercion in the late nineteenth century was not inherent in religious beliefs but was rather a "response to cultural confrontations" between native and immigrant groups in the United States; see pp. 69 and 98. Sidney E. Mead in *The Lively Experiment: The Shaping of Christianity in America* (New York, 1963) has noted that the revivalistic tradition itself reinforced the commitment to persuasion and voluntarism in reform movements. "The revivals had demonstrated the possibilities of persuasion. Subsequently, they taught confidence in it" (p. 113).

very feature of pietism which enables Kleppner, Jensen, and Formisano to link religious values to politics is more ambiguous than they admit.

The nature of church membership in the nineteenth century suggests further limitations to an explanation of political behavior based upon the religious values of different denominations. A large proportion of the population was unaffiliated with a church and thus beyond the scope of party allegiance based upon religious beliefs.[63] Moreover, these historians do not take account of variations in the degree of devotion to religious values which even church members in the electorate possessed. It is doubtful that all those nominally attached to religious groups felt a commitment sufficient to shape their political behavior. In addition, a high proportion of church members then were women, and hence, nonvoters. Particularly in the Protestant denominations, 60 percent or more of those belonging to the church were females, signifying that the proportion of voters who were nonmembers was higher than the percentage of nonchurch members in the entire population.[64]

An interpretation of voting behavior based upon religious values introduces another version of the fallacious assumption that leadership opinions reflect the perceptions of the mass of voters. Ethnoreligious historians have properly distinguished between the beliefs and motives of party leaders and those of voters, but they readily assume that religious leaders succeeded, where politicians failed, in transmitting their opinions directly to the electorate. Even if nineteenth-century pietism had been unam-

63. Jensen estimates that in the Midwest in 1890 fully 27 percent of the population was not church affiliated (*The Winning*, p. 88), and his individual-level data on Illinois and Indiana in the 1870s include huge proportions of voters whose party affiliations cannot be explained by religion (ibid., pp. 59–62; and "Religious and Occupational Roots"). Most of Formisano's tabular presentations of the religious and political preferences of Michigan voting units simply omit those in which the "religiosity" (i.e., ratio of church seats to population) was less than 50 percent (pp. 144, 313, and 315).

64. Henry K. Carroll, *The Religious Forces of the United States* (New York, 1912), pp. lvi–lix.

biguous in its implications for the legal regulation of morality, and even if all voters had been committed church members, a religious world-view explanation of voting would require evidence that ministers, if not politicians, truly shaped the beliefs of voters.

Starting with similar assumptions about what political history ought to be and about the manner in which national parties utilize culturally salient images to attract grass-roots voters, ethnocultural historians describe three different ways in which the ethnic and religious identifications of those voters are translated into political affiliations. Theories of reference group antagonism, cultural defense, and religious world views represent diverse conceptions of the kinds of human aspirations which are politically significant. Those aspirations are not mutually exclusive; indeed, they may function concurrently, either in harmony with one another, or in contradiction to one another. But it is imperative that political historians distinguish between them, both because ethnocultural impulses *can* operate in opposition to each other, and in order to understand what kinds of motives and feelings are politically salient at different times and in different places.

The same issue can be politicized for different members of the electorate in diverse ways. Temperance is easily understandable as an attack on aliens and Catholics, as a defense of the native-American way of living, and as an expression of the evangelical urge to make the community more moral. Sabbatarianism and English language education could similarly be politicized at these three different levels. Thus there is nothing surprising about the variety of historical accounts of the meaning of these issues to grass-roots voters. But because the three levels at which the same public question can be treated reflect diverse kinds of political motives and because different groups of voters could exhibit them, historians must make clear just *how* ethnocultural impulses become political ones. An examination of political rhetoric might indicate, for instance, that in some urban communities temperance was politicized primarily at the level of anti-

Catholicism, that elsewhere it was propagandized principally as a way of defending American cultural traditions, and that in some closely knit evangelical communities temperance was pressed as a way of fulfilling one's Christian duty to reform society.

Each of the ethnocultural historians discussed in this essay gives preeminent attention to one of the three mechanisms whereby cultural impulses become political. A joint examination of these recent studies suggests, however, that historians ought explicitly to take account of the variety of ways in which ethnic and religious aspirations are politically salient. For one thing, the same cultural issue could move different groups of voters in diverse ways. For another, a single voter could be torn between various ethnoreligious impulses and face at the ballot box a choice between his hatreds, his habits, and his beliefs.[65]

An ethnocultural interpretation of past political behavior is fashioned as an explicit alternative to the "progressive" view that socioeconomic divisions are the most important determinants of voting behavior and of party coalitions. Yet the most significant theoretical question raised by ethnocultural history is not whether grass-roots voting is economically determined but whether electoral behavior is rational and goal oriented at all. Given the deep importance of cultural concerns to voters, it is surprising how minimal were the fruits of their prejudices and values. Only a small proportion of public policies in the nineteenth century were culturally oriented, and the question arises as to why the American electorate was so strikingly unsuccessful at

65. Some ethnoreligious conflicts have no political salience. Hostility between different nationality groups in the Catholic Church rarely produced political divisions, though analogous antagonisms in Protestant churches frequently found political expression. A theory of ethnocultural politics ought to specify not only the variety of cultural conflicts which are politically meaningful, but also the circumstances under which those conflicts will fail to achieve political significance.

getting results on the ethnoreligious and ethnocultural factors that mattered most. From the perspective of the ethnocultural challenge to progressive history, it is ironic that most of the government's actions related to those economic issues deemed of such small significance in the determination of voting behavior. The most important message conveyed by ethnocultural analysis is not that voters are ethnically and religiously motivated, but that grass-roots concerns are so irrelevant to public policymaking.

Voting can be understood as the expression of deeply felt personal impulses without assuming that its goal is to further the implementation of particular programs, even ethnocultural ones. The wide range of human feelings and motives upon which appeals for temperance and Sabbath observance were based suggests that desire for specific public policies is not what moves the mass of the electorate. Most voters respond to group likes and dislikes, to fondness for their own way of living, or to a perception of what their God requires. The relation between particular government actions and these deeply personal aspirations is never very direct or obvious. Political rhetoric is designed to establish the connections and to popularize specific public programs by relating them to what men feel. Since most decisions about governmental acts are not overtly cultural, leaders undertake to make those connections for other kinds of issues as well.

If voting behavior is a response to carefully fashioned rhetoric and does not signify the demand for particular government policies, then where and how do public policy programs arise? And if voters care most passionately about cultural rather than material matters, then why is so much of the political rhetoric and so much of the government's activity devoted to economic affairs? Ethnocultural history raises the question of what, if any, relation the processes of mobilizing voters into political parties and determining economic policies bear to one another. It is important to ask how thoroughly ethnocultural historians have transcended a rational, goal-oriented view of politics and to see how directly they have faced the question of the relation between mobilizing voters and making economic policies.

Though most ethnoculturalists are not concerned with the sources of economic policies,[66] they take for granted that these programs are formulated by elites rather than by grass-roots voters. Formisano says that in Michigan "The parties' mass supporters tended to follow the positions on economic issues marked out by national and state leaderships." Kleppner points out that leadership decisions are a "visible limitation" on party rhetoric: "When the national and state leaders of the party commit themselves . . . to a high tariff policy, the party's campaign propaganda cannot very well depict the organization as a vehicle for free-trade sentiment."[67] Ironically, while ethnocultural historians assume policies are the creations of leaders, they analyze them only from the perspective of their influence upon voters. If leaders have any purposes other than the mobilization of the electorate, these are ignored by historians who take as their subject grass-roots behavior. Thus McSeveney says that "Republican leaders had for some time sought to maintain unity among various groups within the party's coalition by stressing the tariff as the bond that united Republicans."[68] The questions of why leaders chose the tariff and a protective stance on the tariff issue are answered only with regard to the effects of the strategy on voters. Policy program decisions are treated simply as the tactics of coalition makers.

Typically, ethnocultural historians consider economic policies "in terms of their symbolic meaning for the masses."[69] Both Holt and Formisano conclude that in the 1850s tariff and homestead questions were of small importance to the growth of the Republican coalition.[70] When such issues were raised, however, they often were formulated in a culturally symbolic manner. The

---

66. Hays ("Community-Society Continuum," p. 152), Jensen (*The Winning*, p. xiii), and Formisano (p. 11) explicitly disavow interest in policymaking. Other ethnocultural studies are so evidently preoccupied with voting patterns that a direct disclaimer regarding policymaking is unnecessary.

67. Formisano, p. 55; Kleppner, *The Cross*, p. 150.

68. McSeveney, *Politics of Depression*, p. 87.

69. Formisano, p. 11.

70. Holt, p. 5; Formisano, p. 280.

tariff could easily be argued as a call for the protection of native-American workers against foreigners. Homestead policy proposals for the distribution of land to "citizens" rather than "persons" could similarly take on ethnoreligious significance.[71] In the 1890s, too, economic issues were politicized in a cultural context. Kleppner notes that Democrats attacked activist Republican economic policies as threats to the "personal liberty" of voters, and, along with Jensen and McSeveney, he points to the Republican reliance on both tariff and currency questions to mute the party's anti-immigrant image.[72]

Ethnoculturalists are not thoroughly consistent in treating economic policy proposals as cultural symbols. Holt, for instance, regards national economic issues as symbolic but accepts local ones at face value. Pittsburgh Democrats, he says, "attempted to build a new coalition based on . . . popular outrage at railroads." In Holt's analysis, there was nothing false or symbolic about the local railroad issue; only when Pittsburgh Republicans themselves adopted an antirailroad stance could they neutralize Democratic gains.[73] Jensen ambivalently treats economic policy questions in 1896 as both symbolic and substantive. Much of his analysis of the presidential campaign that year suggests that the "real battle" was over culturally sensitive moral questions.[74] But Jensen also handles the currency question in a traditional, rational fashion. "Republicans," he writes, "had literature for everybody. Farmers and coal miners, wool growers and steel workers, mechanics and lumberjacks, each could read carefully prepared analyses of the relative effects of gold and silver on his own well-being. . . . Evidently most of the [200 million] pamphlets reached their target audiences and were read and reread."[75] The ethnocultural approach to political analysis

71. Holt, pp. 243 and 258; Formisano, p. 294.
72. Kleppner, *The Cross*, pp. 155-156 and 367; Jensen, *The Winning*, pp. 291 and 305; McSeveney, *Politics of Depression*, pp. 185-186.
73. Holt, pp. 221, 228, and 251-253.
74. Jensen, *The Winning*, pp. 269, 278-279, 292-296, and 305.
75. Ibid., p. 288.

embodies a denial that voters respond wholly rationally to different party policies on economic questions, but some of these
historians are reluctant to pursue that insight consistently.[76]

The ambivalence apparent in ethnocultural history about
what political parties are and what they do is another sign of
reluctance to move beyond a rational, goal-oriented view of politics to a more symbolic perspective. For the most part, these
historians regard parties as coalitional instruments. As Kleppner
puts it, hedging slightly, "Whatever else it may be, a political
party is a device for mobilizing voters." Formisano agrees, opening his book with a discussion of "parties as coalitional systems,"
and Silbey takes as his central theme in the 1840 to 1860 period
the struggle of the Republican party to reconcile "a combination
of social groups."[77] But ethnocultural historians also treat parties
as vehicles for the expression of the policy goals of grass-roots
party members. Benson regards "the pursuit of [both cultural
and economic] goals by individuals or groups" as one of the three
"categories of voting determinants." Kleppner refers to the way
in which the coalitional purposes of parties may be threatened by
the efforts of different groups to implement their demands
through the party. McSeveney upholds both a goal-oriented perspective and a coalitional view of parties. "Each party," he
writes, "contained cultural groups that sought to attain their
goals through politics." And Silbey, too, combines both interpretations of what political parties do.[78]

76. McSeveney (*Politics of Depression*) also treats economic issues in 1896 as
both substantive and symbolic. Republicans argued that a protective tariff and
gold currency would reduce unemployment and raise wages (p. 177). But these
economic issues were also symbols of the cultural inclusiveness of the GOP
(p. 220). Bryan failed because northeastern workers rejected his economic argu-
ments (p. 219) and because his moral rhetoric on the currency question was
offensive to some groups (p. 182).

77. Kleppner, *The Cross*, p. 93; Formisano, p. 3; Silbey, *The Transformation*,
especially pp. 28–32.

78. Benson, pp. 281–283; Kleppner, *The Cross*, p. 93; Samuel T. McSeveney,
"Voting in the Northeastern States During the Late Nineteenth Century," in
Silbey and McSeveney (eds.), p. 202; Silbey, *The Transformation*, p. 4.

There is nothing inherently contradictory about assigning to political parties both coalitional and goal-oriented functions; indeed, traditional political history has always assumed parties perform both kinds of tasks. Nevertheless, if voters respond most decisively to cultural images and symbols, and if leaders, rather than masses, formulate party programs, then political parties ought not to be regarded as vehicles of grass-roots demands. A coalitional definition of party functions is the most logical one for ethnocultural historians to adopt.

In its major thrust, ethnocultural political analysis recognizes that the formation of economic policy programs and the processes of voter mobilization are not intrinsically related to one another. These historians assume that economic policies are formulated by cosmopolitan leaders, refashioned as cultural symbols by local leaders, and perceived by voters in the light of cultural, not material, impulses. Nevertheless, there is an unwillingness among ethnocultural historians to accept the separation of economic policymaking from grass-roots concerns. They sometimes treat voters as goal oriented on economic policies and occasionally regard party voting as the expression of particular material demands.

The problem is dual: on the one hand, ethnoculturalists ignore the question of the origin of economic policies, and on the other hand, they sometimes imply that those policies are formulated to advance the political goals of voters. Ethnocultural historians neglect the question of how policies are formed by treating party programs only from the perspective of their strategic impact upon mass voting. Private motives of elites, as well as long-range patterns of social and economic development, are ignored as sources of economic policy. The reply that policy formation is another problem and that historians should not be criticized for the topics they select is insufficient here. Ethnocultural history purports to explore the bridges between local and national orientations in politics, between leaders and masses, and between economic policy programs and the personal aspirations of voters. Bridges cannot be studied from one bank of the river only.

If political history is not to become a branch of social history, then we need ultimately to know what determines the agenda of issues and policies that are up for decision. In effect, the ethnoculturalists have told us where not to look for an answer: the electorate. Voters have other things on their minds. Sometimes, however, ethnocultural historians imply that the electorate is the place to look. They suggest that voting *is*, in part, the expression of political goals, and that the processes of building majorities and fashioning policies are intimately related. The dangers of an exclusive focus on coalition-making are twofold: it ignores the traditional "Who gets what how?" problem, and it risks the implication that in explaining why people vote it has answered the traditional question as well.

Ethnocultural history—for all the theorizing of its practitioners—leaves us without a theory of what electoral politics have to do with policymaking. Old ideologically oriented interpretations of American politics and not-so-old class theories at least had the advantage of giving coherence to the electoral and policymaking processes. They implied that voters were goal oriented, that leaders implemented the desires of their constituents, and that the process was a rational one between two (or more) groups of voters and leaders. Ethnoculturalists have quite properly introduced elements of symbolism and myth making into our understanding of electoral behavior. They have distinguished between leadership perceptions and mass behavior, and between economic policies and cultural impulses. Indeed, they have done the job thoroughly enough to suggest that perhaps the pieces cannot be put back together again. Electoral politics and policymaking may not have a great deal to do with one another.

The symbolic patterns which politicians create to link decisions about government action to the personal aspirations of voters are available for politicizing noncultural issues as well as explicitly cultural ones. Indeed, any public question can be expressed as a reference group conflict, a life-style problem, or a question of values. The greatest single issue of the nineteenth century, slavery, was propagandized in the North at all these

levels. Abolitionists attacked the peculiar institution as sinful
and morally wrong, and thereby politicized it at the level of
beliefs and values. As Eric Foner has shown, Republican politicians more typically decried the slave system as hostile to free
labor and to the northern way of life based upon free labor.[79]
And, as several ethnocultural historians have suggested, slavery
was politically salient as a reference group issue too. Formisano,
Holt, and Silbey contend that the antislavery issue was often
most powerfully argued in the North as anti-southernism and
anti-Negroism.[80] Much of the current debate among historians
about the meaning of the slavery issue to the northern electorate
comes down to a question of the style by which it was most
frequently politicized. Slavery was a moral problem, a life-style
issue, and a negative reference group question. Like ethnocultural issues and economic ones, the slavery question could be
made salient through symbolic rhetoric at all these levels, and so
move northern voters to strong feelings about government policy
toward an institution remote from their daily lives.

While ethnocultural historians have been neither thoroughly
consistent nor fully explicit about the use of political symbolism
on other than cultural issues, their studies strongly suggest that
carefully fashioned appeals to deeply felt personal impulses,
rather than demands for particular government policies, most
decisively activated voters and helped create and maintain their
partisan loyalties. But these historians have failed to explain
adequately why political history should concentrate so much
attention on voting behavior. Election campaigns and party
loyalties were important forms of entertainment and of social
and cultural expression in the nineteenth century, but what they
had to do with other aspects of the political system remains
unclear.

79. Eric Foner, *Free Soil, Free Labor, Free Men: The Ideology of the Republican Party Before the Civil War* (New York, 1970), especially chapters 1 and 2.
80. Silbey, *The Transformation*, p. 17; Formisano, pp. 244, 265, 267–272, 278–
281, 287–288, 326–327, and 329; Holt, pp. 55–56, 193–199, 304–305, and 312.

The most unfavorable thing there is to say about the ethnocultural school is that its members have not pursued their own fine insights far enough. Unless political history becomes a subdivision of social history, it is important to specify precisely how cultural identifications become politically salient, and to face squarely the question of what, if anything, mobilizing voters has to do with making policies.

2

The Realignment Synthesis in American History

It is not difficult to agree with Allan G. Bogue that the idea of periodic electoral realignments separating successive political eras has become "the dominant conceptual picture" of American political history. By this I do not mean—nor do I suppose Bogue meant—that most political historians design their research around the realignment model. Most of them probably still study individual leaders, laws, or locales. But if one looks at the most innovative and influential research—the studies that interpret long spans of time, make use of social science theory and of quantitative methods, and consciously seek to integrate the different elements of the American political system—then the "realignment perspective" looms dominant, although not universal (19). This interpretation focuses on a series of electoral turning points, commonly said to have occurred around 1800, 1828, 1860, 1896, and 1928–1932, that resulted from major social and economic crises and shaped the political eras that followed. Not a narrow notion, the realignment idea suggests a comprehensive way of studying American political history.[1]

This article originally appeared as a review essay of Jerome M. Clubb, William H. Flanigan, and Nancy H. Zingale, *Partisan Realignment: Voters, Parties and Government in American History* (Beverly Hills, 1980). The page numbers given parenthetically in the text refer to that book.

1. Allan G. Bogue, "The New Political History in the 1970s," in Michael Kammen (ed.), *The Past Before Us: Contemporary Historical Writing in the United States* (Ithaca, 1980), 237.

Although this perspective has flooded the historical and political science journals only within the past decade, the realignment concept is not new. It dates from the publication of V. O. Key's article, "A Theory of Critical Elections," in 1955, and thus has reached a venerable age. At such a juncture, amidst an increasing flow of realignment studies, this ambitious book by Jerome M. Clubb, William H. Flanigan, and Nancy H. Zingale (a historian and two political scientists, respectively) is particularly welcome. Modestly billing their task as "integrative as much as innovative," the authors set out to synthesize and reformulate the realignment perspective on American political history (7). They do so—and much else.[2]

Many of their findings call into question the simplistic view that realignments, occurring at regular intervals, each abruptly ended one era of political and governmental stability and inaugurated another. Observing more long-term continuity and more short-term variability than previous studies have suggested, the authors raise doubts about whether the major realignments were associated with lasting, massive, and permanent electoral changes. Noting significant variations in the manner in which different realignments occurred, they question how much these upheavals have in common with one another and, by implication, ask if realignments actually form a common class of historical events.

Clubb, Flanigan, and Zingale do not reject the realignment perspective; rather, they revise it by shifting attention from voting behavior to policymaking. In place of the thesis that electoral change constitutes "the primary driving force in American politics," the authors suggest that the actions taken by governing elites in the aftermath of realignments have greater analytical and practical importance than do the voting changes themselves (14). Thus they depart from, even while building on, Walter Dean Burnham's view that American political history can usefully be conceptualized as a succession of party systems, separated

2. Valdimer O. Key, Jr., "A Theory of Critical Elections," *Journal of Politics*, XVII (1955), 3–18.

by regularly spaced electoral upheavals that define the distinctive forms taken by politics and governance in each subsequent era. The publication of their book offers an opportunity to review the development of the realignment perspective, to observe how Burnham's formulation of it became the prevailing one, to discuss the significance of the authors' new findings, and to ask whether the realignment perspective ought to retain its conceptual dominance.[3]

Key's original article is usually remembered for the definition it offered of a critical election. Less commonly recalled are the reasons Key was interested in such elections and the considerable pains he took to distinguish the patterns of behavior underlying the two realignments that he identified, those of 1896 and 1928. As the opening and closing sections of his article make plain, Key's purpose in categorizing elections was to advance the "understanding of the democratic governing process." Critical elections, he implied, were ones in which the voters acted to change the direction of the government. Precisely what the linkages were between elections and governance Key did not say, for his article ended with a series of questions about the relationship between types of elections and the political system as a whole. Too much "of the study of electoral behavior," he chided, "has only a tenuous relation to politics."[4]

Within the context of this larger purpose, Key directed attention to a category of elections he called "critical" and identified two of them: the elections of 1928 and 1896 in New England. Although he insisted that each of these elections merited the label "critical" because it produced "a sharp and durable electoral realignment between parties," Key devoted considerable space to showing that the behavioral patterns underlying the two realign-

---

3. Walter Dean Burnham evidently collaborated with Clubb, Flanigan, and Zingale during the early stages of their work (7).

4. Key, "A Theory of Critical Elections," 3, 17.

ments were different. There was much "reshuffling of voters" in 1928, with some towns moving toward the Democratic party and others away from it; in 1896, by contrast, Key concluded that all social and economic groups shifted toward the Republican party. Key's article has been enormously influential. But some of those who have adopted his definition of critical elections have forgotten the larger set of questions in which Key was interested and have ignored his insight that critical elections are not all alike.[5]

In the years following the publication of "A Theory of Critical Elections," three lines of research deepened our understanding of the phenomenon that Key had described. One line involved further classification of elections beyond the single type, "critical," and tested Key's idea in specific eras and locales. In 1960, Angus Campbell and his colleagues added the concepts of "maintaining" and deviating" elections; Gerald Pomper later filled out the typology by identifying "converting" elections. Pomper ambitiously categorized every presidential election as either realigning, maintaining, deviating, or converting, and other scholars subsequently added to the typology and matched their classification against his.[6]

In the same year that Campbell published his study, Duncan MacRae, Jr., and James A. Meldrum proposed what has now become a widely accepted revision of Key's concept of critical elections: a "critical period" during which a realignment occurs over the course of several elections. Their study focused on Illinois from 1888 to 1958 and began the scholarly tradition of testing and refining the Key-Campbell-Pomper typology for different places and periods. This literature, which is still flourishing, has established that not all critical elections are analytically

5. *Ibid.*, 4, 16, 5.
6. Angus Campbell et al., *The American Voter* (New York, 1960), 531–538; *idem* et al., *Elections and the Political Order* (New York, 1966), 63–77; Gerald Pomper, "Classification of Presidential Elections," *Journal of Politics*, XXIX (1967), 535–566. For an interesting subsequent effort at further classification, see William L. Shade, *Social Change and the Electoral Process* (Gainesville, 1973).

identical and not all states experience them at the same time.[7]

A second research trend, related to the classificatory literature, delineated the progress of electoral cycles over the long course of American history. Lee Benson and Charles Sellers were the two pioneers. Benson focused on nineteenth-century New York State, and Sellers applied his analysis to the whole country from 1789 to 1960. Each identified a succession of realignments, marking the transitions from one stable, or equilibrium, voting phase to another.[8] Pomper's classification scheme also lent itself to a description of an electoral pattern in which critical realignments periodically disrupted long periods of stability. These cycles were not, however, regular or identical, according to Benson, Sellers, and Pomper. Benson's first stable phase lasted twenty-one years (from 1832 to 1853); his next one endured half again as long (1860 to 1892). Sellers, too, resisted the temptation to equate a cyclical pattern with a regular one. He focused attention on numerous aberrant elections and noted how irregularly the cycle had operated in the twentieth century. Pomper similarly observed that "the length of time between" critical elections "varies considerably."[9]

E. E. Schattschneider's brief, brilliant discussions of the political and governmental consequences of the realignments of 1896 and 1932 marked the third type of analysis that appeared during

7. Duncan MacRae, Jr., and James A. Meldrum, "Critical Elections in Illinois, 1888–1958," *American Political Science Review*, LIV (1960), 669–683. Two important studies of the 1928 election illustrate the specialized applications of the critical-election concept: John L. Shover, "Was 1928 a Critical Election in California?" *Pacific Northwest Quarterly*, LVIII (1967), 196–204; Clubb and Howard W. Allen, "The Cities and the Election of 1928: Partisan Realignment?" *American Historical Review*, LXXIV (1969), 1205–1220.

8. Lee Benson, *The Concept of Jacksonian Democracy: New York as a Test Case* (Princeton, 1961), 125–131; Charles Sellers, "The Equilibrium Cycle in Two-Party Politics," *Public Opinion Quarterly*, XXIX (1965), 16–38.

9. Benson, *The Concept of Jacksonian Democracy*, 128; Sellers, "The Equilibrium Cycle," 19–22, 35; Pomper, "Classification of Presidential Elections," 561. Benson has since renounced the concept of voting cycles; see Benson and Joel H. Silbey, "American Political Eras, 1788–1984: Toward a Normative, Substantive, and Conceptual Framework for the Historical Study of American Political Behavior," paper presented at the Social Science History Association meeting (1978).

the early phase of critical-election study. Without citing Key, Schattschneider nonetheless laid out the paths taken by much of the subsequent research on these two realignments. The upheaval of 1896, he said, "determined the nature of American politics from 1896 to 1932." Two sectional minorities, a northern, Republican, business elite and a southern, Democratic, bourbon elite, took advantage of the decline of party competition in both sections and imposed conservative policies on the nation. More than a generation later, Schattschneider contended, the upheaval of 1932 made the Democratic party "the reluctant instrument" of "a profound change in the agenda of American politics." A national political alignment replaced the sectional one established in the 1890s, and two-party competition returned to many areas of the country. These developments profoundly affected govermental policies. Supreme insight, if not deep research, thus led Schattschneider to sketch out bold interpretations supporting Key's belief that the study of critical elections would advance our knowledge "of the democratic governing process."[10]

It was Burnham, however, who in 1967 and 1970 synthesized—and revolutionized—understanding of critical elections. Burnham went beyond the literature of classification and case-study, discovered more regularity in American voting cycles than had previous scholars, and attributed to each electoral realignment the system-changing characteristics that Schattschneider had seen in the upheavals of the 1890s and 1930s. Critical elections, he said, are the "mainsprings" of American politics. They are "constituent acts" which occur with "remarkably uniform periodicity," reorganize the partisan coalitions, and bring about decisive governmental responses to problems that politics-as-usual cannot solve.

10. Eric E. Schattschneider, "United States: The Functional Approach to Party Government," in Sigmund Neumann (ed.), *Modern Political Parties: Approaches to Comparative Politics* (Chicago, 1956), 194–215 (quote 201); Schattschneider, *The Semisovereign People: A Realist's View of Democracy in America* (New York, 1960), 78–96 (quotes 86, 88).

Burnham's work provided the theory of critical elections that Key had labeled, but no one had done much to advance. This theory fit vital features of the American political system, especially its nondevelopmental character and its "chronic . . . tendency" not to respond to emergent socioeconomic demands; it offered a comprehensive scheme for dividing the political past into five "party systems" separated by critical realignments; and it connected elections with the larger political order (just as Key wanted to do) by suggesting that periodic voting upheavals determined the succeeding patterns of politics and governance.[11]

Like any masterful theory, however, Burnham's simplified the historical realities it explained. Although it revealed patterns not previously seen, and elevated discussion of the future course of American politics, it also disguised anomalies, classified disparate events as though they were alike, and forged linkages between critical elections and public policy mainly by assertion. Burnham readily noted, for example, that at the state and local levels there was a "humbling" complexity to patterns of "electoral movement over time," but in his generalizations about realignment such complexity gave way to regularity. He judged as correct Pomper's finding that critical elections were not evenly spaced, but nonetheless found them to have occurred "approximately once a generation, or every thirty to thirty-eight years." Applying his considerable knowledge of American political history, Burnham described each party system as a unique entity but, at the same time, gave the ahistorical impression of a cyclical pattern in which similar sequences of events were regularly repeated. Above all, although Burnham insisted that critical elections shaped the subsequent course of public policy, he had much more to say about the elections than about policies.[12]

---

11. Burnham, "Party Systems and the Political Process," in *idem* and William Nisbet Chambers (eds.), *The American Party Systems: Stages of Political Development* (New York, 1967), 277–307; Burnham, *Critical Elections and the Mainsprings of American Politics* (New York, 1970), 10, 8, 27. For an earlier discussion by Burnham of the 1896 election, see "The Changing Shape of the American Political Universe," *American Political Science Review*, LIX (1965), 23–26.

In the years after the publication of Burnham's major works, the study of realigning eras went in two directions. Most researchers continued to examine voting behavior apart from policy, and the early 1970s brought forth detailed analyses of electoral changes, especially during the 1850s and 1890s. Not decisively influenced by Burnham, such works as those by Michael F. Holt, Ronald P. Formisano, Paul Kleppner, Richard Jensen, and Samuel T. McSeveney nonetheless were congruent with Burnham's conception of these realignments as fundamental political (if not governmental) turning points.[13] Other voting studies continued the tradition of examining individual elections—particularly that of 1928—in diverse locales to see if they met the definition of "critical." The result that most forcefully emerged from such research was the enormous variation from place to place in the pattern and timing of realignments.[14] A few

---

12. Burnham, *Critical Elections*, 24, 26. For two early critiques of Burnham's formulation, see: David R. Mayhew, "Party Systems in American History," *Polity*, I (1968), 134–143; Douglas Price, "'Critical Elections' & Party History: A Critical View," *Polity*, IV (1971), 236–242. In 1973 Burnham, working with Clubb and Flanigan, suggested some modifications of his earlier views in "Partisan Realignment: A Systemic Perspective," paper presented at a Mathematical Social Science Board conference. Here Burnham, Clubb, and Flanigan reported the existence of considerable electoral shifts between the major realignments and placed greater stress on post-realignment policy changes than had Burnham in his earlier work. This significant paper was published later in Silbey, Bogue, and Flanigan (eds.), *The History of American Electoral Behavior* (Princeton, 1978), 45–77. It contains the seeds of many of the ideas developed in the book under review.

13. Michael F. Holt, *Forging a Majority: The Formation of the Republican Party in Pittsburgh, 1848–1860* (New Haven, 1969); Ronald P. Formisano, *The Birth of Mass Political Parties: Michigan, 1827–1861* (Princeton, 1971); Paul Kleppner, *The Cross of Culture: A Social Analysis of Midwestern Politics, 1850–1900* (New York, 1970); Richard Jensen, *The Winning of the Midwest: Social and Political Conflict, 1888–1896* (Chicago, 1971); Samuel T. McSeveney, *The Politics of Depression: Political Behavior in the Northeast, 1893–1896* (New York, 1972). A subsequent book by Kleppner makes explicit, extended use of Burnham's formulation: *The Third Electoral System, 1853–1892: Parties, Voters, and Political Cultures* (Chapel Hill, 1979).

14. Besides the articles by Shover and by Clubb and Allen cited above, see the following studies of the 1928–1936 realignment: Shover, "The Emergence of a

scholars, ignoring such diversity in favor of retaining the chronological and geographical breadth that had characterized Burnham's work, offered theories of their own to explain the regular cycles of stability and change that he had observed. James L. Sundquist focused particular attention on the way in which powerful issues, cutting across the existing alignments, brought about the upheavals of the 1850s, 1890s, and 1930s. Paul Allen Beck ingeniously but speculatively suggested that generational change—the "entry of new age cohorts into the electorate"—acccounted for the remarkable periodicity of these realignments. Largely absent from all of this work was the Key-Schattschneider-Burnham insight that critical elections were critical because they had something to do with governance.[15]

Beginning in the early and mid-1970s, a small number of researchers did pursue that insight. After coding and analyzing the contents of party platforms and federal statutes, Benjamin Ginsberg concluded that realigning eras were marked by high degrees of ideological difference between the parties and by significant transitions in national policy. David W. Brady and several coworkers marshaled evidence of heightened party voting in Congress and of the adoption of "clusters of policy changes" following the realignments of the 1890s and the New Deal era.[16]

Two-Party System in Republican Philadelphia, 1924–1936," *Journal of American History*, LX (1974), 985–1002; Bernard Sternsher, "The Emergence of the New Deal Party System: A Problem in Historical Analysis of Voter Behavior," *Journal of Interdisciplinary History*, VI (1975), 127–149; Allen and Erik W. Austin, "From the Populist Era to the New Deal: A Study of Partisan Realignment in Washington State, 1889–1950," *Social Science History*, III (1979), 115–143; David F. Prindle, "Voter Turnout, Critical Elections, and the New Deal Realignment," in *ibid.*, 144–170.

15. James L. Sundquist, *Dynamics of the Party System: Alignment and Realignment of Political Parties in the United States* (Washington, D. C., 1973); Paul Allen Beck, "A Socialization Theory of Partisan Realignment," in Richard G. Niemi et al., *The Politics of Future Citizens* (San Francisco, 1974), 199–219 (quote 203).

16. Benjamin Ginsberg, "Critical Elections and the Substance of Party Conflict: *1844–1968*," *Midwest Journal of Political Science*, XVI (1972), 603–625; *idem*, "Elections and Public Policy," *American Political Science Review*, LXX

Other scholars contributed related findings.[17] They contended, for the most part, that governmental policy in the United States undergoes only incremental change during periods of electoral stability. According to Ginsberg, "stable partisan alignments are, in effect, the electorate's choice in favor of the continuation of a particular set of policies." Periodically, however, an electoral realignment brings with it the possibility of major governmental innovations by offering the voters clear policy choices and by putting in office a party committed to enacting measures addressing the causes of the crisis that precipitated the realignment. Beck recently summarized this literature and concluded that Burnham was right: "the electoral cycle serves as the mainspring of American politics" and "realigning periods are typically times of comprehensive change in the direction of public policy."[18]

Conceptually important as they were, the studies linking realignments with policy shifts often relied on the simplest, most ahistorical versions of critical-election theory. They tended, for

---

(1976), 41–49; David W. Brady and Naomi B. Lynn, "Switched-Seat Congressional Districts: Their Effect on Party Voting and Public Policy," *American Journal of Political Science*, XVII (1973), 528–543; Brady and Phillip Althoff, "Party Voting in the U.S. House of Representatives, 1890–1910: Elements of a Responsible Party System," *Journal of Politics*, XXXVI (1974), 753–775; Brady, "Critical Elections, Congressional Parties and Clusters of Policy Changes," *British Journal of Political Science*, VIII (1978), 79–99.

17. Barbara Deckard Sinclair, "Party Realignment and the Transformation of the Political Agenda: The House of Representatives, 1925–1938," *American Political Science Review*, LXXI (1977), 940–953; *idem*, "The Policy Consequences of Party Realignment—Social Welfare Legislation in the House of Representatives, 1933–1954," *American Journal of Political Science*, XXII (1978), 83–105; Michael R. King and Lester G. Seligman, "Critical Elections, Congressional Recruitment and Public Policy," in Heinz Eulau and Moshe M. Czudnowski (eds.), *Elite Recruitment in Democratic Polities: Comparative Studies across Nations* (New York, 1976), 263–299; Clubb and Santa A. Traugott, "Partisan Cleavage and Cohesion in the House of Representatives, 1861–1974," *Journal of Interdisciplinary History*, VII (1977), 375–401. See also a number of the articles in Bruce A. Campbell and Richard J. Trilling (eds.), *Realignment in American Politics: Toward a Theory* (Austin, 1980).

18. Ginsberg, "Elections and Public Policy," 49; Paul Allen Beck, "The Electoral Cycle and Patterns of American Politics," *British Journal of Political Science*, IX (1979), 129–156 (quotes 155, 154).

one thing, to generalize about realigning eras (listed by Ginsberg as 1798–1800, 1826–1836, 1852–1860, 1874–1880, 1892–1896, and 1928–1936) without regard to gross differences between them.[19] In some critical periods, new parties were established; in others, only moderate shifts took place in the balance of power between the existing parties. Some of these periods involved basic changes in the character of the electorate, and in others it remained little altered. It would be surprising if electoral upheavals so distant from one another in time and character exerted comparable effects on policy. The early efforts to connect realignments and governance assumed, moreover, that critical elections gave voters real opportunities to choose new policies. Yet, for example, few students of the 1932 election would agree with Brady that "the parties differed markedly over the role that government was to play in curing the Depression. The Democrats favored active government involvement; the Republicans favored voluntarism and non-intervention."[20]

Besides simplifying the realignments, these studies failed to identify the policy transformations they purported to explain. Brady's analysis notwithstanding, neither the Dingley tariff nor the Gold Standard Act was either a major policy change or a significant response to the underlying conditions that caused the realignment of the 1890s. And Ginsberg's nominal categorization of United States statutes did not provide a way to identify important governmental turning points.[21]

By the late 1970s realignment theory was in disarray. The larger group of studies it had inspired, which had concentrated on describing critical elections, had uncovered enough excep-

19. Ginsberg, "Elections and Public Policy," 41–42.
20. *Idem*, "Critical Elections," 622–624; *idem*, "Elections and Public Policy," 45; Brady, "Critical Elections," 84.
21. Brady and Lynn, "Switched-Seat Congressional Districts," 541; Brady, "Critical Elections," 80, 94–95. For a critique of Ginsberg's method, see W. Lawrence Neuman and Alexander Hicks, "Public Policy, Party Platforms, and Critical Elections: A Reexamination," *American Political Science Review*, LXXI (1977), 277–280.

tions and irregularities to raise questions about both the comparability and the periodicity of realignments. Some critics pointedly asked what, precisely, a critical election was and how, exactly, to know when one had occurred.[22] Others openly doubted that American electoral patterns could be separated into periods nearly as neatly as Burnham and others had suggested.[23] The smaller group of critical-election studies, those that ambitiously sought a causal connection between realignments and governance, had taken such a simple view of each that they could only be regarded as marking the bare beginnings of the solution to a difficult problem. One might have wondered whether the theory of critical elections could possibly be made to fit historical reality and also to clarify the linkages between elections and government, the task for which Key had originally intended it.

Clubb, Flanigan, and Zingale believe that the realignment perspective can do both, if properly reformulated. Their strategy of revision is, accordingly, twofold: first, the application of a new method for measuring and describing electoral realignment and second, the presentation of evidence suggesting that only effective policy action by the governing party can confirm a realignment and cause it to endure. The result of their work is a serious, plausible response to the problems encountered by critical-election theory. It is not, however, the only possible response.

22. Allan J. Lichtman, "Critical Election Theory and the Reality of American Presidential Politics, 1916–40," *American Historical Review*, LXXXI (1976), 317–351; J. Morgan Kousser, "History — Theory = ?" *Reviews in American History*, VII (1979), 157–162; *idem*, "Key Changes," in *ibid.*, IX (1981), 23–28.

23. Benson, Silbey, and Phyllis F. Field, "Toward a Theory of Stability and Change in American Voting Patterns: New York State, 1792–1970," in Silbey, Bogue, and Flanigan (eds.), *The History of American Electoral Behavior*, 78–105; Benson and Silbey, "American Political Eras." For an important critique of the use of the realignment concept as an organizing principle for the study of American political history, see Everett Carll Ladd, Jr., and Charles D. Hadley, *Transformations of the American Party System: Political Coalitions from the New Deal to the 1970s* (New York, 1975), especially 24–27, 332–333.

Commonly, the authors observe, scholars have stressed "the differential shifting of social and geographical bases of support for the political parties as the sole indication of a realignment" (49–50). Some groups and locales move toward one party; others shift in the opposite direction. Widespread as this understanding of realignments is, it is not correct, they suggest—at least to judge from correlation analysis of presidential and congressional elections from 1840 to 1978. Neither states nor counties experienced pronounced and enduring changes in the relative degree of their support for one party or the other at times when realignments are conventionally said to have occurred. "Breaks in the correlations at the expected times, if they appear at all, are less substantial than we might have supposed, or indicate a deviating election rather than a realignment" (61). Over the long time-span examined, Clubb, Flanigan, and Zingale find American voting behavior to have been remarkably stable, broken erratically by disruptions that were as often temporary as permanent. The problem, they say, is "not that correlations are inappropriate for analyzing election data," but that correlations can capture only differential shifts in voting behavior (74). To understand realignments, across-the-board changes—those that affect most segments of the electorate in approximately the same way—must also be taken into account.

This the authors do using a technique for the two-way analysis of variance that enables them to separate differential (or interactive) change from across-the-board (or surge) change and, further, to distinguish lasting from temporary shifts.[24] Table I shows how they conceptualize and name these different forms of electoral change (83). By calculating the deviations of each state and county, both from the mean vote in every election and from the unit's own expected vote (based on a twelve-year moving average), the authors derive measures of the relative amounts of each type of change for every presidential and congressional election.

24. The technique is explained in more detail in Flanigan and Zingale, "The Measurement of Electoral Change," *Political Methodology*, I (1974), 49–82.

Table 1   Types of Electoral Change

	Temporary	Lasting
Across-the-board	Deviating Surge	Realigning Surge
Differential	Deviating Interactive Change	Realigning Interactive Change

They present such an analysis both for the nation as a whole, from 1836 to 1978 (using states as units), and for six different regions of the country, from 1854 to 1966 (using counties).

What their calculations show is how relatively little lasting, interactive electoral change there has been over the course of American history and yet how constantly voting changes of some sort have taken place. All three of the "major" realignments—those of the 1850s, the 1890s, and the New Deal era—were marked by differential voting shifts of a temporary nature, but even more by permanent, across-the-board changes. Of the three realignments, the authors say, only that of the 1930s "involved the sharp, massive, pervasive, and lasting electoral change that is often taken as a general characteristic of historical realignments" (114–115). Their regional analysis also supports these observations, although they detect some surprising variations, too numerous and complex to note here.

Of equal importance, the authors find that many other elections, besides those thought of as critical, also displayed varying degrees of surge and differential change. Indeed, realignment "has been virtually a constant property of the historical political system" (115). This observation leads the authors to a revisionary analysis of the so-called decay periods after the major realignments. Using various aggregate indicators designed to tap the deterioration of standing voting patterns, they conclude that only the New Deal realignment gave way to the type of decay which is commonly said to have followed all realignments.

Not all of these findings are entirely new. As the authors note, Key's original article distinguished differential from across-the-

board electoral change. So have some subsequent studies. McSeveney's analysis of the realignment of the 1890s in the northeast, for
instance, used correlations to reject an interpretation based on
interactive change and concluded that almost every group in the
electorate shifted toward the Republican party. In addition, the
authors' emphasis upon frequent deviations and regional variations is not unprecedented. Numerous local critical-election
studies have prepared us for the patterns that they describe.[25]

Sophisticated as their electoral analysis is, moreover, it relies
on less than a complete enumeration of the types of change
underlying realignments. Nonvoting, in particular, is unac-
counted for in their method, although the qualitative discussion
in the book strongly suggests the likelihood that in each realignment some eligible voters entered the active electorate while
others left it (267–268).[26] This problem notwithstanding, Clubb,
Flanigan, and Zingale treat over a century of voting behavior in
sufficient detail, and with such disarming recognition of oddities
in the data and of limitations in their own analysis, that most
readers will acccept the conclusion reached in the first half of the
book: that electoral changes alone do not provide an adequate
basis for identifying unmistakable turning points in American
political history. There is too much long-term continuity and
short-term variability for that assertion to be valid.

To allay the confusion produced by electoral analysis, the
authors turn to policymaking, not simply as an important byproduct of realignment but as an element essential to completing
and confirming the transformation. Impressionistic evidence,
they say, suggests that each of the leading realignments was
followed by "major policy innovations" (157). Perceived as effec-

25. McSeveney, *The Politics of Depression*, 228.

26. Two studies of realignment that take explicit account of nonvoting
through regression estimates of transition probabilities are: Ray M. Shortridge,
"The Voter Realignment in the Midwest during the 1850s," *American Politics
Quarterly*, IV (1976), 193–221; Dale Baum, "Know-Nothingism and the Republican Majority in Massachusetts: The Political Realignment of the 1850s," *Journal
of American History*, LXIV (1978), 959–986. See also Prindle, "Voter Turnout."

tive, the new policies served to solidify the preceding electoral shifts and enabled them—unlike those "which might have been"—to "earn" the designation "realignment" (264, 191-192). It is this combination of electoral change and meaningful policy action that leads us to think of the 1850s, the 1890s, and the New Deal era as political watersheds of the first importance.[27]

Rather than study the new policies themselves, however, Clubb, Flanigan, and Zingale explore patterns of partisan control over both national and state governments and the behavior of one key policymaking elite, the members of Congress. What they find is that the realignments of the Civil War era, the 1890s, and the New Deal period inaugurated uniquely long eras of domination by the advantaged party over both Congress and the presidency. Such control, together with the wide margins by which it was accomplished, "provided the necessary conditions for policy initiatives" (184). To judge from congressional roll-call analysis, the two parties became more polarized (although not more internally cohesive) after each major realignment. At the state level, too, the authors present evidence of increased partisan control over government agencies following the realignments. Here, as elsewhere throughout the book, Clubb, Flanigan, and Zingale avoid overstating their findings. Just as electoral behavior has exhibited remarkable continuity throughout American history, so have the patterns of partisan domination over state governments. "Conditions approaching national crisis," they point out, "have been required to bring about even . . . modest shifts" in the party balance of most states (214).[28]

Carefully qualified as is their discussion of governance, the authors are bold enough to move from their data to a conclusion

---

27. Clubb, Flanigan and Zingale are not the first to suggest that effective policy actions are necessary to complete an electoral realignment: see Samuel Lubell, *The Future of American Politics*, (New York, 1965; 3rd ed. rev.), 55-63; Campbell et al., *The American Voter*, 554-555.

28. The findings that are summarized all too briefly in this paragraph follow and extend those previously reported in Clubb and Traugott, "Partisan Cleavage and Cohesion" and in Burnham, Clubb, and Flanigan, "Partisan Realignment."

of enormous importance for the study of American political history: leaders, not voters, are the driving elements in the political system. Effective policy changes, not critical elections, are the mainsprings of the political process. Whether or not a realignment proves lasting, whether new political attitudes emerge, and whether workable policies are enacted are all much more dependent on what governing elites do after an election than on how citizens voted. Successful political changes come about when leaders make use of the opportunities offered by electoral victories; political failures, correspondingly, indicate "failures of leadership" (296). The authors consciously observe the need to redirect scholarly "attention away from the role of electoral change" and toward "political leadership and governmental performance" (16, 295). Theirs is a daring position, plainly at odds not only with much of the existing literature on critical elections but also with the most visible recent trends in the study of American political history. It is nonetheless, I think, a correct position.[29]

Whether their data actually show leadership and policy innovation to be the driving forces in American politics is another matter, however. As the authors acknowledge, they have studied neither the policies themselves nor the relationships between electoral and policy processes.[30] Instead, they have gathered data on several surrogates for policy, especially partisan control of governmental agencies. But how meaningful are their surrogates? If one party gains and maintains control of the government after a realignment, that helps establish that there was an electoral realignment. It may even suggest that a possibility existed for carrying out a party program. But it says nothing in itself about new policies, let alone the effect such policies may have in sustaining and confirming a prior electoral shift. Indeed, the argument is circular because it affirms the existence of a link between critical elections and policy changes through the use of

29. For two prior calls for a shift from the study of elections to policy, see Richard L. McCormick, "Ethno-Cultural Interpretations of Nineteenth-Century American Voting Behavior," *Political Science Quarterly*, LXXXIX (1974), 371–377; Lichtman, "Critical Election Theory."

30. The authors issue this caveat a number of times: 15, 161, 221, 244, 254.

essentially electoral data (the partisan affiliations of elected officials) as indicators of policy. To establish such a linkage more firmly would require a number of things, above all some method for describing and categorizing policy changes over time and for identifying major governmental turning points. That is a tall order, and it would be unfair to say that Clubb, Flanigan, and Zingale should have done something that they repeatedly note they did not set out to do.

Even without making a detailed study of the relationship between elections and policy innovations, the authors have performed a signal service by renouncing, at least implicitly, the assumption that all casual lines run in one direction. Most previous studies of realignments and governance—in fact, most works of all types in American political history—regard policies as byproducts of elections. Clubb, Flanigan, and Zingale propose that the reverse is also true: effective policies can cause electoral realignments to endure. They are vague, however, about how this happens, and to explain it they rely on the impressionistic evidence that each of the major realignments was followed and confirmed by important new policies. For the Civil War and New Deal realignments, their argument is uncontroversial. Few historians would deny that the Republicans after 1860 and the Democrats after 1932 undertook new policies of enormous significance and, in so doing, solidified their hold on office. But the case is much less persuasive for the realignment of the 1890s, which was not followed by an immediate policy departure.

My object here is not to nitpick over the one realignment for which the authors freely acknowledge their argument to be weak, but rather to raise two theoretical questions of the first importance: (1) What are the connections between political changes (broadly understood here to include realigning elections) and policy innovations? and (2) Can realignment theory explain those connections if only two cases in American history fit the theory?

If William Jennings Bryan had defeated William McKinley in 1896, significant governmental changes might have followed. But Bryan lost, and for approximately another decade, until after the passage of the regulatory measures of 1906, national policies remained little altered. What is more, the specific policy disputes of the realigning years, currency and tariff, soon abated and scarcely shaped the major clashes over governance during the succeeding era (although the tariff issue flashed again into prominence around 1909). The main economic policy question of the decade after 1896 involved the search for a new and more satisfactory balance between the promotion and regulation of industry by government. This issue had been only barely raised in 1896. And when it later did come to the fore it was not in any clear way a Democratic-versus-Republican question. These are difficult facts for realignment theory to accommodate.

The difficulty is apparent in the writings of those who have connected realignments with governmental innovations. Beck recognizes that there were no "significant policy changes" after 1896; Ginsberg finds "critical conflict" between the parties that year but mentions no policy shifts; Brady notes "major policy changes" in one article, but in another says that the realignment of the 1890s was significant because it prevented such changes from being enacted. These uncertainties are also present in the book by Clubb, Flanigan, and Zingale—although, to their credit, they acknowledge them whenever the subject comes up. The policy actions of the late 1890s are "difficult to identify and describe precisely," but they had something to do with making big business "more legitimate" (157, 158). Elsewhere the authors hypothesize that it was not a policy change but an economic recovery that caused voters to confirm the electoral shift to the Republicans (262).[31]

31. Beck, "The Electoral Cycle," 150; Ginsberg, "Critical Election"; *idem*, "Elections and Public Policy"; Brady and Lynn, "Switched-Seat Congressional Districts," 541; Brady, "Elections, Congress, and Public Policy Changes: 1886–1960," in Campbell and Trilling (eds.), *Realignment in American Politics*, 187. For an interesting comment on these inconsistencies, see Seligman and King, "Political Realignments and Recruitment to the U.S. Congress, 1870–1970," in *ibid.*, 175. For the authors' comments on the electoral realignment of the 1890s, see 57, 98–100, 111, 114. They conclude that it was more moderate and diffuse than it is commonly said to have been.

Unrecognized in their study, as in those by Beck, Ginsberg, and Brady, is the fact that the realignment of the 1890s *was* followed by one of the more significant governmental transformations in American history—the emergence of meaningful regulatory and administrative policies in the early twentieth century. But this change did not represent a straightforward result of the electoral crisis of the 1890s, nor was it fought out along the party lines laid down in that decade, nor did it become visible for a decade after 1896. Its connection with the realignment of the Bryan-McKinley years is enormously complex; no historian or political scientist has yet worked out that relationship. The realignment of the 1890s was also followed by a series of lasting changes in the nature and structure of political participation; party voting declined and interest-group politics became more important. These and other related political changes no doubt bore some connection to the electoral upheaval of the 1890s, but precisely what that connection is remains to be fully explored.[32]

The path-analytic diagram in Figure 1 sketches out some of the findings scholars have made about the political and governmental changes of this era. It is not intended to present a comprehensive interpretation of those changes but rather to illustrate the complexity of a transformation that, in the broadest sense, was caused by industrialization and resulted in the creation of new forms of politics and governance. The realignment of the 1890s has a secure place in that causal pattern, as the diagram suggests. Both the decline of electoral competitiveness throughout much of the country and the achievement of governmental control by the Republicans resulted from that realignment and contributed significantly to the new political order that emerged. But the realignment scarcely explains everything that changed. Rather, it may be termed a crucial intervening episode between economic

32. For an interesting effort to link the realignment of the 1890s to one form of public policy, see Charles V. Stewart, "The Federal Income Tax and the Realignment of 1890s," in Campbell and Trilling (eds.), *Realignment in American Politics*, 263–287.

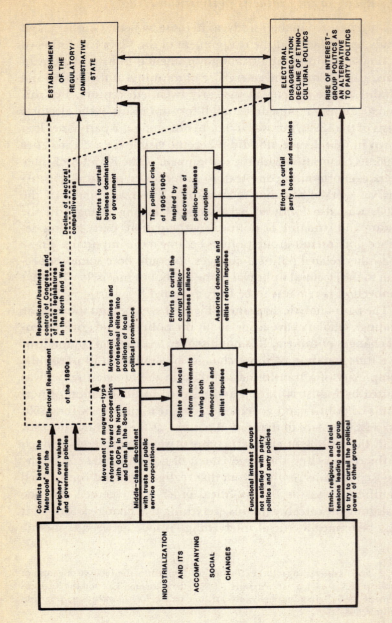

Fig. 1 Creation of the Early Twentieth-Century Political Order of the United States, 1890–1917

and social developments, on the one hand, and the creation of new political and governmental forms, on the other. Giving realignment no role in an interpretation of these changes would be a major error; so would assigning it the leading part. If the political changes that occurred in other eras of American history were as complex as those of the late nineteenth and early twentieth century—and surely they were—then the conceptual dominance over scholarship that realignment theory now exerts ought to be broken.[33]

If the theory is flawed, the perspective nonetheless remains valuable, particularly as formulated by Clubb, Flanigan, and Zingale. In their hands, the notion of realignment retains many of the strengths that have made it central to the newer, more systematic American political history of recent years. This history prides itself on being oriented toward long-term developments, not isolated incidents; on suggesting connections between different elements of the political system; and on linking the study of mass behavior with elite decision-making. Clubb, Flanigan, and Zingale accomplish these goals without being insensitive to historical exceptions and anomalies. They offer, as well, a persuasive argument for shifting the study of political history toward the subjects of leadership and governance. These achievements add up to a volume with a valuable perspective on the American political past: in the aftermath of realigning elections come truly critical moments when the leaders of the majority party have the opportunity to take advantage of their victory. The way that they perform can shape politics and government in the years to come.

But Clubb, Flanigan, and Zingale also present a great deal of

33. No reader need accept the entire diagram in order to grasp the point that the realignment of the 1890s was only one element of a much larger political transformation. For a discussion of the political crisis of 1905–1906, see McCormick, "The Discovery that Business Corrupts Politics: A Reappraisal of the Origins of Progressivism," *American Historical Review*, LXXXVI (1981), 247–274.

evidence that makes it difficult to accept realignment (or critical-election) theory. Invented by Key, and brought to maturity by Burnham, that theory posits a sequence of developments rigidly divided into periods in which long eras of stability are regularly broken by sharp electoral realignments that determine the subsequent contours of voting behavior and governmental policy. The combination of constant flux and "major inertia" found by the authors of this volume will not accommodate such an account (214). The inertia is probably more damaging than the flux. No one who compares American history with that of other countries from, say, 1865 to the present can fail to be struck by the nation's fundamental electoral stability or by the relative ease and placidity that have accompanied major policy innovations. As framed by Burnham, critical-election theory attributes such governmental stability to periodic electoral upheavals. Realignments have been America's surrogates for revolution. But, as Clubb, Flanigan and Zingale make plain, the nation's electoral history has been nearly as calm as its policy transitions. What really needs to be explained is the inertia underlying both realms of American political experience.

Equally damaging to the theory of critical elections is that it fits only two cases: the Civil War and the New Deal. In each era, an electoral realignment made possible immediate and substantial policy changes. At no other moment in American history was the relationship between elections and governance nearly so direct. Even in these two cases, few would argue that the realignments represent anything close to a complete explanation of the subsequent policy transitions. Many would agree that the differences between these two realignments are too great to warrant grouping them together. How useful can a theory be if it fits, at best, but two instances? The realignment perspective affords one valuable angle of vision on American political history. Nothing more.

Yet something more is needed. Because elections in America, even critical elections, do not offer voters the opportunity to make clear policy choices, the connections between politics and governance are not simple. Traditional scholarship on political history commonly took for granted the existence of reasonably close relationships between voting and policymaking, but recent research has challenged these connections. Many of the newer historical studies of electoral patterns consider voting to be essentially a form of social behavior.[34] A corresponding literature, produced first by political scientists and now beginning to be emulated by historians, suggests that election results do not make much difference in the formation of governmental decisions.[35] The realignment perspective offers one way of exploring—and restoring—the linkages between politics and policy in American history. But this perspective has the limitations noted above and is not very helpful in explaining some of the most important governmental changes, for example, the decline of state legislative authority in the 1840s and 1850s or the regulatory revolution of 1906–1914.

The answer would seem to lie in making the study of governmental policy as systematic as is the study of elections. There is an urgent need for a satisfactory typology of governmental policies, for new methods of describing and categorizing those policies, and for new ways of identifying the significant governmental transformations in American history. Legislative turnover, nominal policy categories, and expenditure levels all may have their place in such a typology, but none is adequate alone. Once the important turning points in governmental policy have been identified, the question of what politics have to do with them can be addressed. There is no reason to assume, however, that politics determines policies. In fact, the causal lines have often run in the opposite direction, as Clubb, Flanigan, and Zingale imply. To

34. See note 13 above.
35. For an introduction to this literature, see Thomas R. Dye, "Politics versus Economics: The Development of the Literature on Policy Determination," *Policy Studies Journal*, VII (1979), 652–662.

3

The Social Analysis of American Political History— After Twenty Years

When Samuel P. Hays called for a "social analysis" of American political history twenty years ago, neither he—nor anyone else— could have foreseen what a successful intellectual venture it would prove to be.[1] Particularly within the last half-dozen years, an outpouring of studies has begun to delineate the communal, familial, class, and cultural context of past political beliefs and behavior more fully than any previous body of historical scholarship in America. These works are not all of a piece, and they have not yet yielded a new interpretive synthesis in American political history—although that may be just around the corner. Nor, for the most part, do the authors of these studies mean the same thing Hays meant by a "social analysis" of politics. Together, however, they have made giant strides toward fulfilling the promise which he saw in social analysis—nothing less, that is, than "the revitalization of political life as the central focus of [American] history."[2]

1. Samuel P. Hays, "The Social Analysis of American Political History, 1880–1920," *Political Science Quarterly* 80 (September 1965): 373–94. This essay, along with others written in the same period, is included in Samuel P. Hays, *American Political History as Social Analysis* (Knoxville, 1980).
2. Hays, *American Political History as Social Analysis*, p. 88.

Hays presented his vision for political history in a series of
articles written during the late 1950s and 1960s.[3] Welcomed almost immediately for staking out a bold prospect for future
scholarship, these provocative, articulate essays still repay reading two decades later. Hays's articles were not, however, *sui
generis*. Ever since the late 1940s, the field of American political
history had been in a state of quiet ferment, with numerous
younger scholars—first individually and then in some cases collectively—engaged in a search for new concepts and new directions. Some began to borrow ideas from the social sciences and to
break down the historical guild's long-standing resistance to that
approach. Others were stimulated to pursue the insights so vigorously put forward in Arthur Schlesinger, Jr.'s *The Age of Jackson*, although, as often as not, Schlesinger's unabashedly progressive—and methodologically old-fashioned—account of the
heroic Jacksonians served as a negative model. Certainly it
worked that way for Hays and also for Lee Benson, who was
perhaps the single most influential member of the 1950s generation of new political historians. Allan G. Bogue, Noble E. Cunningham, Jr., Richard P. McCormick, Charles G. Sellers, Jr., and
(from an earlier generation) Roy F. Nichols also had a hand in
the ferment and helped stir up the field. Hays's great contribution was to synthesize and shape some of the fruits of this search,
add his own suggestions, and present in his essays the boldest
definition of what a reinvigorated political history could be.[4]

3. Besides "The Social Analysis of American Political History," these include
"History as Human Behavior" (1959); "New Possibilities for American Political
History: The Social Analysis of Political Life" (1964); "Political Parties and the
Community-Society Continuum" (1967); and "A Systematic Social History"
(1971). All are reprinted in Hays, *American Political History as Social Analysis*.
4. On these developments see Hays's autobiographical essay in *American
Political History as Social Analysis*, pp. 3–45; Allan G. Bogue, "Inside the 'Iowa
School,'" in Bogue, *Clio & the Bitch Goddess: Quantification in American
Political History* (Beverly Hills, 1983), pp. 19–50; Bogue, "The 'New' Political
History," reprinted in *ibid.*, pp. 57–78; and David M. Potter, "Roy F. Nichols and
the Rehabilitation of American Political History," in Don E. Fehrenbacher, ed.,
History and American Society: Essays of David M. Potter (New York, 1973), pp.

Central to Hays's vision was what he called the "social analysis" of politics, that is, studying political behavior for what it revealed about the underlying human relationships involved rather than focusing—as political history usually had—upon top leaders, official ideologies, dramatic episodes, and key policy decisions. "Political life," he declared, "involves the origin, clash, and resolution of all value conflicts in society . . . the resolution of differences in every realm of human affairs." So broad an understanding of political history meant studying the people involved, "the circumstances in which they lived and thought," and, as Hays frequently repeated, the ways in which they expressed their different "goals and values." Fundamental to this type of analysis was a single pivotal question which can be paraphrased as follows: What is the social setting from which political behavior springs? Or, as Hays put it in declarative rather than interrogative form, "Participation in the wider political system was a product of participation in smaller units of social life." Quite properly, Hays claimed a good deal for the possibilities of this sort of analysis. "The range of political life," he wrote, "is as broad as the scope of society itself. . . . Political history, thus conceived, can well restore itself as the major integrative context of history."[5]

As Hays himself has recognized, his early essays were important less for their substantive findings than for "pointing out limitations of past historical work and setting a tone for new approaches."[6] They contained warnings about the subjects *not* to study, as well as imaginative suggestions about where research *should* be focused. Political leadership, for example, had at-

---

192–217. Although Benson's work, especially *The Concept of Jacksonian Democracy: New York as a Test Case* (Princeton, 1961), had a greater influence on the field of American political history than did Hays's, I have stressed Hays's role here because of his conscious emphasis upon a *social* analysis of politics. Benson's own imaginative and influential essays are gathered together in Lee Benson, *Toward the Scientific Study of History* (Philadelphia, 1972).

5. Hays, *American Political History as Social Analysis*, pp. 15, 97–98, 132, 164.
6. Hays, *American Political History as Social Analysis*, p. 50.

tracted more than its share of attention from traditional historians who frequently assumed that entire movements were but
reflections of those at the top. Of greater value than further studies
of the leaders would be intensive investigations of their grass-
roots supporters.[7] Isolated, episodic events—such as "the drama
of the single legislative decision"—likewise had filled too much
space in the history books. More significant than headline-grab-
bing episodes or so-called "major" decisions were the "persistent
patterns of values" held by those on all sides.[8] Perhaps above all,
Hays warned against the study of ideology, particularly if public
statements such as speeches and party platforms were taken at
face value. "Too often," he wrote, historians have read such
ideological evidence ". . . as accurate descriptions of the past
rather than ideas generated by a movement to establish its legitimacy."[9] Hays did not suggest that leadership, policy decisions, or
ideology deserved to be ignored completely, only that inquiry
ought to be focused on the patterns of human experience and
values that lay behind these formal products of "politics."

To encourage such inquiry, Hays proposed a far-reaching
agenda for studying the ways in which social relationships were

7. Hays, *American Political History as Social Analysis*, pp. 53–54, 70–74, 92–
93.

8. Hays, *American Political History as Social Analysis*, pp. 85, 92–93 (quote
93), 96–97, 101, 115, 137–38 (quote 137). Political historians, in Hays's view,
whether studying election results or governmental decisions, ought to place less
emphasis on the particular outcomes than on the underlying attitudes and values
of those involved (pp. 78, 91, 137–38, 293–94).

9. Hays, *American Political History as Social Analysis*, pp. 69, 100, 113–14,
140–41 (quote 141). Hays's most celebrated single essay, "The Politics of Reform
in Municipal Government in the Progressive Era," calls into question a "liberal"
interpretation of progressivism by challenging its reliance on ideological evidence; Hays, *American Political History as Social Analysis*, pp. 205–32. For a
recent discussion which implicitly recognizes greater possibilities for using ideological evidence than did Hays's earlier essays, see Hays, "Politics and Society:
Beyond the Political Party," in Paul Kleppner et al., *The Evolution of American
Electoral Systems* (Westport, Conn., 1981), especially pp. 246, 256–57. J. Morgan
Kousser, "History as Past Sociology in the Work of Samuel P. Hays: A Review
Essay," *Historical Methods* 14 (Fall 1981): 181–86, provides an important critical
evaluation of Hays's views of political history.

given political expression. Each level of society, he suggested—from the grass-roots up to a national elite—generated its own distinctive patterns of political activity. In the local communities of nineteenth-century America, distant from cosmopolitan influences, differences of ethnicity, religion, and nationality shaped the most serious political conflicts. There, Hays speculated, partisan divisions tended to be "cultural, not economic, in nature," and electoral choices expressed "deeply rooted social values" rather than positions on national issues. Repeatedly Hays urged historians to test these hypotheses through quantitative analyses of popular voting behavior.[10] As time passed, he went on, the nation's towns and countrysides were gradually overtaken by outside political forces—wrought by science and technology and issued forth from cosmopolitan America. The resulting upward shifts in decision-making and the values reflected in those shifts offered a fertile field for historical study. In particular, Hays urged, attention could profitably be directed to the middle reaches of authority where the forces of centralization met and interacted with people whose values derived mainly from the local community. From this perspective, a wide range of research possibilities came into view, including the entry of organized economic groups into politics, the clash of values between urban and rural America, the impact of science and technology on government, and the growth of bureaucracy and administration.[11]

Given the extraordinary breadth of Hays's interests in social and political life, his relative neglect of one subject stands out, and that subject is class. Hays was by no means oblivious to economic differences in society (he noted the need for studies of inequality and social mobility, for example), nor did his research program explicitly exclude class conflict. But it was only infre-

10. Hays, *American Political History as Social Analysis*, pp. 54–56 (quote 54), 77–81, 97–98, 150–52, 157 (quote), 298–302.
11. Hays, *American Political History as Social Analysis*, pp. 74–77, 81–85, 94, 95–96, 126–28, 153–56, 293–325.

quently mentioned—a fact which the 1980s reader cannot help noticing.[12]

Hays's agenda-setting articles were widely cited, and, as the footnotes in his own volume of collected essays demonstrate, his calls for work to be done found willing hands. In any number of areas where he urged research, we know far more today than we did in 1965—a record of progress due in no small part to Hays. Yet however influential his articles may have been, one—and only one—body of work stands out in exemplification of what *he* meant by the social analysis of politics: the ethnocultural voting studies. Even here, of course, Hays was not alone in giving inspiration; Lee Benson's role in formulating the ethnocultural model was probably even greater than Hays's. But many of these studies prominently cite Hays's articles, and, more pertinently, they embrace crucial elements of his vision for political history. Like Hays, they treat voting as a form of decision-making that occurred in local communities, often far distant from the centralizing forces that political historians had traditionally emphasized. Just as Hays and Benson had predicted, moreover, most of the historians who researched voting behavior found evidence that ethnicity and religion were important determinants of nineteenth-century partisan choices. Particularly in the earliest works of this genre, economic class was specifically relegated to a secondary status in influencing voting. Like Hays, too, these historians tended to be wary of ideological evidence—especially if it emanated from top leaders—and to eschew the study of governmental institutions and policymaking. Above all, they shared with him an interest in political behavior chiefly for what it expressed of the human values held by grass-roots Americans.[13]

12. One exception is "The Politics of Reform in Municipal Government in the Progressive Era" where Hays attributed reform to "the upper class" rather than "the lower and middle classes." See also Hays, *American Political History as Social Analysis*, pp. 94–95.

13. Richard L. McCormick, "Ethno-Cultural Interpretations of Nineteenth-Century American Voting Behavior," *Political Science Quarterly* 84 (June 1974): 351–77.

During the 1970s, the ethnocultural interpretation of nineteenth-century voting behavior made its way into the textbooks and came to be recognized (often reluctantly) as a valuable corrective to earlier economic interpretations of the party alignments. But there was a slowing of the pace at which the voting studies appeared and a quickening of dissatisfaction with them. From the perspective of political history, they had failed to produce a satisfactory account of the motives for political participation—which, after all, had something to do with affecting government, not merely expressing cultural values.[14] Nor did such studies seem to lead toward a general social history of politics—not even of the sort Hays had sketched out (with different forms of political activity emanating from each level of society), much less a social history of politics that included class conflicts and ideological differences as integral parts of the story. Some critics of ethnocultural history explicitly questioned what they saw as a false dichotomy between "culture" and "economics." Not surprisingly, many social historians read the voting studies with, as one of their number put it, "varying degrees of boredom and hostility."[15] Perhaps it is not too much to say that by the late 1970s the social analysis of American political history, as originally conceived, was at a dead end.

But such analysis was also about to be reborn, as interest in the subject began to emerge from diverse—even unlikely—quarters. One of the most important was the new social history itself. In its earliest years, of course, the new social history had little use for politics. Family life, class formation, ethnic history, women's sphere, social mobility, community development, sexuality, criminality, and demography were among its subjects—but parties, voting, public policies, and the like usually were not. There were

14. Richard L. McCormick, "Political Parties in the United States: Reinterpreting Their Natural History," *The History Teacher* 19 (November 1985): 15–32; Eric Foner, "The Causes of the American Civil War: Recent Interpretations and New Directions," in Foner, *Politics and Ideology in the Age of the Civil War* (New York, 1980), especially pp. 16–19.

15. Sean Wilentz, "On Class and Politics in Jacksonian America," *Reviews in American History* 10 (December 1982): 48.

exceptions, to be sure; some of the community studies, for example, included accounts of how different social groups carried their concerns into the public arena and how local elites worked their will on the polity. But these *were* exceptions—until recently, that is, when the tide has seemed to turn, carrying social history with it toward the shores of politics. Two related factors seem to account for the still nascent blending of the new social history with political history. One is a growing recognition among social historians that a full history of American society simply could not afford to leave out the struggles for governmental power between contending social groups, or even the party battles which so animated nineteenth-century Americans. The second is the simple fact that most younger American historians today, including most with an interest in politics, were trained during an era when the new social history was attaining enormous influence and making significant contributions to knowledge. It was inevitable that when some of those historians settled on politics as their subject they would bring to it many of the methods and assumptions of social history. And so they have.[16]

Renewed interest in the social history of politics has also sprung from another seemingly unlikely quarter, the studies of republican ideology. When it first emerged in the 1960s, the new appreciation of eighteenth-century Anglo-American republican thought seemed antithetical to a social analysis. As formulated by Bernard Bailyn, republicanism was a consensual American ideology—"a single configuration of thought," in John Higham's words—articulated by a Revolutionary elite but apparently shared equally and identically with other social groups as well. Soon, however, that earlier republican paradigm came under significant challenge. Conceding the pervasiveness of certain bedrock republican notions, historians nonetheless found important variations in the way those ideas were expressed and in the

---

16. Peter N. Stearns, "Toward a Wider Vision: Trends in Social History," in Michael Kammen, ed., *The Past Before Us: Contemporary Historical Writing in the United States* (Ithaca, 1980), pp. 205–30; Eric Foner, *Politics and Ideology*, pp. 5–9, 30; Wilentz, "On Class and Politics."

meaning they carried for people. Besides its political implications, republicanism also appeared to have had profound economic and social connotations. Although they talked in nearly the same terms, different groups of Americans found republican ways of expressing their conflicts and of articulating competing conceptions of what their society should become. Republicanism thus emerged as something quite different from what it had first seemed to be: a powerful analytic tool for examining what differing Americans thought of their social arrangements and their government. The study of political ideology and social analysis turned out to be one and the same.[17]

From within the field of history and beyond, other influences have also helped inspire a fresh examination of the social history of American politics—especially cultural anthropology, works on modernization, and studies of political culture around the world. The collective result of these trends has been a range of recent forays across the boundary between political history and social history. Undertaken for the most part by younger scholars writing their first monographs—but also by several well-established historians—the new work constitutes a diverse but significant body of scholarship genuinely worthy of the label "the social analysis of political history." Although Hays's sweeping definition of that term was broad enough to embrace what these historians have done, his actual suggestions for research pointed away from the social and political phenomena in which most of them proved interested, including ideology, class conflict, and battles over government policies. Not surprisingly, perhaps, the recent works indicate little debt to Hays.

While each of the newer studies makes distinctive contributions, they fall into two groups, one somewhat more unified than the other. First there are those that employ Marxist insights to illuminate the lives of workers and farmers and to place their

17. Robert E. Shalhope, "Republicanism and Early American Historiography," *William and Mary Quarterly* 39 (April 1982): 334–56; John Higham, *History: Professional Scholarship in America*, Johns Hopkins Paperbacks Edition (Baltimore, 1983), pp. 251–53 (quote 253).

political beliefs and behavior in a social setting. Second are the studies of "political culture," a rich—if occasionally elusive—concept upon which a number of historians have constructed accounts of the consciousness and expectations underlying political action. Following an analysis of each of these "schools," we may ask what, precisely, they have contributed to American political history and what insights, in turn, a more traditional political history can bring to the social analysis of politics.

The social historians of politics who make up the first group, including Alan Dawley, Sean Wilentz, Leon Fink, Steven Hahn, and Eric Foner, are perhaps most appropriately termed cultural Marxists. Indifferent or blatantly hostile to the ethnocultural voting studies, they frequently express debts to E. P. Thompson, Eric J. Hobsbawm, and, among Americanists, Eugene D. Genovese, Herbert Gutman, and David Montgomery. Although scarcely united on a single interpretation, Dawley, Wilentz, Fink, Hahn, and Foner share a sympathetic interest in the lives led by workers and farmers in commercializing, industrializing America and a common commitment to a class analysis. But because they are anything but economic determinists and unafraid to interpret ideological evidence, their studies place great emphasis upon the role of ideas in class formation and, more generally, upon the interplay between ideas and social and political reality. To these historians the social analysis of politics means exploring how ideologically charged class relations were expressed in political acts directed toward obtaining power and controlling the government.[18]

18. The works to be discussed here include Alan Dawley, *Class and Community: The Industrial Revolution in Lynn* (Cambridge, Mass., 1976); Sean Wilentz, *Chants Democratic: New York City & the Rise of the American Working Class, 1788–1850* (New York, 1984); Leon Fink, *Workingmen's Democracy: The Knights of Labor and American Politics* (Urbana, 1983); Steven Hahn, *The Roots of Southern Populism: Yeoman Farmers and the Transformation of the Georgia Upcountry, 1850–1890* (New York, 1983); Eric Foner, *Nothing But Freedom:*

To be sure, their studies differ considerably in the extent of attention paid to politics, and some of these authors may not consider themselves political historians at all. But academic labels aside, each of them actually has a lot to say about the political beliefs and behavior of the men and women (mainly men) they study. Their books place the workers' and farmers' formal political activities—such as joining parties and casting ballots—right alongside their street actions, strikes, mass meetings, organizational efforts, and ideological pronouncements. From this perspective, the "political" and the "social" tend to disappear as separate categories. Both realms of experience are understood to emanate from the everyday lives—and ideas—of nineteenth-century Americans.

Alan Dawley's story, in its largest sense, is about the impact of the industrial revolution upon a community and its people. More specifically, he tells how the shoe industry of Lynn, Massachusetts, was transformed from small shops where a master and his artisan journeymen worked side by side to large factories where industrial workers operated machines according to the impersonal dictates of the foreman and the clock. As production was revolutionized, Dawley says, the inequalities of the patriarchal household gave way to the new inequalities of industrial capitalism. Keenly experiencing the pains and hardships of the new order, the workers of Lynn organized unions, struck the factories, and expressed what Dawley calls the doctrine of "equal rights"—the equality of all producers and the right of each person "to live in comfort and dignity." To Dawley, their songs

---

Emancipation and Its Legacy (Baton Rouge, 1983); and Foner, *Politics and Ideology*. These are not, of course, the only works I might have dealt with. To name but two others, Edward Countryman's *A People in Revolution: The American Revolution and Political Society in New York, 1760–1790* (Baltimore, 1981) and Lawrence Goodwyn's *Democratic Promise: The Populist Moment in America* (New York, 1976) could well have been included. So might any number of other excellent studies. But the works discussed in the following pages are representative of the best and most important contributions to what I have termed the cultural Marxist analysis of American political history.

and their printed statements leave no doubt that Lynn's shoe workers became aware of the class conflict between themselves and the factory owners. In the words of their newspaper, "capital and labor stand opposed."[19]

Although politics occupies little more than a chapter of Dawley's book, it is politics upon which his interpretation of class conflict finally rests. Democracy and capitalism arrived in the United States together, he says, and proved mutually supportive. Just as resolutely as commerce and industry created new inequalities, democratic politics disguised them because workers identified with the political system and considered it their own. Initially disposed to trust the State because of a Revolutionary tradition which taught that government in America was the people's government, workers deepened their attachment to democracy when they heard friendly appeals from party politicians and saw men of their own class elected to positions of authority. Ultimately, according to Dawley, it was this confidence in politics and government that discouraged workers from deepening their recognition of class conflict and pursuing its implications.[20]

For much of the nineteenth century, the workers of Lynn gave their votes to candidates of the major parties—despite the parties' support for the policy programs of the local shoe manufacturers. The workers' faith in democratic politics was deep. Even on the occasions when they withdrew their votes from the regular parties, that faith remained. Embittered by the use of the city's police force against striking factory hands in 1860 and again in 1878 and 1890, workers put up their own local candidates, and they elected several mayors and numerous councilmen. But except for removing three offending police chiefs, workingclass officials continued the same basic policies that the Democrats and Republicans had supported. The Workingmen's party "did not enact a program of municipal reform because it had no such program." Never did the party's mayors raise the issue of class struggle. For

19. Dawley, *Class and Community*, pp. 2, 64.
20. Dawley, *Class and Community*, pp. 66–72, 97–104, 194–219, 235–41.

workingmen who identified with the political system, winning public office proved to be an end in itself. As a result, the shoe workers of Lynn failed to follow up their radical economic perceptions with radical politics. "The ballot box," Dawley dramatically declares, "was the coffin of class consciousness."[21]

Despite some important similarities to Dawley's book, Sean Wilentz's study of the New York City workingclass in the early nineteenth century takes a somewhat different view of the relationships among class formation, ideology, and politics. Just as Dawley does—although with more richness of detail—Wilentz describes how changes in the means of production and distribution during the decades after 1815 transformed the crafts and trades, created a new breed of entrepreneurs, and reshaped the work and lives of artisans. Like Dawley, too, Wilentz finds in the workers' words and phrases evidence of a developing class consciousness and a critique of the inequalities of the marketplace. But in analyzing those words Wilentz offers a far more nuanced reading of what he terms "artisan republicanism" than Dawley gives to the doctrine of "equal rights." Dissecting not only speeches and pamphlets but also public ceremonies and craft symbols, Wilentz finds that a historic republican language was subtly rearticulated by both entrepreneurs and workers—and, indeed, by various constituent elements within each class. For entrepreneurs, the old ideology justified individualism, economic competition, and moral self-improvement; for workers, it signified mutuality and cooperation and a rejection of exploitation and inequality. At the heart of Wilentz's study is his interpretation of the many meanings which New Yorkers gave to republicanism—meanings which reveal the extent, the terms, and the shades of the process by which they continually worked out their class conflicts.[22]

21. Dawley, *Class and Community*, pp. 70, 202.
22. For Wilentz's treatment of republicanism, see *Chants Democratic*, especially pp. 13–15, 61–103, 145–71, 237–48, 271–86, 302–6, 315–25, 331–35, 393–96. For a related discussion see Sean Wilentz, "Artisan Republican Festivals and the Rise of Class Conflict in New York City, 1788–1837," in Michael H. Frisch and Daniel J. Walkowitz, eds., *Working-Class America: Essays on Labor, Community, and American Society* (Urbana, 1983), pp. 37–77.

When he turns to politics, then, Wilentz is not looking for some imagined, unified workingclass movement. He has no expectation of finding it, and so he is not disappointed. Wilentz, in fact, rejects the question of why the American workingclass evidenced less political solidarity than its supposed European counterpart, and he looks instead at the variety of political forms workers created, often in competition with one another. Writing of the New York City Working Men of 1829–30, for example, Wilentz shows how an initially radical "movement" was supplanted by a much more moderate "party" and then foundered completely. No less than three different factions, struggling to control the Working Men, "all resorted to the same political language, that of the artisan republic." Yet behind their words, says Wilentz, "lay fundamentally different meanings and motives"—on which he lavishes impressive analytical attention. Wilentz brings a similar, if less detailed, analysis of ideology to the question of why many workers were attracted to the Democrats and the Whigs, despite the entrepreneurial outlook shared by both major parties. The answer lay in the party leaders' ability to blur their true aims "with broad republican rhetoric" that echoed the language used by workers themselves. Elsewhere, turning to the growing political and cultural conflict between Protestant and Catholic workers in the 1840s, Wilentz shows how the words employed by lower-class Protestants expressed not only their nativism but also their economic grievances against capitalist employers.[23]

What all this adds up to is an account of the class basis of political conflict grounded primarily on an analysis of ideology. To judge solely from the political *actions* of New York City's workers, they were thoroughly divided—between the major parties and their own factionalized organizations, between different trades and crafts, and between Protestants and Catholics. Class

23. Wilentz, *Chants Democratic*, pp. 15–16, 172–216 (quotes 213–14), 266–69, 276 (quote), 315–25, 343–49. See also Sean Wilentz, "Class, Democracy, and the Labor Movement," a paper presented at the Annual Meeting of the Organization of American Historians, Los Angeles, California, April 1984.

politics in the familiar sense of the term would be hard to find. But looking instead at what workers *said* and at the symbols they displayed, Wilentz uncovers the extensive, complex ways in which class perceptions shaped political behavior. As for governance, it is scarcely part of Wilentz's story because, unlike their counterparts in Lynn, the workers of New York City never succeeded in electing their chosen representatives to office. If they had, it seems fair to predict from Wilentz's analysis that we would discover the class basis of the workers' policies chiefly in what they *said* about their programs rather than in any governmental actions themselves.

Like the studies by Dawley and Wilentz, Leon Fink's book on the Knights of Labor grapples with the difficult subjects of ideology, class conflict, and power. But by focusing on the Knights' electoral struggles at the local level, Fink places these matters more concretely in a political context than do Dawley and Wilentz. Moreover, because the Knights actually came to power in the cities and towns he studies, Fink has a great deal to say about labor's view of the State and about the nature of government under workingclass control.

To explore these matters, he turns first to ideology. Influenced, just as Wilentz has been, by the literature on republicanism, Fink provides a subtle account of how "inherited values" were put to "radical ends." Although the Knights shared many commonplace beliefs of the Victorian culture they inhabited, they rejected the "possessive individualism" of their wealthier neighbors and considered the wage system of labor to be in "inevitable and irresistible conflict" with republican government. Taking seriously "the ideal of a republic of producers," the Knights held to mutuality, collective action, and the "vision of a cooperative industrial future." Although their notion of class lines was "rather elastic," they perceived "an ultimate social division . . . in the world around them." When it came to government, however, the Knights' ideas were much fuzzier—as Fink shows in a superb account of the workers' limited conception of the State. Unlike later Socialists, the Knights often entered politics without a specific program of reform in mind. "In many cases," Fink writes, "the Knights did not set out do anything dramatically unconventional with political power." A natural "spillover effect" of union organizing, labor's quests for public office were intended to demonstrate that workers were capable of governing and, in some instances, "to curtail state repression" of their movement. Less often did the Knights come to politics with "specific class-related legislation" in mind, much less to change the basic nature of American governance.[24]

These themes are explored in the five case-studies that make up the heart of Fink's book. In Rochester, New Hampshire; Rutland, Vermont; Kansas City, Kansas; Richmond, Virginia; and Milwaukee, Wisconsin, local Knights capitalized on their union's victories in the great strikes of the mid-1880s and put together electoral coalitions that held or shared power for several years. As Fink shows, however, class conflict alone does not explain these triumphs, for workers were often sharply divided, and in each case racial or ethnic divisions crucially shaped the political confrontation. (With the ethnocultural political studies in mind, Fink specifically rejects "misguided" efforts to isolate class from cultural influences in politics or to treat either as "unchanging, ahistorical categories.") Once in office, the Knights "exercised power with great restraint." In Rochester they assumed only "a limited caretaker role," while in Rutland they advocated "fairly modest reforms." Milwaukee's Knights similarly envisioned "a positive yet still limited role for government." In each city, local circumstances propelled workers into battles for political control, but—just as Dawley finds in Lynn—

24. Fink, *Workingmen's Democracy*, pp. 4, 9, 12, 14, 30, 31. Fink's important discussion of workers and the State may also be found in Leon Fink, "The Uses of Political Power: Toward a Theory of the Labor Movement in the Era of the Knights of Labor," in Frisch and Walkowitz, eds., *Working-Class America*, pp. 104–22. As Fink acknowledges, David Montgomery's insights on this subject provided one crucial starting point for analysis; see Montgomery, *Beyond Equality: Labor and the Radical Republicans, 1862–1872* (New York, 1967), especially pp. 259–60; and Montgomery, "Labor and the Republic in Industrial America: 1860–1920," *Le Mouvement Social* 111 (April–June 1980): 201–15.

they evidently regarded their governmental power less as a means to statist ends than as an affirmation of republican ideals.[25]

Industrial workers were not alone in making ideological struggles for control of nineteenth-century American government: farmers made them, too, according to Steven Hahn and Eric Foner. Hahn's subjects are the yeomen of Upcountry Georgia whose traditional social relations were undone when the market economy penetrated their region during the decades after the Civil War. In the 1850s, when his account begins, the self-sufficient, patriarchal household was the focus of production; exchange networks tended to be local; and an array of popular customs governing economic life enabled farm families to preserve their familiar ways. Then, within the space of a few decades, the Upcountry economy was swiftly transformed by the relentless spread of cotton cultivation. Despite the resistance of a yeomanry that was deeply suspicious of economic development, a new class of merchants, possessing a monopoly over credit, practically forced farmers to grow the staple crop for sale in distant markets. Yeomen now lost their self-sufficiency—and frequently their land, too. "Once the domain of yeoman freeholders, the Upcountry [fast become] . . . a territory of the dispossessed."[26]

To make sense of how Georgia farmers experienced these economic woes, Hahn turns to their culture, specifically to a preindustrial republican ideology which he says was "still vital" in postbellum America. Linking "freedom and independence with control over productive resources," republican ideas underpinned a yeoman culture distinguished by its prebourgeois qualities and by the "habits of mutuality" which it supported. Hahn

25. Fink, *Workingmen's Democracy*, pp. 57, 58, 94, 209, 222, 231n.

26. Hahn, *The Roots of Southern Populism*, pp. 15–49, 137–203 (quote 168). On related aspects of northern rural life see Christopher Clark, "Household Economy, Market Exchange, and the Rise of Capitalism in the Connecticut Valley, 1800–1860," *Journal of Social History* 13 (Summer 1979): 169–89; and Michael Merrill, "Cash Is Good To Eat: Self-Sufficiency and Exchange in the Rural Economy of the United States," *Radical History Review* 3 (Winter 1977): 42–66.

points to the prevalence of cooperative work patterns; to customary definitions of property rights; and to traditional patterns of exchange, indebtedness, and tenancy as testimony to the strength of "the republican producer ideology." Despite the spread of market relations that profoundly challenged these customary ways, Upcountry farmers seem to have adhered to their old beliefs, according to Hahn's reading of the evidence. In the 1880s, the Southern Farmers' Alliance gave expression to the traditional ideology, as did the Populist party in the following decade.[27]

Politics, to Hahn, was the terrain on which these social and cultural tensions were articulated and fought out. Before the war, most Upcountry farmers voted Democratic because they shared that party's expressed opposition to the spread of market relationships and, in particular, its suspicion of banks. After the war, yeomen tended to support independent candidates against the nominees of the Democratic party, which was now frankly oriented toward commercial development. Increasingly Upcountry politics came to reflect a class division between those who favored the new market economy and those who wanted to maintain an earlier way of life. By the 1880s, the conflict had come to focus on a group of local policy questions—especially the customary right of farmers to let their livestock roam freely through the woods—that were as much a matter of culture as of economics. Essential to the small producer's livelihood, common grazing rights also "embodied distinct ideas about labor, community, independence, and the role of the state." At issue in the political battles that preceded Populism, says Hahn, was nothing less than the survival of what Georgia yeomen considered to be a cooperative, productive, republican society.[28]

27. Hahn, *The Roots of Southern Populism*, pp. 1–11 (quotes 2, 3), 50–85 (quote 52), 239–89 (quote 283).

28. Hahn, *The Roots of Southern Populism*, pp. 86–133, 204–68 (quote 252). See also Steven Hahn, "Common Right and Commonwealth: The Stock-Law Struggle and the Roots of Southern Populism," in J. Morgan Kousser and James M. McPherson, eds., *Region, Race, and Reconstruction: Essays in Honor of C. Vann Woodward* (New York, 1982), pp. 51–88; and Hahn, "The Transformation of the Rural South," a paper presented at the Annual Meeting of the Organization of American Historians, Los Angeles, California, April 1984.

Foner, too, is concerned with the linkages forged by southern farmers between ideology and political power—in this case by the planters and freedmen of the immediate postwar era.[29] No problem was more hotly debated during Reconstruction, Foner says, than labor, specifically the question of the legal and economic arrangements under which the former slaves would work. Would the Black Codes of 1865 and 1866, which so strictly regulated the freedmen's labor, be permitted to stand? What rights to land did the former slaves possess? Could they graze their animals and hunt and fish in the woods? Who would have the first lien on a man's crop? Would the black sharecropper be taxed? From a comparative perspective, American Reconstruction was unique in that the former slaves enjoyed political rights and thus were able to take public part in deciding these questions, so central to their livelihoods. The result, writes Foner, was that throughout the South "state and local government . . . became a battleground between contending social classes, including the black laborer." Depending on which party was in power the issues all were decided differently. Under Radical Republican regimes, the power of the State was used in support of black economic opportunities; under Democratic Redeemers, it was not.[30]

Just as Hahn finds in Upcountry Georgia, the political battles described by Foner were laden with ideological significance. To the Republicans who came south to assist the freedmen (and themselves), the North's own "free labor" ideology offered the answer to the South's economic problems. The market itself, they believed, would "provide the incentive . . . [to] make self-disciplined free laborers of the blacks." To southern planters, northern-style free labor was a hopeless illusion. Only by "legal and physical compulsion," as embodied in the Black Codes, could the former slaves be made to work hard. To blacks themselves, just learning the doctrines of republican citizenship, their

29. The following discussion draws on three of Foner's works: *Nothing But Freedom*, especially chapter 2; *Politics and Ideology*, especially chapter 6; and Eric Foner, "Reconstruction and the Black Political Tradition," in Richard L. McCormick, ed., *Political Parties and the Modern State* (New Brunswick, N. J., 1984), pp. 53–69.

30. Foner, *Nothing But Freedom*, pp. 39–73 (quote 46).

own productive labor entitled them to the land and to the full fruits of their toil. What freedmen chiefly wanted was autonomy, that is, "independence from white control" and freedom from the dictates of the "impersonal marketplace." Here, according to Foner, were three different views of black labor and, by implication, of the kind of society the South ought to become. Those competing visions, above all, defined the politics of the Reconstruction South.[31]

Despite some obvious differences in subject matter and interpretation, Dawley, Wilentz, Fink, Hahn, and Foner share essential elements of a common view of nineteenth-century politics and society. At the heart of that view is a recognition of class conflict, in particular a division between people who welcomed commercial or industrial development and those who clung to more traditional ways. To judge from these studies, that cleavage formed an enduring aspect of American life. Across great spans of time and space and under widely varying circumstances, the question of economic "progress" persisted in inspiring bitter contention. Yet however pervasive it may have been, the class conflict which these historians find was not simple; nor is it easily interpreted. Rejecting an older progressive formulation that equated classes with "fixed social categories," Dawley, Wilentz, and the others generally prefer E. P. Thompson's understanding of class formation as a dynamic process, and class consciousness as existing in myriad forms.[32] They acknowledge that classes were seldom monolithic and that class conflict was only infrequently expressed in hard and fast political lines. Often class oppositions became entangled with racial, ethnic, and religious

31. Foner, *Politics and Ideology*, pp. 97–127 (quotes 101, 103, 107, 109); Foner, "Reconstruction and the Black Political Tradition," pp. 58–65. On the "free labor" ideology, see Eric Foner, *Free Soil, Free Labor, Free Men: The Ideology of the Republican Party Before the Civil War* (New York, 1970).

32. E. P. Thompson, *The Making of the English Working Class* (New York, 1964); Dawley, *Class and Community*, pp. 4–5; Fink, *Workingmen's Democracy*, p. 219; Wilentz, *Chants Democratic*, pp. 7–12 (quote 7), 17–19; Wilentz, "On Class and Politics," pp. 49–50.

divisions—and the mixture defies disentanglement by historians. Perhaps most important, these authors recognize the difficulty of discerning and interpreting class consciousness, and they rely on close readings of ideological evidence to probe their subjects' states of mind. The care brought by the cultural Marxists to the subject of class should not, however, be taken as an indication of interpretational ambivalence. Fortified by so sophisticated an approach, they firmly insist upon class conflict as the central fact of the nineteenth-century American experience.[33]

Politics was one means—and frequently an important one—by which competing social classes expressed and contested their differences. Although some of these studies are more centrally concerned with politics than others, Dawley, Wilentz, Fink, Hahn, and Foner all view political action as arising predominantly from economic conflicts within local communities, often inseparably from nonpolitical activities. This was true of Workingmen's parties in both the Jacksonian era and the Gilded Age, just as it was of black politics in the South Carolina rice country during Reconstruction.[34] But these historians agree, too, that nineteenth-century workers and farmers did not automatically look to political solutions for their problems; many were reluctant to do so, and they often quarreled among themselves over whether to form a separate party, endorse candidates, or ask for government help. The workers' and farmers' complex, often bitter, relationships with the major political parties typified these problems. All five historians find evidence of troubled connec-

33. Some readers will find that, despite the recognition they give to racial and ethnocultural differences, these historians are too insistent on the primacy of class conflict over all other social divisions. See James Oakes, "The Politics of Economic Development in the Antebellum South," *Journal of Interdisciplinary History* 15 (Autumn 1984): 312; and Dan T. Carter, "Politics and Power: Emancipation in Comparative Perspective," *Reviews in American History* 12 (September 1984): 396.

34. Wilentz, *Chants Democratic*, pp. 172–216; Dawley, *Class and Community*, pp. 199–207; Fink, *Workingmen's Democracy*, pp. 38–218; Foner, *Nothing But Freedom*, pp. 74–110; Hahn, *The Roots of Southern Populism*, pp. 91–105, 216–38.

tions between tradition-oriented Americans and development-oriented parties: in Lynn, Massachusetts, Upcountry Georgia, and New York City alike. Sometimes partisan rhetoric proved highly alluring to workers and farmers, but the results of an encounter with a party frequently turned out to be deeply disappointing.[35]

The record of such bitter experiences raises the difficult problem of explaining the motives which drove workers and farmers to turn to politics when they did. Although the cultural Marxists inevitably leave this puzzle at least partially unsolved, they do offer two related answers. First, workers and farmers took political action as a means of articulating ideologically rooted convictions about their society, especially when they felt the need to defend it against unwanted changes. And second, they entered politics to get control of the government, both for its own sake and as a means of protecting themselves against their class enemies. Both answers, one concerning ideology and the other governance, are significant—but each stands in need of further refinement.

Although Dawley, Wilentz, and the others would probably agree with Samuel P. Hays that there are dangers in taking ideological statements at face value, they are far more willing than he to probe such evidence and to try to ferret out its meanings. Convinced that masses do have coherent beliefs, these historians make imaginative efforts, employing traditional written sources as well as other cultural expressions, to bring those beliefs to light. Wilentz is the most innovative in this regard, but Hahn, in particular, and the others are not far behind. Reconstructing mass belief systems is a difficult task, of course, because

35. Dawley, *Class and Community*, pp. 66–72, 97–104, 209–10; Wilentz, *Chants Democratic*, pp. 172–75, 206, 235–37, 276, 326–35, 383–86; Fink, *Workingmen's Democracy*, pp. 53–54, 81–82, 87–88, 95–101, 123–29, 134–35, 164–69, 196–204; Hahn, *The Roots of Southern Populism*, pp. 99–105, 204–16, 225–38. Several of these studies take particular note of the attractiveness of the Democrats' anti-bank rhetoric to workers and farmers; see Wilentz, *Chants Democratic*, pp. 240–41; and Hahn, *The Roots of Southern Populism*, pp. 101–5.

the ideological evidence left by lower-class Americans does not admit of easy interpretation. To what extent do the statements of leaders reflect the ideas of their followers? Are newspaper editorials and stump speeches valid indicators of mass opinion? What meanings can be found in ceremony and symbol? These are perennial questions for social and political historians, and the cultural Marxists have not shied away from the difficulties.[36]

What distinguishes their approach from that of most previous American historians is the tendency—more pronounced in some of these works than others—to treat ideologies as patterns of meaning rather than functional creeds. Influenced by anthropological scholarship, these historians take their subjects' words, symbols, and behavior chiefly as clues to what they felt or meant or understood. Only secondarily do they regard ideologies as purposive instruments of conscious goals—such as means to mobilize popular support or gain legitimacy. These historians thus tend to *believe* their subjects' ideologies, to trust them as valid indicators, seldom to denigrate them as merely instrumental poses. To these scholars ideological expressions are texts full of evidence about the ways in which nineteenth-century people gave meaning to—and found meaning in—their lives and the world around them.[37]

The possibilities, as well as the limitations, of this approach to ideology can be seen in the cultural Marxists' analyses of republicanism, the ideology held to by the workers and farmers they describe. Building on earlier studies documenting the suspicions with which eighteenth-century republicans regarded commercial development, Wilentz, Fink, and Hahn (and to a lesser extent Dawley and Foner) trace precapitalist republicanism into the

36. Dawley, *Class and Community*, pp. 58–66; Wilentz, *Chants Democratic*, pp. 13–15 and passim; Hahn, *The Roots of Southern Populism*, pp. 1–4, 50–52, 282–83; Foner, *Politics and Ideology*, pp. 18–19.

37. For recent discussions of how American historians interpret ideology, see Shalhope, "Republicanism and Early American Historiography"; and Daniel Joseph Singal, "Beyond Consensus: Richard Hofstadter and American Historiography," *American Historical Review* 89 (October 1984): 976–1004.

nineteenth century.[38] What they find is that the historic ideals continued to provide workers and farmers with an alternative to the "liberal" marketplace values fostered by economic development. Rejecting possessive individualism and capitalist competition, many Americans retained an older republican commitment to cooperation, mutuality, and an identification of the citizen with the independent producer. When they entered politics, whether in New England, New York, or Georgia, they carried with them a powerful vision of what their society was—and had been—and a profound moral commitment to keeping it that way.

This is a provocative and appealing thesis, likely to have considerable influence on the writing of American history. But it rests upon an interpretation of meaning which defies verification. The problem is not only the scarcity of evidence about what lower-class people believed but also the great difficulty of knowing what they *meant* by what they said and did. Some of the same statements which these historians interpret one way could be read by others as indicative of liberal values. How can one be sure, moreover, that the workers' and farmers' ideological expressions did not primarily have strategic, functional purposes which the "meaning" was intended to disguise? The reader is left in the position of either grasping the interpretation or not, of seeing the point or not, of accepting it or not.[39] Some will and some won't.

38. Wilentz, *Chants Democratic*, pp. 13–15, 61–103, 145–71, 237–48, 271–86, 302–6, 315–25, 331–35, 393–96; Fink, *Workingmen's Democracy*, pp. 3–15, 21, 48–49, 224; Hahn, *The Roots of Southern Populism*, pp. 1–4, 50–52, 107–9, 252–54, 282–89; Foner, *Politics and Ideology*, pp. 10, 58–59; Dawley, *Class and Community*, p. 229. On eighteenth-century republican attitudes toward commerce, see J. G. A. Pocock, "Virtue and Commerce in the Eighteenth Century," *Journal of Interdisciplinary History* 3 (Summer 1972): 119–34. Two related studies documenting the precapitalist mentality of eighteenth-century Americans are Michael Zuckerman, *Peaceable Kingdoms: New England Towns in the Eighteenth Century* (New York, 1970); and James A. Henretta, "Families and Farms: *Mentalité* in Pre-Industrial America," *William and Mary Quarterly* 35 (January 1978): 3–32.
39. This sentence is a paraphrase of an observation by Clifford Geertz in *The Interpretation of Cultures* (New York, 1973), p. 24. For a discussion of the difficulty of verifying cultural interpretations, see Paul Shankman, "The Thick and the Thin: On the Interpretive Theoretical Program of Clifford Geertz,"

To the cultural Marxists, workers and farmers entered politics not just to express their ideologies but also to obtain governmental power. Although only a minor theme in Wilentz's study, the struggle to win control of government and shape its policies is given prominence by Dawley, Fink, Hahn, and Foner. In Lynn, workers sought office to avenge the use of the local police force against strikers; in South Carolina, black fieldhands voted Republican to protect their opportunities for collective action against the rice planters; in Milwaukee, the Knights of Labor nominated their own candidates to protest militia violence against workers and to further their campaign for the eight-hour day; in Upcountry Georgia, yeoman farmers repeatedly opposed local ordinances requiring the fencing of livestock.[40] Behind these struggles lay the protagonists' ideological values, but even more prominently at stake were some very specific intentions for getting and using the power of the State.

Taken together, the studies by Dawley, Fink, Hahn, and Foner add significantly to our knowledge of what nineteenth-century workers and farmers wanted from government. What they mainly desired, it seems, was protection of the right to earn their livings and conduct their lives without undue interference. This meant that the State should not become the tool of their class enemies, that the community's customary economic practices should be maintained, and that each person's (or at least each white man's) opportunity to be a productive citizen ought to be upheld. In Hahn's words, the State was portrayed "as defender of the public good, as protector of communities of petty producers." In a sense, that was a great deal to ask of the State—far more, as it turned out, than development-minded government officials were willing to grant. But from another perspective, the workers' and

Current Anthropology 25 (June 1984): 261–70. For a passionate challenge to the contention that republicanism pervaded nineteenth-century America, see John Patrick Diggins, *The Lost Soul of American Politics: Virtue, Self-Interest, and the Foundations of Liberalism* (New York, 1984).

40. Dawley, *Class and Community*, pp. 199–207; Foner, *Nothing But Freedom*, pp. 74–110; Fink, *Workingmen's Democracy*, pp. 188–98; Hahn, *The Roots of Southern Populism*, pp. 254–68.

farmers' agenda was extremely limited, certainly compared with
that of their capitalist opponents who asked so much in the way
of public assistance for their enterprises. According to Fink, who
explores this subject more fully than anyone else, workers did not
look to government for imaginative efforts or novel experiments,
but rather for the "consolidation and preservation" of what they
already had.[41]

These insights into how workers and farmers regarded government are extremely important, and yet they remain regrettably
vague and undeveloped in the cultural Marxist studies. Dawley
largely fails to connect his observations about the workers' limited demands on government to his provocative thesis that their
faith in politics killed class consciousness. Hahn refers several
times to the yeomanry's conception of the State but does not
really pursue the question. Even Fink, who gives the Knights'
view of government a thorough theoretical discussion, somewhat
loses sight of it in his case-studies.[42] That lower-class Americans
had an essentially defensive and preservationist policy program
while merchants and entrepreneurs asked for aggressive and revolutionary governmental actions would seem to be a fact of critical
importance to an understanding of nineteenth-century politics.
It might, if pressed far enough, help explain why the State bent
to the will of the capitalists and, yet, why workers and farmers
retained such confidence in the political process—from which
they asked so little. At the very least, these historians have persua-
sively challenged the notion that ordinary Americans were
mainly absorbed by ethnic and religious conflicts and paid little
attention to economic policy issues. Even more important, these
studies have opened up—if not satisfactorily answered—the vital
questions of how social classes compared in their demands upon

41. Hahn, *The Roots of Southern Populism*, p. 3; Fink, *Workingmen's Democracy*, p. 32. See also Dawley, *Class and Community*, pp. 201–2.

42. Hahn, *The Roots of Southern Populism*, pp. 2–3, 252. For examples of
instances where Fink might have done more to connect his broad discussion of
how workers viewed the State with the specific policies proposed or enacted by
workingclass administrations, see *Workingmen's Democracy*, pp. 124–25, 131–33,
156–57, 196–97.

government and what effects their differential expectations had on politics and society.

Whatever limitations their works have, the cultural Marxists possess an admirably clear vision of what it means to do a social analysis of political history. All insist on the pervasiveness of class conflict, on the durability and believability of popular ideology, and on the significance of political struggles to shape the government's economic policies. These historians thus share an interpretation of the social setting of nineteenth-century American politics that differs on almost every vital point from that of Hays and the ethnocultural historians. They depart from Hays, as well, in their implicit theory about the fundamental cause of social and political change. To Hays, the great watershed in American history and the primary engine of political conflict was the transformation, rooted in science and technology, from a land of local communities to a cosmopolitan, administrative society. To the cultural Marxists, the great turning point and the cause of subsequent political struggles was the revolution in commerce and industry which altered nearly everything about the way people earned livings and conducted their lives. Hays's great watershed, of course, came decades (or more, depending on the locale) after the commercial and industrial revolution, and so the contrast between him and the cultural Marxists comes down, in part, to a matter of their different chronological foci. But it is rooted, too, in a philosophical difference between them, in conflicting conceptions of how the ambiguous, troubled relationship between a democratic polity and a capitalist (Hays would say "modern") society came into being.

Fundamental questions of this sort also inform some recent books by a second group of social historians of politics, including Jean H. Baker, Harry L. Watson, Ronald P. Formisano, and Robert H. Wiebe.[43] To these four, however, a social analysis of

43. The books to be discussed here include Jean H. Baker, *Affairs of Party: The Political Culture of Northern Democrats in the Mid-Nineteenth Century*

political history does not mean what it does to either Hays or the cultural Marxists. In the broadest terms, Baker, Watson, Formisano, and Wiebe examine the origins and nature of the democratic political culture of the early and mid-nineteenth-century United States. Each has a distinctive approach. Baker focuses on the generation of northern Democrats who reached maturity during the era of the Civil War; Watson and Formisano recount the rise of the Democrats and Whigs in a single county and state, respectively; Wiebe presents a general American social history in which parties emerge amidst broader developments. All mainly construe politics to mean party politics, and, in general, they focus on the major parties. Unlike the cultural Marxists who confine their attention to particular social groups, these authors include everyone who participated in politics and, in Wiebe's case, others as well.

What distinguishes the works by Baker, Watson, Formisano, and Wiebe—and gives common ground to a somewhat disparate group of historical writings—is the study of political culture. Each of these historians is concerned with the popular beliefs and expectations that gave meaning to the political process and guided the conduct of politics and government.[44] All agree that American political culture was fundamentally transformed during the era when mass parties came into being, and (with differ-

---

(Ithaca, 1983); Harry L. Watson, *Jacksonian Politics and Community Conflict: The Emergence of the Second American Party System in Cumberland County, North Carolina* (Baton Rouge, 1981); Ronald P. Formisano, *The Transformation of Political Culture: Massachusetts Parties, 1790s–1840s* (New York, 1983); and Robert H. Wiebe, *The Opening of American Society: From the Adoption of the Constitution to the Eve of Disunion* (New York, 1984).

44. Baker, Watson, and Formisano all employ the term "political culture," and all give it clear—albeit varying—definitions. Wiebe does not use the phrase itself, although he does portray the "democratic culture" of nineteenth-century America in a way that bears significant comparison with the treatments given political culture by the other three historians. Daniel Walker Howe's fine study of *The Political Culture of the American Whigs* (Chicago, 1979) could logically have been included here. But I chose not to discuss Howe's work because it is mainly an intellectual history of twelve prominent Whigs and does not attempt a social analysis of popular political behavior and beliefs. For Howe's definition of political culture, see *The Political Culture of the American Whigs*, p. 2.

ent emphases) all seek to understand that transformation by examining the social context in which parties arose and the values that Americans came to express in their partisan behavior. Although these historians all recognize economic and ethnoreligious conflicts (indeed, Watson and Formisano emphasize such differences in accounting for party origins), each portrays aspects of a partisan political culture shared by white, male Americans across the boundaries of class and ethnicity.

Unlike any previous study of American political history, Jean H. Baker's book takes for its subject an entire generation of party members—from the time of their socialization by family and school to their days as mature leaders and followers of the Democratic party. What she traces out, moreover, are not their external political actions, such as votes, roll calls, or party-building activities, but rather their internal lives as Democrats—the "beliefs, expressive symbols, and values" which defined for them "the situation in which political action . . . [took] place." Baker traces, in other words, their political culture. Building on the insights of anthropologists and political scientists, she assumes that "the attitudes, sentiments, and cognitions that inform and govern politics are not random arrangements, but represent . . . coherent patterns that together form a meaningful whole." Through the study of political language, of campaign rituals, of party symbols, and of popular cultural expressions, Baker's purpose is to reconstruct that whole. In doing so, she makes explicit what Wilentz and Hahn leave implicit: that she is interested in the meaning, rather than the function, of her subjects' words and behavior. Democratic ideological statements are examined not to explain how the party mobilized its ranks but to reveal the symbols and traditions through which Democrats made sense of their political experiences. Election rituals are described not for the purpose of analyzing how or from whom the Democrats obtained votes but to probe what voting meant to nineteenth-century people.[45]

45. Baker, *Affairs of Party*, pp. 9-14 (quotes 12), 19-24, 146-47, 262-64. In these pages Baker expresses particular debts to Sidney Verba and Clifford Geertz;

Baker's book is organized, then, to explore first how men learned to be Democrats, then what they believed as party members, and finally how they behaved. Her starting points are the institutions in which political socialization began: the home and the community, where the seeds of partisanship were planted in young men; and the schoolhouse, where they learned to be republicans and patriots irrespective of party. Baker's analysis of "Schooling and Political Culture" is particularly perceptive and original. Classrooms were organized like little republics in order to teach the rules of membership in a political community; American history lessons emphasized the Revolution and ignored partisan conflict; a "hidden curriculum" instilled attitudes and behavior considered appropriate for future citizens of the American republic.[46] By the time northern Democrats reached manhood, they had come to share distinctive beliefs which Baker probes in successive chapters: their views of party itself in an age that was just transcending the antipartyism of an earlier day, the particularly literal interpretation which Democrats placed on classical republican ideas, their virulently racist portrayal of blacks as lacking the self-control for republican citizenship, and (less systematically) their attitudes toward government. Finally Baker explores what it meant to behave as Democrats—above all, to participate in election rituals that expressed the party's distinctiveness but also affirmed a deep loyalty to the American nation. Even as Democrats learned and held to attitudes uniquely their own, they shared with other Americans elements of a national (or at least northern) political culture.

Baker thus provides a social analysis of politics of a special kind. She specifically rejects Hays's prescriptions for research, eschews any concern to discover which social groups voted Democratic, and declares of the quantitative voting studies that "the

see Lucian W. Pye and Sidney Verba, eds., *Political Culture and Political Development* (Princeton, 1965); Lucian W. Pye, "Political Culture," in David L. Sills, ed., *International Encyclopedia of the Social Sciences*, vol. 12 (New York, 1968), pp. 218–25; and Geertz, *The Interpretation of Cultures*.

46. Baker, *Affairs of Party*, pp. 71–107 (quote 87).

limits of such interpretation have been reached."[47] What she offers instead is a close look at the social institutions that instilled beliefs and attitudes in party members and a semiotic analysis of the social settings in which they expressed what they had learned. Among Baker's most effective chapters is her study of minstrelsy, a form of popular entertainment that had "no rival" in mid-nineteenth-century society. Attending minstrel shows afforded white Americans (and northern Democrats in particular) "concrete versions" of their abstract belief that blacks "threatened the sacred dream of a virtuous republican society." In describing (and portraying through pictures) minstrelsy's racist symbolism and imagery, Baker illustrates how richly the study of popular culture can reveal the values and beliefs underlying political behavior.[48]

To Harry L. Watson, too, the social analysis of politics means attending to political culture—to the "values and expectations which explained [to citizens] what government ought to be and ought to do, who political leaders should be and how they ought to be chosen, what a man's civic duties were and how he should perform them."[49] Watson's definition of political culture is thus similar to Baker's, but his book's scope and methodology are very different. By confining his attention to Cumberland County, North Carolina, during the Jacksonian era, Watson is able to employ the techniques of the new social history for analyzing community life and to trace the emergence of parties amidst the wrenching social changes experienced in a limited locale. The result is a bold and thickly detailed history of how Cumberland's Democrats and Whigs came into being, of the social origins of their leaders and supporters, and of the values which those on each side expressed through their partisanship.

Watson's starting point is the prepartisan, republican mentality that Cumberland citizens shared with most white, male Amer-

47. Baker, *Affairs of Party*, p. 11.
48. Baker, *Affairs of Party*, pp. 212–58 (quotes 213, 218, 248).
49. Watson, *Jacksonian Politics and Community Conflict*, p. 60.

icans before the 1820s. Thinking and speaking in terms learned
from their Revolutionary forebears, North Carolinians condemned political controversy, regarded government chiefly as a
moral endeavor, and considered a man's character rather than his
legislative program the true test of fitness for office. Into this
traditional setting came two disruptive forces: the Transportation Revolution and Andrew Jackson. Like Wilentz and Hahn,
Watson finds a basic cleavage between people who welcomed the
spread of commerce and called upon the government to promote
it and those who clung to earlier forms of work and community
life and remained suspicious of public support for economic
development. Central to Watson's book is an account of how
local Jacksonian leaders and their Whig opponents each fashioned distinctive republican appeals persuading competing
groups of Cumberland citizens to link their own economic concerns with national political issues. For Democrats, Watson
argues, hostility to commerce and banking and admiration for
Jackson "became a coherent package of interests, symbols, and
convictions," while for Whigs enthusiasm for economic development and dislike for Jackson "became an equally consistent and
attractive collection of attitudes." Political conflict thus mainly
expressed an economic contention between town and country
over nothing less than the kind of society Cumberland ought to
be.[50]

By the 1840s, the dual forces of commercial development and
Jackson's personality had profoundly altered the county's political culture from what it had been before 1820. Above all, it was
now a partisan political culture. Amidst the social and economic
changes wrought by the Transportation Revolution, political

---

50. Watson, *Jacksonian Politics and Community Conflict*, p. 198. Watson is
cautious in summarizing his analysis of electoral cleavages in Cumberland, and
he acknowledges that "a residual cultural conflict between Scots and non-Scots"
modified the economic division he finds; Watson, *Jacksonian Politics and Community Conflict*, pp. 198–213 (quote 213). For Watson's critique of the ethnocultural interpretation of nineteenth-century voting behavior, see *Jacksonian Politics and Community Conflict*, pp. 5–7.

organizers had created two parties holding different images of Cumberland's future, and they had hitched that local division to the national conflict between Jacksonians and Whigs. Political controversy was now an accepted fact of county life, and many men looked to government not only as a font of morality but also as a purveyor of positive action. But Watson is no admirer of the new culture of two-party politics. In persuading citizens to adopt party loyalties, Cumberland's leaders had institutionalized a political response to the social problems of that single moment when the Transportation Revolution first challenged the county's citizens. Keeping to their original appeals long after that moment had passed, the Whigs and Democrats each offered "stock answers" to familiar problems but failed to respond to subsequent social developments. Both parties fell in behind economic "progress," and they diverted any objections to that course "into noisy but harmless rituals." At the heart of Cumberland's partisan political culture, Watson bitterly concludes, lay values and expectations that were outdated almost as soon as they were created.[51]

Ronald P. Formisano's study of Massachusetts also traces the social origins of the culture of mass politics. Like Watson, he gives particular emphasis to the revolutions in transportation and communication and takes a critical view of the two parties that emerged from the social and political turmoil of the 1820s and 1830s. More centrally, Formisano shares with both Baker and Watson a concern with political culture. All agree that the transition to mass politics involved not only changes in organization and participation but also new "perceptions" and "expectations" on the part of citizens. Placing the term "Political Culture" in his title, Formisano defines it to mean those aspects of political life that are obvious, consensual, and taken for granted.[52] Although looser and briefer than the definitions given by Baker and Watson, this concept significantly assists Formi-

---

51. Watson, *Jacksonian Politics and Community Conflict*, pp. 14, 324.
52. Formisano, *The Transformation of Political Culture*, pp. 3–4.

sano in recounting the Bay State's passage from the prepartisan
"Politics of the Revolutionary Center" in the 1790s to the Democratic and Whig contentions of the 1840s. All told, it was a
halting, difficult passage. Massachusetts took a half-century to
make the leap from a deferential, centrist, antipartisan style of
politics to a more participatory, less consensual, highly divisive
political culture. Even then, the transformation was not complete—or entirely benign.[53]

An eclectic study, Formisano's book takes a number of tacks in
tracing the transformation of political culture, including quantitative analyses of electoral behavior, anecdotal portraits of individual men and communities, and careful readings of ideological
pronouncements.[54] The interpretive framework is accordingly
complex, and Formisano is appropriately cautious in stating his
conclusions. But amidst the welter of evidence, a theory stands
out linking changes in society and economy to the creation of a
partisan political culture. The key developments, felt decisively
during the 1820s, were the invention and spread of new means for
transporting people and products and for communicating news
and ideas. These innovations increased the "technical potential"
for mass politics, while at the same time they unleashed short-
lived but intense crusades marking "an extraordinary development of new forms of public participation by average citizens."
In Boston in the early 1820s, the newly organized "Middling
Interest" focused attention on a group of "improvement"-related
issues that sharply divided middle-class citizens from the established elite. Less than a decade later, the Anti-Masons surged into

53. Formisano has previously treated these themes in a number of important
articles: Ronald P. Formisano, "Political Character, Antipartyism, and the Second Party System," *American Quarterly* 21 (Winter 1969): 683–709; Ronald P.
Formisano, "Deferential-Participant Politics: The Early Republic's Political Culture, 1789–1840," *American Political Science Review* 58 (June 1974): 473–87; and
Ronald P. Formisano, "Federalists and Republicans: Parties, Yes—System, No,"
in Kleppner et al., *The Evolution of American Electoral Systems*, pp. 33–76.

54. Paul Goodman, "Putting Some Class Back into Political History: 'The
Transformation of Political Culture' and the Crisis in American Political History," *Reviews in American History* 12 (March 1984): 80–88.

public life to restore "an uncorrupted republican polity" and express their conception of a moral political order. In the same years, the Workingmen's party put forward a radical critique of the emerging economic system and a vision of "a fairer order of things." Although Formisano does not fully succeed in explaining how, these diverse social movements paved the way for the creation and acceptance of mass parties. Groups formerly quiescent had been roused to action, new means of political organizing had come into practice, and fresh expectations now shaped the governmental agenda. By the 1840s, the Whigs and Democrats had "absorbed and channeled" the protest movements of the 1820s and 1830s into their own organizations, and together the new parties carried on "a different kind of politics" than Massachusetts people had known before.[55]

Formisano offers a mixed conclusion about the new politics. On the positive side, the Democratic and Whig parties gave expression to genuine social and ideological differences among the state's citizens. Formisano's analysis of the social cleavages between the parties is complex, but basically he finds the Whigs to have represented the cultural and geographic "Core" of Massachusetts, while the Democrats tended to win the support of voters on the "Periphery."[56] Ideologically, too, the parties generally stood for different approaches to state government, with the

55. Formisano, *The Transformation of Political Culture*, pp. 15–18 (quotes 16, 17), 173–267 (quotes 233, 243, 246, 261).

56. For discussion of the concepts of Core (or Center) and Periphery, see Formisano, *The Transformation of Political Culture*, pp. 5–7, 14–20, 149–54, 250, 268–69, 278–79, 289. It is interesting to note the difference between Formisano's electoral analysis of Massachusetts and that given in his earlier study of Michigan, *The Birth of Mass Political Parties: Michigan, 1827–1861* (Princeton, 1971). The Michigan book, a key volume in the ethnocultural "school," places predominant emphasis upon a religious division in the electorate; see *The Birth of Mass Political Parties*, especially pp. 102–94. The Massachusetts study presents a much more complicated picture of electoral choices, with fewer firm generalizations. Religion mattered to Massachusetts voting behavior, but religious differences interacted with economic status, regional variations, and migration patterns. All these factors, moreover, are regarded as undergirding (or, in some cases, cutting across) the Core-Periphery division at the heart of Formisano's electoral analysis.

Whigs favoring the public promotion of "material and moral improvement" and the Democrats opposing governmental activism on the grounds that it contributed to social inequality.[57] But Formisano has grave reservations about how democratic these parties were. Just as Watson finds in North Carolina, the Democrats and Whigs often bottled up demands for change and, despite their official ideologies, tended to obscure controversial issues rather than offer meaningful policy choices to the electorate. Amidst the participatory culture of mass politics, significant elements of deference, elitism, and resistance to democracy all persisted.[58]

Robert H. Wiebe, too, would explain the political culture of democratizing America, but he remains as aloof from the details as Baker, Watson, and Formisano are enmeshed in them. Wiebe's book is a work of social history on a grand scale. Tracing "The Opening of American Society" from the 1780s to the 1850s, he places the emergence of mass politics in the context of a social and cultural sea change of which political behavior was but one reflection. From a nation monitored, as it were, by a self-conscious Revolutionary elite, the United States was metamorphosed by the 1840s into a "formless" society in which all the old centers of authority had weakened. Propelled by what Wiebe calls a "revolution in choices" (the "pivot" of his study), men and women everywhere exhibited a "popular passion" to extend the "exhilarating" rights and opportunities which they perceived as theirs. Particularly after 1820, the relentless westward drive for new land, the democratization of economic opportunities, the rage for popular politics, and the assertion of the right to "spiritual self-determination" all assisted in creating "America's society of choices." "Overwhelmingly," Wiebe writes, "Americans grasped the power of choice as soon as they spotted it and protected it jealously once they had it." Of course, not everyone had

57. Formisano, *The Transformation of Political Culture*, pp. 269–77 (quote 270), 316–20.
58. Formisano, *The Transformation of Political Culture*, pp. 321–43.

it, as Wiebe makes plain in the final section of his book where he traces the consequences of the "revolution in choices" for family and community life, education, religion, politics, and the relations of class and race and section. Still, he contends, the quest to make personal choices was the determining characteristic of nineteenth-century American society—shaping the institutions inhabited even by those who possessed only the desire for self-determination, not the reality of it.[59]

Among those institutions were political parties, and Wiebe has a theory about how the parties emerged and the place they occupied in a "democratic culture."[60] The dynamic factor here was what Wiebe labels the "politics of development." Where the first parties of the 1790s had been mobilized by a national gentry on the basis of "the powerful passions for [maintaining the nation's] independence" from Europe, the new parties of nineteenth-century America originated in the far more mundane and localistic passions for economic opportunity unleashed after 1800, and especially after 1815. Promotional ventures of all sorts now became the stuff of state politics, obliterating old loyalties and testing the coalition-building skills of a new breed of leaders. Enterprise and politics seemed to go together, and (although Wiebe is a bit vague on the details), the politics of development, "like its gentry predecessor, also gravitated toward a two-party division."

By the time the Democratic and Whig parties reached maturity in the 1840s, party affairs had come to typify the society of choices Wiebe describes. Composed of "a volatile mass of little parts," each organization offered to its leaders the chance "to turn politics into a personal lane of opportunity" and to its members endless occasions for celebrating the "egalitarian style" of the day. Indeed, of all the "institutional webbing" that "gave social

59. Wiebe, *The Opening of American Society*, pp. xii, 146, 158, 164, 167, 251. For Wiebe's key discussion of the "Revolution in Choices," see pp. 143–67.

60. On America's "Democratic Culture" and its "Institutional Web," see Wiebe, *The Opening of American Society*, pp. 265–320.

expression to . . . [America's] democratic culture," the parties were the most inclusive because virtually every white male enjoyed the privilege of voting. Yet the parties' very openness, as Wiebe shrewdly observes, called forth a "division of politics into two spheres that usually had no relation with each other"—the electoral arena, which was inclusive, and the legislative arena, which economic elites preserved for themselves. Within a culture of choices, the lure of economic development had encouraged the creation of mass parties, but the right to make decisions about the fruits of that development remained restricted to those "above the class line."[61]

Although many details remain obscure and politics is but a part of his story, Wiebe provides an overarching interpretation linking social change, political innovation, and the emergence of a democratic culture. Written on a different scale from the monographs of Baker, Watson, and Formisano, *The Opening of American Society* is not fundamentally concerned with the consciousness and expectations of individuals or with the local cultural milieus in which party politics developed. But it *is* a study of the assumptions and beliefs that Americans carried with them into politics (as well as into other endeavors) and that guided their understanding of what went on there. Like the works of Baker, Watson, and Formisano, Wiebe's book bases a social analysis of political history upon the study of what we may term (even if he does not) "political culture."

As social analysts of American political history, Baker, Watson, Formisano, and Wiebe have somewhat less in common than do the cultural Marxists. Their books differ in subject and method, in the questions they address, and, not least, in geographical scope. In some respects, then, these four are unlikely candidates for inclusion in a single historiographic "school." What they do

61. Wiebe, *The Opening of American Society*, pp. 80–89, 123–25 (quote 123), 152–56, 194–208 (quote 205), 291–98 (quotes 292, 297), 348–52 (quotes 349, 351).

share, however, is an interest in the values and expectations that gave meaning and order to partisan political behavior and in the social and economic environment from which those values sprang. They share, too, elements of a common interpretation of nineteenth-century politics and government—and a failure to carry that interpretation as far as they might.

In itself, a concern with the beliefs and values informing political action does not distinguish Baker, Watson, Formisano, and Wiebe either from Hays and the ethnocultural historians or from the cultural Marxists. Such a concern, broadly conceived, is a common denominator of contemporary writing on American political history—expressed alike in studies of "pietists" versus "liturgicals" and in works on republican ideology. What distinguishes these four is the effort to document and explain changing attitudes toward the political process itself. With varying degrees of explicitness, they ask such questions as: "What sort of men did nineteenth-century citizens look to for leadership?" "Why and when did they accept the legitimacy of political parties?" "What kinds of actions did they believe the government ought to take?" and "What satisfactions did they derive from political participation?" These historians inquire, that is, into the content of American political culture.[62] And their answers, although not profoundly startling, add significantly to our knowledge of these matters and bring it to a new level of sophistication. Watson and Wiebe trace the decline of concern with personal character and reputation as criteria for evaluating political leaders. Baker and Formisano probe the stages by which Americans came to recognize the value of political parties. All except Baker show how the development of commerce transformed the citizenry's expectations for government.

Yet while they ask common questions, these historians answer them in three distinct ways. Baker alone is interested in the psychological dimensions of political culture, certainly the most

---

62. See Pye, "Political Culture" for an effective introduction to the questions and problems addressed by those who study political culture.

difficult to document. Tracing the stages of political socialization and interpreting the symbols and imagery associated with
Democratic politics, she leaps daringly to sensible (if ultimately
unverifiable) conclusions about the meanings men found in political life. Her approach is utterly original in American political
history, although (perhaps fortunately for our confidence in her
methods) Baker's substantive findings tend to confirm and extend those attained by more traditional means. Watson and Formisano are less interested in the internal lives of partisans than in
the manifest content of their beliefs. Paying little attention to
ritual and symbol, they scrutinize written documents for opinions and ideological statements attesting to the transformation of
political culture. One of Formisano's chapters looks at election
sermons and Fourth of July orations for evidence of changing
attitudes toward parties, while among Watson's most insightful
contributions is an analysis of platforms and editorials showing
how Whig and Democratic leaders crafted, by trial and error, two
competing "republican" responses to the issues raised by the
Transportation Revolution.[63] Unlike the other three historians,
Wiebe's vantage point on political culture is the whole society.
Presenting a broad panorama of social and political change, he
relies on anecdotal evidence, as well as the works of other historians, to support his interpretation. It is, of course, an unprovable
interpretation, but Wiebe marshalls fact and analysis with such
skill that his conclusions are sure to shape subsequent studies of
American democratic culture.

In another respect, too, these historians differ in their approach to political culture: the relative importance they assign to
the locality, the state, and the nation in shaping political values
and expectations. Was a citizen's immediate environment the
most significant determinant of political consciousness in nine-

---

63. Formisano, *The Transformation of Political Culture*, pp. 84–106; Watson,
Jacksonian Politics and Community Conflict, pp. 151–97. Baker does not completely reject the study of the manifest content of political documents; see, in
particular, her chapter on the republicanism of Democrats; *Affairs of Party*, pp.
143–76.

teenth-century America? Or was it the state? Or the nation? Watson, Formisano, Baker, and Wiebe all have something to say on that subject, but collectively their books are far from conclusive. Watson's study focuses on a county, Formisano's on a state, Baker's on a region, and Wiebe's on the whole country—and each contends implicitly for the significance of his or her chosen geographical unit in molding political values. Each, however, recognizes the limitations of such a focus, and Watson, in particular, makes real efforts to show the connections between local and national concerns.[64] All four would probably acknowledge that future studies of political culture should do even more to sort out the relationships among influences operating at various distances from the individual citizen.

Yet for all their differences in scope and approach, Watson, Formisano, and Wiebe offer similar theories about the social and economic origins of nineteenth-century political culture.[65] Each begins with relatively familiar developments in commerce, transportation, and communication, and each ties these changes—together with the social consequences they wrought—to new demands on government and new patterns of political organization. Watson shows Cumberland County citizens to have divided deeply over policy measures to encourage "progress" and their quarrels to have led, by stages, to the formation and acceptance of parties. Uncovering elements of a similar division in Massachusetts, Formisano traces the emergence of political protest movements whose fervor and methods the Whigs and Democrats later copied. From his more olympian position, Wiebe describes how the social and economic changes of the post-1815 years led to a revolution in personal choices that was reflected, among other ways, in the partisan politics of development. Of

64. Watson, *Jacksonian Politics and Community Conflict*, pp. 9–10; Baker, *Affairs of Party*, pp. 9–11; Wiebe, *The Opening of American Society*, pp. 374–75.
65. Baker does not explicitly treat this question. She deals with the social institutions in which individual Democrats learned their political values but not with the social and economic developments from which the culture of mass politics emerged.

the three, Watson's account of the linkages between society and politics is the most persuasive, although his success in connecting them so concretely derives in part from the local nature of his study. Formisano's contention that parties triumphed by tapping the wellsprings of social and political insurgency is a fertile idea—not yet fully worked out. The same may be said of Wiebe's insight that parties sprang from the quest for policies of economic development. Although this is a provocative thesis about the social origins of partisanship, Wiebe's account of the connections between the policies and the parties remains regrettably vague.[66]

Implicit in all these works, whatever their limitations, is an interpretation of party politics and party government. In some respects, Baker, Watson, Formisano, and Wiebe concur in the relatively appreciative view of parties that now dominates scholarship on nineteenth-century American politics. As described in their books, party life was arousing and participatory. The major parties addressed voters' real concerns, voiced distinctive principles and values, and tried to enact the programs they promised.[67] This is the same general interpretation subscribed to by the ethnocultural historians, although not by the cultural Marxists. To this benign picture of party politics, however, Baker, Watson,

66. Formisano recounts the emergence of the Democrats and Whigs and the development of their party organizations. But the connections between the growth of parties and the insurgent social movements of the previous decades remain shadowy; see *The Transformation of Political Culture*, pp. 245–67. Wiebe suggests (accurately, I think) that the politics of development assisted in undermining the old Republican and Federalist parties and in bringing forth new party organizations within the states. But he sketches these processes in such broad strokes that the "fit" between developmental politics and the new sort of partisanship never comes clearly into focus; see *The Opening of American Society*, pp. 194–208.

67. Baker, *Affairs of Party*, pp. 261–316; Watson, *Jacksonian Politics and Community Conflict*, pp. 198–213, 246–81; Formisano, *The Transformation of Political Culture*, pp. 268–301; Wiebe, *The Opening of American Society*, pp. 294–98. On the pervasiveness within recent scholarship of a favorable view of nineteenth-century parties, see McCormick, "Political Parties in the United States."

Formisano, and Wiebe add some darker tones. Where the ethno-cultural voting studies emphasize the Democratic party's commitment to defending the personal liberties of white, male Americans, Baker stresses the other side of that commitment: the intense racism at the core of Democratic beliefs. Watson and Formisano recognize the legitimate bases of the parties' popularity, but they suggest that over time Democratic and Whig leaders increasingly failed to respond to social changes and grass-roots demands. Wiebe's criticism of the parties is perhaps the harshest of all. In his view, party leaders secured the voters' loyalty by basing election appeals on cultural issues, but they and their wealthy allies kept economic policymaking to themselves.[68] Together these books provide a mixed and critical appraisal of nineteenth-century party politics—and a valuable corrective to the all too flattering portrait in some of the voting studies.

Central to the critique of parties by Watson, Formisano, and Wiebe is their observation of the gap between participatory politics and elitist policymaking. These historians are not, of course, the first to observe that gap, but their contributions to this subject acquire originality from the dynamic role which each assigns to policy expectations in calling forth mass politics. All three, as we have seen, regard the demand for novel uses of governmental power to promote economic enterprise as a mainspring of early nineteenth-century political development. To Watson, Jacksonian politics originated in the clash between "progress"-minded Cumberland citizens and their traditionalist opponents. To Formisano, the quarrel over "improvements" helped set in motion events that led to the formation of the Whigs and Democrats. In Wiebe's account, the "politics of development" plays a similar role. These are powerful insights. What they suggest is that the motive force behind the transformation of

---

68. Baker, *Affairs of Party*, pp. 177–258; Watson, *Jacksonian Politics and Community Conflict*, pp. 287–300; Formisano, *The Transformation of Political Culture*, pp. 321–43; Wiebe, *The Opening of American Society*, pp. 348–52.

American political behavior may have been the prior emergence of a new vision of government.[69] If that were shown to be so, it would constitute a conclusion of the first importance about the political culture of early nineteenth-century America—and perhaps of other eras as well.

But documenting such a conclusion is not easy. And despite what Watson, Formisano, and Wiebe have accomplished in pointing a direction for research, the twisted pathways from new policy expectations to new forms of politics are still to be mapped. When that map is drawn, it will probably show that the Democrats and Whigs aroused electoral enthusiasm by taking opposing ideological approaches to economic development but that both parties actually employed governmental power to support it. This, at least, is a finding reached, in different ways, by all three of these historians. Whigs made the case for "progress"; Democrats made the case against it; both parties won the loyalty of citizens intensely interested in the question; and "progress" went on—with the government's assistance and with unequal benefits for different groups.[70] Watson, Formisano, and Wiebe all contribute to our understanding of these matters, but much more work is needed to explain the complex relationships among

69. Of the three, Watson is the most explicit in citing "demands for novel applications of governmental power" as a stimulus for political change (*Jacksonian Politics and Community Conflict*, p. 15), but Formisano and Wiebe implicitly suggest the elements of a similar causal argument.

70. Watson, *Jacksonian Politics and Community Conflict*, pp. 14–16, 151–213, 246–313, 324; Formisano, *The Transformation of Political Culture*, pp. 268–77, 316–20; Wiebe, *The Opening of American Society*, pp. 249–51, 350–52. None of these historians deals entirely convincingly with these matters. Watson tends to exaggerate the extent to which Democrats and Whigs offered "alternative world views" in response to the issues raised by the Transporation Revolution. By his own account, Cumberland County Democrats straddled the issue of internal improvements right from the beginning; see *Jacksonian Politics and Community Conflict*, pp. 162 (quote), 188. Formisano raises but never effectively addresses the question of whether the Democrats would have been likely to govern Massachusetts any differently than the Whigs did; see *The Transformation of Political Culture*, pp. 319–20. Baker occasionally gives hints concerning Democratic views of the economy, but she never develops the subject; see *Affairs of Party*, pp. 157, 320.

economic development, party ideologies, political participation, and governmental policymaking. Embedded in these studies of political culture is the outline of a new interpretation linking demands on government to the emergence of mass politics in nineteenth-century America—but the job of working out that interpretation remains to be done.

In the hands of these scholars, political culture emerges as a powerful tool for the social analysis of American political history. Although they rely on somewhat different definitions of that concept, Baker, Watson, Formisano, and Wiebe all employ it as a means of connecting the values and expectations that people brought to politics, the social settings in which their values were formed, and the sorts of politics and government they carried on. Many of the findings presented by these four historians extend and confirm what is already known about nineteenth-century American politics. In that sense, they are perhaps less revisionary than their contemporaries, the cultural Marxists, or than the ethnocultural historians were a decade or more ago. Still, in giving unprecedented attention to mass beliefs and expectations, Baker, Watson, Formisano, and Wiebe may well have laid the groundwork for a fresh understanding of a political culture in which participation was relatively democratic but the fruits of government far less so.

Such are the recent contributions made by nine scholars to the social analysis of American political history. They are not the first to have explored the social bases of past politics, but collectively they have advanced our knowledge of that subject far beyond its former state. Variously employing the methods and insights of the "new" histories of the 1960s and 1970s—the new social history, the new labor history, the new intellectual and cultural history—these historians depict political behavior as flowing naturally from the experiences and values of nineteenth-century people. Whether forming a Workingmen's party in New York or Lynn, fighting against a fence law in Upcountry Georgia, marching in a torchlight parade in Illinois, or casting Whig ballots in Massachusetts, men turned to political action not as an escape to some other world called "politics" but as an integral expression of their beliefs and life situations. In a sense, this is a truism about political behavior everywhere. But these authors have made an obvious truth palpable by documenting the intricate linkages between society and politics. In so doing, they have written highly innovative books—different, as we have seen, from earlier social analyses of political history and, more obviously, different from traditional political histories of national elites and their policy programs.

Yet even as they elaborate previously unrecognized connections between society and politics, these studies also contribute materially to some familiar subjects in American political history. This is not accidental, for each of these books is firmly grounded in the traditional historical literature and the questions it addressed. As a result, all of these studies have something to say about the content of political ideas, the development of parties, and the nature of government. But a careful reading of their contributions to these subjects suggests that a social analysis of political history is not the same as a political analysis, however mutually supportive the two may be. By returning briefly to some of the conclusions reached in these books, we can see how more conscious attention to political questions could have enabled the authors to carry further the insights obtained from a social analysis of political history.[71]

Take the matter of ideology. That nineteenth-century citizens held to meaningful belief systems, or ideologies, is among the most important findings made by the studies considered here,

71. For related observations and an intense (if inconclusive) scholarly debate on these matters see J. Morgan Kousser, "Restoring Politics to Political History," *Journal of Interdisciplinary History* 12 (Spring 1982): 569–95; Terrence J. McDonald, "Putting Politics Back into the History of the American City," *American Quarterly* 34 (Summer 1982): 200–209; Paul F. Bourke and Donald A. DeBats, "On Restoring Politics to Political History," *Journal of Interdisciplinary History* 15 (Winter 1985): 459–66; J. Morgan Kousser, "Are Political Acts Unnatural?" *ibid.*, pp. 467–80; and Samuel P. Hays, "Society and Politics: Politics and Society," *ibid.*, pp. 481–99.

especially those of the cultural Marxists. Far from an exclusively elite possession, the doctrines of republicanism provided workers and farmers with core beliefs about their society and government and, equally important, grounds for a powerful critique of economic development. Together with Watson, the cultural Marxists show that for many people politics and government had a moral dimension, and that for them republicanism offered the basis for righteously rejecting men and measures they opposed. These are provocative findings—made even more interesting by corresponding accounts of the political organizations that propagated versions of republican ideology. From these books we learn that the regular political parties often attracted the support of workers and farmers through "broad republican rhetoric" and partisan expressions of resistance to economic progress. Frequently, however, that rhetoric proved false—forcing workers and farmers to look to their own organizations to defend the old ideals. Even then, they often found themselves ideologically divided or, worse, persuaded by their own leaders to support the unrepublican policy programs of their class enemies.

In pursuing their analyses of mass beliefs, the cultural Marxists could profitably have paid more attention to these connections between ideology and organization. As political scientists have told us, it is chiefly through organizations that ideologies achieve the power to affect political conflict. In Samuel H. Barnes's words, "No idea has ever made much headway without an organization behind it. . . . Whenever ideologies seem to be important in politics they have a firm organizational basis." And yet, as Barnes and others have observed, the internal imperatives of maintaining an organization's strength can "work profound transformations" on the ideology itself.[72] These considerations

72. Samuel H. Barnes, "Ideology and the Organization of Conflict: On the Relationship between Political Thought and Behavior," *Journal of Politics* 28 (August 1966): 513–30 (quotes 522, 523, 530). For related comments see Giovanni Sartori, "From the Sociology of Politics to Political Sociology," in Seymour Martin Lipset, ed., *Politics and the Social Sciences* (New York, 1969), pp. 65–100. And for some pertinent questions about the linkages between ideology and political behavior see Bogue, *Clio & the Bitch Goddess*, p. 97.

suggest the need for sustained political analyses of the organizations to which nineteenth-century Americans turned for expression of their ideological goals. Under what circumstances, we may ask, did the political parties voice the pure republican doctrines that many of their constituents evidently wished to hear? What organizational imperatives militated for and against the persistence of partisan republicanism? When and why did the parties abandon or water down the old ideals? How did their members react to the transformation of ideology? Similar questions might be asked of reform movements, labor unions, and farmers' organizations. The point is *not* to supplant a social analysis of mass beliefs but to deepen our knowledge of them through political analyses of the organizations that, in the end, were capable of sustaining or destroying republican ideals.

Or consider, in a related vein, the political parties. Parties are more central in some of these books than in others, but all nine authors advance our knowledge of the parties' development, persistence, and nature in nineteenth-century America. Dawley, Wilentz, Watson, Formisano, and Wiebe describe aspects of the social and economic setting in which mass party politics emerged, while Hahn, Fink, Foner, and Baker recount the circumstances under which the parties continued to flourish. Particularly from the writings of the cultural Marxists, as well as Formisano's, we also learn a good deal about third parties—about the social conditions that called them forth, the opportunities and dangers they presented to their supporters, and the reasons they so commonly met defeat. Collectively these historians tend to confirm contemporary scholarly wisdom by documenting the powerful appeal of the major parties and by comprehending the good reasons for which nineteenth-century citizens voted the party tickets.

But these studies also subtly revise that wisdom in at least three ways. For one, several of these works suggest that the voters' loyalty to the major parties was scarcely immutable and, for many, was perpetually tested by changing social realities. Implicit, at least, in the writings of Dawley, Wilentz, Fink, Hahn, and Formisano is a view of the nineteenth-century electorate as more frequently discriminating and less habitually partisan than is commonly thought today. Second, as noted earlier, most of these works give a tough-minded interpretation of the major parties. To the cultural Marxists, the parties were often irrelevant—or blatantly hostile—to workers and farmers, while to Watson, Wiebe, and Formisano the parties governed with diminishing concern for grass-roots policy demands. Finally, these historians tend to see the third parties in a favorable light. Realistic enough to recognize why the minor parties usually failed to achieve electoral victory, Wilentz, Hahn, Fink, and Formisano nonetheless regard them as responsive to important segments of the popular will and as instrumental in supporting policy innovations that the major parties initially spurned.

These are revisionary conclusions. But confirming and elaborating them will require supplementing a social analysis of political history with a more explicitly political analysis. Just as organizational imperatives affected the content and longevity of republican ideology, so, too, the internal operations of the political parties shaped their ability to maintain both their popularity and their responsiveness to grass-roots demands. Watson and Formisano tell us that the Whigs and Democrats ceased to react creatively to social changes, but they do not explain why the party leaders chose, or felt compelled to adopt, such an insensitive course. Foner alerts us to the significance of the freedmen's politicization during Reconstruction, but he does little to probe the extent to which the Republican party proved capable of training black leaders and spreading among blacks the doctrines whose name it bore. A corresponding political analysis would assist the cultural Marxists in carrying forward their insights into third parties. Dawley and Fink record the limited degree to which even victorious Workingmen's parties tried to enact class legislation, but they do much less to sort out the contradictory pressures inevitably faced by a mass party seeking to represent a particular social class. These examples all suggest the need to ask political questions recognizing that nineteenth-century parties led semi-

autonomous lives—independent, in significant ways, of the social conditions out of which they came.[73]

Take, finally, the subject of governance, to which the social
historians of politics have made especially important, if under-
developed, contributions. None of their books is centrally concerned with the policymaking process or with specific governmental decisions. But almost all of them deal with the question
of what citizens expected from government and with the social
and economic origins of their expectations. Focusing on workers
and farmers, the cultural Marxists observe the relatively limited
and defensive view of the State held to by members of those
groups. Rather than look to government for individual benefits,
they tended to seek protection of their customary rights and the
maintenance of regulations minimizing economic risk. Their
capitalistic enemies, by contrast, shared an extensive and ambitious conception of the governmental benefits that they and
their developing enterprises ought to receive, although, to be
sure, they competed fiercely among themselves for the available
resources. Here the contributions of Watson, Formisano, and
Wiebe also become relevant. As they have suggested, the developmental vision of government came to maturity in the years after
1815, altered the public agenda decisively, and played a dynamic
part in fostering the transition to mass party politics. Men who
wanted governmental promotion of economic development
tended to group with the Whigs, while those who opposed it
responded to Democratic rhetoric—but both parties came to be led
by elites who favored "progress." Together these historians have
significantly advanced our understanding of what Americans
wanted from government. Certainly their findings belie the notion that political contests mainly expressed cultural antagonisms and had little to do with the quest for economic policies.

73. For two excellent studies that take account of the social origins of parties
but also recognize that party organizations and party leaders came to operate, to a
significant degree, independently of their social surroundings, see J. Mills Thornton III, *Politics and Power in a Slave Society: Alabama, 1800–1860* (Baton Rouge,
1978); and Michael F. Holt, *The Political Crisis of the 1850s* (New York, 1978).

Of potentially greater importance, these studies indirectly provide evidence for an interpretation linking expectations for government to the structure of nineteenth-century politics. Over the course of the first few decades of the 1800s, development-minded entrepreneurs—possessing a clear vision of what government could do for them—managed to place their demands for allocative benefits at the top of the political agenda. They met opposition both from those who had other priorities for government and from those who did not want public resources used in support of economic progress. But the developers won, and their victory had seminal consequences not only for governmental policy and economic growth but also for politics. For, although no one seems to have anticipated such a result, policies of allocation and distribution proved remarkably conducive to the formation and persistence of parties. At an ideological level the parties won devoted adherents by battling over "progress," while on a day-to-day basis their leaders thrived on the mundane job of passing out economic benefits—just as they distributed patronage—to their coalitions of supporters. Once firmly established, the party organizations did everything in their power to ensure that allocational questions remained at the top of the political agenda. From time to time, republican-minded workers and farmers burst loose from the major parties. But they usually proved unable to articulate an alternative policy program—much less to win consistent electoral victories—and the regular parties with their policies of development remained dominant. The sectional crisis drastically disrupted the party leaders' plans, but by the 1870s the partisan politics of distribution had returned to preeminence, and not until the early 1900s did this structure of politics and policy finally succumb to forces beyond the leaders' power.

Such would be the rough sketch of an interpretation building upon a social analysis of nineteenth-century political history—but going beyond it. Documenting this interpretation would necessitate explaining how entrepreneurial elites succeeded in setting the policy agenda in the face of opposition from others. It

would require asking by what stages the parties emerged from the
politics of development and through what means those organizations kept distributive issues to the fore despite contravening
demands and expectations. Perhaps most important, it would
involve asking how political elites wielded power and directed
policy.[74] These are political questions. To ask them is to recognize the social basis of politics but to reject any form of social
determinism in political history. Nineteenth-century politics and
government can scarcely be understood apart from the social life
from which they emerged—and of which they formed essential
parts. But neither can they be understood without respectful
attention to what went on within their own distinct spheres.
Even in such skilled hands as those of Wilentz, Watson, Wiebe,
and the rest, the social analysis of political history is, in itself, no
substitute for political history.

74. For examples of some recent studies that give political answers to questions about politics and government, see J. Morgan Kousser, *The Shaping of
Southern Politics: Suffrage Restriction and the Establishment of the One-Party
South, 1880–1910* (New Haven, 1974); William E. Nelson, *The Roots of American
Bureaucracy, 1830–1900* (Cambridge, Mass., 1982); Stephen Skowronek, *Building
a New American State: The Expansion of National Administrative Capacities,
1877–1920* (Cambridge, England, 1982); and Richard P. McCormick, *The Presidential Game: The Origins of American Presidential Politics* (New York, 1982).

PART TWO

THE POLITICAL PARTIES

4

Political Parties in American History

Ever since the late seventeenth century, political parties have been organized to achieve and exercise influence over government in America. The earliest parties, often termed factions, appeared in the assemblies of several colonies before 1700, although they and their successors had precarious and irregular careers until well after the American Revolution. During the early 1800s, with the burgeoning of popular electoral competition for public offices, parties took on recognizably modern attributes and gained increased legitimacy and stability. They persisted and changed further through the sectional crises, electoral realignments, and vast expansions of governmental authority of the 1800s and 1900s.

During their long history, American parties assumed numerous forms and filled divergent roles: as cliques of officeholders, as electoral machines, as instruments of political socialization, as formulators of public policy, and as ideological movements. A band of gentry formed to oppose a royal governor's policies is hardly the same phenomenon as an electoral machine organized to win the loyalty of immigrant voters, and both differ markedly from a mass-based ideological movement such as populism or socialism. Over time, American parties varied significantly in structure and organization, in leadership and membership, in ideological purity, and in their relationship to government.

Yet, as much as they changed, American parties have had some common characteristics. The first was the name *party*, a word used more or less synonymously with *faction* in colonial America and later employed to designate groups that sought to win control of the government, usually through electoral competition with other parties. Second, parties also shared the goal of achieving governmental power, normally by winning public office and guiding the actions of the chosen officials. In every era, the parties' characteristics were largely molded by the rules and opportunities for capturing public positions and by the prevailing norms and expectations for governance. Third, American parties have shared the burden of trying to survive amidst some surprisingly continuous, though not unvarying, antipower and antiparty attitudes. Whatever forms they took, parties were always limited in what they could do with the governmental authority that they won. And although they have been among the most durable of political institutions, parties always struggled for power within an environment that was in many ways hostile to their existence.

Innumerable factors account for the historic changes, as well as the continuities, in the forms that American parties have taken and the roles that they have filled. Scholarship is replete with evidence of the social, economic, and ideological influences upon the parties, and the discussion that follows will refer repeatedly to these subjects. What stands out, and gives structure to the history of environmental influences upon politics, is the intimate connection between the history of parties and the history of governance. Opinions about what the government ought to do, its actual policies, and the rules for filling offices and influencing the officeholders have been among the most important avenues through which social, economic, and ideological changes have impinged upon the parties. Collectively these governmental matters—beliefs, policies, and rules—have been the mainsprings of American party history.

Because parties were formed, above all, to contest for position and power in government, it should not be surprising that changes in the nature of governance have, in turn, repeatedly transformed the parties. Even the smallest attitudinal change toward government, the most routine adjustment of policy, or the merest tinkering with the rules for filling offices has inevitably, if only minutely, affected the conduct of party politics. In studying the history of parties, one must trace and explain the changes that have been of enduring importance and distinguish these changes from less significant or temporary transitions. From this perspective, the history of American parties is the history of adapting politics to the demands of winning power under changing conditions of governance. It is also the history of practices and beliefs that persisted, relatively unchanged, even as the political and governmental universe was successively transformed.

The political parties that appeared in the English colonies of North America during the late seventeenth and eighteenth century were far less stable, cohesive, or inclusive than the parties that emerged in the United States after 1820. With some notable exceptions, the colonial parties comprised shifting networks of elites who cooperated on some causes and parted, often explosively, on others, who never wrote political platforms, who relied on the deference paid them in their local communities, and who only intermittently cultivated followings in the electorate. Yet, considering the intense antipartyism of the Anglo-American world that they inhabited and the dearth of well-regarded examples of political organizing, the colonial parties were remarkably innovative and successful. And although no straight lines connect them to the Democrats, Whigs, and Republicans of a later age, the struggles of colonial parties to shape themselves around the opportunities for achieving governmental power were destined to be repeated.

That parties were evil was a widespread conviction in England and America, reinforced by both ideology and experience. Thinkers of almost every political persuasion agreed that society was, or ought to be, a harmonious whole. Rooted in medieval corporate ideas, the organic conception had no place for the community's division into competing parts. People differed in rank and wealth, but bonds of deference and responsibility were believed to unite them in a common interest. The reality, of course, did not match the ideal. Seventeenth-century England was convulsively and violently divided along religious and constitutional lines, with those on each side organizing not only parties but armies, too. The Whig triumph in the Glorious Revolution (1688–1689) largely settled the most divisive issues, but partisanship lived on, most commonly among factions in Parliament and occasionally in the form of armed conflict.

The lessons of England's divisive partisanship were not lost on Americans. As heirs to the same basic corporate ideas as other English people, the colonists derived their antipartyism most particularly from several strands of Anglo-American belief. One was Puritanism, with its central doctrine of the covenant. In fulfillment of what they regarded as their duty to God, Puritan covenanters pledged to subordinate themselves to a civil society governed in the common interest according to His laws. To engage in partisanship was to break the covenant, and generations of New England ministers and magistrates decried parties. Of more general influence within the colonies than Puritanism were the ideas put forward in England late in the seventeenth and early in the eighteenth century by a disparate amalgam of "country," or opposition, writers. Often partisans themselves, country spokesmen nonetheless warned bitterly of the dangers to liberty emanating, as they saw it, from selfish factions within the English government.

Although the country opposition never became very influential in England, it provided the language and rationale for a critique of partisanship which would have a long life in America. According to this understanding, preserving personal liberty in the face of governmental power presented a constant problem to a free people, because power was inherently aggressive and liberty passive. The only answer lay in an independent citizenry, committed more to the common good than to private interests and sufficiently virtuous to root out abuses of power wherever they appeared. The formation of parties, or factions, offered a sure sign that some men were conspiring to place their special interests above those of the community. Conflict and disorder, the growth of tyrannical power, and the loss of liberty were sure to result from these formations. That parties might contribute to achieving the common good was seldom recognized, at least until late in the colonial period.

Despite condemnation, factions and parties abounded in colonial America. They were local to each province, however, and never attained any semblance of intercolonial organization. The usual sources of partisanship were conflicts of interest and ambition among rival elites, although in no two colonies were political cleavages alike. Practically any economic, cultural, or political division was capable of shaping party lines: mercantile interests against landed ones, coastal towns versus interior villages, Presbyterians against Anglicans (or Quakers), proponents of economic and territorial expansion versus nonexpansionists, and many others. Sometimes several cleavages reinforced one another, adding solidity and durability to party conflict; more frequently one line of division would wreak havoc upon another, rendering politics shifting and chaotic.

In the South, the parties tended to be short-lived, and they became rarer as the colonial era ended. South Carolina, which had been through decades of unstable factionalism—reflecting religious, regional, and economic rivalries—fell under the rule of a unified eastern elite after about 1740. Virginia followed a similar political pattern: years of divisiveness were followed by the emergence of a governing class of planters who quarreled with the royal governor but avoided serious internal rivalries. Of all the southern colonies only North Carolina remained torn by political strife—not only between the governor and the assembly but also between the more settled eastern areas and the rapidly expanding South and West. These conflicts did not produce even the beginnings of stable party politics, however.

In the culturally heterogeneous middle colonies, partisanship developed much further. Notables, competing for legislative supremacy, divided along reasonably well defined lines, and, especially in Pennsylvania and New York, party organizations achieved a comparatively advanced stage of development. At times in all the middle colonies, and for long periods in some, politics assumed a court-versus-country pattern, with one segment of the elite allied to the governor (or proprietor) and one or more others opposed to him, usually from a base in the assembly. This was the case in Maryland, where the issue usually came down to the privileges and powers of the Baltimore family, although regional variations also caused division. In Pennsylvania, where a Quaker party provided the major opposition to the proprietary interest for much of the eighteenth century, the bases of partisanship included not only the Penn family's privileges but also trade policies, Indian relations, and religion. In New York, the most culturally diverse colony, tangled factional alliances formed and reformed along economic, regional, religious, and family lines—with the royal governor usually exercising his influence on one side or another and with different factions sometimes tied to cliques of officeholders in England.

New England presented variations on the types of party politics seen further south, plus one configuration that was unique—Rhode Island's. There, after alternating eras of calm and chaos, two parties appeared, which, unlike any others in colonial America, functioned above all as electoral machines. The competing organizations, led by Samuel Ward and Stephen Hopkins, were centered in Newport and Providence, respectively, but each extended throughout the colony. The main issue between them was nothing more than which elite should dominate Rhode Island's political and economic life. To advance its interests, each side nominated candidates, campaigned vigorously for them, assisted (and bribed) voters on election day, and spread the spoils of office.

No other colony had such evenly matched or well-developed machines as Rhode Island, but certain elements of modern electoral politics appeared elsewhere. This happened especially in colonies in which factional competition was intense, including Maryland, Pennsylvania, New York, and Connecticut, but it was also the case in nonpartisan Virginia. Although no uniform system of making nominations ever emerged in colonial America, political organizations experimented with a variety of popular devices, including rudimentary caucuses and conventions. To get their nominees elected, faction leaders sometimes organized elaborate campaigns featuring newspaper appeals, pamphlet warfare, the treating of voters to lavish spreads of food and drink, and sometimes outright bribery. On election days, if a contest appeared to be close, partisans might round up potential supporters and bring them to the polls. To judge from incomplete evidence, voter turnout was highest where partisan competition was most vigorous.

As these evidences of machine politics suggest, the parties of colonial America were, in some respects, forerunners of those that came later. Their creative responses to the demands of winning office, the diversity of the social cleavages on which they were based, their shrewdness in playing politics amidst competing interests, and their experiences with peaceful transitions in and out of office all anticipated nineteenth-century party politics. By the mid-1700s, especially in the middle colonies, some people were publicly, if tentatively, recognizing that party competition might actually be valuable in preserving liberty, not a sign of its imminent loss. But the parties of the colonial era were actually far from modern, and the glimmering of a pro-party rationale was not a sign that parties soon would be accepted. The key to understanding these parties lies not in a comparison with the latter-day organizations that they partially anticipated but in the mix of governmental conditions that they, in their own day, faced.

The institutions of governance in early America and the expectations surrounding them encouraged the emergence of parties but worked against the parties' obtaining of power. That parties formed at all was due to the opportunities available for contesting seats in the assemblies and to the widely shared belief that those bodies would make policies of importance to the people. Despite disputes over the nature and authority of the colonial legislatures, no one denied the right of the legislatures to exist or to exercise creative powers over a whole range of essential matters, including land, public improvements, schools, trade, and Indians. Not only that, but as new towns or counties were established (by the assemblies) their representatives took legislative seats, fully expecting to continue the tradition of directly serving their constituents' interests through whatever political means were presented. Factions and parties thus arose within the assemblies as a response to the opportunity to govern. When necessary the parties devised ways for winning support in the electorate, and when conditions permitted they stabilized their positions and endured. The partial success that they enjoyed in some colonies during an antiparty age measures the potency of governmental conditions in calling them forth.

That most parties remained weak and unstable was due to other, less hospitable elements of governance in colonial America. Particularly damaging were the perpetual conflicts between the royal governors and assemblies and, especially later in the colonial era, the grave disagreements about where sovereignty lay. Governors were formally vested by the crown with a host of rights and prerogatives, but they were actually given few tangible means of making good their claims. Precariously situated themselves, the governors almost always found it in their interest to do what they could to prevent concentrations of power in the hands of the colonists. Given the widespread suspicion of parties, the lack of precedents for them, and the opportunities for exploiting cleavages that cut across existing factions, it was not hard to undermine the stability of political lines. Of perhaps even greater importance were the ultimately unresolvable conflicts concerning where final authority over colonial matters rested: with the king and Parliament or with the people of America. Under such conditions the extent and scope of the governmental powers for which the parties were contending were never clarified and, indeed, became more controversial over time. The parties thus remained fragile bodies, with even their purposes in doubt. Under suspicion from the start, they were further weakened by the instabilities and ambiguities of governance in colonial America.

The Revolution intensified the contradictory pressures for and against political parties. From the establishment of Britain's new imperial policies after 1763 through the adoption of the federal Constitution in 1788, more Americans than ever before entered into public affairs and experimented with fresh forms of political participation. As the governmental dilemmas of the colonial era came to a head and successive crises were weathered, Americans created—though scarcely by design—many of the elements of what would become a partisan political culture. Even as they did so, the Revolution placed severe constraints upon political parties—some of them practical, some ideological, some constitutional. By 1788, parties were probably more roundly condemned in America than they had been a quarter-century before. The Revolution's antipartyism, no less than the experiments in partisanship that the conflict encouraged, endured and complicated the new nation's political and governmental life.

Even before the outbreak of war in 1775, the crisis with Britain had done much to popularize politics. As imperial quarrels called into question existing governmental authority, men unaccustomed to the public arena became active, long-suppressed social tensions received expression, and the language of everyday politics acquired a more popular tone. The Sons of Liberty appeared in 1765, as did committees of public safety and committees of observation during the next decade. In the countryside, aggrieved tenants sometimes rose up against landowners, while in the cities men and women took street actions that occasionally turned into riots. None of these activities bears direct comparison with political parties, but collectively they politicized more Americans than ever before and helped prepare them for the party politics to come. Beginning in 1776 when the states wrote their constitutions, many of the new documents strengthened popular politics through provisions increasing backcountry representation in the legislatures, widening the suffrage, and making possible increased scrutiny of public officials.

These changes confused existing political alignments and established new ones. Those who refused to support the Revolution were now excluded from politics; in New York the powerful DeLancey party turned loyalist, as did many members of Pennsylvania's Quaker party. Into their places came new elements, often men of modest standing who had first gained political experience in the turbulent atmosphere of the 1760s and 1770s. In Massachusetts, representatives of the formerly quiescent backcountry emerged as a political force early in the Revolution and took positions on economic, political, and constitutional matters that differed sharply from those of the eastern elite. In Pennsylvania, where party lines were drawn more firmly than in any other state (due mainly to a division over the highly democratic constitution of 1776), politics also had class and regional overtones, although ethnicity and religion continued to be factors too.

By the early and mid-1780s, party politics of a highly contentious, if often disorganized, sort was visible in the legislatures of many states. Especially on economic issues such as taxation, debtor relief, and paper money, a rough division emerged between cosmopolitan (eastern, urban, commercial) legislators and their localist (western, rural, agricultural) opponents. In some states the competing parties went beyond the legislative halls into the electorate by making nominations, issuing campaign appeals, and getting out the vote. It seems fair to speculate that by mobilizing political expression and representing the interests of people formerly distant from the public arena, the parties of the Revolutionary era did much to establish the popularity and legitimacy of the new state governments.

Yet most Americans of the day were unwilling to acknowledge the utility of parties. From a practical point of view, unity was of the essence if independence was to be secured. In most states, party divisions remained in check until after the cessation of hostilities in 1782. But unity was more than a practical matter; it had ideological meaning as well. Whatever their social background, almost all Revolutionaries believed that the preservation of the American republic depended on an extraordinary degree of loyalty to the common good by a virtuous people. Like the country opposition writers whose ideas had contributed so greatly to American republicanism, people of the Revolutionary generation regarded the emergence of parties as proof that political self-interestedness was on the rise and that liberty was imperiled by those who grasped for power. Even as they organized parties, Americans of the 1770s and 1780s warned of the dangers that partisanship posed and worried about the power that parties were acquiring.

The movement leading to the formation of the federal Constitution—as well as the document itself—reflected the contradictory tides of partisanship and antipartisanship in the Revolutionary era. On the one hand, the drives for the Philadelphia Convention and, later, for the Constitution's adoption were well-organized, partisan movements by men who had much to gain from a stronger national government. Opposed to them in the struggle over ratification was a party nearly as well organized as their own. On the other hand, the Federalists (as they shrewdly called themselves) intensely disliked and feared the contentious party politics that had developed in a number of the more democratic states by the mid-1780s. If they conceived of their movement as a party, it was a party to end parties.

The Constitution plainly expressed the Federalists' aversion to factionalism and partisanship. Not only did it fail to mention parties but it established a series of mechanisms designed to check their growth. Nowhere can the desire to frustrate parties be better seen than in the elaborately crafted provisions for election of the president by an electoral college, a body as securely insulated from partisanship as the minds of the Founding Fathers could make it. Yet even as they contrived against parties, some of the authors of the Constitution recognized not only that divisions among the people were inevitable but also that a multiplicity of

factions might actually promote liberty by preventing the emergence of a party of the majority. This was, of course, the message
of James Madison's *Federalist* number 10, an essay brilliantly
expressive of his generation's experience with parties—and wari-
ness of them.

Neither Madison nor any of his fellow Federalists in 1788
anticipated that the Constitution, by establishing a national government and a national political arena, would lead almost immediately to the creation of two great national parties. Still less did
anyone imagine that Madison himself would emerge as one of
the leaders of the majority party. These were among the ironies of
partisanship in the Revolutionary age—an era that closed with
the inauguration of a national government designed to restrain
parties but that actually ushered in a time of unprecedented
partisan bitterness.

Within a few years after the adoption of the Constitution, two
political parties started to form within the new government for
the purpose of imposing their leaders' beliefs upon the new
nation's policies. No other major parties in American history
would ever equal their ideological intensity. Before many more
years had passed, these same parties began to establish state
organizations designed to win elections. And by 1800 the Federalists and Republicans were able to conduct a nationwide presidential contest with the most highly developed party machinery ever
seen. Yet, compared with parties of a later day, those of the first
American party system remained rudimentary in organization,
and they competed only inconsistently. After 1815 they virtually
ceased to contest elections at the national level. These were political parties of a transitional sort, formed in response to unique
governmental conditions, within a setting of culture and beliefs
soon to pass away.

The opportunities for national policymaking offered by the
new Constitution proved highly stimulating to the emergence of
parties. First within President Washington's cabinet, and then
within the House of Representatives, divisions over policy fo-

mented contending cliques and, by the mid-1790s, increasingly firm voting blocs. The bases of the conflict were numerous and complex, including ideological disagreements concerning the character of the young republic, clashes of sectional and economic interests, and highly personal likes and dislikes. Almost at the outset, contention emerged over an ambitious economic program put forward by Secretary of the Treasury Alexander Hamilton that was designed to stimulate commerce and manufacturing. Thomas Jefferson, the secretary of state, came to oppose Hamilton's proposals, as did a faction in the House led by James Madison. Beginning in 1793 and 1794, differences over relations with revolutionary France, as well as with Britain, paralleled the contention over the economic program and gave added stimulus to the formation of parties.

Those who filled the offices in the republic's capital had come to hold sharply different views of the new nation and its government. In the broadest terms the Federalists, as they were most commonly called, envisioned a swiftly developing commercial society, tied closely by trade with England and assisted by an energetic central government. Their opponents, the Republicans, hoped that the nation's basic character would remain agrarian, that its agricultural surplus would be marketed to many countries, and that the government would do little. The men on each side deeply distrusted those on the other, as their language made plain. To Republicans, the Federalists were monarchists bent on destroying liberty. To Federalists, the Republicans were anarchists inclined toward mob rule.

That these ideological parties soon spread beyond the national government owed much to the Constitution's provisions for electing the president. Despite the Founding Fathers' hopes for a nonpartisan executive chosen by electors remote from the people, the placement of a powerful elective office at the center of the nation's political arena created just the conditions for carrying party strife into the states. In 1796 and, more spectacularly, in 1800 the presidential candidacies of the Federalist John Adams and the Republican Thomas Jefferson stimulated the widespread formation of party organizations and the development of new electioneering methods. Almost everywhere the Republicans took the lead in these actions, but the Federalists often were not far behind. Characteristically, state party affairs came to be managed by caucuses composed of legislators and, sometimes, other leading party members. The caucus took responsibility for nominating candidates, supervising the networks of state and local party committees, and issuing appeals to the voters. By 1800, when Jefferson was elected president, politics in most of the states was conducted along Federalist-Republican lines. And in the following years party machinery continued to be developed, not only by the victorious Republicans but also by a second generation of Federalist leaders determined to match their opponents in perfecting a popular party organization.

Despite such efforts, the parties of the early 1800s always remained in flux, never quite complete, with even their names often disputed. At the national level, the Republican congressional caucus nominated candidates for president and vice president from 1796 to 1824, but almost from the start the caucus was shadowed by doubts about its legitimacy. The Federalists, whose strength was chiefly concentrated in New England, never established a regular means of agreeing upon national candidates. Within Congress, party voting was sporadic; foreign-policy crises tended to harden party lines, although at other times the divisions were barely visible. In the states, party development varied greatly, and in only a few did vigorous competition persist for all (or even most) of the first party system's life. In general terms, state-level party competition developed furthest and endured longest in certain of the New England and middle states; it was less in evidence in the heavily Republican South and hardly existed at all in the newer western states. So great were the differences among the states that it is hazardous to generalize about such matters as partisan loyalty in the electorate, party voting in the legislature, and party patronage practices.

Amidst the variations, two distinguishing features of the first party system stand out: the degree of ideological conflict and the incompleteness of partisan organization. Most of the men who responded to the opportunity to govern the new nation were deeply committed to the doctrines of the Revolution and were imbued with a strong sense of responsibility for the republic's survival. Although Federalists and Republicans interpreted these doctrines differently, those on both sides fought for their causes with loftier intensity than ever would be seen again in American politics. Their conflicts, however, did not always take the form of a partisan war for the people's support. Party divisions were still regarded as signs of social decay, and it was with reluctance that many leaders organized and maintained party organizations. The United States, moreover, remained a deferential society. Despite the upsurge of popular politics during the Revolution, most people still assumed that recognized elites would dominate public affairs. Both parties were organized from the top down, and although voter turnout sometimes reached great heights in closely contested elections, little was done to create mass loyalties of the sort that developed later.

These considerations help to explain the course of the first party system during its later years. Instead of seeking new issues that might have planted partisan loyalties deeply in the popular consciousness, both parties continued to respond almost exclusively to the ideologically charged, but increasingly outdated, concerns about national character and foreign policy that had given rise to parties in the first place. Seldom did party life acquire routines of its own apart from the weighty issues placed on the political agenda by respected leaders. The foreign-policy crises before and during the War of 1812 rekindled the partisan fires, but after 1815 they died down again. By the early 1820s most people probably had come to share President James Monroe's opinion that with the great questions settled there was no basis for maintaining the old parties. Loyalties, never strong, faded. Machinery, never perfected, rusted.

During the quarter-century after the War of 1812, the world's first nationwide mass parties appeared in the United States. Called forth by social, economic, and ideological developments, the new parties emerged awkwardly, by stages, through decades of political instability. The results of the process were far from accidental, however, for the new parties owed much of their character to the work of shrewd political leaders. By 1840 the Democrats and Whigs were competing virtually everywhere, not only for the presidency but also for state and local positions. Highly organized at the state level and professionally managed, they enjoyed the loyalty of most adult white males and filled nearly all the offices. Although the party system formed by the Democrats and Whigs would have a relatively brief life, many of these parties' characteristics became enduring features of American politics.

That modern parties appeared when they did was due in part to the establishment of certain preconditions for mass politics. The liberalization of suffrage requirements, the shift to popular choice of presidential electors, and the multiplication of elected officials together created a legal and constitutional environment conducive to widespread political participation. At the same time, technological and economic changes made possible revolutionary advances in transportation and communication. Roads, canals, railways, and (by the 1840s) the telegraph enabled delegates to attend party conventions, candidates to mount statewide campaigns, leaders to consult across great distances, and—above all—more voters than ever before to reach the polls. These developments were necessary pieces of the foundation upon which political leaders built mass parties, but they were not sufficient. More fundamental were new issues that prepared men to join parties and to accept political conflict.

With the "great" questions of foreign policy and national survival settled after 1815, competition between the Federalists and Republicans waned, but the political calm was short-lived. The quickening of entrepreneurial activity, the burgeoning and diversifying of population, the spread of religious revivals, and the opening up of the continent to expansion placed fresh concerns on the political agenda. Many of the new issues were economic. The Panic of 1819 and the depression that followed caused men and women to look to government for assistance. Some wanted relief from their debts; others called for the promotion of economic growth; still others demanded the regulation, or even abolition, of privileged corporations, especially banks. Fueling conflict nearly everywhere and inspiring factional politics in a number of states, these issues accustomed men to some of the routines and expectations of party politics. The same may be said of another group of issues that emerged during the 1820s and 1830s—those involving social and moral reform. Spurred by religious revivals, men and women embarked on crusades against intemperance, Sunday mail delivery, and slavery; others set out to establish schools, asylums, and prisons.

Compared with the policy issues of the 1790s and early 1800s, the issues of the post-1815 era had greater potential for arousing and sustaining partisan conflict. For one thing, there were now more issues; with the republic's survival seemingly assured, there was no end to the subjects that could be safely politicized. For another, the new issues were both heavily ideological and, under the right circumstances, highly compromisable. Economic questions, in particular, could be contested either loftily, as though they involved differing visions of American society, or much more mundanely, in terms of whose enterprises were to receive preferential treatment. Social-reform issues could also be debated on several planes. Party leaders who spoke to such questions thus had the opportunity to appeal to their followers' highest values—and then to bring home tangible rewards based on compromise with other groups having different values. This was possible, finally, because so many of the policy choices of the post-1815 years were highly divisible. They could be expressed, or decided, one way in one locale, another way in the next, and a third way in both places the following year. All in all, these governmental policy decisions were marvelously suited to partisan conflict: numerous, arousing, compromisable, and particularistic.

Many Americans were troubled by the continued political conflict. With the momentous questions of an earlier era no longer so frightening, parties seemed unnecessary. Given the old ideal of social harmony—still strong in the United States—parties appeared pernicious and selfish. In time, however, other Americans turned the classic antiparty position on its head: with the republic secure, no great harm could come from contesting legitimate differences among the people. More than that, there were positive advantages in party conflict: it checked those in power, maintained the people's vigilance, promoted majority rule, and militated against sectional conflict. Put forward first in New York by members of the highly pragmatic Albany Regency, the new rationale for parties never received unanimous acceptance. Whigs especially tended to resist it, even as they organized their own party. But the defense of parties unquestionably seeped into the consciousness of Americans, more and more of whom recognized and tolerated divisions within their society.

Even in such a propitious environment, the Democrats and Whigs took a long time emerging. During the 1820s, politics in most states remained chaotic; and even where party lines became more settled, party politics bore little relationship to national affairs. In New York a division in the old Republican party produced two factions with most of the attributes of modern parties; until the approach of the presidential election of 1828, however, New York politics was largely a state matter. In Georgia, too, parties emerged after the War of 1812, but for many years they had no connection to national politics. Party lines in other states during the 1820s were even less well formed than in New York and Georgia. Everywhere, however, the new issues of the post-1815 era were prominent. Kentucky, where debt relief became the basis of brief party alignments, provides a conspicuous example. Even so, politics began to assume the professional, pragmatic air of a slightly later day. Leaders used issue appeals to arouse the electorate, but most tried to keep their organizations as free from principled positions as they could.

The history of the Anti-Masonic party, which flourished in several northern states during the late 1820s and early 1830s, illustrates these generalizations. Anti-Masonry began in upstate New York as a moral crusade against the alleged exclusiveness, secrecy, and political power of the Masonic order. Based in evangelical districts, Anti-Masons tended to favor temperance, Sabbatarian laws, educational reforms, and even fair treatment of the Indians. Soon their fervor was channeled into partisan lines by politicians like Thurlow Weed in New York and Thaddeus Stevens in Pennsylvania. Under such leadership the party published dozens of newspapers, developed effective organizations in at least four states, and held the first national nominating convention in 1831. By the mid-1830s most Anti-Masons had been further guided by their leaders into one of the emerging major parties, their passionate issue-orientation having been turned to the service of passionate partisanship.

All these elements of a nascent partisan political culture might never have culminated in the formation of two national parties except for the developments surrounding the successive presidential elections from 1824 to 1840. Dulled by the dominance of the Virginia dynasty (Jefferson, Madison, and Monroe) after 1800, the presidential contest was revived in 1824 by Virginia's inability to offer an acceptable successor to Monroe and, even more, by the emergence of Andrew Jackson. Over the course of the next sixteen years, the presidential election became the crucible of national party politics, with Jackson the central figure. After Jackson's defeat in 1824, a pragmatic interstate coalition of leaders, led by Martin Van Buren of New York, engineered Jackson's triumph in 1828 and his reelection in 1832. In every state the Jacksonians appealed to the electorate's issue concerns, but the main issue was Jackson himself, a hero whose policy positions were difficult to discern.

The actual sequence of party formation owed much to the regional identifications of the presidential candidates. Broadly speaking, national parties solidified first in the middle states, where voters divided between Jackson the Tennessean and John Quincy Adams of Massachusetts in 1828; next in New England, which divided between Jackson and Henry Clay the Kentuckian in 1832; and finally in the South and West, where many voters rejected the northerner, Van Buren, as Jackson's successor in 1836. The key years for party formation were 1834–1836, when a

Whig opposition appeared in many states that had been solidly Jacksonian. In due course the Whigs would succeed in identifying themselves with some distinctive policy positions; but when their party was forming, the main dogma on which it could agree nationwide was the defeat of Van Buren. In 1840 both parties presented presidential candidates, conducted rousing campaigns on their behalf, and drew more men to the polls than ever before. An unprecedented form of party politics had come into existence, born of distinctive social and cultural developments and forged by determined leaders in the cauldron of presidential politics.

The party system of Democrats and Whigs lasted less than two decades, but the kind of parties established in the 1830s endured. In organization, in the voter loyalties that they inspired, in the nature of their campaign appeals, and in their relationship to government, these parties proved to be the prototypes for American parties throughout the rest of the nineteenth century and, in some respects, well beyond. But the continuities should not be exaggerated. The Whigs collapsed in the mid-1850s, the sectional crisis seriously interrupted national party conflict, and the third party system of Democrats and Republicans was far less sectionally balanced than the second party system of Democrats and Whigs had been. Through it all, however, much that was essential to American party politics remained unchanged.

One enduring characteristic was two-partyism. Although "minor" or "third" parties repeatedly emerged, the basic pattern of competition between two major parties was seriously threatened only during the gravest political crises. Technical as well as cultural factors account for the two-partyism. The United States always had winner-take-all elections and, for the presidency, a requirement that the winner receive a majority of the electoral votes. These rules discouraged parties with little or no chance to win elections and, given the president's symbolic importance, particularly hurt parties that had no hope of obtaining a majority of electoral votes. Over time the two-party system acquired sanctity, and its presumed benefits became rhetorical weapons not only against minor parties but also against a major party that seemed too dominant. The American inclination toward pragmatic consensus also contributed to the two-party preference. Two strong parties tend to gravitate toward the middle of the political spectrum, a process that has intrigued political scientists and given comfort to people wary of ideological extremes.

In the nature of their organizations, too, the Democrats and Whigs established long-lasting patterns. Where party affairs in the early republic had been entrusted to small, often secretive bodies, the new parties relied on corps of activists, organized from the smallest electoral units up to the national level and assigned to committees whose tasks were specialized and well understood. The most distinctive and important components of party organization were the delegate conventions, held at every level to secure agreement upon candidates and write platforms. During the 1820s and 1830s, the convention system became well established in most states, and in the 1832 presidential election it made its appearance on the national scene. Compared with the old caucus system of nominations, the convention ostensibly gave ordinary party activists a chance to participate in party affairs and thus obtained greater legitimacy for the resulting nominations. In practice, party conventions tended to be dominated by insiders and activists. Compared with any previous party organizations, however, those of the nineteenth-century United States were notable for their inclusiveness and their adherence to democratic forms.

After the nominations, the most important tasks of the party organization were to arouse the voters and get them to the polls. From the "log cabin" campaign of 1840 through the presidential elections of the early 1900s, the parties put on dramatic spectacles featuring mass rallies and torchlight parades with banners, bands, songs, and uniforms. Besides their political functions, the campaigns also served social purposes. For white men the parties were fraternal organizations, offering entertainment, carrying on ritualistic celebrations, and perhaps even providing a definition of manhood. For families and communities, too, parades and campaign rallies were occasions for enjoyment and satisfaction, central to nineteenth-century American culture. Before the election, local party organizations frequently conducted complete canvasses of the eligible voters. Loyal workers made sure that the party's ticket was in the hands of every elector who might reasonably be persuaded to cast it. And when election day came, there was no dearth of assistance and incentive for those who wished to vote.

The aim of all the hoopla was to arouse the party faithful rather than convert the enemy. Voter turnout was high (averaging around 75 percent in presidential elections from the 1840s to the early 1900s), and most men seem to have remained loyal to their parties over time. The sources of partisan choice were complicated and varied; ethnic, religious, communal, occupational, and sectional factors could all be relevant. Whatever the precise influences upon a man's choice of party, casting a ballot expressed group solidarity and affirmed the shared values of one's community. Fathers typically passed partisan loyalties on to their sons, just as mothers inculcated religious beliefs in their children. Not surprisingly, in light of these intergenerational influences, many towns and counties tended to show the same patterns of partisan division at election after election.

The voters who cast their ballots so loyally and consistently probably had fairly definite images of the parties that they were supporting. Certainly the party leaders worked hard to impress such images upon the electorate. In platforms, stump speeches, editorials, and the character of their candidates, the parties expressed distinctive styles and beliefs that voters recognized and with which they identified. In the 1840s and 1850s the Democrats presented themselves as the opponents of big government and special privilege, the defenders of states' rights and personal liberties (including the liberties of white ethnic and religious minorities), and, above all, the champions of the common man. The Whigs tended (a bit less consistently) to emphasize their party's commitment to energetic government in pursuit of progress, to the promotion of stable economic growth, and to the preservation of Protestant moral values. One important stylistic difference was each party's view of "party" itself, with the Democrats adopting the more positive position and the Whigs taking a more skeptical stance. Democratic presidential candidates tended to identify themselves with their party and the party with the people. Whig nominees, by contrast, stood a bit above the party and made their aloofness a point of pride. Both sides portrayed themselves as the preeminent protectors of republican liberty, and each sought to symbolize for voters the contrasting means through which they would fill that role in office.

In office the Democrats and Whigs made good on some of their promises, particularly after the Panic of 1837 when the two parties increasingly held to divergent economic and social programs. Except on foreign policy, Democrats tended to voice, and vote for, the doctrines of the negative liberal state: the less the government interfered in private affairs, the greater would be the general prosperity and the smaller the risk of creating inequalities and special privileges. At the national level this meant divorcing the government from the banking system, halting internal improvements, and opposing protective tariffs. In the states it meant restricting or even abolishing banks, resisting the incorporation of private businesses, and opposing interference in people's personal and social affairs. Whigs tended to support the dogmas of the positive liberal state: active governmental policies would promote the well-being of all and knit the nation together. This implied creating a new national bank, levying protective tariffs, and aiding transportation projects. At the state level, Whig doctrines pointed to the support of banks and other corporations, assistance to internal improvements, the establishment of schools, and the enactment of social and moral reforms.

But there were grave limitations upon the parties' ability to govern in accordance with their professed ideologies—just as there have been for American parties ever since. Even during the peak years of programmatic conflict, the policy positions described above were never hard and fast; by the early 1850s the

Democrats and Whigs seemed to be losing their distinctiveness altogether. As mass parties seeking majority support in all sections, they found it difficult to adhere rigidly to particular doctrines or programs. "Democratic" complaints against big government and special privileges were so popular that the Whigs echoed them, just as "Whig" policies of economic promotion proved irresistible to the Democrats.

It is doubtful that most Americans were distressed by the parties' inability to govern strictly in accordance with their ideologies. Nineteenth-century citizens were profoundly ambivalent about public power. Expecting the government's assistance for their enterprises, they also distrusted its actions and continually sought to assure its subservience to the people. The parties of the day proved well suited to the popular mood. They excelled in deciding the particularistic policy issues, the emergence of which had helped call forth the parties in the first place. And they proved supremely capable in carrying out the related task of building and maintaining socially diverse electoral machines. But the parties were less successful in the strong and consistent exercise of public power, a quality that probably enhanced the trust that voters placed in them.

The political turmoil of the Civil War era disrupted and rearranged American parties, but it left much about them surprisingly unchanged. In magnitude and duration the disruption was considerable, and it encompassed a striking sequence of developments, including the collapse of the Whigs, the division of the Democrats, and the triumph of the Republicans. What is notable, however, is the extent to which politics-as-usual persisted, especially in the North, during the Civil War and Reconstruction, and how familiar were many elements of the party system that stabilized at the end of the era. The explanation for these continuities lies in two circumstances. First, although the crises of the 1850s–1870s revolutionized national and sectional power relations, those crises also reinforced many of the loyalties and practices of the existing political system. Of equal importance, the sectional upheavals did not permanently reshape governance in the United States; as a result, the same sorts of parties that had managed the policy processes of the 1830s still remained useful and effective in the 1880s.

Party politics under the Democrats and Whigs had always borne a curious and complex relationship to the sectionally divisive slavery issue. From the outset, these national parties seemed to exist precariously, in defiance of North-South differences over black servitude. Many Democrats and Whigs tried hard to prevent slavery from disrupting their parties by banning the subject from national politics whenever possible and compromising slavery-related matters when they could not be stifled. Ultimately these efforts broke down, largely over the question of slavery's expansion into new territories in the West. By the early 1850s, both the Democrats and Whigs had well-defined southern and northern wings. The Whigs soon disappeared as a party, while in 1860 the Democrats broke into halves.

But slavery's relationship to the party system was not that simple. For two decades the Democrats and Whigs had survived—and even profited by—the slavery issue. At the national level slavery was dangerous to party unity, but at home in the North and South it provided grist for partisan mills as spokesmen for each side competed to outdo the other in defense of their section's interests. Even the question of slavery in the territories, although it ultimately proved unresolvable through political means, at first presented Whigs and Democrats with opportunities to reinforce partisanship by defending alternative positions.

The slavery issue alone, moreover, cannot explain the reorganization of parties in the 1850s. To be sure, the initial challenges to the party system of Democrats and Whigs came from the abolitionist Liberty party in 1840 and 1844 and from the Free Soil party in 1848. But the Liberty party won less than 3 percent of the popular vote in its best year, and the Free-Soilers (although they captured 10 percent in 1848) could not prevent major party lines from holding firm. Even as the slavery question gained salience in the 1850s, other matters came to the fore—chief among them the moral and social threats that Protestants perceived from the influx of Catholic immigrants, especially the Irish. In fact, by 1854, the year in which the Kansas-Nebraska Act outraged northerners by opening new territories to slavery, the antiforeign American (or Know-Nothing) party was the fastest growing political organization in many parts of the country and had more to do with giving Whiggery its deathblows than did the nascent Republicans. In the end, though, the nativist party was the vehicle of assorted social and political protests and an instrument of realignment—but not a survivor. Instead it was the Republicans who fashioned winning appeals out of the discontents of northern voters.

Made up of former Democrats as well as Whigs, abolitionists and negrophobes, nativists and men of tolerance, the new party staked out popular positions and shrewdly adjusted them for local constituencies. On slavery, the Republicans stood for free soil—no more extension of black servitude. On economic questions, most supported Whig policies of governmental promotion. On cultural issues, the Republicans made concessions to the Know-Nothings when they thought they had to. Perhaps the heart of the Republican appeal was anti-southernism, composed particularly of the notions that the Slave Power's aggressions endangered liberty and that slavery's expansion threatened the northern way of life. In 1860, when the Democrats broke up over the slavery expansion issue and named two rival candidates for president, the Republicans capitalized on the division and elected Abraham Lincoln to the White House. During the war, they labeled themselves the Union party and wrapped their cause in patriotic appeals. Perfecting the spectacular campaign techniques first seen a generation earlier, leaders instilled in their supporters a lifelong passion for Republicanism.

That party competition persisted during the Civil War was a remarkable, and probably fortuitous, feature of northern life. Shrunken in size, the Democratic party nonetheless remained highly competitive in the central block of states from Connecticut to Illinois. To a great extent the Democrats' viability rested on traditional appeals for Jacksonian economic policies, tolerance of the foreign-born, and white supremacy. On the issue of the war itself, most Democrats walked a thin line—for union and for peace. One important consequence of the northern Democrats' survival was that most opposition to the Lincoln government in the North was moderated and safely channeled to the ballot box. Republican partisanship proved equally beneficial to the northern cause. It offered a means of engendering enthusiasm for the war; it gave Lincoln ways of influencing and disciplining leaders throughout the North; and it compelled cooperation even among Republicans discontented with the purposes and progress of the war.

The southern Confederacy, lacking parties, also lacked the means of moderating internal opposition and of focusing support for the regime. In the lower South, party politics had largely collapsed a decade before the war, while in the upper South it had persisted. North Carolina, in fact, continued to have statewide party competition until 1863, and Virginia and Tennessee might have done so, too, had they not been battlegrounds. But in the Confederacy as a whole, President Jefferson Davis had no party behind him, nor did he face a loyal opposition. Although southerners trumpeted the virtues of their nonpartisanship, comparison with the North suggests that their cause was hurt by it.

Following the North's victory in 1865, the political parties entered upon perhaps the most trying years of any between the 1830s and early 1900s, but years from which they emerged strong, stable—and bland. In ideological intensity, the party warfare of the early Reconstruction years rivaled that of the early republic. Radical and moderate Republicans joined together to transform the South socially and politically, while Democrats in both sections tried to stop them. Helped by the army's presence, black and white Republicans organized state governments throughout the South, politicized the freedmen, and carried out programs of reform. Before a half-dozen years had passed, however, many Republicans were retreating from the goals of Reconstruction, and state after state in the South was being "redeemed" by the Democrats. In both sections this uncommon political era was marred by unusual levels of apparent corruption. Although the major parties survived the scandals, a small but influential body of reformers fashioned an enduring image of party politics as inherently corrupt. That image remained confined to a minority of Americans for the rest of the nineteenth century, but early in the 1900s it would become commonplace.

As Reconstruction waned, two-party equilibrium returned to the nation. Despite the Republicans' best efforts to smear them as traitors, the Democrats reemerged as a national party, aided both by the return to (almost) exclusively white rule in the South and by a widespread, if unspectacular, shift toward the Democrats in the industrial states of the North, where the depression of the 1870s was felt most severely. At the national level the Democrats and Republicans were now highly competitive, just as the Democrats and Whigs had been, but most states were less closely balanced than in the earlier era. The South voted strongly Democratic (although by no means as "solidly" as it would in the twentieth century), while the upper North voted predominantly Republican. Only in the industrial heartland from Connecticut to Illinois was party competition intense. In crucial ways, the geography of partisanship and power had been transformed by the Civil War.

But the continuities of party politics were impressive too. Among the war's legacies was a set of symbols and appeals that was used to sustain a partisanship even more intense than that formerly inspired by the Democrats and Whigs. The bloody shirt, race baiting, and memories of heroism and defeat all became the stuff of stump speeches, and all assured that the loyalties forged and confirmed by war would not be forgotten on election day. Late nineteenth-century parties thus excelled as electoral organizations, rooted in deeply felt cultural and communal experiences, just as those of the Jackson period had. They excelled, too, in managing the particularistic policy decisions that still dominated American governance. Although the war and its aftermath had seen considerable governmental innovation, by the 1870s both the states and the nation were abandoning their activism. The net result was a body of public policies somewhat larger than, but not fundamentally different from, that of the prewar era. Well suited to particularistic decisions of a basically distributive, piecemeal nature and to organizing the legislative bodies that still predominated in the national and state governments, the major political parties, now more popular than ever, embarked upon their most vigorous years.

As organizations and as objects of loyalty, the major parties enjoyed their golden age during the last three decades of the nineteenth century. Although only loosely coordinated at the national level, the Democrats and Republicans each boasted awesome machines in localities where they were competitive, and on election days they shepherded enthusiastic and committed followers to the polls. Based on cultural and communal identities as well as memories of the Civil War, the partisan loyalties of most voters tended to persist over time. Few were independents, and until the 1890s third parties made little headway. So long as the mass of voters remained generally satisfied with the limited governmental policies that the major parties promoted, those loyalties endured—for good reasons.

The Democrats' greatest asset was their party's appeal to the electorate. They captured control of the House of Representatives in 1874 and retained it for sixteen of the next twenty years; in all but one of the presidential elections from 1876 to 1892 the Democrats won more popular votes than the Republicans. This was a remarkable record for a party still burdened with the stain of wartime disloyalty, fragmented between its rural southern and urban northern wings, lacking in distinguished national leaders, and empty of a national program. Yet these apparent liabilities were also the party's sources of strength. For it was in local communities that the Democrats made their appeals—to white supremacists in the South; to Roman Catholics, German Lutherans, and other nonevangelical Protestants in the North; to men everywhere who believed in limited government and personal liberty—as they defined these things out of their own experiences. It is doubtful that highly visible national spokesmen or ringing policy programs could have sustained the Democrats nearly as well as did the appeals to tradition and the parochial images fashioned by the party's local leaders.

The Republicans had a somewhat different balance of strengths and weaknesses. Secure only in the upper North, they were a sectional party whose relevance was in doubt once the most serious North-South differences had been resolved. To add to the Republicans' burdens, demographic trends—especially urbanization and European immigration—seemed, all told, to favor the Democrats. The Republicans could count on the loyalties of most northern evangelical Protestants, but the number of Catholics and other nonevangelicals in the population was growing rapidly. Yet the Republicans were scarcely without resources. Compared with the Democrats, they had a larger and better known corps of national leaders, many of whom had distinguished themselves on Civil War battlefields and—like their party as a whole—could claim the glory of having saved the Union and abolished slavery. The Republicans appeared, moreover, to be the party with ideas, the party unafraid to use the government to solve problems, the party of energy and change. Although these were mixed blessings in an age of low expectations for government, over the long run they worked to the Republicans' advantage.

In the short run, it was well for both parties that most late nineteenth-century voters seem to have accepted the existing policy process. Anxious for material progress, they welcomed the government's grants of resources and privileges to their enterprises but were only beginning to see benefits in regulation, administration, or planning. The resulting economic policies were well suited to two heterogeneous parties, each eager to please nearly every particular constituency and loathe to antagonize large groups. When social or cultural matters came to the fore, as they often did in the late nineteenth century, the same particularism generally suffered. Each major party's ideology assisted in explaining why the government should not undertake policies distinguishing one group from another or adjusting social differences. According to the Republicans, the various interests in society were fundamentally harmonious and whatever helped one helped all. The Democrats tended to see social conflict more clearly but believed that the preservation of liberty required weak government. Both parties enjoyed dispensing, and fighting about, policies benefiting particular constituencies, but both opposed any significant expansion of public authority. The perennial question of how much tariff protection to place on scores of separate products perfectly fit the major parties of the late nineteenth century.

So, at a different level of governance, did actions assisting city residents, whose needs inspired the creation of urban party machines beginning in the 1860s and 1870s. Within the growing industrial cities of America, government remained rudimentary, communication and transportation limited, and social welfare programs utterly lacking. Party machines, such as William Marcy Tweed's in New York, scarcely solved all the problems, but they did offer contacts and services provided by no one else— from funding for a streetcar line to flowers at a funeral. Along the way, the machines broke the laws by paying off each constituency in whatever currency it wanted most, but demands for the parties' assistance continued unabated. In return for their help, the machines expected support on election day as well as indulgence in using the governmental powers they won. Despite cries for reform, the machines endured, both because they filled so many voids and because they thrived in a particularistic polity where most groups scarcely knew what the others were getting.

Not all Americans of the late nineteenth century supported the major parties or were satisfied with the government that they provided. One small but vocal body of dissenters, known as Mugwumps or independents, was made up of well-to-do urban easterners. Less concerned with the substance of party policies than with the allegedly corrupt manner in which government was conducted, men of this sort were put off by the scandals of the Reconstruction era, by the apparently corrupt bonds between national party politicians and big business interests, and above all by the seemingly sordid quality of machine politics in the large cities. Mostly Republican in their background, they bolted their party in the presidential elections of 1872 and 1884 and in numerous state and local elections as well. The Mugwumps were conservative, and their remedies for the ills of party government tended to be structural changes—especially civil service reform. Their elitist independence from the major parties harked back to the antipartyism of an earlier era and foreshadowed the resurgence of distrust of the parties during the early 1900s.

More numerous, if less socially prominent, than the Mugwumps were those who joined the third parties of the late nineteenth century, especially the Prohibition party and the various farmer-labor parties. With the Democrats and Republicans so closely balanced, the minor parties sometimes assumed an influence disproportionate to their actual numbers. In half of the era's congressional elections, for example, the small parties' combined vote exceeded the difference between the major parties' totals. First formed in 1869, the Prohibitionists spread their organization to a majority of states in the mid-1880s and captured a small but loyal corps of supporters (drawn mainly from among native-born Republicans) for the "dry" cause. Often larger, but with a less continuous electoral base, were the assorted Greenback and Labor parties that appealed to discontented economic groups with demands for putting more money into circulation, regulating commerce, and taxing incomes. Helped by the nationwide labor unrest of 1877, a reorganized Greenback party increased its vote from 81,000 in 1876 to over a million (12 percent of the total) in the off-year elections of 1878. But by 1880 the party had faded, and most of its supporters were back in Republican or Democratic folds.

What distinguished these minor parties from their larger counterparts was their support for activist governmental policies that plainly assisted some groups while restraining others. Whether oriented toward cultural minorities (as were the Prohibitionists) or economic constituencies (as were the Greenbackers and Laborites), the minor parties explicitly recognized the clashes of interest within American society and demanded that the government do so too. For the Democrats and Republicans, these were demands of the kind they could not or would not fulfill.

The most important third party of the late nineteenth century, the Populists, frightened the majority of Americans by appealing for policies directly benefiting farmers. An outgrowth of the Farmers' Alliance, whose touring lecturers had aroused and educated the growers of cotton, wheat, and corn, the nascent Populists elected numerous state legislators and congressmen in the West in 1890. In the South, Alliance-backed candidates ran strongly under the Democratic banner. Meeting at Omaha, Nebraska, two years later, western and southern Populists united behind James B. Weaver for president and adopted a platform that combined a radical critique of the emergent industrial order with a series of specific proposals designed to help the farmer. These included an increase in the money supply, national ownership of the railroads, a plan to support crop prices, and a graduated income tax. Denounced as dangerous lunatics by the Democrats and Republicans, the Populists won nearly 9 percent of the presidential vote in 1892 and 12 percent of the congressional vote in 1894. Almost certainly their vote in both years would have been higher except for frauds committed by the major parties, especially the southern Democrats.

The growth of the Populists was an important element of a major realignment of party voters during the 1890s. And that realignment, in turn, assisted in creating the conditions for an even more fundamental political transformation during the early 1900s. The sequence of events was swift. Amidst a serious depression that brought not only widespread unemployment but also industrial violence, the Republicans made heavy gains in the congressional elections of 1894. Two years later the Democrats and Populists allied behind William Jennings Bryan for presi-

dent and supported his vigorous demands for the free and unlimited coinage of silver. Excoriated by wealthy conservatives and
abandoned by industrial workers who feared that free silver
meant continued depression and higher food prices, Bryan went
down to defeat at the hands of the Republican William McKinley. In an election that marked the end of partisan equilibrium,
voters from almost every social group in the North and Midwest
shifted toward the Republicans and gave them a national majority that they would enjoy for more than a generation. Suddenly
the party loyalties of the post-Civil War years no longer seemed
so firm, and class conflict was an undeniable reality. What remained to be seen was whether the major parties, especially the
now-dominant Republicans, could make governmental policies
that recognized, and adjusted, the clashing interests of an industrial society.

The first years of the twentieth century brought great changes to
the political parties of the United States. Under attack from many
quarters for the ills of government, they emerged less popular,
more closely regulated, and, overall, less able to dominate the
now-expanded institutions of government. But the major parties
survived the changes by becoming tamer and more respectable,
and they even turned some of the new restrictions to their own
advantage. As electoral machines the Democrats and Republicans gained formal powers that they had not possessed before,
and the major parties were now securely embedded in law. All
told, these changes compare in importance to those of the 1820s
and 1830s, when modern mass parties first appeared. Just as in
the earlier era, many social and political elements had a hand in
the transition, and no one could have anticipated all the results.

One unexpected blow to partisanship came from the realignment of the 1890s. After the electoral shifts culminating in 1896,
many areas of the nation fell under the domination of a single
party. In the former Confederate states of the South, where assorted oppositions had commonly challenged (if not defeated)

the Democrats in the post-Reconstruction era, politics now became utterly noncompetitive. Similarly, in many areas of the North and West, where the Democrats had remained viable during the 1870s and 1880s, the Republicans achieved almost uncontested dominance. During the late nineteenth century, well over half of the population had resided in states where elections were closely contested; by the early twentieth century that proportion was less than a third. Over time, the waning of partisan competitiveness contributed to lower levels of popular interest in politics, falling voter turnout, and weakening of the party machines.

An even more fundamental cause of change lay in the widespread dissatisfaction with the methods and results of American governance and in the determination to shape new patterns of policy. No social group had a monopoly on the demands. Elite urban independents assailed the corruption and inefficiency of city government and urged the establishment of what they called businesslike administration. Professionals of all sorts wanted public recognition of their expertise and official authorization to give the population the benefit of their skills. Economic interest groups sought regulation of their rivals and more assistance for themselves. These demands were not easy for the major parties, with their large and heterogeneous coalitions, to meet. To many, the Republicans and Democrats both seemed outmoded, their historic ideologies irrelevant to an urban-industrial society. The Republican doctrine of the harmony of interests conflicted conspicuously with social realities; the Democratic belief in limited government appeared hopelessly out-of-date. Early in the twentieth century, disclosures of rampant politico-business corruption furthered the public's conviction that the major parties were inadequate to the tasks of government.

The most visible result was the appearance of new third parties with bold and specific governmental programs. Under Eugene V. Debs's leadership, the Socialist Party of America reached a peak of strength between 1910 and 1912 when dozens of towns and cities elected Socialist mayors and Debs won nearly a million votes as a presidential candidate. Central to the Socialists' appeal was the demand for collective ownership of many industries and the strong governmental regulation of others. Less long-lived but far larger was the Progressive party, which nominated Theodore Roosevelt for president in 1912 and captured over a quarter of the popular vote. Roosevelt's popularity was the main reason for the new party's showing, but its chief legacy was its platform—a remarkable compendium of nearly every social and political reform then talked of in the United States. Binding the Progressive platform together was one of the most striking visions ever to come out of American party politics, that of a collective democratic society presided over by a strong federal government to regulate and protect every interest. By 1916 Roosevelt had returned to the Republican party, and the Progressives collapsed. But the Progressive party's vision (and, to a lesser extent, that of the Socialists) survived as a significant influence upon twentieth-century American governance.

As government expanded and took on more and more regulatory tasks, many of them proposed by the Socialists and Progressives, the major parties inevitably felt the effects. Many of the government's new duties were given not to partisan legislators but to independent boards of experts entrusted with significant powers of investigation and enforcement. By no means wholly immune to partisanship, the new administrative agencies nonetheless made policies with less regard for the parties than nineteenth-century legislatures ever had. Party leaders naturally resisted their own loss of influence, but the twentieth-century trend toward nonpartisanship in certain policy areas may actually have been helpful to the Democrats and Republicans. Well-suited to particularistic distributive decisions, the parties found policies of regulation and intervention highly dangerous to their coalitions. Now the government was explicitly assisting some groups at the expense of others, and votes were sure to be lost. To be sure, the major parties continued to promote and enact governmental programs when their partisan interests required it. But the party organizations never again dominated the institutions of government as fully as they had in an earlier era.

Nor would they again conduct elections in the freewheeling manner of the nineteenth century, when parties had been largely untouched by law. Before the 1890s, parties had chosen their candidates, printed and distributed their tickets, and gotten out the vote pretty much as they chose. Then, beginning in the last years of the nineteenth century, laws passed in almost every state converted the parties from private into public organizations. Governments took over the task of printing the ballots, which now listed the candidates of every party, and of assuring that they were cast in secret. Ballot reform inevitably involved the state in the regulation of party nominations, and by the early 1900s the direct primary was sweeping the country. Corrupt-practices acts clamped down on many of the old techniques that the parties had once used to get their supporters to the polls, while voter registration laws curtailed the ease of voting. Other laws forbade corporate contributions to party campaigns, limited election expenses, and threw restrictions around the appointment of loyal partisans to public office. Together these measures encased the parties in the web of law and contributed to the decline of the hoopla and excitement, as well as of the high levels of voter participation, which had characterized nineteenth-century elections.

In its details, however, the web of law was largely woven by the parties themselves. Placed on the defensive by the widespread dissatisfaction with party government and by the growth of third parties, the Democrats and Republicans had no choice but to accept restraints on their own actions. The determination to rein in the party organizations was real and widespread; often, it was indeed the common denominator of otherwise antagonistic interest groups and reform-minded organizations. Recognizing the inevitability of change, major-party legislators set out to write rules that they could live with—and this they did. The new laws governing ballots and nominations curtailed the worst abuses of the past, but they also made independent and minor-party candidacies more difficult to mount than before. Other measures restricted the political participation of many electors who might have been among the most likely to cast third-party—especially

Socialist—ballots. The decline of spectacular campaigns and of electoral turnout was not necessarily damaging to the major parties. Secured in law and guaranteed a near monopoly over nominations, they equipped themselves well to survive in an antiparty age.

Overall, the beleaguered Democrats and Republicans of the early 1900s exhibited a degree of flexibility and responsiveness, mixed with self-interestedness, that surprised their critics. Guided by charismatic national leaders, both parties abandoned the most out-of-date elements of their historic doctrines. Under Theodore Roosevelt, the Republicans enacted social and economic measures frankly recognizing the clash of group interests. Led by Woodrow Wilson, the Democrats gave up their rigid insistence on limited government. In the states and cities, too, party leaders demonstrated a remarkable eagerness to try new programs and had striking success in adapting to the new political and governmental environment. Parties in America had always been under suspicion—and had always endured it. Those of the early 1900s were no different in this regard.

None of this came easily, and both major parties went through troubled times. It took the Democrats until 1910 to recover from the crises of the 1890s, and by the end of the Wilson administration a decade later they were once again deeply divided. The 1920s marked a nadir for the Democrats; out of power everywhere except in the South, they fought among themselves over the most serious economic and cultural questions dividing the nation as a whole (which was perhaps to their credit) but showed little promise of being able to govern if they got the chance. The Republicans dominated national elections more frequently in the first decades of the twentieth century, although from 1910 to 1916 they were split into conservative and progressive wings. Reunited in the 1920s, the Republicans elected successive presidents who encouraged, but also suffered from, the apathy that had settled over American politics.

By the 1920s, political parties occupied a very different position in America than they had a generation before. Less popular, they inhabited a political world where electoral participation counted for less than it had in the nineteenth century. Their relationship to government had changed, too, and many newer policy areas were out of the parties' control. Interest groups of many sorts now competed with them (as well as with each other) for the loyalties of citizens and for influence over the government. All in all, the parties were now less central to the polity, but they were by no means ready to go away. Fewer people than ever contested the parties' control over nominations and elections, and the Republicans and Democrats alike parlayed their historic strengths as electoral machines into means of survival.

During the early 1930s, the most dramatic development in twentieth-century party politics took place: the rise of a new majority coalition behind the Democratic party. More issue-oriented and group-based than its nineteenth-century predecessors, the New Deal coalition, as it has been aptly called, would last for more than a generation. The new majority was complex in its origins and owed a great deal to the politics of the 1920s, the depression of the 1930s, and the election of Franklin D. Roosevelt. But its most important source of strength and the primary cause of its longevity was the set of governmental programs around which the party coalesced, particularly between 1933 and 1936. New Deal policies put an end to the political apathy of the 1920s, temporarily rekindled partisanship, and fixed issues and alignments for decades to come. The creation of this coalition demonstrates as clearly as any event in history the proposition that American parties have endured because they have repeatedly transformed themselves in response to new opportunities to exercise governmental power.

Accomplishing the transformation was not easy, and the Democrats required almost a decade to complete it. Having received the support of only one eligible voter in seven in 1924 (when Robert M. La Follette's Progressive campaign drained votes from both major parties), the Democrats sharply improved their popular showing in 1928. Although Alfred E. Smith, the party's presidential candidate, was soundly defeated by the Republican Herbert Hoover, Smith, a New York City Catholic, drew to the Democrats thousands of urban, immigrant, Catholic voters, many of whom had not bothered to vote before. Even before the onset of the Great Depression, then, the Democrats had begun to stake their party's future upon the cities, the Catholics, and the poor. The hard times that commenced in 1929 increased the Democrats' opportunity to pursue this strategy. Led by Franklin D. Roosevelt, whose sunny personality inspired optimism about economic recovery, the Democrats captured the White House in 1932.

Yet while the depression had given the party its majority, to keep it the Democrats had to devise governmental programs perceived as successful. Under Roosevelt they did so. During the famed Hundred Days of 1933 and again during 1935, the president proposed and Congress enacted numerous and unprecedented laws designed to achieve relief, recovery, and reform. A magnificently skilled politician, Roosevelt patiently explained his policies to the people in "fireside chats" over the radio, and he brought confidence and hope to millions. As a result, the Democratic landslide of 1932 gave way to an even more overwhelming victory in 1936. Roosevelt was reelected with over 60 percent of the popular vote and carried every state but Maine and Vermont. The Democratic coalition would never be quite this big again, but its basic elements persisted. Included were most first- and second-generation immigrant Americans, among them a majority of Catholics and Jews; a very high proportion of the native-born industrial work force; a majority of northern blacks (southern blacks were mainly disfranchised); and almost all white southerners.

In some ways, the emergence of the New Deal coalition restored nineteenth-century-style party politics. Voter turnout rose, partisan competitiveness increased (at least in the North), and a rising generation of men and women signed on to do party work. But the parties of the New Deal era actually differed significantly from those of the nineteenth century. The minority Republicans differed most. Until the 1950s they were mainly in the position of reacting (often inconsistently) to the Democrats and of trying to attract whomever the Democrats alienated. It was a far cry from the loyal, passionate Republicanism of an earlier era. The majority Democrats *had* loyalty and passion—especially for the magnetic Roosevelt—but they hung together mainly by virtue of a vigorous program of governmental policies that recognized and regulated many different interest groups. The special relationship between labor unions and the Democrats offers the best case in point, but other groups had close ties to the national party machinery too. After Roosevelt's death in 1945, the Democratic party increasingly became the sum of the constituencies that its programs rewarded. In an age of big government, that was not an unreasonable basis for a mass party. But it carried long-term risks.

In the short run, however, the Democrats put the new policies of relief and recovery to work as instruments of political rejuvenation. Across the country, federal money and programs gave politicians unprecedented means for establishing followings among the poor and the needy. "Little new deals" sprang up in some states and offered further opportunities for party building. The Democrats benefited almost everywhere from these developments, but as time passed the New Deal's luster proved more durable in some regions than in others. In the industrialized Northeast and the Midwest, the effects were long-lasting; almost every state moved in the Democratic direction, and some (such as Pennsylvania and Michigan) that had been heavily Republican now embarked on lengthy eras of intense two-party competition. In the South, which was already solidly Democratic, New Deal policies were received well at first and even emulated in a few states. By the middle and late 1930s, however, conservative southern Democrats had become wary of the social and racial implications of the new programs, and they distanced themselves from the national party. To the west, many farming states swung toward the Democrats in 1932 and 1934, but afterward they shifted back in the Republican direction. The region's renewed Republicanism was in part an expression of ingrained western resistance to big government, but it also reflected a widespread perception that New Deal agricultural policies had not succeeded.

The New Deal had important and complicated implications for party politics in the cities, especially for the party machines that still flourished there. On the whole, city voters tended to retain the Democratic loyalties forged in the 1930s longer than did their rural counterparts, and most urban regions of the nation continued to support the party of Roosevelt long after he was gone from the scene. Such enduring loyalties owed much to the ability of local leaders to use federal (and, to a lesser extent, state) largess for the benefit of the party organization. No matter where the jobs and money ultimately came from, the cities and counties enjoyed the benefits of distributing them. But the New Deal also had countervailing effects on the city machines. For one thing, the reform spirit associated with Roosevelt and his program probably was a factor in the downfall of some of the more corrupt city bosses, such as Thomas Pendergast of Kansas City. Of more importance, federal welfare policies increasingly rendered obsolete many of the social services that local parties had provided to earlier generations of urban poor. The long-term decline of the city machines, which was visible by the mid-1900s, was at least partly due to such obsolescence.

A coalition as large as the one assembled during the early New Deal years was bound to suffer losses as groups became unhappy with the party's policies. Conservative white southerners objected to the federal government's social and economic activism, but bound to the Democrats by tradition and racism, they saw no place else to go—until 1948, that is. Under President Harry S. Truman, Roosevelt's successor, the national Democratic party had begun cautiously to take up policies of civil rights and racial equality. In response, a States' Rights ("Dixiecrat") party nominated J. Strom Thurmond for president, and he carried Alabama, Louisiana, Mississippi, and South Carolina. That same year, a faction of liberal Democrats also abandoned the party. Convinced that Truman's vigorous policies of containing communism threatened world peace, a new Progressive party supported Henry A. Wallace for president. Other elements of the New Deal Democracy drifted away, too. As workingclass and middle-class families recovered from the hard times and moved from city to suburb, many began to cast Republican ballots. Through it all, however, the heart of the coalition remained intact, including a majority of Catholics, Jews, northern blacks, industrial workers and their families, and (except for 1948) white southerners. In 1952 and 1956 many of them cast presidential ballots for the Republican Dwight D. Eisenhower, but they still thought of themselves as members of the party of the New Deal.

Their loyalty is not hard to understand. Led by Roosevelt, the Democrats had identified their party with compassion and recovery, and in thousands of communities they shaped New Deal programs to the task of strengthening the organization. The result was a party unlike any other before it in American history—one that evoked passionate loyalties *and* used big government to assist many elements in the population. But dangers lay in the very programs that had established the New Deal coalition. Leaders of even the most loyal groups learned to balance the degree of their commitment to the party against the benefits they received. Every group, moreover, now found the government doing at least some things harmful to its members. Just as nineteenth-century party leaders had known, the more the government did, the greater the potential for dissatisfaction with government. In time the Republicans as well as the Democrats became vulnerable to the discontent because their party, too, fell in behind many of the new policies.

So long as Roosevelt—or personal memories about him—remained alive, love for him dampened and disguised these risks, at least for the Democrats. But by the 1950s, and even more during the 1960s, young men and women with no recollections of Roosevelt entered the electorate. When they felt dissatisfaction with government, they expressed it by turning away from the parties.

From this perspective the New Deal years appear as aberrant ones amidst the long-term decline of party loyalty that began in the early 1900s. One party temporarily reversed the decline by identifying itself with vastly enlarged governmental programs. Both parties then paid the price when more people than ever came to blame the government for their problems.

The 1960s and 1970s saw a major decline in the percentage of Americans who considered themselves members of a political party and a rising tide of independents. Election days brought relatively fewer voters to the polls, while public opinion surveys revealed widespread disaffection from the party leaders. Other signs of party decay also appeared: the electorate's volatility from year to year, the growing tendency for candidates to play down their party labels, and the rise of single-interest groups that channeled citizens toward causes independent of the parties. Many factors assist in explaining the erosion of party strength, but at the root of the matter was a loss of confidence in the parties' ability to make governmental policies that solved problems. The distrust of parties was hardly new, but never before had there been such cause to wonder whether the Democrats and Republicans still possessed their historic ability to adapt themselves to new demands on government.

Beginning in the 1950s, and especially by the 1960s, issues emerged that tested that ability. Racial conflict, the war in Vietnam, feminism, and a series of other social issues—including drugs, abortion, and prayer in the schools—aroused great numbers of people and split them along new and contradictory lines. Just as they often had before, the Democrats and Republicans found it difficult to take firm positons on controversial questions. As a result, the new issues of the 1960s weakened the loyalties that had been formed during the New Deal era but did not put new party commitments in their place. Considerable evidence suggests that dissatisfaction with the parties was most pronounced among younger voters who had no personal memories of Roosevelt and the Great Depression. To them, the parties and the government—which were supposed to have solutions to problems—were evading the most important issues of the day. Apathy, alienation, and low voter turnouts were the results.

During the 1970s a new and even more intractable set of problems emerged for which the parties had no answers: inflation and unemployment. Accustomed to the prosperity that had endured for most of the 1940s, 1950s, and 1960s, Americans now faced declining real incomes and, for many, the prospect of either joblessness or part-time work. No one knew for sure how to solve these economic problems, and every proposed solution hurt some while it assisted others. Yet people expected the government to have answers—just as it had seemed to have during the 1930s. When those in office failed to produce remedies, much of the blame fell on the parties. Asked by polltakers whether they had confidence in the Democrats and Republicans to solve the nation's economic problems, great numbers of people declared they did not.

The electoral instabilities evident in the presidential contests of the era suggest the depths of disaffection from the parties. In four of the six elections from 1960 to 1980, the party of the incumbent president was defeated for the White House, while in the other two—1964 and 1972—the incumbent won by a landslide. Both types of elections were revealing. Unsatisfied with both major parties and less and less loyal to either, the voters usually opted for change—with a vague expectation that it would bring more successful policies. Thus a Democrat was chosen to replace a Republican president in 1960 and 1976, while the reverse occurred in 1968 and 1980. Besides a change of parties in the White House, 1968 also saw a strong third-party candidacy by Governor George Wallace of Alabama, the nominee of the American Independent party. A hero to workingclass whites who were frightened by campus radicals protesting against the war in Vietnam and, even more, by the specter of black men and women demanding equality, Wallace won almost 14 percent of the vote and carried five states.

The two exceptional elections of the era, when the president was reelected, were characterized not so much by expressions of confidence in the incumbent as by aversion toward his opponent. In 1964, members of the conservative wing of the Republican party managed to nominate Senator Barry Goldwater, who blazoned his right-wing ideology and won less than 40 percent of the popular vote. Eight years later, amidst the Vietnam War, the Democratic Left engineered the choice of Senator George McGovern, who ran even less well than had Goldwater. For some voters the nomination of men who were perceived as extremists inspired a renewal of faith in the capacity of the parties to present genuine choices to the people. But to most citizens the events of 1964 and 1972 gave further reason for rejecting the parties. Overall, the presidential elections of the 1960s and 1970s were marked by high instability and declining participation—exactly the reverse of the conditions that had prevailed during periods when parties were at a peak of strength.

These events elicited a variety of responses from Americans— some seeking to arrest the decline of parties, others hoping to profit by it, still others trying only to endure the changes. So recent and complex are these developments that it is difficult to be certain which contributed to the weakening of parties, which merely registered a reaction to their decay, and which—if any— may have begun to restore party strength. Although it is too early to assess their full implications, three related phenomena merit particular attention: the tendency of political leaders to distance themselves from the parties, the growth of extraparty political organizations, and the efforts to reform the parties through new laws and new party rules.

Where candidates of an earlier era had proudly identified themselves with their parties, those of the 1960s and 1970s were understandably less inclined to do so. In speeches and campaign advertisements they played down their partisanship and emphasized their independence. This was true not simply of local and state candidates, for every president of the period sought in some way to rise above his party. Jimmy Carter in 1976 and Ronald Reagan in 1980 consciously campaigned as outsiders. Top politicians increasingly established personal machines separate from the regular party apparatus, as John F. Kennedy had done in the 1950s. They raised money, created images of themselves (often through the use of television), and appealed for votes largely as individuals. Their behavior both reflected and encouraged the decline of party loyalties.

While those who sought office usually remained at least nominally partisan (because the Democrats and Republicans still had a near monopoly on the nominating machinery), citizens who wanted not offices but particular governmental policies increasingly ignored the parties. Many worked instead through interest organizations of various sorts, including the newer cause-oriented advocacy groups as well as the more familiar trade associations. These bodies raised money, lobbied officials, and powerfully influenced policy on such matters as abortion, gun control, and the environment. More and more of the new organizations learned to employ computer technology to contact their members and spread their appeals. Through such means, the new groups competed with the parties for the most precious political resources, including time and money. Often they won—and so contributed to the further erosion of the parties.

Seeing the parties in trouble, various forces sought to reform them, either through law or through changes in the party rules. Many groups and motives were behind the reforms of the 1960s and 1970s, but most of them shared the historic aim of making the parties into public rather than private organizations. Above all, this meant regulating party nominations and assuring that rank-and-file members (including women and ethnic minorities) had their share of influence. Both parties, but especially the Democrats, took significant steps in this direction. Other important reforms altered the manner in which campaigns were financed, by limiting the size of monetary contributions and providing that all such gifts be publicly reported. Together, the party reforms had contradictory effects. On the one hand they eliminated some obvious abuses and perhaps increased the parties' opportunities to attract the young, the women, and the minorities. On the other hand the reforms probably contributed to weakening the party organizations by reducing their role in recruiting and nominating candidates and in financing the campaigns. (The finance-reform laws were conspicuously candidate-oriented rather than party-oriented.) Above all, the reforms failed to address the basic reason for the contemporary decline of parties: the seeming inability of the Democrats and Republicans to use government to solve problems.

The parties' prospects for renewal would seem to depend upon their capacity to bring forward remedies for social and economic ills. Doing so will be difficult, not only because effective answers are so elusive, but also because the solutions are likely to hurt as many people as they help and to increase dissatisfaction with the party perceived as responsible. Yet this is the dilemma that the Democrats and Republicans face in post-New Deal America: they are expected to make vigorous use of government at all levels and are widely blamed for their nearly inevitable failures. It may well be that the parties will collapse, unable to survive this dilemma. But the record of the past suggests otherwise. Probably the parties will adjust to the new demands on government, just as they always have. Probably, too, significant numbers of Americans will remain ever suspicious of the political parties.

A central pattern characterizes the long history of political parties in America: they have repeatedly shaped themselves in response to changes in the nature and structure of government, but they have always found it difficult to exercise the governmental powers they won. All the major turning points in party history have been governmental turning points. Parties first emerged in response to opportunities to make policies in the colonial assemblies. They became national in scope and far more organized with the creation of the new federal government. From the 1830s to the early 1900s the parties presided over legislative bodies that were mainly geared to particularistic policies of promotion and distribution, and they enjoyed their golden age. When demands for regulatory policies became irresistible in the first years of the twentieth century, the parties responded by relinquishing both authority and popularity, while securing their (nearly) sole right to nominate candidates to office. During the New Deal years, one party temporarily regained nineteenth-century-style popularity by identifying itself with vastly expanded governmental powers of regulation and redistribution. But the parties' identification with big government plagues both the Democrats and the Republicans of the contemporary era because they seem unable to make successful use of their powers.

The apparent failure of today's parties to govern is not surprising in the light of party history, for while policies and policy-making institutions have always exercised determining effects upon the parties, the reverse is not true. Parties face great problems in governing. The more the government does, the greater will be the discontent with government and with the party responsible. At the root of this is the historic American aversion to power and distrust of authority. But the problem is more than an abstraction, because almost every governmental policy helps some people only at the expense of hurting others. Those who are assisted will likely overlook their aversion to power and commend both the policy and the party. But for those who are harmed, the ingrained distrust of authority will be heightened by personal grievances against the policy and the policymakers.

The more specific and particularistic the policies, the less danger they pose to parties. If expectations are minimal, if resources are (or appear to be) sufficiently plentiful, and if most people remain only vaguely aware of what the rest are getting, then policymaking can actually be a source of partisan strength. It is no coincidence that parties achieved their greatest popularity during the nineteenth century when the policy structure came closest to this model. Even in the twentieth century, parties have been able to benefit conspicuously from distributive policies of the "pork barrel" variety. By contrast, regulatory and redistributive policies that inherently distinguish one group from another—the "helped" from the "hurt"—can seldom assist the parties, and the parties have seldom been very effective in making such policies. The New Deal years are the great exception. For a brief span of time, in an atmosphere of crisis, a majority of the people regarded themselves as among the "helped," and their gratitude was increased by their affection for Franklin D. Roosevelt. But when the depression was over, both parties discovered what thankless tasks big government had thrust upon them.

Fortunately for the parties, they long ago carved out other, more successful roles for themselves, especially those of recruiting and nominating candidates and getting them elected. As early as the eighteenth century, the parties displayed great creativity in accomplishing these functions. They perfected spectacular means for carrying them out during their peak years of nineteenth-century popularity, and they won legal authorization for continuing to perform their electoral tasks amidst the renewed antipartyism of the twentieth century. Their strengths as nominating and electing organizations have enabled the major parties to survive and prosper. They have governed only at their peril, but they have filled the offices.

BIBLIOGRAPHY

Arthur M. Schlesinger, Jr., ed., *History of U.S. Political Parties*, 4 vols. (New York, 1973), is an excellent reference work and a fine starting point for the study of party history. It contains articles by numerous scholars on both major and minor parties, together with a wealth of supporting documents. William Nisbet Chambers and Walter Dean Burnham, eds., *The American Party Systems: Stages of Political Development* (New York, 1967), includes ten essays, many of which have had considerable impact upon scholarship. A more recent compilation of articles on political parties and voting behavior is Paul Kleppner et al., *The Evolution of American Electoral Systems* (Westport, Conn., 1981). For the most successful study of party realignments, see Jerome M. Clubb, William H. Flanigan, and Nancy H. Zingale, *Partisan Realignment: Voters, Parties, and Government in American History* (Beverly Hills, Calif., 1980). V. O. Key, Jr., *Politics, Parties, and Pressure Groups*, 5th ed. (New York, 1964), provides a comprehensive analysis by one of the most influential political scientists of the twentieth century. A more recent effort to synthesize both the historical and contemporary nature of American parties is Samuel J. Eldersveld, *Political Parties in American Society* (New York, 1982).

For the beginnings of American politics during an antiparty age, the indispensable starting point is Bernard Bailyn's brief but brilliant analysis of ideology and practice in colonial America, *The Origins of American Politics* (New York, 1968). A more detailed treatment of the principles underlying the hostility to parties in the eighteenth century may be found in Richard Hofstadter, *The Idea of a Party System: The Rise of Legitimate Opposition in the United States, 1780–1840* (Berkeley, Calif., 1969). Robert J. Dinkin, *Voting in Provincial America: A Study of Elections in the Thirteen Colonies, 1689–1776* (Westport, Conn., 1977), describes the nuts and bolts of colonial elections, including the methods employed by nascent factions and parties to work their will on the electorate. The best account of a single colony's politics is Patricia U. Bonomi, *A Factious People: Politics and Society in Colonial New York* (New York, 1971). Finally, for a pathbreaking analysis that is somewhat different from Bailyn's, see Jack P. Greene, "Changing Interpretations of Early American Politics," in Ray Allen Billington, ed., *The Reinterpretation of Early American History: Essays in Honor of John Edwin Pomfret* (San Marino, Calif., 1966).

Patricia U. Bonomi, ed., *Party and Political Opposition in Revolutionary America* (Tarrytown, N.Y., 1980), contains a series of articles charting the ambivalent course of parties between 1763 and 1788. A number of studies of individual states also show the relationship of parties to the Revolution. Among the most interesting are Stephen E. Patterson, *Political Parties in Revolutionary Massachusetts* (Madison, Wis., 1973); and Edward Countryman, *A People in Revolution: The American Revolution and Political Society in New York, 1760–1790* (Baltimore, 1981). Jackson Turner Main, *Political Parties Before the Constitution* (Chapel Hill, N.C., 1973), provides a state-by-state account of party development in the legislature during the 1780s. Hofstadter, *The Idea of a Party System*, explores the Founding Fathers' ideas about political parties.

The best studies of the actual functioning of political parties in the early republic are two volumes by Noble E. Cunningham, Jr.: *The Jeffersonian Republicans: The Formation of Party Organization, 1789–1801* (Chapel Hill, N.C., 1957); and *The Jeffersonian Republicans in Power: Party Operations, 1801–1809* (Chapel Hill, N.C., 1963). For a detailed account of the beginnings of the Republican party in a single state, see Alfred F. Young, *The Democratic Republicans of New York: The Origins, 1763–1797* (Chapel Hill, N.C., 1967). David Hackett

Fischer, *The Revolution of American Conservatism: The Federalist Party in the Era of Jeffersonian Democracy* (New York, 1965), shows that after 1800 a new generation of Federalist leaders emulated the party-building of their Republican opponents. But several articles by Ronald P. Formisano raise important questions about the extent of party development in the young republic: "Deferential-Participant Politics: The Early Republic's Political Culture, 1789–1840," in *American Political Science Review*, 68 (1974); and "Federalists and Republicans: Parties, Yes—System, No," in Kleppner et al., *The Evolution of American Electoral Systems*.

The emergence of modern parties after 1815 has been the subject of considerable scholarly disputation. Richard P. McCormick, *The Second American Party System: Party Formation in the Jacksonian Era* (Chapel Hill, N.C., 1966), emphasizes the role of the successive contests for the presidency between 1824 and 1840. Robert V. Remini, *Martin Van Buren and the Making of the Democratic Party* (New York, 1959), focuses on his subject's pivotal part in putting the Jacksonian coalition together. Very different is Harry L. Watson, *Jacksonian Politics and Community Conflict: The Emergence of the Second American Party System in Cumberland County, North Carolina* (Baton Rouge, La., 1981), which traces the social sources of partisanship. Daniel Walker Howe, *The Political Culture of the American Whigs* (Chicago, 1979), explores that party's ideology through a study of the political ideas of a dozen of its leading members. Joel H. Silbey, *The Shrine of Party: Congressional Voting Behavior, 1841–1852* (Pittsburgh, 1967), demonstrates the strength of partisanship in Congress even as sectional tensions were building.

Michael F. Holt, *The Political Crisis of the 1850s* (New York, 1978), is a brilliant interpretation of the relationship between party politics and the coming of the Civil War. For a comprehensive treatment of the politics of abolitionism and free soil, see Richard H. Sewell, *Ballots for Freedom: Antislavery Politics in the United States, 1837–1860* (New York, 1976). Eric Foner, *Free Soil, Free Labor, Free Men: The Ideology of the Republican Party Before the Civil War* (New York, 1970), analyzes the beliefs that united, and divided, the party of Lincoln. Among the best state-level studies of partisan behavior during the Civil War era is Marc W. Kruman, *Parties and Politics in North Carolina, 1836–1865* (Baton Rouge, La., 1983), which demonstrates the existence of significant political continuity even amidst secession and war. For a seminal essay probing how parties benefited the northern cause, see Eric L. McKitrick, "Party Politics and the Union and Confederate War Efforts," in Chambers and Burnham, eds., *The American Party Systems*.

Paul Kleppner, *The Third Electoral System, 1853–1892: Parties, Voters, and Political Cultures* (Chapel Hill, N.C., 1979), gives a compre-

hensive and sophisticated analysis of party alignments and voting behavior from the Civil War era through the late nineteenth century.
Morton Keller, *Affairs of State: Public Life in Late Nineteenth Century
America* (Cambridge, Mass., 1977), provides an interpretive synthesis
of both politics and government during most of the same long era.
Robert D. Marcus, *Grand Old Party: Political Structure in the Gilded
Age, 1880–1896* (New York, 1971), focuses heavily on the top Republican
leaders but offers, as well, a provocative interpretation of party life in the
1880s and 1890s. Lawrence Goodwyn, *Democratic Promise: The Populist Moment in America* (New York, 1976), is a sympathetic and strongly
argued study of the Populist party.

Much of the seminal work on the transformation of political parties
in the early twentieth century has been done by Walter Dean Burnham
and Samuel P. Hays. Burnham has emphasized that the decline of partisanship contributed to insulating an industrializing elite from mass
pressures; see especially "The Changing Shape of the American Political
Universe," in *American Political Science Review*, 59 (1965); and "The
System of 1896: An Analysis," in Kleppner et al., *The Evolution of
American Electoral Systems*. Hays has stressed that political parties
found it difficult to serve functionally organized groups whose interests
transcended the local community; see "Political Parties and the Community-Society Continuum," in Chambers and Burnham, eds., *The
American Party Systems*. For a state-level study of party politics and
governmental change that builds on Burnham and Hays but also departs
from their interpretations, see Richard L. McCormick, *From Realignment to Reform: Political Change in New York State, 1893–1910* (Ithaca,
N.Y., 1981). The nature and fate of the Socialist party are treated in
David A. Shannon, *The Socialist Party of America: A History* (New
York, 1955). On the Democrats, see David Burner, *The Politics of Pro-
vincialism: The Democratic Party in Transition, 1918–1932* (New York,
1968).

John M. Allswang, *The New Deal and American Politics: A Study in
Political Change* (New York, 1978), provides a splendid overview of the
subject given in its title. Allan J. Lichtman, *Prejudice and the Old
Politics: The Presidential Election of 1928* (Chapel Hill, N.C., 1979), is
based upon a detailed analysis of voting patterns from 1916 to 1940 and
thus delivers a good deal more than its title promises. Like Lichtman,
Kristi Andersen has analyzed the formation of the New Deal coalition,
but her conclusions are somewhat different; see *The Creation of a
Democratic Majority, 1928–1936* (Chicago, 1979). V. O. Key, Jr., *Southern Politics in State and Nation* (New York, 1949), analyzes party politics in the most Democratic region of the United States during the New
Deal era. Bruce M. Stave, *The New Deal and the Last Hurrah: Pitts-*

burgh Machine Politics (Pittsburgh, 1970), offers one of the best accounts of machine politics in an age of big government.

The decline of parties in the contemporary era is a topic of great interest to political scientists and historians. One of those most responsible for bringing the subject to prominence is Walter Dean Burnham, whose essays on the subject may be found in *The Current Crisis of American Politics* (New York, 1982). For a systematic analysis of the transformation of voting patterns since the 1950s, see Norman H. Nie, Sidney Verba, and John R. Petrocik, *The Changing American Voter*, enl. ed. (Cambridge, Mass., 1979). Another important study of contemporary voting patterns is Everett Carll Ladd, Jr., and Charles D. Hadley, *Transformations of the American Party System: Political Coalitions from the New Deal to the 1970s* (New York, 1975). Austin Ranney, *Curing the Mischiefs of Faction: Party Reform in America* (Berkeley, Calif., 1975), scrutinizes the American tradition of reforming the parties, with particular emphasis on the rules changes of recent years. Finally, for a dissent from the view that American party organizations are growing ever weaker, see the final chapter of Eldersveld, *Political Parties in American Society*.

The notions about parties and governance that are central to this article owe a great deal to the insights of Theodore J. Lowi; see especially his article "Party, Policy, and Constitution in America," in Chambers and Burnham, eds., *The American Party Systems*.

5

The Party Period and Public Policy: An Exploratory Hypothesis

When historians in any field simultaneously become uncertain about the relationships among the most important classes of events they study and have fundamental disagreements about periodization, their field may be said to be experiencing a crisis. Such is the condition of American political history. Voting and elections, on the one hand, and government policies, on the other, provide the substance of political history, yet today scholars are wondering how, if at all, these bedrock phenomena affected one another in the American past. Their uncertainty contributes to the second problem, the lack of consensus on a periodizing framework. While the presidential synthesis no longer commands wide support among political historians, they are divided on the leading alternative that has been proposed— the concept of successive party systems separated by periodic critical elections. The two problems are related because without a theory that connects voting and policy, a periodizing scheme based on successive electoral alignments covers, at best, only half the subject matter of political history.

Until twenty years ago, something like a responsible-party-government model implicitly guided most historical study of elections and policymaking. Party leaders were depicted as voicing support for government programs and receiving votes on that basis. Once in office, it was assumed, they tried to enact the promised policies. The presidential synthesis lent support to such an approach by suggesting the correspondence between a president's election and the programs of his administration.

Thomas C. Cochran challenged the presidential synthesis in 1948,[1] but not until the 1960s did scholars question the assumption that party programs linked voters and policies or offer an alternative periodizing formulation. Taking numerous different approaches, researchers within the past two decades have cast doubt on whether policy divisions led to party formation, questioned whether partisan rhetoric on policy matters should be taken at face value, shown that parties were often weak instruments of government decision-making,[2] and suggested that ethnoreligious values shaped voting choices far more than did policy demands.[3] None of this research has proved voting and governance to be unrelated, but all of it makes plain that whatever relations existed were more complex than historians traditionally assumed them to be.[4]

While historians were reexamining the connections between

1. Thomas C. Cochran, "The 'Presidential Synthesis' in American History," *American Historical Review*, LIII (July 1948), 748–59.

2. Richard P. McCormick, *The Second American Party System: Party Formation in the Jacksonian Era* (Chapel Hill, 1966); Lee Benson, *The Concept of Jacksonian Democracy: New York as a Test Case* (Princeton, 1961); Samuel P. Hays, "Political Parties and the Community-Society Continuum," in *The American Party Systems: Stages of Political Development*, ed. William Nisbet Chambers and Walter Dean Burnham (New York, 1967), 152–81; Theodore J. Lowi, "Party, Policy, and Constitution in America," in *ibid.*, 238–76.

3. Benson, *Concept of Jacksonian Democracy;* Paul Kleppner, *The Cross of Culture: A Social Analysis of Midwestern Politics, 1850–1900* (New York, 1970); Richard Jensen, *The Winning of the Midwest: Social and Political Conflict, 1888–1896* (Chicago, 1971); Ronald P. Formisano, *The Birth of Mass Political Parties: Michigan, 1827–1861* (Princeton, 1971); Michael F. Holt, *Forging a Majority: The Formation of the Republican Party in Pittsburgh, 1848–1860* (New Haven, 1969); Samuel T. McSeveney, *The Politics of Depression: Political Behavior in the Northeast, 1893–1896* (New York, 1972); William Gerald Shade, *Banks or No Banks: The Money Issue in Western Politics, 1832–1865* (Detroit, 1972).

4. Richard L. McCormick, "Ethno-Cultural Interpretations of Nineteenth-Century American Voting Behavior," *Political Science Quarterly*, LXXXIX (June 1974), 371–77; Paul Kleppner, *The Third Electoral System, 1853–1892: Parties, Voters, and Political Cultures* (Chapel Hill, 1979), 357–82.

voting and policymaking, a political scientist, Walter Dean Burnham, offered a new formulation for periodizing American political history. He delineated five successive party systems, covering the 1790s to the 1960s, each with its own policy patterns as well as distinctive voting characteristics. While Burnham's formulation plainly rested more heavily on electoral behavior than on policymaking, his work suggested, just as did studies by historians, that the relations between voting and policy were far from simple.[5]

Researchers are currently following two lines of inquiry into the complex connections between elections and policy formation in American history. One approach, based on quantitative studies of electoral and legislative behavior, suggests that political parties appealed to different cultural groups in the electorate and employed distinct governmental means to promote the public welfare.[6] A second tack, being taken by scholars testing Burnham's contention that electoral changes from one party system to the next were accompanied by corresponding policy transformations, has produced studies associating critical elections with new patterns of congressional recruitment, sharper party conflict in Congress, and innovations in national legislative policy.[7]

While these two approaches have yielded useful results, and

5. Walter Dean Burnham, "Party Systems and the Political Process," in *American Party Systems*, ed. Chambers and Burnham, 277–307; Burnham, *Critical Elections and the Mainsprings of American Politics* (New York, 1970).

6. Benson, *Concept of Jacksonian Democracy*, esp. 86–109, provides the starting-point for this literature. Other works include Joel H. Silbey, *The Shrine of Party: Congressional Voting Behavior, 1841–1852* (Pittsburgh, 1967); Thomas B. Alexander, *Sectional Stress and Party Strength: A Study of Roll-Call Voting Patterns in the United States House of Representatives, 1836–1860* (Nashville, 1967); Herbert Ershkowitz and William G. Shade, "Consensus or Conflict? Political Behavior in the State Legislatures during the Jacksonian Era," *Journal of American History*, LVIII (Dec. 1971), 591–621; Shade, *Banks or No Banks*; Peter D. Levine, *The Behavior of State Legislative Parties in the Jacksonian Era: New Jersey, 1829–1844* (Rutherford, N.J., 1977); and Michael F. Holt, *The Political Crisis of the 1850s* (New York, 1978).

7. Walter Dean Burnham, Jerome M. Clubb, and William H. Flanigan, "Partisan Realignment: A Systemic Perspective," in *The History of American Electoral Behavior*, ed. Joel H. Silbey, Allan G. Bogue, and William H. Flanigan (Princeton, 1978), 45–77; Benjamin Ginsberg, "Critical Elections and the Sub-

will continue to do so, it seems important to find a broader way of dealing with the historic connections between voting and policymaking.[8] Several large and growing bodies of scholarship facilitate such a perspective. First are the recent voting studies—quantitative, theoretical, and, even to their critics, immensely exciting. Second is an older, but still vital, literature on economic policymaking that has yet to be integrated with the new accounts of electoral behavior. Finally, there are the burgeoning community studies by social historians with much to say about the perceptions of Americans, including their expectations for politics and government. Taken together with certain key concepts from political science, these works suggest that for most of the nineteenth century there was a complementary relationship between voting and one major category of government decisions, economic policies.

Indeed, the decades from the 1830s to the early 1900s form a distinctive era in American political history, with patterns of party politics, electoral behavior, and economic policy that set it apart from the eras that came before and after. Covering the second and third party systems, in addition to some of the fourth, this was the period when parties dominated political participation and channeled the flow of government policies. Even as the

stance of Party Conflict: 1844–1968," *Midwest Journal of Political Science,* XVI (Nov. 1972), 603–25; Benjamin Ginsberg, "Elections and Public Policy," *American Political Science Review,* LXX (March, 1976), 41–49; Michael R. King and Lester G. Seligman, "Critical Elections, Congressional Recruitment and Public Policy," in *Elite Recruitment in Democratic Polities: Comparative Studies across Nations,* ed. Heinz Eulau and Moshe M. Czudnowski (New York, 1976), 263–99; Jerome M. Clubb and Santa A. Traugott, "Partisan Cleavage and Cohesion in the House of Representatives, 1861–1974," *Journal of Interdisciplinary History,* VII (Winter 1977), 375–401.

8. One attempt to take a broad view of the voting-policy connection is Robert Kelley, "Ideology and Political Culture from Jefferson to Nixon," *American Historical Review,* LXXXII (June 1977), 531–62. For an essay that suggests a new periodization of the history of electoral behavior, see Lee Benson, Joel H. Silbey, and Phyllis F. Field, "Toward a Theory of Stability and Change in American Voting Patterns: New York State, 1790–1970," in *History of American Electoral Behavior,* ed. Silbey, Bogue, and Flanigan, 78–105.

nation grew in size and numbers, fought the Civil War, and industrialized, parties continued to perform these functions and retained their dominance. They did so because they admirably filled two roles: as objects of vital attachments grounded in the people's cultural backgrounds and as vehicles for managing the limited sort of economic policies that nineteenth-century conditions called forth. From the age of Andrew Jackson to that of Theodore Roosevelt, the parties' fulfillment of these roles gave American politics its distinctive character. An understanding of how the parties performed and why their efforts broke down after 1900 provides a new perspective on the voting-policy connection and the related problem of periodization.

From the 1830s until the early 1900s parties shaped campaigns and elections into popular spectacles featuring widespread participation and celebration. Three-quarters of the nation's adult male citizens voted in presidential elections and nearly two-thirds also participated in off-year contests. Most of them cast straight tickets conveniently supplied by the party organizations. While illicit voting may have swelled the electoral totals and fraudulent counting likely reduced the recorded levels of split ballots, it is probable that the great majority of adult males voted honestly, enthusiastically, and partisanly.[9]

In an age when sources of information and diversion were limited, parties and elections provided crucial forms of education and entertainment. Newspapers were almost uniformly partisan and heavily political in their content. Party speakers were often

---

9. Richard P. McCormick, "New Perspectives on Jacksonian Politics," *American Historical Review*, LXV (Jan. 1960), 288–301; and Ronald P. Formisano, "Deferential-Participant Politics: The Early Republic's Political Culture, 1789–1840," *American Political Science Review*, LXVIII (June 1974), 473–87, discuss the rise of electoral participation at the beginning of the era. Walter Dean Burnham, "The Changing Shape of the American Political Universe," *American Political Science Review*, LIX (March 1965), 7–28, describes the decline in voter turnout after 1900. There is no reason to suppose that fraudulent electoral techniques always inflated recorded turnout rates; some illicit practices kept voters from the polls.

centers of attraction at community gatherings such as fairs and market days. At least once a year, election campaigns offered drama and aroused emotions. Attending primaries and conventions, joining in parades and rallies, hearing speeches, waiting for the returns, and celebrating victories—all provided enjoyment and social satisfaction as well as a feeling of political participation.[10]

Recent studies show that voting alignments commonly followed ethnoreligious lines and suggest that citizens found parties effective vehicles for the values they learned in their homes and churches. Though they did not always abide by their ideologies, the parties voiced distinctive beliefs and exhibited characteristic styles which citizens recognized and with which they identified. Casting a ballot expressed group solidarity and affirmed the shared values of one's community. Partisan loyalties typically passed from father to son, just as religion did. Partly as a result, towns, counties, and states displayed considerable electoral stability from year to year and decade to decade.[11]

For two-thirds of a century, through political cataclysms of the first magnitude, electoral behavior followed these patterns far more often than not, in far more places than not. When voter turnout dropped, it usually rose again before long; when party loyalties faded, they soon were restored or replaced by new ones; when politicians failed to voice values the people cared for, leaders who did soon replaced them. The persistence of these patterns suggests the validity of designating the era as the "party period" of American political history, when voting was more partisan and more widespread than ever before or since.

Electoral alignments were, however, far from static during the

10. Besides the works cited in note 3, see Robert Gary Gunderson, *The Log Cabin Campaign* (Lexington, 1957); and Robert D. Marcus, *Grand Old Party: Political Structure in the Gilded Age, 1880–1896* (New York, 1971).

11. To date, historians have found the ethnoreligious interpretation mainly applicable outside the South. Even the South, however, shared the other electoral characteristics noted here, including high participation, long-term stability, and voting choices grounded in community values.

party period. Twice during the era—in the 1850s and 1890s—a combination of new electors, abstainers, and voters shifting from one party to another, created fresh coalitional patterns. As a result of the upheaval of the 1850s, the major parties became more sectionally polarized and, in the North, more strongly divided along religious lines than they had been in the Jackson period. In the lower South, interparty politics broke down for a period of time.[12] But it would be misleading to exaggerate the disruption in the party period's electoral style caused by either the realignment of the 1850s or the Civil War. Several recent studies, especially Joel Silbey's volume on the Democratic party, have stressed the electoral continuity of the Civil War era and the war's effect in strengthening preexisting voting patterns. The issues and appeals, the structure of the vote, and the meaning and importance of political participation were surprisingly unaltered by war and continued into the Gilded Age.[13] Even when fewer places had close interparty competition, electoral turnout remained as high as it had been in the 1840s. The basic structure of party organizations persisted, as did their techniques for mobilizing the voters.[14] In the 1890s, coalitional lines were once again redrawn, and the parties' sectional polarization was further enhanced. In time, that polarity would help diminish electoral turnout. But for almost a decade after the realignment of the 1890s, except in the South, the fundamental behavior of a highly mobilized, partisan electorate persisted.[15]

Throughout the party period, while these characteristic forms

12. Holt, *Forging a Majority*; Formisano, *Birth of Mass Political Parties*. On the breakdown of party politics in the lower South, see Holt, *Political Crisis*, 219–59.

13. Joel H. Silbey, *A Respectable Minority: The Democratic Party in the Civil War Era, 1860–1868* (New York, 1977); Jean H. Baker, *The Politics of Continuity: Maryland Political Parties from 1858 to 1870* (Baltimore, 1973).

14. Burnham, "Changing Shape"; Marcus, *Grand Old Party*; J. Morgan Kousser, *The Shaping of Southern Politics: Suffrage Restriction and the Establishment of the One-Party South, 1880–1910* (New Haven, 1974), 11–44.

15. Kleppner, *Cross of Culture*; Jensen, *Winning of the Midwest*; McSeveney, *Politics of Depression*; Kousser, *Shaping of Southern Politics*.

of voting continued, economic policymaking manifested distinctive patterns of its own. The government's most pervasive role was that of promoting development by distributing resources and privileges to individuals and groups. An understanding of distributive policies and their centrality in nineteenth-century politics helps establish the complementary relationship between electoral behavior and government decision-making.[16]

The riches that governments bestowed were various indeed. Land formed one such resource, and for almost the whole of the century federal and state officials allocated and sold it. Charters and franchises for banking, transportation, and manufacturing likewise were given away, especially by the states. Special privileges and immunities also came from government: for example, tax exemptions, the right of eminent domain, the privilege of charging tolls on roads and bridges, and the right to dam or channel streams and rivers. Public bounties occasionally encouraged privileged private enterprises, just as government investments sometimes funded mixed corporations. The federal government's tariff also represented a kind of public gift to the individuals and corporations whose products received protection. Public authorities at every level distributed aid by constructing or subsidizing highways, canals, railways, bridges, and harbors.[17]

16. The concept of distributive policies employed here is based on Theodore J. Lowi's seminal typology of policy outputs. See Theodore J. Lowi, "American Business, Public Policy, Case-Studies, and Political Theory," *World Politics*, XVI (July 1964), 677–715.

17. James Willard Hurst, *Law and the Conditions of Freedom in the Nineteenth-Century United States* (Madison, 1956); Carter Goodrich, *Government Promotion of American Canals and Railroads, 1800–1890* (New York, 1960); Louis Hartz, *Economic Policy and Democratic Thought: Pennsylvania, 1776–1860* (Cambridge, 1948); Oscar Handlin and Mary Flug Handlin, *Commonwealth: A Study of the Role of Government in the American Economy: Massachusetts, 1774–1861* (New York 1947); Milton Sydney Heath, *Constructive Liberalism: The Role of the State in Economic Development in Georgia to 1860* (Cambridge, 1954); James Neal Primm, *Economic Policy in the Development of a Western State: Missouri, 1820–1860* (Cambridge, 1954); Harry N. Scheiber, *Ohio Canal Era: A Case Study of Government and the Economy, 1820–1861* (Athens, Ohio, 1969); Morton Keller, *Affairs of State: Public Life in Late Nineteenth*

Forever giving things away, governments were laggard in regulating the economic activities they subsidized. At the federal level the Congress bestowed vast land grants on the transcontinental railroad companies but virtually ignored the rules it established for them. In the states, where regulation was considered a basic function of government, the forms it took often bespoke developmental purposes rather than restrictive ones. Corporation charters commonly specified operating procedures, the quality of service, and maximum rates. General laws, too, frequently regulated banks, insurance companies, transportation corporations, and other public utilities. But through weak laws and weaker enforcement, the results of regulation usually proved meager.[18]

Administration, too, was difficult to accomplish for nineteenth-century governments. According to Leonard White, federal administrative practices remained as rudimentary at the end of the century as in the 1830s. Historians of state politics have similarly observed the limits of administration, including the

---

Century America (Cambridge, 1977). Robert A. Lively, "The American System: A Review Article," *Business History Review*, XXIX (1955), 81–96, provides a review of the books by Hartz, the Handlins, Heath, and Primm, and argues that American governments maintained their promotional policies throughout the nineteenth century. For two recent assessments of this literature, see Harry N. Scheiber, "Government and the Economy: Studies of the 'Commonwealth' Policy in Nineteenth-Century America," *Journal of Interdisciplinary History*, III (Summer 1972), 135–51; and Harry N. Scheiber, "Federalism and the American Economic Order, 1789–1910," *Law and Society Review*, X (Fall 1975), 57–118.

18. Wallace D. Farnham, " 'The Weakened Spring of Government': A Study in Nineteenth-Century American History," *American Historical Review*, LXVIII (April 1963), 662–80; Hartz, *Economic Policy and Democratic Thought*, 96–103, 148–60, 204–7, 262–67, 292–95; Heath, *Constructive Liberalism*, 357–67; Keller, *Affairs of State*, 171–81, 409–38; Scheiber, "Federalism," 100, 104–5; Carter Goodrich, "American Development Policy: The Case of Internal Improvements," *Journal of Economic History*, XVI (Dec. 1956), 457–58; Lee Benson, *Merchants, Farmers & Railroads: Railroad Regulation and New York Politics, 1850–1887* (Cambridge, 1955), 1–9; Jeremy P. Felt, *Hostages of Fortune: Child Labor Reform in New York State* (Syracuse, 1965), 17–37; Allan G. Bogue, "To Shape a Western State: Some Dimensions of the Kansas Search for Capital, 1865–1893," in *The Frontier Challenge: Responses to the Trans-Mississippi West*, ed. John G. Clark (Lawrence, Kansas, 1971), 203–4.

states' unwillingness to rely on independent commissions for policy formation, fact finding, and day-to-day regulation.[19]

A paucity of planning also characterized government in the party period. According to Willard Hurst, "We often made policy piecemeal and in disconnected efforts and areas, where a more rational practicality would have told us to link our efforts, fill in gaps, and move on a broad front." Even states that experimented with economic planning, as some did, particularly in the area of transportation, saw their efforts ultimately fall victim to interest-group conflicts and localistic rivalries. "Policy" was little more than the accumulation of isolated, individual choices, usually of a distributive nature.[20]

It seems pointless and present-minded to blame nineteenth-century authorities for these "failures." From everything we know, the American people got roughly the economic policies they wanted. Given a choice between governmental promotion and restraint, they clearly preferred the former. Except for the abolition of slavery, the distribution of economic benefits proba-bly represents the outstanding achievement of nineteenth-cen-

19. Leonard D. White, *The Jacksonians: A Study in Administrative History, 1829–1861* (New York, 1956); Leonard D. White, *The Republican Era: A Study in Administrative History, 1869–1901* (New York, 1958); Scheiber, "Government and the Economy"; Gerald D. Nash, *State Government and Economic Development: A History of Administrative Policies in California, 1849–1933* (Berkeley, 1964); Seymour J. Mandelbaum, *Boss Tweed's New York* (New York, 1965), 155–68; Hartz, *Economic Policy and Democratic Thought*, 148–60; Keller, *Affairs of State*, 98–108, 307–18.

20. James Willard Hurst, "Legal Elements in United States History," *Perspectives in American History*, V (1971), 63; James Willard Hurst, *Law and Social Process in United States History* (Ann Arbor, 1960), 28, 63–69, 104, 120–25; Hurst, *Law and the Conditions of Freedom*, 33–70; Harry N. Scheiber, "At the Border-land of Law and Economic History: The Contributions of Willard Hurst," *American Historical Review*, LXXV (Feb. 1970), 744–56; Harry N. Scheiber, "Urban Rivalry and Internal Improvements in the Old Northwest, 1820–1860," *Ohio History*, LXXI (Oct. 1962), 227–39; Scheiber, "Federalism," 65–67, 92; Scheiber, "Government and the Economy," 143–47. For a related analysis of the absence of planning in social policymaking, see Gerald N. Grob, "The Political System and Social Policy in the Nineteenth Century: Legacy of the Revolution," *Mid-America*, LVIII (Jan. 1976), 5–19.

tury American government. Certainly it formed the most characteristic achievement.

Distributive decisions may have been roughly what the American people wanted, but the details of such policies perpetually fueled conflict. For one thing, there were never enough of the choicest resources and privileges to go around. Competition for the best land, the most lucrative charters, and the finest transportation facilities inspired battles at every level of government. Inevitably, those who lost called into question the legitimacy of bestowing special privileges on some and depriving others. From the 1830s forward, politics reverberated with the Jacksonian complaint that virtually everything the government did helped only the few. That accusation in turn aroused the historic American distrust of public power and brought forth recurring efforts to preserve liberty by scaling down governmental authority.[21]

For most of the century, however, countervailing circumstances dampened conflict and distrust sufficiently to permit the continuance of a policy structure based on distribution. Land and natural resources remained abundant, while new communities offering charters and privileges to entrepreneurs continually opened up. These favorable circumstances, deriving from the extent and richness of the national domain and from the ongoing spread of population, mitigated scarcity or at least disguised it.

A second set of encouraging circumstances lay in the policy process itself and in the inherent qualities of distributive goods. At every governmental level, the dominant legislative branch threw open its doors to special, local interests demanding assistance and decrying restraints. The very nature of the benefits they

21. Several recent studies of nineteenth-century politics point to the centrality of the urge to secure liberty against governmental authority: J. Mills Thornton III, *Politics and Power in a Slave Society: Alabama, 1800–1860* (Baton Rouge, 1978); Holt, *Political Crisis;* and Lloyd Ray Gunn, "The Decline of Authority: Public Policy in New York, 1837–1860" (Ph.D. Diss., Rutgers University, 1975). For the background of these beliefs, see Bernard Bailyn, *The Ideological Origins of the American Revolution* (Cambridge, 1967); and Gordon Wood, *The Creation of the American Republic, 1776–1787* (Chapel Hill, 1969).

sought facilitated legislative acquiescence. While public revenues were limited, and heavily taxed citizens sometimes insisted on the reduction of spending, some distributive policies conveniently generated the revenue to support others. Land sales did this at every level of government, just as tariff protection did at the federal level. Of equal importance, distributive policies were highly divisible. Voting tariff protection for one commodity did not preclude protecting others; aiding one canal company was no bar to helping a second and a third. As Harry N. Scheiber puts it, "repeated trips to the public trough are possible, both for those who come away empty-handed and for those already well fed. If interests X and Y have already been well served—say, by grants of land to aid railroad projects, or by grants of a franchise to build a log boom or a millrace dam—similar gifts can be devolved upon Z the next year."[22]

A crucial transformation in the form of distributive policies provided a third force for sustaining a policy structure based on such outputs. Occurring from the 1830s through the 1860s, the shift involved making benefits available to everyone who met certain requirements rather than to favored recipients only. At the state level, free banking and general incorporation laws embodied the new approach, as did the related shift from special to general legislation in other fields. At the federal level, the Homestead Act and National Banking Act similarly embraced the principle of allowing all who qualified to avail themselves of benefits.[23]

Finally, distribution was facilitated by an ideological counterweight to the dread of government authority. As a general prin-

22. On the legislative process, see Hurst, "Legal Elements"; Hurst, *Law and Social Process*; Hurst, *Law and the Conditions of Freedom*; White, *Republican Era*; White, *Jacksonians*; Farnham, "'Weakened Spring of Government'"; and Keller, *Affairs of State*. On the divisibility of distributive goods, see Scheiber, "Federalism," 89; and Lowi, "American Business," 690–95.
23. Benson, *Concept of Jacksonian Democracy*, 89–104; Handlin and Handlin, *Commonwealth*; Shade, *Banks or No Banks*; L. Ray Gunn, "Political Implications of General Incorporation Laws in New York to 1860," *Mid-America*, LIX (Oct. 1977), 171–91.

ciple, nineteenth-century citizens accepted public assistance to industry; they possessed only an imprecise conception of the distinction between what was public and what was private. Robert Lively remarks how regularly "official vision and public resources" were "associated . . . with private skill and individual desire." That association was possible, according to Carter Goodrich, because "Americans did not feel themselves bound by any permanent and unalterable demarcation of the spheres of state action and private enterprise." Thus an ideology permitting the spread of government aid, in combination with other favorable circumstances, encouraged distributive policies to thrive, despite the conflicts they continually inspired.[24]

The same party organizations that mobilized citizens on election day also structured their receipt of government goods. The divisibility and abundance of distributive benefits, the general acceptance of their legitimacy, and the diversity of forms in which distributive matters could be debated and decided all made them excellent grist for partisan mills. The policy equivalent of patronage, distribution strengthened the parties and helped build bridges between their voters, leaders, and representatives in office.[25]

Party leaders took various approaches to managing distribution. Especially in the Jackson period, public promotion of economic development ideologically divided the two major parties. Acting on a vision of social harmony, Whig leaders claimed that subsidies for some meant economic growth for all. Perceiving divisions instead of harmony, Democratic leaders denied the assumption about shared benefits and frequently opposed dis-

24. Lively, "American System," 94; Carter Goodrich, "The Revulsion against Internal Improvements," *Journal of Economic History*, X (Nov. 1950), 169; Michael H. Frisch, *Town into City: Springfield, Massachusetts, and the Meaning of Community, 1840–1880* (Cambridge, 1972).

25. Theodore Lowi's insights concerning parties and distributive policies have influenced the paragraphs that follow. See Lowi, "Party, Policy, and Constitution," 273–74. On the tripartite structure of parties, see Frank J. Sorauf, "Political Parties and Political Analysis," in *American Party Systems*, ed. Chambers and Burnham, 37–39.

tributive policies. Through such appeals, often voiced together
with ethnoreligious keywords, the leaders of both parties transformed the debate over distribution into an ideological conflict
that aroused their members and mobilized them to vote.[26]

While the evidence is not yet all in, the ideological debate over
promoting private enterprise, which marked one phase of the
second party system, seems to have formed a special case in the
parties' management of distributive issues. By the late 1840s and
early 1850s, the Democrats were succumbing to the lure of public promotional ventures, particularly railroads, and thereafter
distribution ceased to divide the parties so starkly. Especially at
the state and local levels, Democrats as well as Whigs and Republicans granted charters, aided transportation companies, and
sought tariff protection for local industries. To have abjured
would have been as remarkable as to have declined to appoint
men to office. While both parties thus took up the "Whig"
approach to economic policy, both voiced the "Democratic"
complaint against special privilege. Just as neither party could
resist constituent demands for public benefits, neither could ignore the long-standing distrust of active government. Undeni-
ably, there remained a tendency for those with the most expansive
conceptions of public policy to group in opposition to the Democrats, and for those with the most limited notions of government to support the party of Jackson. Especially at the national
level, and particularly in connection with the tariff and currency
issues, ideology remained a feature of nineteenth-century politics. Nonetheless, the key to party management of distribution
usually lay not in its ideological potential but in its infinite
variety and divisibility.[27]

26. Benson, *Concept of Jacksonian Democracy,* 86–109, 216–53; Silbey, *Shrine
of Party;* Alexander, *Sectional Stress;* Ershkowitz and Shade, "Consensus or Conflict?"; Shade, *Banks or No Banks;* Holt, *Political Crisis,* 17–38; James Roger
Sharp, *The Jacksonians versus the Banks: Politics in the States after the Panic of
1837* (New York, 1970).
27. For discussion of the blurring of party principles in the 1850s and the
Democrats' adoption of policies promoting economic development, see Holt,
Political Crisis, 101–38. Even in the 1830s and 1840s, Herbert Ershkowitz and

With policy recipients organized geographically like the parties themselves, log-rolling legislators fashioned awesome combinations of benefits that won widespread support. From the 1830s on, such schemes were common. In Illinois in 1837, the Whig majority crafted a package of internal improvements that satisfied a large constituency. In North Carolina in 1855, the Democratic legislature assisted the residents of a majority of the state's counties by voting money for three large railroads, smaller lines, plank roads, and river improvements. In New York in the 1890s, the Republican legislature combined improvements on the Erie Canal with state aid for macadam roads in non-canal counties. While such projects often received bipartisan support and rarely drew strict party lines, the party organizations usually provided the means of channeling demands and deciding on the successful policies. With so much similarity between managing a party coalition and devising a socially acceptable package of benefits, parties and distributive policies fit one another well.[28]

Divisible as they were, distributive benefits were not unlimited. Tremendous tensions sometimes built up within the parties, as

---

William G. Shade find that on internal improvements questions (which the authors call "the chief preoccupation of the period") Democratic and Whig legislators alike usually voted the interests of their local districts and that most charters for business corporations were granted unanimously by the state legislatures. Ershkowitz and Shade, "Consensus or Conflict?" Levine, *Behavior of State Legislative Parties,* also finds evidence of the promotional impulse in both parties, as does Formisano, *Birth of Mass Political Parties,* 109–10. See also Marvin Meyers's brilliant essay, "The Judges and the Judged: A View of Economic Purposes," *The Jacksonian Persuasion: Politics and Belief* (Stanford, 1957), 92–107. To date, state legislation in the Gilded Age has not received nearly the attention paid to it in the Jackson period. One excellent study of the subject finds that national ideologies were irrelevant to economic policymaking in Colorado; James Edward Wright, *The Politics of Populism: Dissent in Colorado* (New Haven, 1974), 85–102.

28. Benjamin P. Thomas, *Abraham Lincoln: A Biography* (New York, 1953), 55–62; Marc Wayne Kruman, "Parties and Politics in North Carolina, 1846–1865" (Ph.D. diss., Yale University, 1978), 104–7; Richard L. McCormick, "Shaping Republican Strategy: Political Change in New York State, 1893–1910" (Ph.D. diss., Yale University, 1976), 320–27. On the role of parties in channeling distributive measures, see Lowi, "Party, Policy, and Constitution," 273–74; and Levine, *Behavior of State Legislative Parties,* 106, 126, 191, 230.

well as between them, over who would get what. But because the claimants were usually small, geographically based groups, rather than broad occupational, sectional, or cultural classes, distributive measures did not delineate irrevocable social divisions. Almost everyone basically wanted the same thing: his own share (or more) at the least possible cost to himself. In this respect, distributive issues were relatively safe ones for party leaders to take up. Unlike regulatory questions, sectional issues, or cultural matters, distributive decisions seldom threatened consensus or risked unmanageable divisions in the party coalitions.

Although distributive policies predated the 1830s and continued beyond the early 1900s, the manner in which they came to be decided and the dominance they achieved in that period mark it as a distinctive era in public policymaking, just as it formed an identifiable era of electoral behavior. Before the 1830s, distribution was based on the Federalist conception of government aid to an economic elite. The events of that decade, including the Bank war and depression, effectively killed the old approach and replaced it with a more democratic one. As Lee Benson has shown in his study of New York, both parties broke "irrevocably" with Federalist policies and "adopted programs whose *stated objectives* were to democratize American enterprise."[29] Even when Jacksonian rhetoric wore thin, the essential character of economic policy discussions begun in the 1830s persisted. The attack on special privilege and the inauguration of the movement toward the more general form of distribution began an era of economic policymaking that lasted until the first years of the twentieth century.

While distributive policies were characteristic of the party peı.od, that long era was far from monolithic in its economic policies. In both the states and the nation, the amounts and types of government aid changed over time. Sometimes the passage of power from one party to the other precipitated policy transformations. At the beginning of the era, Jackson's administration

29. Benson, *Concept of Jacksonian Democracy*, 105.

cut back numerous federal ventures which the Republicans revived a generation later. Economic conditions also caused changes in the level of distribution. In general, prosperity encouraged contentment with distributive policies and brought on demands for more, while hard times led to dissatisfaction and cries for retrenchment. At the state and local levels, the effects of the economic cycle may be observed most clearly. There, throughout the century, authorities alternately extended and withdrew aid to private enterprises.[30]

Over the long run, governmental undertakings significantly expanded. The growth and diversification of the population alone assured higher levels and new forms of aid. The Civil War also brought about an enlargement of governmental activity. While, as Morton Keller has shown, localism, cultural diversity, and economic conflicts later forced retreats from the most advanced wartime projects, public activity and expenditures never returned to their prewar levels. The postwar decades saw a continuing debate about the scope of public duties and a steady rise of pressures to assume new ones.[31]

Amidst these cyclical and long-term changes in policy, distribution continued to form the government's basic economic activity. Not until early in the twentieth century did social and economic developments permanently enlarge governmental responsibilities by strengthening both regulation and administration. The new policies, when they came, coincided with the decline of partisan voting. Together the two developments marked the end of an era when parties shaped the political

30. For the antebellum era, the ebb and flow of state aid to private enterprises may be traced in the studies cited in note 17. For the postwar era, see Keller, *Affairs of State.*

31. Keller, *Affairs of State,* 85–121. On the increase in expenditures that accompanied the Civil War, see Paul B. Trescott, "Federal Government Receipts and Expenditures, 1861–1875," *Journal of Economic History,* XXVI (June 1966), 206–22; and Lance E. Davis and John Legler, "The Government in the American Economy, 1815–1902: A Quantitative Study," *Journal of Economic History,* XXVI (Dec. 1966), 514–52.

participation of the great majority of male citizens and managed economic policies of the single type they universally expected.

The chronological correspondence of massive, partisan voting and distributive policymaking suggests a significant relationship between electoral behavior and governance in the nineteenth century. The parties' central role in managing both strengthens the suggestion. It remains to be worked out, however, just what the connection was and what shaped it. Admittedly, such an analysis must be somewhat speculative, for the question has not previously received the attention it merits from historians. Moreover, because the relationship between voting and policymaking was less direct than might be anticipated, it must be defined with appropriate qualifications.

Some, but not all, of the evidence points to responsible party government. Especially at the state and local levels, and particularly in the short run, policymakers were extremely responsive to the voters. Legislators, as we have seen, readily acquiesced in constituent demands for government assistance or, when times were hard, for retrenchment. Out of a desire to be reelected to office, public authorities in both parties behaved in this manner. Such a responsive policy process was not confined to the economic matters treated here. When sectional or cultural questions were at stake, leaders championed their constituents' values and sought to preserve them through government action. On all these subjects, voters evidently paid attention to what the authorities did and were capable of casting their ballots accordingly.[32]

Because they molded both voting and policymaking, the political parties formed the linkage between the two processes. In

32. Two case-studies illustrating the responsiveness of legislatures and voters to one another on cultural issues are Roger E. Wyman, "Wisconsin Ethnic Groups and the Election of 1890," *Wisconsin Magazine of History*, LI (Summer 1968), 269–93; and Ballard C. Campbell, "Did Democracy Work? Prohibition in Late Nineteenth-Century Iowa: A Test Case," *Journal of Interdisciplinary History*, VIII (Summer 1977), 87–116.

ways already suggested, the management of distributive policies strengthened the parties as electoral machines and enhanced participation. Distribution, by affording relatively safe issues at every level of government, enabled parties to satisfy disparate constituencies through the allocation of aid. It is not necessary to believe that material benefits formed the people's highest political priority or that economic issues determined partisan alignments in order to conclude that the parties' management of the particular sort of economic policies citizens expected helps explain the devotion and participation the parties inspired.

Correspondingly, the parties' virtuosity as electoral organizations strengthened their policy roles and influenced government decision-making. In close contact with the people, the party leaders who got out the vote also learned what the citizens wanted. Successful in electing candidates to office, the party organizations placed men in positions to procure the desired benefits. Party voters were confident in the men elected and gave officials relative freedom to determine the details of policy outcomes. It is not necessary to assume a complete identity of interests between party voters, party organizers, and party legislators to see that these connections—all deriving from the parties' electoral strength—helped shape the final form of public policy.

The parties' two roles interacted in other ways. To attract and maintain a broad constituency, party leaders encouraged distribution, which was widely accepted, and forestalled regulation and administration, which were far more divisive.[33] Electoral politics thus influenced the details of economic policy, through the agency of party. The reverse was also true. A party's role in managing distributive outputs affected its electoral performance by setting limits on how it fashioned its appeals and to whom they were directed. If a party's congressmen voted against tariff protection on a certain product or party legislators approved

33. For studies showing the reluctance to enact and enforce regulatory measures, see Felt, *Hostages of Fortune*, 17–37; and Benson, *Merchants, Farmers, & Railroads*, 141–73.

aid for one of several competing railroad lines, the local party organization could not very well make fresh inroads among producers of the unlucky commodity or in towns bypassed by the chosen railroad. Policymaking thus made its mark on the details of electoral behavior.

What all this suggests is that at the level of party politics, the interactions between voting and policymaking were numerous and complex. Because the parties structured both processes, the different needs of party voters, party organizers, and party office-holders caused elections and policy to influence one another in ways that may always defy complete historical analysis.

While they intensely affected one another, however, voting and policymaking were sufficiently independent to cast doubt on the responsible-party-government model. Nineteenth-century voting choices reflected long-term commitments, grounded in cultural, communal, and geographic factors. Although they sometimes fluctuated in accord with policy demands, those loyalties were largely determined by factors outside the process of governance. By the same token, policy patterns transcended elections. While a new administration might reverse some of its predecessor's deci-sions, the fundamental continuities in nineteenth-century eco-nomic policymaking suggest that more was at work in shaping government action than elections alone.

The responsible-party-government model is also flawed by its basis in the assumption that people voted because they wanted the government to do things. Actually, nineteenth-century citi-zens were profoundly ambivalent about public authority. Expect-ing the government's assistance for their enterprises, they also distrusted its actions and continually sought to assure its subser-vience to the electorate. In the Jackson period, the same state constitutional coventions that reduced legislative authority also extended popular control over the choice of government offi-cials.[34] Far from a means to secure expansive policy programs,

34. James Schouler, *Constitutional Studies, State and Federal* (New York, 1897), 253–66; Bayrd Still, "An Interpretation of the Statehood Process, 1800–1850," *Mississippi Valley Historical Review*, XXIII (Sept. 1936), 189–204; Gunn, "Decline of Authority," chap. 5.

the spread of electoral participation thus helped assure the extension of restrictions on government action. Far from contradictory, both developments bespoke the long-standing aim of securing liberty against authority.

The relationship between curtailing public power to act and enlarging popular participation is difficult to understand only if we assume that people vote chiefly to get tangible goods from government. But their participation may have other purposes entirely, and it may be more intimately related to confidence in weak government than to gratification by strong and active public authorities.

Indeed, for voters who distrusted power, specific benefits from government often proved less important than general satisfaction with the process of governance. Some policies had symbolic meanings that provided psychic benefits when the actual results were inconsequential, impossible to trace, or contrary to the policy's declared purpose. The Bank veto, the Homestead Act, and the Sherman Antitrust Act all had such symbolic value. Many nineteenth-century citizens presumably found satisfaction in the basic methods of government as well as in the general patterns of public policy. Taken together, such satisfactions produced what David Easton calls "diffuse support" for the political system. Independent of particular policies, such support encouraged political participation by citizens no matter what specific programs the officials enacted.[35]

These considerations all imply that, however much voting and policymaking interacted in the short run, neither was fundamentally determined by the other. This is precisely the conclusion suggested by recent political science studies showing that socioeconomic factors are better than purely political factors in ex-

35. David Easton, *A Systems Analysis of Political Life* (New York, 1965); Murray Edelman, *The Symbolic Uses of Politics* (Urbana, Ill., 1964); John C. Wahlke, "Policy Demands and System Support: The Role of the Represented," *British Journal of Political Science,* I (July 1971), 271–90. Two historians have treated the ways in which party speakers gave culturally symbolic meanings to economic issues. On the banking question, see Shade, *Banks or No Banks;* on the tariff, see Kleppner, *Cross of Culture,* 155–56.

plaining contemporary policy outcomes. Using expenditure levels as policy indicators, comparative state analyses have demonstrated that such variables as wealth, education, industrialization, and urbanization statistically account for more policy variance than do such political variables as participation, competitiveness, and election type. Limited in some respects, these studies nonetheless offer a suggestive insight for analyzing nineteenth-century electoral behavior and policy formation: both processes were fundamentally shaped not by one another but jointly by factors beyond politics.[36]

According to such a hypothesis, voting and policy interacted only within limits set by the socioeconomic environment. Empirical evidence for this theory lies beyond the scope of the present essay, but crucial support is provided by studies—especially those of individual communities—exploring the conditions and perceptions of nineteenth-century Americans. These works suggest how social circumstances led to widespread political participation and to an economic policy structure based on distribution. Political factors, operating through the parties, helped shape the precise forms these processes took, but the fundamentals of voting and policy were products of a common environment, not of one another.

Historians have already done much to explain how the people's social and cultural conditions led to high degrees of party loyalty and electoral participation. Varied and fragmented as a nation, urban as well as rural Americans lived in "island communities," each closely knit by bonds of culture and history. Through a diversity of organizations and activities, they discov-

---

36. Richard I. Hofferbert, "State and Community Policy Studies: A Review of Comparative Input-Output Analyses," *Political Science Annual*, III (1972), 3–72, summarizes the state of this literature as it existed in the early 1970s. For historical applications of this approach, see Richard E. Dawson, "Social Development, Party Competition, and Policy," in *American Party Systems*, ed. Chambers and Burnham, 203–37; and J. Rogers Hollingsworth, "The Impact of Electoral Behavior on Public Policy: The Urban Dimension, 1900," in *History of American Electoral Behavior*, ed. Silbey, Bogue, and Flanigan, 346–71.

ered their group's identity and expressed its distinctive beliefs. Political parties filled these purposes well, while campaigns and elections offered the means to show commitment to the community and its values. These forms of behavior are understandable without assuming they were mainly directed to determining government action.[37]

Correspondingly, policy formation originated independently of electoral behavior, in the conditions and aspirations of the American people. The economic circumstances underlying distribution are well known. A developing economy, where entrepreneurial opportunity primarily befell individuals and small groups, called for governmental assistance without excessive restraints. With land and capital heavily in the control of public authorities, and with no abstract theory holding Americans back from demanding aid, government policies spreading the resources naturally found support.[38]

Community studies disclose how often mercantile elites succeeded in persuading their towns to pave streets, subsidize railroads, and build public docks. These studies also suggest why such policies proved so widely acceptable. Part of the answer lies in the capacity of promoters to convince others that the desired benefits would advance the town's general prosperity. Pointing to the fundamental harmony of the producing classes, entrepreneurs argued that what helped one group helped all. With upward (and downward) social mobility sufficient to suggest that class lines were neither impassable nor permanent, the promise

37. One of the best accounts of the rise of political participation in the context of community development is Kathleen Neils Conzen, *Immigrant Milwaukee, 1836–1860: Accommodation and Community in a Frontier City* (Cambridge, 1976), 192–224. In addition, the works cited in note 3 study voting as an expression of community values. The phrase "island communities" appears in Robert H. Wiebe, *The Search for Order, 1877–1920* (New York, 1967).

38. Besides the works cited in note 17, see Alfred D. Chandler, Jr., "Entrepreneurial Opportunity in Nineteenth-Century America," *Explorations in Entrepreneurial Hisotry*, I (Fall 1963), 106–24; and Glenn Porter and Harold C. Livesay, *Merchants and Manufacturers: Studies in the Changing Structure of Nineteenth-Century Marketing* (Baltimore, 1971).

of such prosperity must have been believable to many. Often false, but often plausible, the harmony argument fed the people's hopes for advancement and helped make distributive benefits popular.[39]

But the community studies also show that the nineteenth-century United States was not a harmonious society; Americans were neither unconscious of inequality nor oblivious to the clash of interests. Nor, finally, were they in agreement on industrial values. As Herbert Gutman and others have shown, many Americans clung to traditional perceptions and continued to reject the habits and beliefs of a business civilization. Often they spurned the political leadership of businessmen. These factors increase the difficulty of understanding how entrepreneurial elites obtained community support for their economic programs.[40]

The very nature of distributive goods helps explain how promoters fastened them on a mobile society of unequals who disagreed on economic ends. Dependent on fluidity and plenty, rather than on consensus or an identity of interests, distribution seemed to encourage flexibility in using resources and in interpreting economic development. Unlike regulation, it left large economic classes undefined and unidentified. On the face of things, distributive benefits opened possibilities rather than foreclosed them and permitted differences of opinion about economy and society. Under nineteenth-century conditions, such policies had the appearance of benefiting a diversity of interests. The conditions, not the election returns, explain the policies.

39. Frisch, *Town into City*, 181–83; Roger W. Lotchin, *San Francisco, 1846–1856: From Hamlet to City* (New York, 1974), 142–43, 239–43; Michael B. Katz, *The People of Hamilton, Canada West: Family and Class in a Mid-Nineteenth-Century City* (Cambridge, 1975), 6, 184–87; Stuart M. Blumin, *The Urban Threshold: Growth and Change in a Nineteenth-Century American Community* (Chicago, 1976), 190–211; Stephan Thernstrom, *Poverty and Progess: Social Mobility in a Nineteenth Century City* (New York, 1964).

40. Herbert G. Gutman, *Work, Culture, and Society in Industrializing America: Essays in American Working-Class and Social History* (New York, 1976); Alan Dawley, *Class and Community: The Industrial Revolution in Lynn* (Cambridge, 1976).

This interpretation squares with much that we know about the nineteenth-century American people. Impatient for material progress, they welcomed the government's assistance to their profit-making enterprises but felt little need to weigh up all the costs against the benefits. Individualistic and upwardly mobile, they readily identified with their community and its beliefs but resisted thinking in the class terms that might have led to sterner demands for calculation in government policymaking. Distrustful of power and jealous of their liberties, the people restricted the authority of public officials. But citizens relished joining and participating and expressing group values, and they bestowed on parties a measure of loyalty they never would have given to government itself.

The party period's practices suited a nation that had put aside the recognized political elite of the colonial and early national periods and had not yet succumbed to the interest-group politics of the twentieth century. Addressing a fragmented electorate in litanies that reinforced cultural and social diversity, seldom in broad ideological terms, and granting particularistic distributive benefits rather than comprehensive policy demands, the parties flourished in a society more fluid than it had ever been before or would be again. But as the growing nation modernized, new loyalties and new demands on government threatened the existing patterns of politics. Functional economic organizations began to make stronger policy demands than individuals or ethnoreligious groups ever had. Fresh needs arose that required supplementing distributive decisions with regulatory and redistributive ones. Parties handled these changes with difficulty, and by the early 1900s the party period's practices no longer matched the country's social circumstances.[41]

41. For a cross-national account of why strong party machines may flourish during the period after a society's traditional patterns of deference have declined and before new loyalties based on functional ties of class or occupation have formed, see James C. Scott, *Comparative Political Corruption* (Englewood Cliffs, 1972), 104–12, 145–51. See also Samuel P. Huntington, *Political Order in Changing Societies* (New Haven, 1968), 93–109.

Changes in politics and governance at the beginning of the twentieth century marked the start of a new political era, distinct in its patterns of participation and policymaking from the party period before it. Early in the 1900s, electoral turnout fell and party loyalties became weaker, while new avenues of political participation opened up. In the same years, distributive policies came under sustained assault, while the government's regulatory and administrative functions were strengthened. Brief consideration of what destroyed the party period's characteristic practices may bring the epoch itself into fuller perspective and distinguish it from the political era that followed.

In the presidential election of 1904, voter turnout fell below 70 percent for the first time since 1836; eight years later turnout again dropped sharply, to below 60 percent. While they were highest in the South, the participation losses affected virtually every part of the country. Voter turnout has never returned to its nineteenth-century levels. Beginning in the same year, 1904, high rates of ticket-splitting marked another dimension of the decline in partisan voting. Commentators observed the apathy that seemed to overcome the voters and remarked on the loss of the old excitement that had traditionally accompanied campaigns and elections.[42]

Three things caused the changes in voting behavior. First, the realignment of the 1890s had brought one-party dominance to more places than at any time since before the Jackson period. Although the effects on turnout were not felt immediately, over the course of a decade the loss of competition slowly discouraged

42. U. S. Bureau of the Census, *Historical Statistics of the United States: Colonial Times to 1970* (2 vols., Washington, 1975), II, 1071–72. According to this source, participation in the 1852 presidential election fell to 69.6 percent. See also E. E. Schattschneider, *The Semisovereign People: A Realist's View of Democracy in America* (New York, 1960), 78–96; Burnham, *Critical Elections and the Mainsprings of American Politics;* Burnham, "Changing Shape"; Jerrold G. Rusk, "The Effect of the Australian Ballot Reform on Split Ticket Voting, 1876–1908," *American Political Science Review,* LXIV (Dec. 1970), 1220–38; Richard Jensen, "Armies, Admen, and Crusaders: Types of Presidential Election Campaigns," *History Teacher,* II (Jan. 1969), 33–50.

participation. A second cause lay in efforts to disfranchise allegedly discordant social elements. Southern blacks and poor whites, by participating in the Populist movement, and new immigrants, by supporting the most corrupt city machines and flirting with socialism, convinced elites everywhere that unlimited suffrage fueled disorder. Under the banner of "reform," they enacted registration requirements, ballot laws, and other measures to restrict suffrage and reduce the discipline of party machines.[43]

The third challenge to traditional party voting emanated from the rise of interest-group identities and activities that competed with partisan ones. As urban and industrial growth caused people to become more conscious of their distinct economic interests, they joined together to fulfill the needs of their separate groups. Unable to speak with what Samuel P. Hays calls "a clear-cut, single-interest voice," parties—with their broad coalitions—lost the full loyalty of those who now formed functional economic organizations to represent them.[44]

The same broad forces that changed electoral behavior also contributed to the transformation of policy patterns. Where nine-

43. On the South, see Jerrold G. Rusk and John J. Stucker, "The Effect of the Southern System of Election Laws on Voting Participation: A Reply to V. O. Key, Jr.," in *History of American Electoral Behavior*, ed. Silbey, Bogue, and Flanigan, 198–250; and Kousser, *Shaping of Southern Politics*. Kousser's work astutely relates the southern experience to similar legal changes and electoral transformations elsewhere in the country. For an interpretation of "reform" in the cities, see Samuel P. Hays, "The Politics of Reform in Municipal Government in the Progressive Era," *Pacific Northwest Quarterly*, LV (Oct. 1964), 157–69. On the electoral impact of specific legal innovations, see Rusk, "Effect of the Australian Ballot"; and Philip E. Converse, "Change in the American Electorate," in *The Human Meaning of Social Change*, ed. Angus Campbell and Philip E. Converse (New York, 1972), 263–337.

44. Samuel P. Hays, *The Response to Industrialism, 1885–1914* (Chicago, 1957); Hays, "Political Parties and the Community-Society Continuum," 167; Wiebe, *Search for Order*. A number of state and local political studies treat the rise of interest groups and their significance for early twentieth-century politics: Richard M. Abrams, *Conservatism in a Progressive Era: Massachusetts Politics, 1900–1912* (Cambridge, 1964); Herbert F. Margulies, *The Decline of the Progressive Movement in Wisconsin, 1890–1920* (Madison, 1968); Carl V. Harris, *Political Power in Birmingham, 1871–1921* (Knoxville, 1977); and Mansel G. Blackford, *The Politics of Business in California, 1890–1920* (Columbus, Ohio, 1977).

teenth-century conditions had suggested the plausibility of "the harmony of interests," or at least permitted divergent groups to utilize and interpret government benefits according to their own lights, the scarcities and complexities of an urban-industrial society now made it too plain to deny that government actions helping one group often hurt another. The main casualty was a policy structure based on distributive goods.

All the conditions that had encouraged unrestrained distribution succumbed to new circumstances. The frontier's disappearance only symbolized the scarcity. Rights and immunities bestowed by government clashed inevitably with the rights of others and brought on legal battles or worse. At the same time, the belief in public aid to private enterprise waned. Uncovered by muckrakers, scandals disclosing the extent to which favor-seeking businessmen corrupted government suggested regulation as a more fitting approach to business than promotion. Finally, the growth of large, organized interests, each seeking help from government at the expense of others, reduced the divisibility of distributive goods and heightened the conflict over their allocation. The government scarcely stopped giving things away, but distribution no longer enjoyed the confidence it once had or formed the government's main means of relating to private enterprise.

Into the policy process came what Hurst calls "a new disposition of calculation . . . a new inclination to think in matter-of-fact terms about cause and effect in social relations and to cast up balance sheets of profit and loss in matters of community-wide effect." Such calculation required new and expanded methods of governance. This meant regulation with effective enforcement provisions. It also meant administration to collect information and to perform the calculations that a more rational approach to government required. Emerging at almost exactly the same time as the electoral changes of the early 1900s, the new policy structure flowered during "the creative decade from about 1905 to 1915." These were the years when, at the federal level, the Interstate Commerce Commission finally acquired significant strength and, in the states, newly enlarged and empowered public service commissions began their work. At both levels of government, independent administrative boards invigorated old public functions and assumed new ones.[45]

The transition from distribution to regulation and administration often proved to be complex and subtle, rather than clear-cut. Sometimes the change involved strengthening the regulatory aspects of ongoing policies and curtailing the distributive features. Utility franchises, given away so freely by city governments in the 1870s and 1880s, now came with many more strings attached. Sometimes existing policy areas, such as taxation or utility regulation, were transferred from the legislature, where particularistic forces held sway, to independent agencies, where calculation and planning supposedly prevailed. The changes by no means always hurt the regulated interests, and the promotion of economic development did not cease to be a governmental purpose. Cooperation between public and private interests certainly did not stop. But now government explicitly took account of the clash of interests and fashioned definite means to adjust, regulate, and mitigate the consequences of social disharmony.[46]

The new patterns of voting behavior and policymaking effectively strengthened one another. In several ways the policy changes almost certainly helped to reduce electoral participation. So long as distribution formed the government's main approach to economic matters, individuals and groups routinely became aware only of government actions they favored. But with the adoption of divisive economic policies that assisted some groups at the expense of others, almost everyone found the government doing some things he disliked. Although there are no opinion polls to docu-

45. Hurst, *Law and the Condition of Freedom*, 71–108 (quote 73); Hurst, *Law and Social Order in the United States* (Ithaca, 1977), 33, 36; Nash, *State Government and Economic Development*; Thomas K. McCraw, "Regulation in America: A Review Article," *Business History Review*, IL (Summer 1975), 159–83.

46. Lowi, "American Business"; Gabriel Kolko, *The Triumph of Conservatism: A Reinterpretation of American History, 1900–1916* (New York, 1963); Stanley P. Caine, *The Myth of a Progressive Reform: Railroad Regulation in Wisconsin, 1903–1910* (Madison, 1970).

ment the change, it is probable that fewer people now found satisfaction in the process of governance or in its general policy patterns. In Easton's terms, "diffuse support" for the political system probably declined, and voter turnout fell with it.

The rise of agencies and bureaucracies to perform the burgeoning tasks of regulation and administration encouraged forms of political participation that reduced the importance of voting. Ranging from formal hearings before regulatory agencies to routine communications with administrative officials, these new kinds of contact with government required money and special skills to carry on, just as electioneering did. Inevitably they reduced the resources and manpower available in the electoral arena.

Correspondingly, the decline of loyal, partisan voting strengthened the new policy patterns by weakening the party leaders' old ability to promote distribution and forestall regulation and administration. The removal of discordant social groups from the electorate helped make the government mainly responsive to well-organized economic interests, each served by specialized agencies. These processes of change proved to be cumulative, and, with the progressive decay of the old patterns, voting and policymaking ceased to have so complementary a relationship as they did during the nineteenth century when parties structured both.

It would be misleading to exaggerate the extent of political change at the beginning of the twentieth century. Despite election laws designed to weaken party machines, the structure of party organizations remained traditional, and in the year-in-and-year-out choice of men for public office the parties yielded to no one. Distributive decision-making continued to be an element of legislation, and parties retained a strong voice in shaping such allocation. Even the new administrative agencies, with their client interest groups, sometimes performed their functions in ways that called to mind the old policy patterns.

Yet the political changes of the early twentieth century marked the end of an era when party voting provided the main means of political participation and the distribution of resources and privileges formed the government's most characteristic activity. Basically determined by the conditions and expectations of nineteenth-century Americans, voting and economic policy had met and interacted through the parties that managed them both. When industrialism brought new social conditions, politics mirrored the changes. Participation and policymaking assumed new forms, while the parties only weakly carried on their old function of bringing the two together.

6

Antiparty Thought in the Gilded Age

Few could surpass the young Theodore Roosevelt when it came to stating two sides of the same issue in the space of a few sentences, or even a single sentence. Take the question of partisanship. "There are occasions when it may be the highest duty of any man to act outside of parties," Roosevelt told the Liberal Club of Buffalo in 1893, ". . . and there may be many more occasions when his highest duty is to sacrifice some of his own cherished opinions for the sake of the success of the party." Campaigning as a Republican for mayor of New York seven years earlier, Roosevelt used two sentences to express a similar thought in the form of a plea for votes: "I am, as you know, a strong party man, and I am not ashamed of it. But I appeal to you simply as good citizens."[1] Later as president, Roosevelt won widespread popular support—and invited the spoofing of Mr. Dooley—through the same shrewd tactic of showing simultaneously that he understood two sides of nearly every problem.

What Roosevelt honed as a rhetorical device, others of his age also used, often more clumsily, especially on that matter of the value of partisanship. Considering the strength of party organizations and the intensity of party loyalties during the Gilded Age,

---

1. *The Works of Theodore Roosevelt: Memorial Edition*, 24 vols. (New York, 1923–26), 15:66; 16:124.

many thoughtful Americans displayed a great deal of confusion on the subject and expressed seemingly contradictory viewpoints within the same paragraph, or the same breath. This was true of civics textbook writers, for instance, men who might have been expected to renounce ambiguity for the sake of instructing young minds. Twice in four pages Jesse Macy's *Our Government* (1887) addresses the question of whether parties enable voters to exert an influence over national questions, and in both instances the text first concludes the issue one way and then the other. Worthington C. Ford's *American Citizen's Manual* (1882) does the same. On one page parties are said to have different ideas on government and to contest offices on that basis, while on the very next page they are said often to present candidates without principles and to engage in "a mere scramble for office." What was a poor schoolboy to think?[2]

Ambivalent feelings about political parties were familiar in American politics from the eighteenth century onward, and quarrels about the worth of partisanship had been well rehearsed by the late 1800s. Yet the decades following the Civil War stand out as a special era of uncertainty about the parties. At no other time were the claims made on party's behalf so great or the ambivalence and the quarreling so prominent. Looking backward, it is not hard to see why this was so. The party loyalties that had been forged and confirmed by the sectional crisis still remained powerful, but the issues of wartime and its aftermath had given way to new problems posed by big business and big cities. Parties dominated government more thoroughly than they ever had before or would again, but many people considered the parties' policies and governmental methods inadequate. Charges of corruption, which so pervaded political talk in the Gilded Age, added to the awareness of the parties' limitations.

Some recent scholars have warned against exaggerating the

2. Jesse Macy, *Our Government: How It Grew, What It Does, and How It Does It* (Boston, 1887), pp. 187, 191; Worthington C. Ford, *The American Citizen's Manual* (New York, 1892), pp. 91, 92.

late nineteenth-century dissatisfaction with parties or assuming that the elite intellectual critics of machine politics spoke for their age.[3] These points are well taken. But it is also unwise to overstate the hiatus between the critics and their culture. Most upper-class reformers considered parties both inevitable and useful in a democratic society, just as academic political scientists of the era—the first ever to analyze parties seriously—defended them vigorously even while observing their failures.[4] Ordinary male citizens, for their part, voted Republican and Democratic ballots in record numbers, but many also cast irregular tickets from time to time, bolted to one of the numerous third parties of the age, or sat at home on election day. Parties were the central institutions of Gilded Age political culture. It should hardly be surprising that they were the objects of widespread discussion and suspicion, as well as loyalty, or that they provoked debate and opposition, even as they filled the streets with their banners and the ballot boxes with their tickets.

Of course not everyone felt the ambivalence or was burdened with confusion about the value of partisanship. Among those spared the uncertainty was a small group of men who oposed the parties absolutely and without qualification. Although they shared much with the reformers and academics who merely criticized the parties, Albert Stickney, Charles C. P. Clark, Samuel E. Moffett, and James S. Brown went much further and called for the abolition of party organizations. The names of these antiparty men are unknown today and would not have been widely recognized even in their own day. But their ideas bear examination, as those of dissenters often do for the light they throw on dominant institutions and values. Unlike almost any other Amer-

3. See Richard Jensen, *The Winning of the Midwest: Social and Political Conflict, 1888-1896* (Chicago, 1971); John G. Sproat, *"The Best Men": Liberal Reformers in the Gilded Age* (New York, 1968); and Geoffrey Blodgett, "Reform Thought and the Genteel Tradition," in H. Wayne Morgan, ed., *The Gilded Age*, Revised and Enlarged Edition (Syracuse, 1970), pp. 55-76.

4. On the political scientists, see Austin Ranney, "The Reception of Political Parties into American Political Science," *Southwestern Social Science Quarterly* 32 (December 1951): 183-91.

icans of the 1870s, 1880s, and 1890s, Stickney, Clark, Moffett, and Brown stood unreservedly on one side of an issue upon which their culture as a whole was confused. They pressed hard their conviction that parties brought unmitigated ills, and they tried to imagine what the United States would be like without parties. The books and articles which these men wrote are deeply flawed, even on their own terms. Still, these writings reveal a great deal about the place that parties filled in nineteenth-century America and about the sorts of politics and government that might have existed without them.

For a nation whose public life was so dominated by parties, the United States in its first century produced remarkably few books or even articles dealing systematically with the subject of parties. James Bryce's *American Commonwealth* (1889) noted the scarcity of such studies upon which his own work might draw, and in 1891 political scientist Anson D. Morse complained that "the philosophy of party" had received "little or no attention." According to Austin Ranney's count, Bryan and Morse were right: before 1870 practically no writings gave serious consideration to the nature and role of political parties, and even within the next two decades only six such works appeared.[5] Of these six, Albert Stickney wrote two, *A True Republic* (1879) and *Democratic Government* (1885), and Charles C. P. Clark wrote one, *The Commonwealth Reconstructed* (1878). Stickney followed with *The Political Problem* (1890) and *Organized Democracy* (1906), while Clark published *The "Machine" Abolished and the People Restored to Power* (1900). Samuel E. Moffett's analysis of the party system appeared under the title *Suggestions on Govern-*

5. James Bryce, *The American Commonwealth*, 2 vols. (London, 1889), 1:636–37; Anson D. Morse, "The Place of Party in the Political System," *Annals of the American Academy of Political and Social Science* 2 (November 1891): 300; Ranney, "The Reception of Political Parties into American Political Science"; Austin Ranney, *The Doctrine of Responsible Party Government: Its Origins and Present State* (Urbana, 1954), p. 5n.

ment (1894), and James S. Brown wrote *Partisan Politics: The Evil and the Remedy* (1897). A significant number of the first American treatises on political parties came from the pens of men who were hostile to the parties.

Although far from famous, Stickney, Clark, Moffett, and Brown were successful and respected. A Harvard graduate, Stickney rose to the rank of lieutenant colonel during the Civil War and afterward became a prominent member of the New York City bar. His best known accomplishment was preparing the legal case against the Tweed Ring's Judge Barnard early in the 1870s. Besides his four antiparty treatises, Stickney also authored books, articles, and pamphlets on public policy, the legal profession, and other subjects.[6] Clark, a resident of Oswego, New York, was a physician by trade—apparently specializing in women's ailments—but his most important commitment seems to have been spreading his plan for abolishing parties. In 1894, after years of effort by Clark and other prominent Oswego residents, the state legislature twice approved a city-charter change embodying Clark's system for electing Oswego's municipal officers on a nonpartisan basis. Denouncing the bill and the "new-fangled theories of government" on which it and similar schemes were based, Governor Roswell P. Flower vetoed it both times.[7] Mof-

---

6. For brief biographical sketches of Stickney, see David McAdam et al., eds., *History of the Bench and Bar of New York*, 2 vols. (New York, 1897), 2: 364; and the *New York Times*, May 5, 1908. Among Stickney's other writings are "The Lawyer and His Clients," *North American Review* 112 (April 1871): 392–421; "The People's Problem," *Scribner's Monthly* 22 (July 1881): 353–64, (August 1881): 570–81, (September 1881): 723–32; *Suggestions as to an Amendment of the City Charter* ([New York], [1895]); and *State Control of Trade and Commerce by National or State Authority* (New York, 1897).

7. Accounts of Clark's Oswego plan may be found in Charles C. P. Clark, *The "Machine" Abolished and the People Restored to Power* (New York, 1900), pp. 7–13, 77–83; Walter J. Branson, "The Philadelphia Nominating System," *Annals of the American Academy of Political and Social Science* 14 (July 1899): 31–32; Ernst Christopher Meyer, *Nominating Systems: Direct Primaries versus Conventions in the United States* (Madison, Wis., 1902), pp. 71–72; and the *New York Times*, Feb. 2, 1893, Dec. 23, 1893. Flower's vetoes appear in *Public Papers of Roswell P. Flower, Governor, 1894* (Albany, 1895), pp. 93–99, 205 (quote 97).

fett, too, spent much of his life in New York. A journalist and editor, he filled prominent positions on the staffs of leading newspapers and magazines, and he published articles in journals such as the *Political Science Quarterly, Forum,* and *Harper's Weekly.* In 1907, Moffett earned a Ph.D. in political science from Columbia University by presenting a dissertation entitled *The Americanization of Canada.*[8] All of these men persuaded highly reputable publishing houses to bring out their antiparty books, saw them widely (if often unenthusiastically) reviewed, and enjoyed the satisfaction of having their works cited by better known authors such as Woodrow Wilson, E. L. Godkin, and Moisei I. Ostrogorski.[9]

Despite some real differences among them, the books by Stickney and the rest share enough to warrant grouping and analyzing them together. All offer harsh criticisms of party politics in the United States, and all are larded with historical and contemporary examples of partisan wrongdoing. Each work deals, as well,

Clark published at least one medical article: "The Treatment of Puerperal Eclampsia by Morphine," *American Journal of Obstetrics and Diseases of Women and Children* 13 (July 1880): 533–47.

8. A brief biographical sketch of Moffett may be found at the back of his doctoral dissertation, "The Americanization of Canada" (Ph.D. Columbia University, 1907); see also John W. Leonard, ed., *Who's Who in New York City and State,* Third Edition (New York, 1907), p. 943. Moffett's other writings include *The Tariff. What It Is and What It Does* (Washington, D. C., 1892); "Is the Senate Unfairly Constituted?" *Political Science Quarterly* 10 (June 1895): 248–56; "The Railroad Commission of California. A Study in Irresponsible Government," *Annals of the American Academy of Political and Social Science* 6 (November 1895): 469–77; and "Ultimate World-Politics," *Forum* 27 (August 1899): 665–68.

9. Three of Stickney's antiparty books were published in New York by Harper & Brothers and the fourth in Boston by Houghton Mifflin and Company. Both of Clark's treatises were published in New York, one by G. P. Putnam's Sons and the other by A. S. Barnes & Co. Rand, McNally & Company brought out Moffett's *Suggestions on Government* in Chicago, and the Humboldt Library in New York issued a revised edition in 1899. The J. B. Lippincott Company of Philadelphia published Brown's *Partisan Politics.* Of all the antiparty books, Stickney's received the most attention. His *A True Republic* was reviewed in *The Nation, Scribner's Monthly, Atlantic Monthly,* and the *New York Times,* among other publications; his subsequent works were also widely noticed, as were Clark's two books. Moffett's and Brown's books were somewhat less frequently reviewed.

with governmental ills, especially the alleged incompetence, irresponsibility, and outright dishonesty of officeholders. The reader, in fact, suspects that governmental weaknesses troubled the antiparty writers more than did political ills such as electoral corruption and spoilsmanship. When these men sought to explain the reasons for the wrongs they observed, they agreed that under the existing rules of American democracy the parties' control over nominations and elections, together with the term system of officeholding, gave those organizations enormous power. To eliminate the necessity for parties, Stickney, Clark, and Moffett urged the adoption of new means for choosing men to office, and the methods they proposed made up the heart of their antiparty plans. None of these writers was reluctant to predict the great political improvements that would follow the inauguration of their schemes. Not least among the anticipated benefits was that public officials could be trusted to take on new duties and carry out new policies.

Their proposals for abolishing parties set these writers apart from all others of their day. But the significance of their ideas only becomes clear when the antiparty men are placed in relation to other observers of parties, especially the liberal reformers of "mugwump" fame and the academic political scientists. In their backgrounds and values, Stickney and the rest shared much with the patrician, eastern gentlemen of education and urbanity who spoke for a cluster of well-considered reforms, above all, civil service. Their hatred of "bosses" and "machines," their alienation from contemporary politics, their ideal of leadership by "the best men," and their reluctance to acknowledge the realities of social conflict in America all gave the two groups common ground.[10] But where civil service reformers believed that abolish-

10. On the liberal reformers, see Sproat, *"The Best Men"*; Blodgett, "Reform Thought and the Genteel Tradition"; Geoffrey Blodgett, "The Mugwump Reputation, 1870 to the Present," *Journal of American History* 66 (March 1980): 867–87; Gerald W. McFarland, *Mugwumps, Morals, & Politics, 1884–1920* (Amherst, Mass., 1975); and Michael E. McGerr, *The Decline of Popular Politics: The American North, 1865–1928* (New York, 1986), pp. 42–68.

ing the spoils system would lead the parties to reassume their historic roles as instruments of political principle, the antiparty men thought civil service a paltry response to political ills and derided the notion that parties had principles.[11] It was not spoilsmanship, they believed, that gave the parties their excessive strength, but rather the power to nominate and elect. Taking away that power would do more than any reform the liberals proposed. By focusing so intently on the parties and on the sources of their power, Stickney and the others actually ended up rejecting some basic tenets of late nineteenth-century liberalism.

The antiparty writers also invite comparison with certain trained scholars of their generation, especially men such as Woodrow Wilson and A. Lawrence Lowell who studied the parties carefully and—as they saw it—scientifically. Where the liberal reformers penned graceful essays suitable for public oration, the antiparty men employed the terminology and the tone of social science. Like the academics, Stickney, Clark, Moffett, and Brown placed the parties in their historical settings, analyzed the functions performed by the party organizations, and compared them with their counterparts in England. Perhaps of most importance, the antiparty men shared with the political scientists a recognition that parties were agencies of government and that their behavior significantly affected policymaking. Despite these similarities, however, the antiparty writers were far more hostile to

---

11. For discussion of the liberal reformers' fundamental acceptance of parties, see McGerr, *The Decline of Popular Politics*, pp. 54, 66–67; and Sproat, *"The Best Men,"* pp. 60–61, 63. Characteristic examples of the reformers' belief that the parties had—or once had had—distinctive principles may be found in Dorman B. Eaton, *The "Spoils" System and Civil Service Reform in the Custom-House and Post-Office at New York* (New York, 1881), pp. 38–39, 92–93, 95; and Charles Eliot Norton, ed., *Orations and Addresses of George William Curtis*, 3 vols. (New York, 1894), 2: 145–46, 325–26, 387. The antiparty men denied that very point; see Charles C. P. Clark, *The Commonwealth Reconstructed* (New York, 1878), pp. 180–81; and Samuel Erasmus Moffett, *Suggestions on Government* (Chicago, 1894), pp. 76–79. For the antiparty writers' views of civil service reform, see Clark, *The Commonwealth Reconstructed*, pp. 50–52; Albert Stickney, *The Political Problem* (New York, 1890), pp. 156–61; and James Sayles Brown, *Partisan Politics: The Evil and the Remedy* (Philadelphia, 1897), pp. 205, 213–20.

parties than were the academics. Where Wilson and Lowell emphasized the numerous and indispensable roles which parties performed in a democracy, Stickney and the rest acknowledged the necessity only of the parties' electoral functions and proposed to eliminate even those by substituting other methods for putting men in office. Where the political scientists suggested ways of making the parties more responsible, the antiparty men denied that collective responsibility was possible and instead offered schemes for holding individual officeholders accountable to their constituents. This was social science in the service of a single idea.[12]

It is not surprising that the antiparty writers were less influential in their own day than the liberal reformers and the political scientists or that they have been forgotten since. As contemporary reviewers pointed out, their programs seemed impractical. However ambivalent Americans were about parties, there was little chance of their abolishing them. In the words of one sarcastic critic of Stickney's *A True Republic,* "There you have party disposed of and the golden age returned."[13] One suspects, too, that contemporaries found the antiparty treatises boring. Grounded on the assumption that American society was fundamentally harmonious—except for the baneful influence of party—these works lack the flesh and blood of social conflict and virtually ignore the fierce contention over policy choices.[14] Nor

12. This account of how the academic political scientists regarded parties is based on Ranney, *The Doctrine of Responsible Party Government,* especially his chapters on Woodrow Wilson, A. Lawrence Lowell, Henry Jones Ford, and Frank J. Goodnow. The earliest and most important example of the studies referred to here is Woodrow Wilson, *Congressional Government* (Boston, 1885). For the antiparty writers' rejection of the notion that a party could be held collectively responsible for governmental actions, see Moffett, *Suggestions on Government,* pp. 36–39; Brown, *Partisan Politics,* pp. 144–53; and Albert Stickney, *Democratic Government* (New York, 1885), pp. 131–32.

13. "A True Republic," *Atlantic Monthly* 46 (November 1880): 719. For other reviews making the point that the antiparty writers were "impractical," see the *New York Times,* Feb. 24, 1878; *The Nation* 29 (Sept. 4, 1879): 160–61; *The Nation* 40 (June 25, 1885): 527–28; *The Dial* 6 (July 1885): 73–74; and *Political Science Quarterly* 11 (September 1896): 581.

do these books make real efforts to engage the skeptical reader by conjuring up dreams of a grander future for the American people. Instead, they narrowly enumerate the parties' failings and explain at length how certain changes in the political machinery would bring about their abolition.

So why rescue these men and books from anonymity? Simply put, they are worth remembering because they and their works thoughtfully suggest what late nineteenth-century American politics and government might have been like without parties. The results are both surprising and revealing, particularly their conclusions about government. These writers, moreover, expressed the Gilded Age variant of a long strain of antipartyism in American political culture. In rejecting the parties during their golden age, they recalled and restated notions which had been the conventional wisdom as recently as the 1820s and which, in a progressive guise, soon would be again.[15]

Stickney, Clark, Moffett, and Brown justified their opposition to parties on many of the same grounds cited by generations of

14. For explicit statements of the thesis of social harmony, see Stickney, *The Political Problem*, p. 123; Albert Stickney, *Organized Democracy* (New York, 1906), p. 201; and Brown, *Partisan Politics*, pp. 160, 171, 199.

15. Antipartyism has not yet received the attention it deserves from historians, but there is a growing number of significant works; see especially Ronald P. Formisano, "Political Character, Antipartyism, and the Second Party System," *American Quarterly* 21 (Winter 1969): 683–709; Michael Wallace, "Changing Concepts of Party in the United States: New York, 1815–1828," *American Historical Review* 74 (December 1968): 453–91; Richard Hofstadter, *The Idea of a Party System: The Rise of Legitimate Opposition in the United States, 1780–1840* (Berkeley, 1969); and Michael F. Holt, "The Politics of Impatience: The Origins of Know-Nothingism," *Journal of American History* 60 (September 1973): 309–31. Two excellent state-level studies by Ronald P. Formisano are also very suggestive on the subject of antipartyism; see *The Birth of Mass Political Parties: Michigan, 1827–1861* (Princeton, 1971) and *The Transformation of Political Culture: Massachusetts Parties, 1790s–1840s* (New York, 1983). Finally, for a pathbreaking work that places antipartyism in the context of American political culture, see Jean H. Baker, *Affairs of Party: The Political Culture of Northern Democrats in the Mid-Nineteenth Century* (Ithaca, 1983), especially pp. 108–40.

American antiparty critics, often in the identical republican language used since the eighteenth century. According to Stickney, parties were "only combinations for the purpose of getting place and power," while in Clark's words a party was "little more than a Conspiracy of Self-Seekers." Political parties divided the community for selfish reasons, kept alive differences that otherwise would have been forgotten, and—in Brown's phrase—"conspired to seize and hold the government, with all its . . . offices, and emoluments." Repeatedly these men likened the parties to "standing armies that destroy the political liberties of the people." The parties' growing power signified "the degeneracy of our representative men" and posed "one of the greatest perils of the republic." Each of these writers would have agreed with Brown that "party organizations and party machinery are not needed to maintain a republican form of government."[16]

To these historic objections, the antiparty critics added specific accusations born of the American political experience in the nineteenth century. Like opponents of the machine from Martin Van Buren's era to their own, Stickney and the rest lamented that the parties discouraged the most qualified individuals from seeking office and that—in Clark's words—"men of a trashy sort . . . fill our councils." Those men, moreover, corrupted the political process. "The privilege of nomination is strangled at birth," declared Brown, while "fraud, violence, and intimidation prevail more or less in every important election." Amidst such corruption, said Clark, "we are often obliged to doubt whether we are living under our lawful rulers, and even sometimes know that we are not." The antiparty men also decried the political control gained by wealthy men who funded the parties. According to Stickney, "Vast amounts of money, running into the millions,

16. Albert Stickney, *A True Republic* (New York, 1879), p. 108; Clark, *The Commonwealth Reconstructed*, p. 91; Brown, *Partisan Politics*, p. 7; Stickney, *Democratic Government*, p. 129; Brown, *Partisan Politics*, pp. 8, 202. The description of parties as "standing armies" was employed throughout the antiparty treatises; see, for example, Stickney, *The Political Problem*, pp. 125, 144; and Moffett, *Suggestions on Government*, p. 76.

are paid each year for the support of these great election armies. The men who make the payments expect, and get, an equivalent for their money. They are our shrewdest business men. They pay, because it pays." Such complaints about party politics were more or less common in Gilded Age America. These writers repeated them, even emphasized them, but only rarely did they enliven the charges with any notable originality.[17]

Far more striking—and less derivative—were their criticisms of American government and, especially, their proposals for improving it. All four antiparty critics had thought deeply about governance (perhaps Brown a bit less deeply than the others), all detailed its weaknesses under party domination, and all arrived at some similar conclusions about how policymaking and administration could be made better if parties were got rid of. None of their books, it is important to emphasize, were polemics on particular policy questions. The careful reader may occasionally guess how a certain author felt about the tariff or taxes, but the substance of what these men had to say concerned the process and nature of government, its scope, its methods, its quality. Their emphases differed: Stickney was most interested in the weaknesses of the national government, Moffett in improving state and local affairs. But they agreed that party government was bad government, and they thought they knew what to do about it.

Stickney's *A True Republic* illustrates their preoccupation with government. The book opens in grand style, and with due attention to the English heritage, with two chapters on unsatisfactory forms of government, "Hereditary Monarchy" and "Constitutional Royalty." Then follows Stickney's account of party government in the United States, with special emphasis upon the

17. Clark, *The "Machine" Abolished*, p. 181; Brown, *Partisan Politics*, pp. 71, 74; Clark, *The "Machine" Abolished*, pp. 132–33; Stickney, *The Political Problem*, p. 56. The charge that businessmen corrupted the party organizations was not a major theme of the antiparty books; significantly it was most prominent in Stickney's *Organized Democracy*, published in 1906, which shows clearly the influence of progressive concerns. In various passages both Clark and Stickney took the position that wealth ought to be represented in politics.

abuses of the Lincoln, Grant, and Hayes administrations. The abuses themselves were familiar enough, although in Stickney's telling far less of the blame falls on individual men than on their party. For partisan reasons, Lincoln appointed the corrupt and unqualified Simon Cameron as head of the War Department, and a disastrous waste of public monies followed. Throughout the Civil War, Stickney charged, "The affairs of the Government in all departments . . . were managed by party men on true party principles—that is, the people's offices were used, not for the service of the people, but for the service of party, to reward party men for party work." Under Grant and Hayes, the stakes were less but the mismanagement and wrongdoing just as great. According to Stickney, "The political history of the United States in the years since the war has been a long story of corruption and misconduct on the part of public officers." And the culprit was party. "In the violence and great temptations of party conflict" good men do wrong. And they do it with impunity, Stickney went on, because the party leaders in whom power really lies are not accountable to the people.[18]

Each in his own way, the other antiparty writers echoed Stickney's attack on party government. Taking high ground, Clark opened *The Commonwealth Reconstructed* with a damning account of "the art of government" through history and a warning about "its dubious future." "Considering their mighty powers," he wrote, governments in every age ". . . have done little toward the advancement of society." When he turned to the contemporary United States, Clark found that "Neither government at Washington, nor at any Statehouse or city hall, is held in much respect." Incompetent officeholders, inefficient administration, confused legislation, and widespread corruption were its hallmarks. And affairs were getting worse; within recent decades American governments had outstripped their European counterparts "in rottenness." When Clark asked why government in the

18. Stickney, *A True Republic*, pp. 81, 91, 98; see also Stickney, *Organized Democracy*, pp. 118–54.

United States was so bad and what could be done to improve it, he rejected all kinds of faddish solutions—from civil service to moral rejuvenation—and concluded that the culprit was party itself. "Organizations of Politicians" had seized ". . . from the people the management of affairs." Taking government back from the party politicians was the only answer.[19]

Moffett's book, too, begins with an account of governmental defects. Executive administration was staffed with "amateurs," legislative bodies suffered "paralysis," and local governments had reached a condition of "imbecility." Brown expressed related observations, in a somewhat more formal tone. Through parties, he wrote, "the public service is degraded and its efficiency greatly impaired." So long as those organizations are dominant, he asked, "how can we expect anything but a corrupt and wasteful administration of the affairs of the nation?"[20]

To all four of these writers the worst evils of partisanship lay in government. They emphasized somewhat different problems, and nowhere did any one of them succinctly summarize the antiparty indictment of party government. But it is not difficult to draw together the elements of their fundamentally common critique. Party governments were carried on by ignorant and untrained men who did the public's business haphazardly and inefficiently, while the party leaders who held real authority remained shielded from responsibility. Under such conditions, government was permeated with waste and mismanagement which the people stood helpless to eradicate. Each of these men agreed, in particular, that party governments made unwise policies. "At the beck of this spurious potentate [i.e., party]," declared Clark, ". . . public policy is shaped." Especially regrettable was the extravagant dispersal of resources, including "land grants, steamboat subsidies . . . rich franchises and advantageous charters," by partisan administrators and log-rolling legislators. Ac-

19. Clark, *The Commonwealth Reconstructed*, pp. 9, 14, 18, 36, 60.
20. Moffett, *Suggestions on Government*, pp. 6–7; Brown, *Partisan Politics*, pp. 32, 35.

cording to Moffett, "An average legislative body will pass half a dozen bad measures of which no one, taken separately, would have strength enough even to gain consideration. The advocates of an unnecessary insane asylum at Goshen combine with the champions of a superfluous normal school at Podunk, and with the help of the friends of a useless reformatory at Wayback, a legislative majority is secured for a combined raid on the State Treasury."[21]

Having enumerated the deficiencies of party government, Moffett and the others listed no offsetting virtues it may have had. Indeed, they took pains to deny that parties were of any value at all in giving good government. If the parties had ever served the community by shaping their policies around competing principles (and the antiparty men only grudgingly and inconsistently admitted that they had), they no longer did so. In Clark's words, "neither of our present parties has any principles at all"—a point with which the others agreed. The parties' platform pronouncements, wrote Stickney, were "so vague that they mean anything or nothing." What appeared to be distinctive party positions were but "battle-cries to elect certain men." Nor were the parties of any use in the practical business of getting good laws adopted. "If the administration party, as it is called, brings forward a wise measure," Stickney declared, "the opposition party, if it dare,

---

21. Clark, *The Commonwealth Reconstructed*, pp. 85, 179; see also Clark, *The "Machine" Abolished*, pp. 45–47. Moffett, *Suggestions on Government*, p. 40. For Stickney's extended views of party government see *A True Republic*, pp. 104–53; *Organized Democracy*, pp. 116–99; and *The Political Problem*, pp. 14–66. Moisei I. Ostrogorski, the influential Russian observer of American and British politics, presented a similar, although perhaps even harsher, view of the crippling impact of party upon American government in his *Democracy and the Organization of Political Parties*, 2 vols. (New York, 1902). Like Stickney, Clark, and Moffett, Ostrogorski observed the ill effects of party upon both leadership and public policy, denied the possibility of holding a party collectively responsible for governmental decisions, and proposed the elimination of permanent political parties. Unlike these writers, Ostrogorski envisioned replacement of the existing parties by shifting coalitions which he termed "single issue parties." For an analysis of Ostrogorski's thinking, see Ranney, *The Doctrine of Responsible Party Government*, pp. 113–33.

opposes it, for fear their enemies may gain votes through having done the people good service." To Brown, "Neither society nor civil government has any proper use for . . . [the parties]. . . . They burden rather than facilitate the legitimate labors of the commonwealth." Stickney agreed. The evils of party government, he wrote, "are not mere accidents, but . . . are of the very essence of party; . . . we cannot rid ourselves of these evils unless we rid ourselves of party."[22]

Yet however badly the parties governed, they would be difficult to eliminate. Parties had come into existence, grown powerful, and maintained their hold on government because they met real needs under the existing system of American politics. Stickney, Clark, and Moffett recognized that, and they knew that their goals would not be easy to accomplish. But if other methods were invented for meeting the needs that parties filled, perhaps those organizations would wither away. In examining the parties' functions and proposing new mechanisms for carrying them out, the antiparty men came to the heart of their messages in true social science fashion. If their analyses were heeded and the new means tried, government of a different and better kind would be possible.[23]

It was obvious to Stickney, Clark, and Moffett that the parties' great power rested on their exclusive, continuous role in nominating and electing public officials. "Under our present political system," Stickney wrote, "the highest places in the government . . . are to be won by carrying elections. This work . . . is very large, and recurs at regular and very short intervals. To state

22. Clark, *The Commonwealth Reconstructed*, p. 181; Stickney, *The Political Problem*, p. 72; Stickney, *A True Republic*, pp. 131, 133; Brown, *Partisan Politics*, p. 192; Stickney, *A True Republic*, p. 104.

23. Unlike the other three writers, James Sayles Brown did not explicitly give a functional analysis of the parties' power; nor did he propose other means for performing the parties' tasks. In several passages Brown came close to recognizing that under the existing political rules the availability of offices and spoils inevitably called forth parties. But he did not pursue the implications of his insight, except to propose the legal abolition of political parties. See Brown, *Partisan Politics*, pp.49–51, 159, 176.

it more correctly, the work never ends." Not surprisingly, he continued, there was no shortage of men willing to do the work, and they organized parties to carry it out successfully. According to Clark, in fact, the political rules then in operation made the machine "an absolute necessity and of infinite benefit." Without it, "our condition would be . . . much worse than it is now." Unless politicians organized opinion and nominated candidates, he predicted, "our votes . . . would . . . be scattered all about, and not even a decent plurality of voices, much less a majority would ever chime." "The inevitable result" of the existing system for filling offices, said Stickney, "is the establishment of these large election organizations of professional politicians."[24]

How, then, could the nation ever get along without them? Stickney's first thought on this matter, expressed in *A True Republic* (1879), was simply to abolish the term system of office-holding and reduce the number of elective offices. If governmental positions were no longer regularly vacated and put up to popular vote, there would be no cause to form parties for carrying elections. Let officials serve just as long as they do their jobs well, Stickney suggested, and free public servants from the necessity of protecting their places by constant party work. "The public service must have the same permanence that we find in the service of our great mills and railroads," he declared, "if we hope to be able to find men out, to know what they can really do." Stickney also proposed that more positions be made appointive (and fewer elective) and that public officials be paid larger salaries than those offered in the private sphere. In phrases he often repeated, the nation would then have "Our best men" giving "Their best work." And parties would be destroyed.[25] Yet despite his efforts, *A True Republic* only vaguely explained how talented

24. Stickney, *The Political Problem*, pp. 15–16; Clark, *The "Machine" Abolished*, p. 65; Clark, *The Commonwealth Reconstructed*, p. 108; Stickney, *Organized Democracy*, p. 15. See also Stickney, *Democratic Government*, pp. 56–57, 87, 126–30, 163–64; Stickney, *Organized Democracy*, pp. 4–6; Clark, *The Commonwealth Reconstructed*, pp. 68, 74, 89; *The "Machine" Abolished*, pp. 2–3, 33–35; Moffett, *Suggestions on Government*, pp. 75–77, 82–83, 188–91.

25. Stickney, *A True Republic*, pp. 105–9, 152–69 (quotes 154, 165), 184–203.

officials were to be chosen, incompetent ones removed, and responsibility to the people ensured. In subsequent works, Stickney (along with Clark and Moffett) filled the gap by elaborating mechanisms designed to fulfill the goals laid out in his first book: the elimination of the term system and of frequent elections, the replacement of unworthy officeholders, and the selection of the best men for government work.[26]

The device upon which all three men settled as the basis for politics and government was the local popular assembly. Modeled on the New England town meeting as they imagined it to have functioned at its best, each assembly would deliberate on all public questions properly before a constituency of its size and elect a single person to represent it in choosing higher authorities. Stickney and Clark specifically provided for successive tiers of representatives who would assemble to elect all officials, up to the president of the United States. There would be no fixed terms of office and no periodic election days; each official at whatever level would serve on good behavior until removed from his position. In all likelihood, most would remain in office for long periods of time. Although these writers acknowledged their plans to entail radical departures in American politics, they pointed to historical experiences attesting to the soundness of the forms they proposed. From ancient times to the present day, local assemblies had served as effective instruments of the popular will. And as for the successive layers of elected representatives—that device had been proven sound by the political parties themselves: the very bodies these plans were designed to eliminate.[27]

26. For Stickney's continued commitment to abolition of the term system see *Democratic Government*, pp. 83–120; *The Political Problem*, pp. 38–50, 104–5, 113–38; and *Organized Democracy*, pp. 41–42, 71–73.

27. Stickney, *Democratic Government*, pp. 22–124, 133–36; Stickney, *The Political Problem*, pp. 76–139; Stickney, *Organized Democracy*, pp. 74–115; Clark, *The Commonwealth Reconstructed*, pp. 110–53; Clark, *The "Machine" Abolished*, pp. 67–131; Moffett, *Suggestions on Government*, pp. 9–23, 60–73. For explicit recognition that the antiparty plans mimicked the organization of the parties themselves, see Stickney, *The Political Problem*, p. 82; and Clark, *The "Machine" Abolished*, pp. 2–5.

The advantages of the popular assembly particularly impressed Stickney, Clark, and Moffett. If men came together to resolve common problems and select representatives they would confer, argue, and ultimately reach a consensus that genuinely reflected the will of those gathered. In such a setting, the most persuasive and articulate individuals would have more weight than their peers, just as they should have in the view of these writers. As Clark put it, "The chief root of . . . [the assembly's] virtue . . . is in the gathering of neighbors and acquaintances in actual conference." There, said Moffett, "The man of intelligence can explain his views to the meeting and carry his less acute auditors with him." The usual product of such deliberation, according to Stickney, would be a compromise, yet "Such a result will be properly termed a 'judgment of the people.'" When it came time for the assemblies to elect men to represent them in the choice of state or national officials, those bodies would again prove sure vehicles of the people's will. Composed of men who knew one another well, they would pick good representatives, for, in Clark's words, "Seldom are men who come in frequent contact falsely judged of by each other."[28]

Although similar in outline, the antiparty plans by Stickney, Clark, and Moffett differed in some important ways. Clark's proposal, initially presented in pamphlet form in 1873 and again in books published in 1878 and 1900, was the first to appear and probably influenced Stickney and Moffett. It provided for "primary constituencies" of three or four hundred, each of which would select a "Representative Elector" to act on behalf of the local assembly at higher levels of politics. With that work done, the ordinary voter's political involvement ceased—which Clark

28. On the virtues of popular assemblies, see Stickney, *Democratic Government*, pp. 23–59; Stickney, *The Political Problem*, pp. 76–97 (quote 84); Stickney, *Organized Democracy*, pp. 78–96; Clark, *The Commonwealth Reconstructed*, pp. 119–27 (quotes 123, 126); Clark, *The "Machine" Abolished*, pp. 85–94; and Moffett, *Suggestions on Government*, pp. 10–16 (quote 13), 179–83. Besides the New England town meeting, the Constitutional Convention of 1787 also was held up as a model of the deliberative public assembly; see Stickney, *Democratic Government*, pp. 39–47, 52–53, 151–52.

thought appropriate given the complexity of decisions to be made beyond the local district. All the electors chosen within a town or city would meet to elect the municipal officials, as well as to choose a representative to a statewide assembly of electors. Ultimately the highest category of representatives, the "Presidential Electors," would select the president. Everyone chosen, electors and officials alike, would serve at the pleasure of the assembly appointing him; the various electing bodies would meet only to remove an unworthy official or fill a vacancy. Clark was confident that the electors at every level would "put good men in office" and ". . . keep them there."[29]

Stickney's scheme, first put forward in 1881 and presented again (with modifications) in 1885, 1890, and 1906, came close to Clark's in many details but diverged a bit in its substance. Where Clark considered the assemblies mainly electoral bodies, Stickney placed more emphasis upon their deliberative functions and, at the local level, their capacity for deciding matters of policy. At the highest political level, a body of specially chosen electors would confer together, hear all shades of opinion, and elect the president. Once chosen, however, the president would be removable not by the presidential electors but by the nation's legislature, the highest of the deliberative popular assemblies. In another deviation from Clark's plan, Stickney proposed that the national legislature should control its own membership. An allegedly unworthy representative could be removed only by his fellow members, not by those who first elected him. Just as in Clark's plan, there would be no fixed terms of office—and no need for political parties.[30]

Moffett consciously built upon Stickney's plan but went even further toward empowering the assemblies to make substantive

29. Charles C. P. Clark, *The True Method of Representation in Large Constituencies* (New York, 1873); Clark, *The Commonwealth Reconstructed*, p. 146.

30. Stickney's initial exposition of his plan came in his three-part article, "The People's Problem" (1881). His subsequent books refined and elaborated the scheme. For Stickney's views on choosing and removing the president and the members of the national legislature, see *Democratic Government*, pp. 135–36; and *The Political Problem*, pp. 100–25.

decisions. While praising Stickney for "his luminous exposition of the value of the public meeting as the primary organ of sovereignty," Moffett chided him for failing to appreciate the "full possibilities" of such bodies. In addition to their electoral functions, Moffett's assemblies would have powers of initiative and referendum. They could debate not only local questions but also matters of national policy, and a specified (small) proportion of these bodies could demand a nationwide vote on any subject. Moffett further criticized Stickney's plan for giving the national legislature sole power to remove its own members. That right, he said, ought to remain with the people in their assemblies.[31]

Each of these three men had exercised some real imagination in devising schemes to put good men in office without periodic elections and without parties. Each must have become deeply involved in working out the details of his plan and, along the way, expressing what he considered shrewd observations about American politics. Whether their blueprints would have "worked" is unknowable, but it is hard to quarrel with the contemporary judgment that they had no chance of adoption. It would be unfair, and perhaps misleading, to suggest that Stickney, Clark, and Moffett never expected their electoral plans to be put in operation. Certainly each man insisted upon his scheme's practicality—and even its potential popularity. But one senses, in the end, that these authors felt their plans most important not as alternative systems for electing men to office but as platforms

31. Moffett, *Suggestions on Government*, pp. 10–15 (quote 11), 24–59, 64–65, 69–71. Unlike Stickney and Clark, Moffett did not explicitly provide for successive tiers of electors above the local assembly; his plan for electing state and national officials thus remained a bit vague; see *Suggestions on Government*, pp. 12, 63–64. Starting with rather different assumptions—and placing far more emphasis on democratic participation by citizens—Benjamin R. Barber has recently proposed the adoption of some political machinery very similar to that put forward by Stickney, Clark, and Moffett, namely, "Neighborhood Assemblies" and "A National Initiative and Referendum Process." See Barber, *Strong Democracy: Participatory Politics for a New Age* (Berkeley, 1984), especially pp. 261–311.

from which to propound a vision of what American government could be. One senses, too, that the intellectual process of devising means to eliminate the parties assisted these men in clarifying their views of government.

Without parties, American government would be, above all, government by talented men. Skilled and educated individuals who had been discouraged from entering the public service by partisan political conditions would now return. As Clark put it, "There are plenty of able, cultivated and virtuous men . . . who will be prompt to engage in public life . . . when by this system merit shall be reasonably sure of due encouragement and fair reward." Moreover, because officials would now enjoy security in their positions as long as they performed well, many would gain sufficient tenure to become trained experts. In Stickney's words, they would acquire "a large knowledge of public affairs, and a long experience in their special public work." Here was the merit system, Clark and Stickney noted, applied not merely to the lowliest governmental positions—as civil service reformers contemplated—but to all of them.[32]

Equally important, those in government could now be held directly responsible for their actions. Elected officials, serving on good behavior, would be continuously accountable and removable at any time. Those in appointive positions, too, would hold office only at the pleasure of their superiors. This latter point, while not intrinsic to the electoral plans presented by Stickney, Clark, and Moffett, received emphasis from all of them. "Each chief of a bureau" wrote Moffett, ". . . must have the power of removing any who fail to do good work." Stickney agreed: "At the head of every administrative office and department there must be some one man, who shall have the selection, the control, and the removal of his own subordinates." The result would be a

---

32. Clark, *The Commonwealth Reconstructed*, pp. 188–89; Stickney, *The Political Problem*, p. 119. See also Moffett, *Suggestions on Government*, p. 120. On the application of the merit system to the highest offices, see Stickney, *The Political Problem*, pp. 156–61.

concentration of authority previously unknown in American government. Whenever the public business went awry, the appropriate electoral body or administrative head, having full knowledge of where power lay, could blame—and remove—the man responsible. That was something that could never be done under party government and the term system.[33] Responsibility in government also required the separation of administration from legislation. In place of the checks and balances that mixed and confused executive with legislative authority, Stickney, Moffett, and Clark favored leaving the administration of government entirely to the executive branch and the adoption of policy to the lawmakers. In case of a dire clash between them, the legislature would have the power to remove the chief executive from office.[34]

These changes in government had potentially profound consequences for the nature and scope of public policy. If talented men filled the offices and were held accountable for their actions, then public officials could be trusted to act wisely—and vigorously. All three men insisted on this point. Where the term system of elections was based on the assumption that the people could not trust their officials for long, the new method of politics suggested just the opposite. In Stickney's flowery words, "The servants can be trusted—to serve the people truly." They could also be trusted, as Moffett put it, "to deal with a much wider range of subjects than now." Clark agreed: "The better class of public functionaries that we shall get . . . will enable . . . [governments] profitably to take charge of certain kinds of public business which, as things now are, prudence refuses to them."[35]

33. Moffett, *Suggestions on Government*, pp. 69–70; Stickney, *The Political Problem*, p. 97.
34. Stickney, *A True Republic*, pp. 206–45; Stickney, *Democratic Government*, pp. 120–22, 130–32, 150–51; Stickney, *The Political Problem*, pp. 100–13, 152–53; Stickney, *Organized Democracy*, p. 67; Clark, *The Commonwealth Reconstructed*, p. 136; Clark, *The "Machine" Abolished*, p. 108; Moffett, *Suggestions on Government*, pp. 60–63, 129–66. Unlike Stickney and Moffett, Clark provided for removal of the president by the electors who chose him, not by the legislature.

With the increasing complexity of American society, these men observed, demands upon the government were inevitably growing more numerous. New subjects constantly came before the lawmakers, and forceful responses were expected. Stickney, Clark, and Moffett recognized—and welcomed—these developments. Amidst the "great modern social forces, that are continually growing with the growth of men's knowledge," Stickney wrote, "we must have better government." And stronger government, too, he frequently added. "The real end to be reached in public affairs . . . is *action* . . . the strongest action." Together with Clark and, especially, Moffett, Stickney repeatedly advocated the expansion of government. With skilled, responsible men in office there was no limit to the useful work that government could do or the subjects it could safely address.[36]

"Many matters will at once strike any mind on which national legislation is necessary," declared Stickney. "Education, the care of the poor and the weak, the managment of the public highways, the regulation of commerce, the protection of all the relations of life . . .—all these fall within the sphere of government." The possibilities were endless: a national board of health, a uniform bankruptcy system, the preservation of rivers and forests, national laws of incorporation. Moffett had an even longer list: "International copyright, marriage and divorce laws, the promotion of scientific research, the improvement of the patent

35. Stickney, *A True Republic*, p. 223; Stickney, *Democratic Government*, pp. 100-101, 115-16 (quote 116); Stickney, *The Political Problem*, pp. 132, 149-50; Stickney, *Organized Democracy*, p. 220; Moffett, *Suggestions on Government*, p. 51 (quote); Clark, *The Commonwealth Reconstructed*, p. 195; Clark, *The "Machine" Abolished*, pp. 141 (quote), 190-91.

36. Stickney, *The Political Problem*, pp. 39, 70 (quote); Stickney, *A True Republic*, p. 132 (quote); Clark, *The Commonwealth Reconstructed*, pp. 7, 138-39, 191. As observed above (note 23), Brown's proposal was simply to abolish the parties by law, and he presented no electoral plan comparable to those by Stickney, Clark, and Moffett. He did, however, suggest—as they did—that with the parties gone government could undertake new tasks; see *Partisan Politics*, pp. 156-59, 174-81, 206, 210-12.

system, the development of irrigation, the systematic extension of water transportation, the elevation of Government art and architecture, the increase in the efficiency of the postal service, and the investigation of the best means of relieving poverty, checking vagrancy, and preventing crime, are a few out of hundreds of subjects which might profitably engage the attention of our law-making bodies." Within the municipalities, too, there were great numbers of new tasks that governments might undertake. Particularly at the local level, Moffett implied, the public authorities should be permitted to do anything the people wanted them to do.[37]

So *much* would ensue from the destruction of political parties—especially from the transformation of government which the parties' demise would make possible. It was heady stuff, and these men were not inclined to minimize the social benefits to come. Clark was particularly bold in his predictions: "When justice, honor, and harmony shall be seen to prevail in the high seats of power, they will receive invigoration in all private business and in every household; while contention, greed, falsehood, and intrigue will get a set-back; preachers will deal more righteously with their flocks, and grocers with their customers; children will be more docile, women more womanly, and men more brave; all forms of iniquity will be cowed and every right be strengthened."[38] Perhaps Clark knew he was exaggerating here, but Stickney and Moffett claimed nearly as much. None of them doubted that the reforms they proposed would bring the desired results or admitted to worrying about unexpected consequences. The modern reader is naturally skeptical of their predictions, and so—it must be remembered—were their contemporaries. Still it seems worth inquiring how men who trained their sights so exclusively on the evils of parties and who so enmeshed them-

37. Stickney, *A True Republic*, pp. 219–23 (quote 220); Stickney, *The Political Problem*, pp. 39–41, 70, 186–87; Stickney, *Organized Democracy*, pp. 3, 27–28, 52–53, 233 (quote); Moffett, *Suggestions on Government*, pp. 49 (quote), 106.
   38. Clark, *The "Machine" Abolished*, p. 192.

selves in impractical schemes should have come to a conception of government which their countrymen and women would not arrive at for another generation.

Preoccupation with a single idea is distorting and confining, but it may also be a source of insight and originality. The antiparty writers were nothing if not narrowly focused, and even for an age that abounded in panaceas their solutions to problems look wildly unrealistic. They saw only the evils of partisanship, and they defended far-reaching constitutional revisions that had no chance of acceptance. Along the way, Stickney and the others dismissed the parties' contributions to American democracy, failed to appreciate the social and historical bases for mass partisan loyalty, and exaggerated the unprincipled qualities of political and governmental life. Perhaps most narrow-mindedly, they portrayed a harmonious American society in which the only divisions were artificially created by the parties.[39] As a result, these men ignored the real sources of social and ideological conflict and assumed that if their schemes were enacted some nearly revolutionary governmental policies would automatically be adopted. Their vision was so constricted and their assumptions so faulty that it is difficult to imagine how anything of value could come from their writings. But it did.

For there were intellectual gains as well as losses in pressing to conclusion the antiparty critique of American politics. Constricted though it was, late nineteenth-century antiparty thought profited from its sharp, intense focus and proved far from sterile. Bent on eliminating—not merely reforming—the parties, Stickney, Clark, and Moffett produced a shrewd and essentially accurate analysis of the bases of party power. Where the conventional wisdom of the day held that the parties' main source of strength lay in spoils and patronage, they recognized that the parties gained even greater power from their exclusive control over nom-

39. Stickney, "The People's Problem," pp. 362, 572–73, 728.

inations and elections.[40] In the years ahead, reformers and academics came to share that judgment, although few of them would have endorsed the antiparty proposals for abolishing periodic elections. The point is not that Stickney and the rest changed the course of American reform or political science—only that their single-minded determination to do away with parties led them toward an evaluation of partisan power which proved more advanced and insightful than those of their contemporaries in the Gilded Age.

Of even greater importance, these writers attained a deep understanding of the role of parties in American government. They exaggerated the evils of party government, to be sure, but they also grasped some of its essentials: the difficulty of holding officials responsible for their actions; the frequently inexpert conduct of public business; the unplanned, particularistic nature of the policy process. And they linked these qualities of governance directly to political parties. By marking the parties for extermination, moreover, these men went on to think seriously about what government might be without them. It would be more responsible, more skillfully conducted, more vigorous, and—in all probability—much bigger. Like their judgment that the parties' strength rested on the power to nominate and elect, these conclusions about government contradicted the usual wisdom of the day.

The intellectual accomplishments of the antiparty men can be brought into sharper focus by comparing them with the liberals who favored civil service reform. In their writings, late nineteenth-century liberals frequently mixed and muddled political, moral, and governmental evils. Political corruption emanated from the citizenry's degraded spirit—but also contributed to the popular moral degradation. Governmental ills resulted from a mix of political and moral failings—but the main problem with

40. For examples of the view that the parties' power derived mainly from spoils and patronage, see George William Curtis, "Party and Patronage," in Norton, ed., *Orations and Addresses*, 2: 477–508; and Eaton, *The "Spoils" System and Civil Service Reform*.

government itself seemed to be a moral one, namely, the low ethical standards of those in office. In liberal thought the causal lines between politics, morals, and governance ran in every direction, and the evils came in combinations of all three. Dorman B. Eaton, George William Curtis, James Bryce, and even Theodore Roosevelt all wrote in this way. In some passages they tried to sort out the connections, but typically the mingling of political, moral, and governmental wrongs remained. To Curtis, for example, the spoils system was "subjugating legitimate party action, destroying the moral authority of elections, demoralizing the public conscience, degrading official character, excluding able and upright men from public life, and disgracing the American name."[41] Curtis would probably have acknowledged his difficulty in distinguishing between the political, the moral, and the governmental. They *were* all bound up together, and reform meant nothing less than the concurrent elevation of all three spheres.

What the liberals conflated, the antiparty writers explicitly distinguished. They saw governmental ills, attributed them to political causes, and left the morals largely out. If their electoral plans were adopted, government would be improved: the connection was straight and simple. No doubt this streamlining of analysis entailed some loss of insight, for politics, morals, and government were (and are) mixed and muddled. But Stickney and the rest had little patience for moralizing, and they honestly believed they had political cures for governmental problems. Whatever its costs in insight, their social science reasoning carried the antiparty men well beyond some of the core beliefs of the civil service liberals.

The antiparty writers rejected the emphasis placed on moral rejuvenation by many late nineteenth-century reformers. This was a logical outcome of their thinking: it was not human

41. Norton, ed., *Orations and Addresses*, 2: 125, 181, 275 (quote), 302, 319, 375–76, 502. See also, Eaton *The "Spoils" System and Civil Service Reform*; Bryce, *The American Commonwealth*; and Roosevelt's essays and speeches in *The Works of Theodore Roosevelt*, vols. 15 and 16.

character that required making over but rather the political machinery. "Many [reformers] look to some moral cure," observed Clark. ". . . They say that when the people were good we had a good government, and that we have a bad one now because we ourselves are in a state of moral decline." With this view he had no sympathy. "It has no warrant whatever."[42] In calling on Americans to change not their moral character but their political system, Stickney and Clark also renounced the doctrines of Spencerian determinism. In Stickney's words, many believe "that political institutions develop of themselves, without the agency of man; that we inherit them; that we must accept them, and submit to them. . . . Directly the reverse is the fact. We make, and change, our own political institutions." Clark agreed: "History discredits and reason repudiates the doctrine [of determinism]. . . . Man is the chief circumstance in the environment of man."[43] Above all, these men abandoned the liberals' faith in limited government. Like their rejection of moral cures and of Spencerianism, the renunciation of *laissez-faire* proceeded from the antiparty writers' simple confidence that changes in the political machinery would bring good government. Once the parties were gone, there was no limit to the tasks that government could safely perform. Without apparent foresight and without calling much attention to their achievement, the antiparty men had focused a social science analysis narrowly on the partisan political causes of governmental weakness and, in the process, expressed a significant challenge to conventional liberal thought.

The most important element of that challenge lay in their view of government. It was a distinctly modern view, encompassing not only the enlargement of the government's role but also the reliance on trained experts, the establishment of clear lines of responsibility and accountability, and the separation of administration from legislation. In these respects, the antiparty concep-

42. Clark, *The Commonwealth Reconstructed*, pp. 40, 56.
43. Stickney, *Organized Democracy*, 249; Clark, *The Commonwealth Reconstructed*, pp. 16–17.

tion of government anticipated that of the progressives.[44] What thousands of reformers and academics came to in the early 1900s, Stickney, Clark, and Moffett had reached independently in the Gilded Age. That was no small achievement for men who restricted their sights to the evils of parties.

The antiparty men and the progressives arrived at a modern view of government in somewhat different ways. Stickney, Clark, and Moffett began with an interpretation of American society as fundamentally harmonious, attributed the appearance of conflict solely to the parties, and predicted that if those organizations were eliminated the government could be trusted to take on new tasks—on which there would be general consensus. For these men the path to a conception of a more vigorous and responsible polity was mainly intellectual—a logical byproduct of their starting assumptions and their carefully wrought schemes for abolishing parties. The progressives were much more numerous and diverse, and the paths they took to a new vision of government are less easily characterized. For many of them, however, the acceptance of bigger government grew out of a recognition of social conflict in America and a commitment to ameliorating the problems of a distinctly unharmonious industrial society. These notions were largely foreign to the antiparty men.

Yet despite these differences, progressivism recapitulated in practice the essential dynamic of antiparty thought. Most progressives coupled their expansive conceptions of government with a strong belief in restraining and regulating the political parties. Among their most important reforms were changes in the political machinery designed to accomplish just that. When early twentieth-century governments were given new duties, moreover, most were assigned not to partisan legislatures but to nonpartisan boards of experts. Stickney, Clark, and Moffett would have

44. On the progressives' views of government, see Robert Wiebe, *The Search for Order, 1877–1920* (New York, 1967), pp. 159–95; Stephen Skowronek, *Building a New American State: The Expansion of National Administrative Capacities, 1877–1920* (Cambridge, England, 1982); and Arthur S. Link and Richard L. McCormick, *Progressivism* (Arlington Heights, Ill., 1983), pp. 58–66.

readily understood why, for they had grasped the connections between partisan politics and what they considered undesirable policies. The progressives hardly abolished the parties, of course, and some of their reforms may actually have strengthened the parties' nominating and electing functions. But progressivism did contribute to a significant reduction in the parties' ability to dominate government—the very thing the antiparty writers wanted to achieve. Progressivism emanated from far subtler and more complex impulses than did the antipartyism of the Gilded Age, but at the heart of the political and governmental changes of the Progressive era was the same formula that Stickney, Clark, and Moffett had proposed: strike at parties/strengthen government.[45]

As baldly and bluntly presented by the antiparty writers of the Gilded Age, that formula stood no chance of adoption. Even if their proposals had been more "practical," political and social conditions were not yet conducive to reining in the parties and transforming governance. Considered as reformers, then, the antiparty men must be judged failures. As intellectual critics of the American political system, however, they appear much more successful. For all the limitations of their social vision and the narrowness of their chosen subject, Stickney and the others produced uncommonly astute analyses of the relationship between nineteenth-century party politics and American government. More clearly than others of their generation, these men understood the power which parties derived from their control over nominations and elections and grasped the basic features of government by party. Pursuing restricted but fertile lines of thought, the antiparty men rejected beliefs held strongly by liberal reformers of their own day and foresaw some of the ideas upon which a later generation of liberals would act. The antiparty writers' program was never adopted, but their basic thinking about the connections between politics and government proved both accurate and predictive. When the parties' right to dominate

45. Link and McCormick, *Progressivism*, pp. 47–66.

American government was reduced early in the twentieth century, government itself was simultaneously transformed—along the lines Stickney, Clark, and Moffett had laid out. Although these men had no part in bringing about the transition, their writings provide a revealing analysis of party government in nineteenth-century America and a prescient description of the changes to come.

THREE

POLITICAL CHANGE IN THE PROGRESSIVE ERA

7

Progressivism: A Contemporary Reassessment

Convulsive reform movements swept across the American landscape from the 1890s to 1917. Angry farmers demanded better prices for their products, regulation of the railroads, and the destruction of what they thought was the evil power of bankers, middlemen, and corrupt politicians. Urban residents crusaded for better city services, more efficient municipal government, and, sometimes, the control of social groups whose habits they hated and feared. Members of various professions, such as social workers and doctors, tried to improve the dangerous and unhealthy conditions in which many people lived and worked. Businessmen, too, lobbied incessantly for goals which they defined as reform. By around 1910, many of these crusading men and women were calling themselves progressives. Ever since, historians have used the term "progressivism" to describe the reform movements of the early twentieth-century United States.

Yet many historians today are no longer very comfortable with the term. David P. Thelen, one of the best scholars working in the field of early twentieth-century reform, recently observed that "progressivism seems basically to have disappeared from historiographical and political discussion."[1] Thelen perhaps exaggerated the point, but this much, at least, is true: there is a malaise

1. David P. Thelen to Richard L. McCormick, June 22, 1981.

among historians about the concept of progressivism and a growing urge to avoid the word itself whenever possible.

Three causes account for this situation. For one, the terms
"progressive" and "progressivism" commonly have been in-
voked in a casual way to denote people and changes that are
"good" or "enlightened" or "farsighted." These are the connotations which the progressives themselves gave to the words.[2] Historians, being naturally wary of such value-laden terms, tend to
seek a more neutral language that is better suited to impartial
analysis. Such disinclination to use the word "progressivism"
has been strengthened by the now-common judgment that early
twentieth-century reform was not entirely good or enlightened or
farsighted.

Second, the malaise about progressivism reflects a general discouragement with the liberal reform tradition in American history. I refer not simply to the nation's current political conservatism (for relatively few professional historians share the new
mood) but more generally to a widespread sense, both within and
without academe, that liberalism historically has been characterized by both insincerity and failure. These are the dual criticisms
most frequently leveled against the Great Society programs of the
1960s. They were not genuinely intended to uplift the disadvan-
taged, but rather to assuage guilty liberal consciences. And the
devices upon which they relied, namely, expensive governmental
bureaucracies, proved conspicuously unequal to the problems at
hand.

The same two complaints, of insincerity and failure, underlie
most of the contemporary criticism of the early twentieth-century
liberals who called themselves progressives. They are said to have
used democratic rhetoric only as a cloak for elitist purposes.[3] And
they are berated for placing too much confidence in scientific
methods and administrative techniques that turned out to possess

2. Benjamin Parke DeWitt, *The Progressive Movement* (New York, 1915).
3. See, for example, Samuel P. Hays, "The Politics of Reform in Municipal
Government in the Progressive Era," *Pacific Northwest Quarterly* 55 (1964): 157–
69.

few of the magical powers which the reformers attributed to them.[4] Almost every major political figure of the era is said to have supported remedies that were grossly inadequate to the observed problems.

Often these two criticisms are conjoined in the notion that the progressives never intended their reforms to succeed, only to appear successful. Thus Richard Hofstadter explained the progressives' attraction to "ceremonial," rather than far-reaching, solutions by observing the reformers' own deep need to feel better about American society and their own status within it.[5] Other historians, including Gabriel Kolko and James Weinstein, have suggested that even more consciously selfish motives—specifically the drive of business elites to turn government to their own ends—lay behind the failure of progressivism to solve the problems of an industrial society.[6]

These alleged evils of progressivism—its dishonest rhetoric and its inadequate methods—bring us to an attribute of liberalism that goes a long way toward explaining the sour reputation it has today. Liberals frequently excel in recognizing—indeed, in dramatizing—the social and economic conflicts of American society, but they quickly cover up those conflicts by declaring them solved through expertise and government. The progressives of the early 1900s did this. Conservatives are at least consistent in affirming that capitalism produces a fundamental "harmony of interests," while radicals, for their part, consider social conflict unremitting and unsolvable, save through revolution. But liberals often seem (and seemed) to occupy the foolish, middle position of alternately recognizing and denying the existence of basic social and economic divisions. I call attention to this pattern

4. See, for example, David J. Rothman, *Conscience and Convenience: The Asylum and Its Alternatives in Progressive America* (Boston, 1980).

5. Richard Hofstadter, *The Age of Reform: From Bryan to F. D. R.* (New York, 1955).

6. Gabriel Kolko, *The Triumph of Conservatism: A Reinterpretation of American History, 1900–1916* (New York, 1963); James Weinstein, *The Corporate Ideal in the Liberal State, 1900–1918* (Boston, 1968).

because it strikes me as essential to understanding why so many
of today's historians appear to have lost respect for progressivism
and to avoid the term whenever they can.

The third reason why contemporary historians are dissatisfied
with the concept of progressivism is the awful complexity and
diversity of early twentieth-century reform. Nothing illustrates
this better than the long-standing historiographical debate over
the progressives' identity that flourished during the 1950s and
1960s.[7] Farmers, businessmen, professionals, old middle classes,
and immigrants all were named by one scholar or another as the
key progressives.[8] The historians offering these diverse interpretations were not content with carving out niches within the
reform movement for the groups they studied. Rather they tended
to claim, at least implicitly, that "their" key progressives placed a
distinctive stamp on early twentieth-century reform and to define
progressivism narrowly enough to substantiate that claim. We
learned a great deal from these studies about how different social
and economic groups experienced and responded to the problems
of the early 1900s. But obviously all the historians debating the
identity question cannot have been right about what progressivism was. For while many groups had a hand in it, none exclusively shaped it.

Of all the answers to the question of who the progressives were,
one has exerted an especially pronounced influence upon the

---

7. Historiographic accounts of this literature include Robert H. Wiebe, "The
Progressive Years, 1900–1917," in William H. Cartwright and Richard L. Wat-
son, Jr., eds., *The Reinterpretation of American History and Culture* (Washing-
ton, D. C., 1973), pp. 425–42; David M. Kennedy, "Overview: The Progressive
Era," *Historian* 37 (1975): 453–68; William G. Anderson, "Progressivism: An
Historiographical Essay," *History Teacher* 5 (1973): 427–52. For a superb account
of writings on progressivism published during the 1970s, see Daniel T. Rodgers,
"In Search of Progressivism," *Reviews in American History* 10 (1982): 113–32.

8. See, for example, Russel B. Nye, *Midwestern Progressive Politics: A Historical Study of Its Origins and Development, 1870–1950* (East Lansing, Mich., 1951);
Kolko, *The Triumph of Conservatism*; Robert H. Wiebe, *The Search for Order,
1877–1920* (New York, 1967); Hofstadter, *The Age of Reform*; and John D.
Buenker, *Urban Liberalism and Progressive Reform* (New York, 1973).

field: the so-called "organizational" interpretation. Led by
Samuel P. Hays and Robert H. Wiebe, a number of scholars have
located the progressive impulse in the drive of newly formed
business and professional groups to achieve their goals through
cooperation and expertise. Other groups then copied the organizers, whose bureaucratic methods gave progressivism its distinctive character.[9]

Yet while it has influenced dozens of scholars, the organizational model is too limited to encompass much that we know
about early twentieth-century reform. Hays's and Wiebe's organized, expert progressives seem too bland, too passionless, and
too self-confident to have waged the frantic battles many reformers did. Their interpretations particularly err in downplay-
ing the dramatic events that punctuated the chronology of progressivism, aroused ordinary people, and gave reform its shape
and timing: a sensational muckraking article, an amazing political scandal, or a tragic social calamity.[10] Without taking into
account how the masses of Americans perceived and responded to
such occurrences, progressivism cannot be understood.

More than ten years ago, Peter G. Filene and John D. Buenker
published articles recognizing the progressives' diversity and suggesting ways to reorient historical scholarship on the subject.
Filene proposed the more drastic response to the complexity of
progressivism: abandon the concept of a progressive movement.
It had no unity, either of supporters, or purposes, or ideas.
Indeed, it "displays a puzzling and irreducible incoherence."

9. Samuel P. Hays, *The Response to Industrialism, 1885-1914* (Chicago,
1957); Hays, "The Politics of Reform in Municipal Government"; Wiebe, *The
Search for Order;* Samuel Haber, *Efficiency and Uplift: Scientific Management in
the Progressive Era, 1890-1920* (Chicago, 1964); Louis Galambos, "The Emerging
Organizational Synthesis in Modern American History," *Business History Review* 44 (1970): 279-90.

10. For discussions of the organizational interpretation, see Anderson, "Progressivism: An Historiographical Essay"; Kennedy, "Overview: The Progressive
Era"; and Richard L. McCormick, "The Discovery that Business Corrupts Politics: A Reappraisal of the Origins of Progressivism," *American Historical Review*
86 (1981): 247-74.

Like Filene, Buenker denied there was a unified progressive movement, but he was more optimistic about the meaningfulness of progressivism. Divergent groups, Buenker suggested, came together on one issue and changed alliances on the next. Often, he observed, reformers favored the same measure for different, even opposing, reasons. Only by looking at each reform and the distinctive coalition behind it could progressivism be understood.[11]

Here were two shrewd proposals for coping with the baffling diversity of early twentieth-century reform. Both have been heeded. Filene's pessimism stirred many scholars to abandon the term progressivism altogether. Buenker's call for research on individual reforms helped inspire an outpouring of monographic work on discrete aspects of progressivism. Their two responses offer a classic case of the historical profession's effort to cope with the numbing complexity of the past: give up the game or restore coherence through infinite particularizing.

Neither response will do. We cannot avoid the concept of progressivism—or even a progressive movement—because, particularly after 1910, the terms were deeply embedded in the language of reformers and because they considered the words meaningful. We cannot go on merely particularizing because (however valuable many recent monographs have been) it is important to appreciate and understand progressivism as a whole. The "whole" will scarcely turn out to have been unified or simple, but it is unlikely to have been either incoherent or utterly beyond comprehension. The renewed acceptance of the concept of progressivism may have the added benefit of enabling us to regain respect for the reformers—to see why their rhetoric and their true goals sometimes clashed; to understand why they sometimes failed to achieve their purposes; and to grasp how they, like liberals ever since, often have been confused over whether the

---

11. Peter G. Filene, "An Obituary for 'The Progressive Movement,' " *American Quarterly* 22 (1970): 20–34; John D. Buenker, "The Progressive Era: A Search for a Synthesis," *Mid-America* 51 (1969): 175–93.

United States was, in the final analysis, a harmonious society or a divided one.

Two lines of analysis seem to me useful in achieving such an understanding of progressivism. The first is to identify the basic characteristics that were common, in varying measure, to many (and probably most) progressive reforms. No one list of progressive characteristics will satisfy every historian, but I think we know enough for a tentative enumeration. The second way to proceed is by distinguishing with care the goals of reform, the reasons publicly given for it, and the actual results. Purposes, rationale, and results are three different things, and the unexamined identification of any one with another is invalid.

Progressivism was characterized, first of all, by a distinctive set of attitudes toward industrialism. By the early 1900s, most Americans seem reluctantly to have accepted the permanence of big business. The progressives shared this attitude. They undertook reforms not to dismantle modern industry and commerce but rather to improve and ameliorate the conditions of industrial life. Yet progressivism was infused with a deep, lingering outrage against many of the worst consequences of industrialism. Outpourings of anger and dismay about corporation wrongdoing and of suspicion for industrial values frequently punctuated the course of reform. Both the acceptance of industrialism and the anger against it were intrinsic to progressivism. This does not mean that the movement was mindless or that it must be considered indefinable. What it suggests is that a powerful irony lay at the heart of progressivism: reforms that gained vitality from a people angry with industrialism ended up by assisting them to accommodate to it.[12]

12. The muckraking journalism of the Progressive era illustrates the ambivalence toward industrialism; for the best overall narrative of the subject see Louis Filler, *The Muckrakers: Crusaders for American Liberalism* (University Park, Pa., 1976).

These ameliorative reforms were distinguished, secondly, by a basic optimism about people's ability to improve their environment through continuous human action. Those hurt by industrialization could be protected and their surroundings made more humane. Progressive intellectuals, as well as popularizers, produced a vast literature denouncing *laissez-faire* and affirming the capacity of men and women to better their conditions. Even reformers with little interest in philosophical questions absorbed the era's optimism and environmentalism. Their reforms reflected this habit of mind.[13]

Improving the environment meant, above all, intervening in people's economic and social affairs to channel natural forces and give them order. This attribute of interventionism, of regulation, and even of coercion, constitutes a third essential characteristic of progressivism, visible in almost every reform of the early 1900s. Intervention could be accomplished through both private and public means. Given a choice, most progressives preferred to work through voluntary associations for noncoercive improvements in economic and social conditions. As time passed, however, more and more of their reforms relied on the hand of government.[14]

Progressive reforms may, then, be characterized as interventions in the environment intended to improve the conditions of industrial life. But such a description says little about the ideals behind progressivism or about its distinctive methods. These must make up part of any account of the character of early twentieth-century reform. Progressivism took its inspiration, as well as much of its substance and technique, from two bodies of belief and knowledge: evangelical Protestantism and the sciences, both natural and social. Each imparted distinctive qualities to the reforms of the age.[15]

13. George E. Mowry, *The Era of Theodore Roosevelt, 1900-1912* (New York, 1958), pp. 16–37.

14. John Whiteclay Chambers II, *The Tyranny of Change: America in the Progressive Era, 1900-1917* (New York, 1980).

15. Clyde Griffen, "The Progressive Ethos," in Stanley Coben and Lorman

Progressivism visibly bore the imprint of the evangelical ethos. Basic to this mentality was the drive to purge the world of sin—such as the sins of slavery and intemperance, against which nineteenth-century reformers had crusaded. Now the progressives carried the struggle into the modern citadels of sin, the teeming industrial cities of the nation. No one can read their moralistic appeals without realizing how deeply many of them felt a Christian duty to right the wrongs that sprang from industrialism. The reforms that followed from such appeals could be generous in spirit, but they also could be intolerant. Some progressive reforms were frankly intended to perpetuate a Protestant social order. Not every progressive shared the evangelical ethos, much less its intolerance, but few of the era's reforms were untouched by the spirit and the techniques of Protestant revivalism.[16]

Science, too, had a pervasive influence on the contents and methods of progressivism. Many of the leading reformers considered themselves social scientists—that is, members of the newer disciplines of economics, sociology, statistics, and psychology that came into being between 1880 and 1910. Sharing the environmentalist and interventionist assumptions of the day, they believed that rational measures could be devised and applied to improve the human condition. Their methods inspired elements common to nearly every reform of the age: the investigation of facts, the application of social-scientific knowledge, the entrusting of trained experts to decide what should be done, and the authorization of governmental officials to take the steps that science suggested.[17]

Ratner, eds., *The Development of an American Culture* (Englewood Cliffs, N. J., 1970), pp. 120–49.

16. On the Protestantism of the typical progressive leader, see Robert M. Crunden, *Ministers of Reform: The Progressives' Achievement in American Civilization, 1889–1920* (New York, 1982).

17. Thomas L. Haskell, *The Emergence of Professional Social Science: The American Social Science Association and the Nineteenth-Century Crisis of Authority* (Urbana, Ill., 1977); Roy Lubove, *The Professional Altruist: The Emergence of Social Work as a Career, 1880–1930* (Cambridge, Mass., 1965).

Dispassionate as these methods sound, they actually were compatible with the moralizing tendencies within progressivism. In its earliest days, American social science was infused by ethical concerns. An essential purpose of economics, sociology, and psychology was to improve and uplift people's lives. Progressives blended science and religion into a view of human behavior that was unique to their generation of Americans: people who had grown up in an age of revivals and come to maturity at the birth of social science.

Finally, progressivism was the first (perhaps the only) reform movement to be experienced by the whole American nation. Widely circulated magazines gave people everywhere the shameful facts of corruption and carried the clamor for reform into every town and city of the country. Almost no one in the United States in, say, 1906 could have been unaware that ten-year-old children worked through the night in dangerous factories or that many United States senators served the big business corporations.[18] Progressivism's national reach and mass base vastly exceeded that of Jacksonian reform several generations before. And its dependence on the people for its shape and timing has no comparison in the later executive-dominated New Deal and Great Society. Wars and depressions had previously engaged the whole nation's attention, but never reform.

These half-dozen attributes of progressivism go a long way toward defining the movement as a whole, but they do not tell us much about who was doing what to whom or about what the reforms accomplished. Most progressive crusades shared in the methods and assumptions enumerated above, but they did so in different measure and with different emphases. Some reflected greater acceptance of industrialism, while others expressed more of the outrage against it. Some intervened to improve the environment through private means; others de-

---

18. On the muckraking journalism that was responsible for spreading such knowledge across the country see Filler, *The Muckrakers*; and David M. Chalmers, *The Social and Political Ideas of the Muckrakers* (New York, 1964).

pended on government. Each reform struck a distinctive balance between the claims of Protestant moralism and scientific rationalism.

To move beyond what are essentially a series of continuums along which diverse reforms ranged, we must distinguish goals from rhetoric from results. This is a more difficult task than might be supposed. Older interpretations of progressivism implicitly assumed that the rhetoric explained the goals and that if a reform became law the results fulfilled the intentions behind it. Neither assumption is a good one. Writing in 1964, Samuel P. Hays shrewdly exposed the fallacy of equating the reformers' democratic language with their true purposes. The two may have coincided, but the historian has to show that, not take it for granted.[19] The automatic identification of either intentions or rhetoric with results is also invalid, although it is still a common feature of scholarship on progressivism. Only within the last decade or so have historians begun to examine with care the actual achievements of the reformers.[20] To do so is to observe the ironies, complexities, and disappointments that accompanied progressivism. For the reformers by no means always got what they wanted, or what they said they wanted.

If the two lines of analysis sketched out here were systematically applied to early twentieth-century reform, our comprehension of—and possibly our respect for—progressivism would be substantially enhanced. The existing research and scholarship do not permit that; nor, if they did, is my space here sufficient for it. Instead of being systematic, the following pages are illustrative, taking up, in turn, political reform and social reform. The end in view remains a better understanding of American liberalism and its limits.

19. Hays, "The Politics of Reform in Municipal Government."

20. See, for example, Rothman, *Conscience and Convenience*; Albro Martin, *Enterprise Denied: Origins of the Decline of American Railroads, 1897-1917* (New York, 1971); and Paul Kleppner and Stephen C. Baker, "The Impact of Voter Registration Requirements on Electoral Turnout, 1900-1916," *Journal of Political and Military Sociology* 8 (1980): 205-26.

Shortly after 1900 many of the basic elements of American politics and government were transformed. New patterns of political participation emerged, while the structure and tasks of government changed, too. Ever since the Jackson period, casting party ballots on election day had formed by far the most important means of political expression and involvement. Sectional, cultural, and historical influences all had contributed to shaping men's party loyalties, and to judge from the available evidence most of them took those loyalties seriously indeed. Only under unusual circumstances did ordinary people turn away from their parties and seek other means of influencing the government, although it is worth observing that nonelectoral methods were the *only* possible avenues of political expression for all women and many blacks. Prior to 1900, however, those nonelectoral avenues were difficult to travel and commonly led to failure.

Beginning in the early twentieth century this older structure of political participation gave way to new patterns. Voter turnout fell, ticket-splitting rose, and relatively fewer voters could be counted upon to support the regular party candidates year after year. In the same period, a great variety of interest groups successfully pioneered new ways of influencing the government and its agencies. By organizing their members, raising money, hiring lobbyists, pressuring officials, and inundating the public with their propaganda, the strongest of these groups managed to compel the government to attend to their demands—not just on election day but whenever their interests were vitally affected.[21]

During the same years, the nature and functions of American government also saw significant changes. To a degree unprecedented in the nineteenth century, public officials became widely

21. Walter Dean Burnham, "The Changing Shape of the American Political Universe," *American Political Science Review* 59 (1965): 7–28; Jerrold G. Rusk, "The Effect of the Australian Ballot Reform on Split-Ticket Voting, 1876–1908," *American Political Science Review* 64 (1970): 1220–38; Richard L. McCormick, "The Party Period and Public Policy: An Exploratory Hypothesis," *Journal of American History* 66 (1979): 279–98; Hays, *The Response to Industrialism;* Wiebe, *The Search for Order.*

involved in monitoring and regulating how people lived and worked. In consequence, both the institutions of government and the content of public policy were decisively altered. Legislatures, which had dominated nineteenth-century governments in both the states and the nation, now lost power to increasingly strong executives and, even more importantly, to the recently created boards and agencies that made up a virtually new branch of government. These new agencies, moreover, carried out policies of a sort only rarely seen before. Where nineteenth-century governmental action had mainly concerned discrete groups and locales (to which governments distributed resources and privileges), public authorities now began to recognize and deal with clashing interests throughout the whole society. Inconsistently at first—but with increasing determination—American governments assumed the responsibility for mitigating social conflicts by taking on such previously neglected functions as regulation, administration, and even planning.[22]

These political and governmental changes were important in themselves, quite apart from what they tell us about progressivism. One might, indeed, be tempted to study them on their own terms, with only passing reference to an upsurge of reform. The changes were, after all, products of those all-powerful, ubiquitous forces in modern American history: industrialization, urbanization, and immigration. Historians accordingly have devoted much of their attention to tracing the twisted pathways leading from economic and social developments to the political and governmental responses.[23] Without progressivism, however, the shape and timing and, above all, the results of the political transformation are impossible to understand.

---

22. Morton Keller, *Affairs of State: Public Life in Late Nineteenth Century America* (Cambridge, Mass., 1977); Wiebe, *The Search for Order*; Stephen Skowronek, *Building a New American State: The Expansion of National Administrative Capacities, 1877–1920* (Cambridge, England, 1982); Arthur S. Link and Richard L. McCormick, *Progressivism* (Arlington Heights, Ill., 1983), pp. 58–66.

23. A major achievement of the "organizational" historians has been to trace these pathways; for the pioneering efforts see Hays, *The Response to Industrialism*; and Wiebe, *The Search for Order*.

For in light of the long-term social and economic forces involved, the new patterns of politics and government were established with remarkable speed. In 1900 they were just beginning to make their appearance, but by 1915 they were largely in place. During these years three historic barriers to political and governmental change were significantly weakened: the traditional American devotion to small government, the long-standing unwillingness to enact "class legislation" recognizing the competing needs of different groups, and the intense partisan loyalties of the nineteenth-century electorate. These barriers had largely held throughout the class warfare of the 1880s and the political turmoil of the 1890s. Now they gave way, under assault from a nationwide wave of resentment against bosses and businessmen.

The precipitating crisis came in the form of a series of revelations concerning politico-business corruption. During the two years following Theodore Roosevelt's reelection as president in 1904, while muckraking journalists were trumpeting the details of corruption to a nationwide magazine audience, a remarkable number of cities and states went through wrenching discoveries of how local businessmen bribed legislators, conspired with party leaders, and controlled nominations. In New York State a legislative investigation of the life insurance industry in 1905 unexpectedly disclosed the long-standing alliance between Republican politicians and company executives. In San Francisco the graft trials of city officials in 1906 revealed the politicians' sale of privileges to public utility corporations. To the south that same year, election campaigns in Alabama, Georgia, and Mississippi centered on accusations that the railroads controlled politics. Other cities and states across the country experienced their own versions of these events. In the fall of 1906, party platforms everywhere rang out against corporation domination of politics, and in their annual messages the following winter most state governors of the nation echoed the outcry and demanded action to meet the problem.[24]

---

24. McCormick, "The Discovery that Business Corrupts Politics."

In response, innumerable pent-up proposals for political and governmental reform were enacted. Commonly the progressives presented their plans in moralistic, democratic language, but often the true purposes of many reformers were more complicated. Often, as well, the actual results of reform surprised some of its proponents. On the whole, the anti-boss, anti-business forces that had inspired the outcries of 1905–06 found it difficult to keep control of the complex political developments that followed.

Many new laws redefined the eligible electorate by excluding certain people from voting and including others. Even electors whose eligibility remained unchanged found that the new laws had altered the rules, and even the purposes, of voting. The progressives defended these reforms—together with related measures of direct democracy, including the initiative, referendum, and recall—as efforts to curtail corruption, weaken party bosses, and restore power to ordinary people. But nearly every election-law reform contained fundamental ambiguities, and most brought results that amazed some of their advocates.[25]

A series of laws directed against the party machines provides a case in point. During the years after 1906, most states enacted the direct primary, placing party nominations in the hands of party voters themselves. In practice, this reform eliminated the most blatant abuses of the machine's control over convention nominations, but it left the party leaders substantially in charge of selecting candidates because voter turnout in primary elections tended to be so low.[26] Other progressive measures established

25. On the election-law changes of the Progressive era see Peter H. Argersinger, " 'A Place on the Ballot': Fusion Politics and Antifusion Laws," *American Historical Review* 85 (1980): 287–306; Kleppner and Baker, "The Impact of Voter Registration Requirements on Electoral Turnout"; Lloyd Sponholtz, "The Initiative and Referendum: Direct Democracy in Perspective, 1898–1920," *American Studies* 14 (1973): 43–64; J. Morgan Kousser, *The Shaping of Southern Politics: Suffrage Restriction and the Establishment of the One-Party South, 1880–1910* (New Haven, 1974); and John F. Reynolds and Richard L. McCormick, "Outlawing 'Treachery': Split Tickets and Ballot Laws in New York and New Jersey, 1880–1910," *Journal of American History* 72 (1986): 835–58.
26. V. O. Key, Jr., *American State Politics: An Introduction* (New York, 1956).

stringent governmental regulation of the parties, but in so doing they embedded parties more firmly in the legal machinery of the elections than they had ever been before. In the cities, antimachine elites supported structural reforms, such as commission government, in order to take power from local politicians. But the commissions frequently succumbed to shrewd bosses who learned the new rules of politics. Commission government became the very basis of Frank Hague's rule of Jersey City for three decades.[27]

Governmental policies of economic regulation also were enacted in the aftermath of the exposures of politico-business corruption. Many states established railroad commissions for the first time, while others strengthened their existing boards. Other industries, too, came under effective supervision, not just from state governments but also from the cities and the nation.[28] Yet considerable irony attended the regulatory laws of the early 1900s. Brought forth amidst progressive cries for restraining corrupt corporations and protecting consumers, the new measures usually were opposed by the businesses to be supervised. When it came to shaping the details of regulation, plural, competing interests took a hand in the process and maneuvered to obtain favorable treatment in the law. In actual practice, the regulated corporations often found benefits in the legislation they had initially opposed, although this was not always the case. Perhaps the most significant result of the regulatory revolution of the Progressive era was one that few had expected: the shifting of

27. Bradley R. Rice, *Progressive Cities: The Commission Government Movement in America, 1901–1920* (Austin, 1977); Eugene M. Tobin, "The Commission Plan in Jersey City, 1911–1917: The Ambiguity of Municipal Reform in the Progressive Era," in Joel Schwartz and Daniel Prosser, eds., *Cities of the Garden State: Essays in the Urban and Suburban History of New Jersey* (Dubuque, Iowa, 1977), pp. 71–84.

28. For an excellent survey of the literature on regulation as of the mid-1970s, see Thomas K. McCraw, "Regulation in America: A Review Article," *Business History Review* 49 (1975): 159–83; and for two case-studies see William Graebner, *Coal-Mining Safety in the Progressive Period: The Political Economy of Reform* (Lexington, Ky., 1976); and H. Roger Grant, *Insurance Reform: Consumer Action in the Progressive Era* (Ames, Iowa, 1979).

economic policymaking from the noisy legislative halls to the quiet offices of little-known administrators. There organized interests found a congenial environment for doing their business with the government.[29]

By the end of the Progressive era, the political and governmental system of the United States looked very different than it had in the late nineteenth century. Political parties had been regulated, and the active electorate had become relatively smaller and less enthusiastic. Interest groups had taken over many of the parties' old functions and achieved recognition as legitimate agencies for influencing the now-expanded government. The legislature was less important than before, and the executive more powerful, but many of the government's new roles fell to independent administrative agencies which performed their tasks of investigation and adjustment well outside the public's eye. These changes were not revolutionary, but considering how stable American politics have commonly been (compared, say, with those of Europe) they were changes of great importance.

It would be hard to say whether the new system was more or less democratic than the old one. Voting had become more difficult for many (especially blacks and new immigrants), but for others new avenues of political participation had opened up. The recently created agencies of administrative government often bent to the will of the rich, but so had legislative government in the nineteenth century. Probably we will never have a fully satisfactory answer to the question of whether early twentieth-century American politics became more "progressive" in the casual sense of the word. We can be certain, however, that no one

29. Stanley P. Caine, *The Myth of a Progressive Reform: Railroad Regulation in Wisconsin, 1903–1910* (Madison, Wis., 1970); Morton Keller, *The Life Insurance Enterprise, 1885–1910: A Study in the Limits of Corporate Power* (Cambridge, Mass., 1963); Richard H. K. Vietor, "Businessmen and the Political Economy: The Railroad Rate Controversy of 1905," *Journal of American History* 64 (1977): 47–66; John Braeman, "The Square Deal in Action: A Case Study in the Growth of the 'National Police Power,'" in John Braeman, Robert H. Bremner, and Everett Walters, eds., *Change and Continuity in Twentieth-Century America* (Columbus, Ohio, 1964), pp. 35–80.

could have anticipated the actual results of political and governmental reform—not the ordinary people whose resentment of
bosses and businessmen gave the era its vitality, nor their enemies
either.

Progressive social reform, like economic regulation, was based
on the recognition of group conflict and on a willingness to
intervene in people's lives to mitigate disharmony. Some reformers, inspired by evangelical Protestantism, acted on the basis
of a heartfelt desire to alleviate suffering and bring justice. Others
sought the professional prestige that went with providing scientific solutions for social problems. Still others craved the power
and satisfaction that came to those who imposed what they
considered right forms of behavior on the masses. Few of them
failed to employ the moralistic rhetoric of altruism; fewer still
neglected the needs of their own group or class in determining
how to act.

What distinguished the progressive reformers of the early 1900s
was their conviction that men and women were social creatures.
People who lived in large cities, where social contacts and conflicts were unrelenting, had little choice but to accept their dependence on each other and seek common solutions to problems.
Doctors learned that venereal disease and tuberculosis were indices
of social conditions; curing them meant stamping out prostitution and eradicating the insanitary conditions that accompanied
poverty. Policemen and lawyers saw that crime was most prevalent in certain social circumstances; stopping it depended on
improving the environment and rehabilitating the criminal.
Many progressives blamed social ills on the habits and practices
of the southern and eastern European immigrants who were
crowding into the United States; reform thus meant restricting
immigration, prohibiting the use of alcoholic beverages, and
encouraging the Anglo-Saxon way of life. It might even necessitate preventing unfit people from having children. Whatever
changes they advocated, progressives tended to recognize the need

for solutions that were citywide, statewide, or even nationwide in scope. Whether tolerant or culturally imperialistic, they saw that everybody was bound up in a common social system. It mattered to everyone how employers treated their employees. It even mattered who was having sexual intercourse with whom.[30]

As the foregoing examples suggest, the progressives sought reforms that would acomplish at least two analytically distinct goals: the establishment of *social justice* and the imposition of *social control*. Many reformers focused their efforts on improving the lives of exploited industrial workers and impoverished city dwellers. The progressive campaigns for the abolition of child labor, shorter hours of work and better wages for women, industrial safety and workmen's compensation, improved housing conditions, and the alleviation of poverty were among the leading reforms of this sort. The settlement-house movement was perhaps the most characteristic progressive endeavor for social justice, and Jane Addams of Hull House was the ideal reformer. Traditional scholarship placed predominant emphasis on these progressive campaigns for social justice.[31]

Recent historical writing makes clear that this is too restricted a view. Numerous social reforms of the early twentieth century expressed the progressives' desire to impose uniform living habits on a culturally diverse population whose behavior sometimes seemed to threaten the morality and health of the community. The campaigns for immigration restriction, racial segregation,

30. See, for example, Robert H. Bremner, *From the Depths: The Discovery of Poverty in the United States* (New York, 1956); John C. Burnham, "Medical Specialists and Movements Toward Social Control in the Progressive Era: Three Examples," in Jerry Israel, ed., *Building the Organizational Society: Essays on Associational Activities in Modern America* (New York, 1972), pp. 19–30; Mark H. Haller, *Eugenics: Hereditary Attitudes in American Thought* (New Brunswick, N. J., 1963); Mark Thomas Connelly, *The Response to Prostitution in the Progressive Era* (Chapel Hill, N. C., 1980); and Norman H. Clark, *Deliver Us from Evil: An Interpretation of American Prohibition* (New York, 1976).

31. Harold U. Faulkner, *The Quest for Social Justice, 1898–1914* (New York, 1931); Allen F. Davis, *Spearheads for Reform: The Social Settlements and the Progressive Movement, 1890–1914* (New York, 1967).

sterilization of the mentally defective, and mandatory school attendance demonstrated the reformers' passion for social control. The prohibition of alcoholic beverages was perhaps the prototypical reform of this type.[32]

Weighing the relative gains made by progressives for social justice and social control is a significant problem in historical interpretation. But it is equally important to recognize that most reforms and reformers expressed both goals.[33] There was scarcely any social change that was not advocated, often sincerely, as a means of bringing justice. Yet, in practice, almost every progressive reform gave added control to those who implemented it. This blending of control with justice was not accidental, for most reformers firmly believed that justice in an industrial society depended on systematic interventions in people's lives by both private associations and governments. Wrongdoers and deviants had to be restrained; scientific expertise had to be applied to problems; social conflicts had to be mediated. Protestant American habits of living had to be encouraged, many progresssives probably would have been added. The reformers often argued over how much and what kinds of controls were needed. Many of them, moreover, knew that such interventions posed a risk of repression. But it was a chance they willingly took, for they were convinced that social justice depended on social controls.

Edward Alsworth Ross's classic study *Social Control* (1901) provides insight into that conviction.[34] To Ross, a sociologist at the University of Wisconsin, decent life in modern, industrial

32. Paul Boyer, *Urban Masses and Moral Order in America, 1820–1920* (Cambridge, Mass., 1978); Burnham, "Medical Specialists and Movements Toward Social Control in the Progressive Era"; David B. Tyack, "City Schools: Centralization of Control at the Turn of the Century," in Israel, ed., *Building the Organizational Society*, pp. 57–72; Clark, *Deliver Us from Evil.*

33. Don S. Kirshner, "The Ambiguous Legacy: Social Justice and Social Control in the Progressive Era," *Historical Reflections* 2 (1975): 69–88.

34. Edward Alsworth Ross, *Social Control: A Survey of the Foundations of Order* (New York, 1901).

society—with "its wolfish struggle for personal success, its crimes, frauds, exploitation, and parasitism"—required restraints or, as he put it, "artificial frames and webs that may hold the social mass together in spite of the rifts and seams that appear in it." Ross's book, which made "social control" bywords in the Progressive era, is a compendium of the diverse "frames and webs" available to a society. Some of the controls Ross enumerated were coercive and depended on the threat of punishment. But he preferred those based on gentle, indirect, spontaneous persuasion, such as public opinion, suggestion, art, and what he labeled "social religion."

Justice and control scarcely meant the same things to all progressives. The settlement-house workers, the reforming professionals, and the advocates of such coercive measures as immigration restriction and racial segregation each gave distinctive interpretations to these goals and placed different emphases upon them. Some progressive controls entailed relatively benign environmental constraints; others mandated recognized "experts" to set standards of behavior within the areas of their supposed competence; still other social controls were frankly racist and repressive.[35]

Whatever meaning they gave to justice and control and whatever balance they struck (or failed to strike) between them, most social progressives adopted roughly similar methods. In time a pattern of social reform became familiar, variations of which were followed by progressives in almost every area. They typically began by organizing a voluntary association, investigating a problem, gathering mounds of relevant social data, and analyzing it according to the precepts of one of the newer social sciences. From such an analysis, a proposed solution would emerge, be popularized through campaigns of education and moral suasion, and—as often as not, if it seemed to work—be taken over by some level of government as a permanent public function.

35. Link and McCormick, *Progressivism*, pp. 67–104.

Usually the details of the law were worked out through bargaining among the competing groups interested in the measure.[36]

Certain assumptions guided those who adopted this approach to reform. One concerned the utility of social science in fostering harmony. Progressives knew full well that different groups in American society had competing interests, and they recognized that conflicting social elements often hurt one another. They were not deluded by a belief in a natural harmony of interests. Yet the social sciences, based as they were on a vision of human interdependence, offered the possibility for devising reforms that regulated and harmonized antagonistic social groups. If the facts were gathered and properly understood, solutions could be found that genuinely benefited everyone. Individual reforms might assist one group against another, but a carefully crafted program of reforms would establish a more perfect harmony of interests than ever appeared in nature.

A related progressive assumption held that government could be trusted to carry out broad social reforms. In social policy, just as in the economic area, nineteenth-century American governments had tended to produce haphazard legislative decisions, each having little connection to the next. What Gerald N. Grob has called "clear policy formation and social planning" were largely absent.[37] Most social progressives did not initially set out to expand the limited scope of government. They placed their confidence first in private organization. As time passed, however, the reformers increasingly looked to public agencies to carry out their programs.

Having methods that were largely untried and assumptions that often approximated mere articles of faith, the progressives not suprisingly failed to achieve many of their social purposes. Often they succeeded, however, and their basic approach to social problems has not yet been repudiated in the United States.

36. For illustrations of this approach to social reform see Bremner, *From the Depths*; Lubove, *The Professional Altruist;* and Davis, *Spearheads for Reform.*
37. Gerald N. Grob, "The Political System and Social Policy in the Nineteenth Century: Legacy of the Revolution," *Mid-America* 58 (1976): 5–19.

The foregoing discussion of progressivism has frequently pointed to the differences between the rhetoric, intentions, and results of reform. In every area there were wide gaps between what the progressives said they were doing, what they actually wanted to do, and what they accomplished. It is important to deal explicitly with the reasons for these seeming inconsistencies and to reflect on what they tell us about progressivism.

The failure of reform to fulfill all of the expectations behind it was not, of course, unique to the Progressive era. Jacksonian reform, Reconstruction, and the New Deal all exhibited ironies and disappointments. In each case, the clash between reformers having divergent purposes, the inability to predict how given methods of reform would work in practice, and the ultimate waning of popular zeal for change all contributed to the disjuncture of rationale, purpose, and achievement. Yet the gap between these things seems more noticeable in the Progressive era. So many movements for reform took place in a relatively brief span of time, accompanied by such resounding rhetoric and by such high expectations for improving the American social and political environment. The effort to change so many things at once and the grandiose claims made for the moral and material betterment that would result meant that disappointments were bound to occur.

Yet even the great number of reforms and the uncommonly high expectations behind them cannot fully account for the consistent gaps between the stated purposes, real intentions, and actual results of progressivism. Several additional factors, intrinsic to the nature of early twentieth-century reform, help explain the ironies and contradictions. One of these factors was the progressives' confident reliance on modern methods of reform. Heirs of recent advances in science and social science, they enthusiastically crafted and applied new techniques for improving American government and society. Often their methods worked, but often progressive programs simply did not prove capable of accomplishing what had been expected of them. This was not necessarily the reformers' fault. Making hopeful use of untried methods, they nonetheless lacked a science of society that was equal to all the great problems they perceived. Worse, the progressives' scientific reforms frequently involved the collection of data, making it possible to know just how far short of success their programs sometimes fell. The evidence of their failures was thus more visible than in any previous era of reform. To the progressives' credit, they usually published that evidence—for contemporaries and historians alike to see.

A second aspect of early twentieth-century reform that helps to account for the gaps between aims and achievements was the progressives' deep ambivalence about industrialism and its consequences. Individual reformers were divided, and so was their movement as a whole. Compared with many reformers of the late 1800s, the progressives fundamentally accepted an industrial society and sought mainly to order and ameliorate it. Even reformers who were intellectually committed to socialist doctrines often acted the part of reformers, not radicals. Yet progressivism was infused and vitalized by people truly angry with an industrial society and its conditions. Few of them wished to tear down the modern institutions of business and commerce, but their anger was real, their moralism genuine, and their passions essential to the era's reforms. Progressivism went forward because of their fervor.

Unfortunately, the reform movement never surmounted this ambivalence about industrialism. Much of its rhetoric and popular passion pointed in one direction, while its leaders and their programs went in another. Often the result was confusion and bitterness. Reforms frequently did not measure up to the popular, anti-business expectations for them—and, indeed, never were expected to measure up by those who designed and implemented them.

Perhaps of most significance, progressivism failed to achieve all its goals because, despite their real efforts to do so, the reformers never fully came to terms with the divisions and conflicts in American society. Again and again, they acknowledged the existence of social disharmony more fully and frankly than had nineteenth-century Americans. Nearly every reform of the era was predicated on the progressives' recognition that diverse cultural and occupational groups had conflicting interests and that the responsibility for mitigating and adjusting those differences lay with the whole society, usually the government. Such recognition formed one of the progressives' greatest achievements. Indeed, it stands as one of the most important accomplishments of liberal reform in all of American history. For by accepting social disharmony, the progressives committed the twentieth-century United States to recognizing—and dealing with—the inevitable conflicts within a heterogeneous, industrial society.

Yet significant as it was, the progressives' recognition of diversity was clouded by the methods and institutions they adopted for coping with conflict. Through scientific data-gathering and analysis, they believed that impartial programs could be devised that genuinely benefited every interest. And through expert, administrative government, those programs could be carried out in fairness to all. But science and administration turned out to be less neutral than the progressives expected. No scientific reform could be any more impartial than the experts who gathered the data or than the bureaucrats who implemented the program. In practice, administrative government often succumbed to the domination of special interests.

It would be pointless to blame the reformers for the failure of their new methods and agencies to eliminate the divisions within an industrial society. But it is perhaps fair to ask why the progressives adopted measures which tended to disguise and obscure social conflict almost as soon as they had uncovered it. For one thing, they honestly believed in the almost unlimited potential of science and administration. Our late twentieth-century skepticism of these wonders should not blind us to the sincerity with which the progressives embraced them and imbued them with what now seem magical properties. For another, most progressives were reformers, not radicals. It was one thing to recognize social conflict, but quite another to admit that it was permanent. By and large these men and women were personally and ideologically inclined to believe that America was fundamentally a harmonious society and that such conflicts as existed could be resolved. Finally, the leading progressives' own class and cultural backgrounds often made them insensitive to lower-class immigrant Americans and their cultures. Reducing social divisions sometimes came down to imposing middle-class Protestant ways. Together these factors diminished whatever chance the progressives may have had of eliminating social conflict. Seeing the problem more fully than had their predecessors, the reformers of the early twentieth century nonetheless tended to consider conflicts resolved when, in fact, they had only been disguised by the establishment of scientific policies and the creation of governmental agencies.

Thus progressivism fell short of its rhetoric and intentions. Lest that seem an unfairly critical evaluation, it is important to recall how terribly ambitious were the reformers' stated aims and true goals. They missed some of their marks because they sought to do so much. And despite the shortcomings, they accomplished an enormous part of what they intended to achieve.

The problems with the progressives struggled have, by and large, occupied Americans ever since. And although the assumptions and techniques of progressivism no longer command the confidence which early twentieth-century Americans placed in them, no equally comprehensive body of reforms has ever been adopted in their place. I have criticized the progressives for having too much faith in their untried methods. Yet if this was a failing, it was also a source of strength, now missing from reform in America. For the essence of progressivism lay in the hopefulness and optimism the reformers brought to the tasks of applying science and administration to the high moral purposes in which they believed. The historical record of their aims and achievements leaves no doubt that in the United States in the early 1900s there lived people who were not afraid to confront the problems of a modern industrial society with vigor and imagination. They of course failed to solve all those problems, but no other generation of Americans has done conspicuously better with the political and social conditions it faced.

8

Prelude to Progressivism: The Transformation of New York State Politics, 1890–1910

For a state that produced so many national leaders of what has been called the progressive movement, New York poses unusual frustrations, as well as special opportunities, to the historian of progressivism. If there was such a movement—and most observers from the early 1900s to our own day have believed there was—then Theodore Roosevelt, Seth Low, Charles Evans Hughes, and Al Smith, to name but four New Yorkers, surely qualify as members of it. Yet progressivism proves elusive in the Empire State, especially to the political historian. For one thing, except for brief periods, the political parties there were not discernibly factionalized along lines marking a cleavage between regulars and progressives. For another, there was no explicit agenda of programs upon which any extensive body of reformers agreed. The historian may therefore find it useful to begin not by looking for progressivism, with all its definitional and ideological complexities, but by looking first for something a bit more prosaic: the transformation from nineteenth-century patterns of public policy and voter participation to political practices characteristic of our own century. The careful study of how such changes originated may enable us to take a new approach to what participants and historians alike have always referred to as the progressive movement.[1]

1. For a summary of some of the recent literature questioning traditional views of the Progressive era, see David M. Kennedy, "Overview: The Progressive

In the broadest terms, the political system of New York State from 1890 to 1910 underwent a paradoxical transformation quite similar to the one experienced in the nation at large. During much of the nineteenth century, when partisanship was strong and voter participation was high, American governments performed relatively limited functions. In the economic area, government was most successful where public policy called for the distribution of resources and privileges to promote commercial and industrial growth. Where regulation, or administration, or long-range planning was required, nineteenth-century American governments proved less able. By the early twentieth century, with partisanship eroding and electoral participation declining, governments became more active and seemingly more responsive to a greater variety of demands. Public policies concerning the economy now relied routinely on regulation and administration. In short, party loyalty and voter turnout had flourished in an era when the government chiefly produced particularistic distributive benefits. Devotion and participation then declined when governmental functions broadened.[2]

These patterns may be observed in New York, as in the nation. From the early 1890s to 1910, voter participation rates fell at all types of elections, including presidential and gubernatorial contests, as well as off-year local elections. During the same period,

Era," *Historian* 37 (May 1975), 453–68. Most of the present essay is based on my doctoral dissertation, "Shaping Republican Strategy: Political Change in New York State, 1893–1910," Yale University, 1976. In the notes that follow I generally cite only a minimum of directly relevant sources, including the location of quotations.

2. Some of the studies that have helped shape these generalizations are: James Willard Hurst, *Law and the Conditions of Freedom in the Nineteenth-Century United States* (Madison, Wis., 1956); Walter Dean Burnham, "The Changing Shape of the American Political Universe," *American Political Science Review* 59 (March 1965), 7–28; Theodore J. Lowi, "American Business, Public Policy, Case-Studies, and Political Theory," *World Politics* 16 (July 1964), 677–715; and Samuel P. Hays, "Political Parties and the Community-Society Continuum," in William Nisbet Chambers and Walter Dean Burnham, eds., *The American Party Systems: Stages of Political Development* (New York, 1967), pp. 152–81.

split-ticket voting increased, suggesting that fewer electors than before took partisanship as their sole and constant guide to voting.[3] While turnout and party loyalty weakened in New York, the functions of state government broadened. From 1894 to 1910, the yearly cost of government quadrupled from some $15 million to about $60 million. While much of the increase was devoted to the new thousand-ton barge canal and thus continued the state's traditional role of promoting commercial development, the government now assumed new responsibilities for supervising economic activities it had substantially ignored heretofore. Of most importance, the new Public Service Commissions, established in 1907, took permanent charge of regulating transportation and utility corporations, a task which the legislature and several administrative departments had previously performed only haphazardly.[4]

Such changes are difficult to understand as the deliberate work of any identifiable band of progressives. Instead, it seems more useful to view them broadly as products of the challenges that industrial development and urban growth posed to nineteenth-century political practices. For a variety of reasons, such pressures on traditional politics sharply increased during the period under study here. Then, quite suddenly, two events—which may be termed political crises—brought the forces of change to a climax. These were the municipal elections of 1897, in which independent voters decisively affected the statewide results, and the legislative life insurance investigation of 1905, which revealed the extent of corrupt cooperation between businessmen and politicians. In very special ways, these two events catalyzed long-term pressures on traditional politics and helped transform nineteenth-century political patterns into those of our own century.

3. Chapter 8 and Appendix IV of McCormick, "Shaping Republican Strategy" explain the calculation of turnout and ticket-splitting and discuss their changing levels.

4. For complete data and discussion of state expenditures, see Don C. Sowers, *The Financial History of New York State: From 1789 to 1912* (New York, 1914).

To understand how that happened, it is first necessary to sketch out the characteristics of what I have called the traditional political system in New York. The state's dominant Republican machine, led by the aging Boss Thomas Collier Platt (U. S. senator, 1881 and 1897–1909), exhibited both the strengths and the weaknesses of late nineteenth-century partisan politics. A careful student of the leadership tactics of Thurlow Weed, William H. Seward, and Roscoe Conkling, Platt was skilled in the details of party management—the day-in-and-day-out business of rewarding faithfulness and punishing infidelity, granting patronage, collecting campaign funds, and getting the farmers out to vote on election day. Relying on the habitual Republican loyalties of most rural New Yorkers and on well-established techniques of party control, Platt made the most of partisanship as other bosses had before him. He had little respect for the panacea of civil service reform and "the sincerest and the profoundest contempt" for the doctrine of nonpartisanship in municipal elections.[5]

Platt did not precisely duplicate the methods learned from Weed and Conkling. For one thing, Platt operated as an "easy boss." Requesting and accepting counsel from innumerable local Republican chieftains, he became adept at leading only where others would willingly follow. For another, Platt made it his special concern to control the New York legislature. Even during the Democratic 1880s, Republicans often won majorities in the assembly, and, through careful handling of campaign funds and astute selection of local nominees, Platt consistently maintained his influence in that body. Finally and most characteristically, Platt rationalized and centralized the flow of corporate campaign funds to party coffers. Rather than allow favor-seeking businessmen to deal individually with assemblymen and senators, Platt collected funds, distributed them to friendly candidates, and mas-

    5. Harold F. Gosnell, *Boss Platt and His New York Machine* (Chicago, 1924), especially pp. 12–38; Louis J. Lang, ed., *The Autobiography of Thomas Collier Platt* (New York, 1910), p. 358.

terminded the passage of legislative protection for the generous corporations.[6]

While the techniques of Platt's partisanship were plain, its foundations were obscure. "Were I asked why I became a Republican," Platt wrote, "I might reply that I could not be a Democrat. Early in life I became a believer in the Hamiltonian theory of politics. From that time I have held consistently to the doctrine of government by party, and rule of the party by the regular organization."[7] That *non sequitur*, composed late in life, suggests that Platt's Republicanism was simply an article of faith. Scarcely articulable, it was nevertheless his deepest conviction. Most citizens probably shared Platt's inability to offer a profound explanation for identifying with a party. His leadership was grounded in the truth that the majority of Republican votes came from men, like Thomas C. Platt himself, who habitually voted for the party of Lincoln but who scarcely sounded Lincolnesque when asked why.

With so few ideological components, Platt's partisanship provided him the means to personal power. "He had two definite sentiments," wrote Platt's loyal lieutenant Lemuel Quigg, "perfectly simple and easily understood, not gloriously lofty, but not at all to be despised—faith in the Republican party and a keen enjoyment of the sense of power." Perfecting the technique of casting all his own aspirations in the language of party loyalty, Platt asked for and received support from local leaders, campaign funds from wealthy men, and votes from the faithful on the

6. In addition to the sources cited in note 5, see Lemuel Ely Quigg, "Thomas Platt," *North American Review* 191 (May 1910), 668–77; and William Allen White, "Platt," *McClure's Magazine* 18 (Dec. 1901), 145–53. On the collection of corporate campaign contributions see the typescript of Harold F. Gosnell's interview with Benjamin B. Odell, Jr., Sept. 22, 1922, Columbia University Library; Chauncey M. Depew's testimony in United States Senate, *Campaign Contributions*, Testimony Before a Subcommittee of the Committee on Privileges and Elections, 62nd Congress, 3rd Session, 2 vols. (Washington, D.C., 1913), p. 625; and Platt's own testimony in the life insurance investigation, cited below in note 25.

7. Lang, ed., *Autobiography*, p. xx.

grounds of commitment to Republican success. In all honesty he could write that "the main consideration with me in . . . all . . . matters during the whole period of my activity in politics, was what I considered to be the welfare of the Republican party, which I have never discriminated from the welfare of the State and the nation."[8]

With his party out of power in New York State during the 1880s and early 1890s, Platt's ambition to extend his leadership from the Republican machine to the entire state was frustrated. Then in 1893 and 1894, events largely beyond the boss's power thrust the Republicans into control of the state, and they retained control until 1910. In just three years, under Governors Levi P. Morton and Frank S. Black, Platt demonstrated remarkable ability to use the government to advance his vision of politics.[9]

One key element of Platt's strategy was the expansion of state authority over the large Democratic cities of New York, Brooklyn, and Buffalo. The cities' charters, their boundaries, and, indeed, their very existence, depended on the government at Albany. Through legislative investigations, carefully drawn charter changes, and the creation of bipartisan police boards, Platt could gain for his party a larger share of city power and patronage than the Republicans could command at the ballot box. The most ambitious expression of Platt's policy toward cities came in 1896 and 1897 when the legislature consolidated Brooklyn and New York and approved a charter for the unified metropolis. While sentiment for joining the two cities had existed for decades, and while numerous commercial and civic groups lent support to the move, consolidation was finally achieved only

---

8. Quigg, "Platt," p. 675; Lang, ed., *Autobiography*, p. 357.

9. The best analysis of the Republican victories of the mid-1890s is found in Samuel T. McSeveney, *The Politics of Depression: Political Behavior in the Northeast, 1893–1896* (New York, 1972); for an informative account of the Morton and Black administrations, see DeAlva Stanwood Alexander, *Four Famous New Yorkers: The Political Careers of Cleveland, Platt, Hill, and Roosevelt* (New York, 1923).

when the Republican boss gave it his blessing on terms that offered a real opportunity for Republican control of the new metropolis.[10]

Small-town and rural voters required less attention from Platt and the government at Albany. As Theodore Roosevelt observed, the farmers were simply not accustomed to fulfilling their needs through the agency of the state. Besides, from Platt's point of view, they could be counted on to give Republican majorities at election time no matter what the legislature did. One significant policy innovation did, however, appeal to rural New Yorkers: the 1896 Raines liquor law establishing state regulation and taxation of the traffic in alcoholic beverages. The measure provided multiple benefits for Platt's party organization. It satisfied upstate temperance demands and reduced the Prohibitionist vote; it created a new class of patronage appointments for the Republican party; and it broke the Democrats' alliance with the liquor interests. Incidentally, the measure also provided a significant new source of state revenue and allowed the reduction of property taxes. An imaginative and creative policy, the Raines liquor law richly illustrated Platt's view of how the Republican party of New York State ought to govern.[11]

10. The best study of consolidation is David C. Hammack, "Participation in Major Decisions in New York City, 1890–1900: The Creation of Greater New York and the Centralization of the Public School System," Ph.D., Columbia University, 1973. Several features of consolidation gave Platt optimism. For one thing, the city's new charter assured Republicans of representation on vital boards, including the police board. For another, it was by no means certain that the consolidated city would vote Democratic. In 1894 and again in 1896 the GOP had carried what was now Greater New York. Finally, even without electoral success, a politically unified, uniquely large metropolitan area provided a strong case for the appointment of state (i.e., Republican) commissions to control such local departments as police, fire, and health.

11. *Public Papers of Theodore Roosevelt, Governor, 1899* (Albany, 1899), p. 33. At election time, upstate Republican weeklies repeatedly reminded the voters of the benefits of the Raines law; see *Boonville Herald*, Oct. 14, 1896, Nov. 3, 1898, Oct. 25, 1900; *St. Lawrence Plaindealer*, Oct. 14, 1896, Oct. 26, Nov. 2, 1898, Oct. 24, 1900; *Yates County Chronicle*, Oct. 26, 1898; *Malone Paladium*, Nov. 3, 1898.

On measures affecting large economic interests, Platt proved reluctant to act. Primarily based on geographic and ethnoreligious factors, the Republican coalition embraced widely diverse occupational groups. As a consequence, party leaders were unwilling to take measures explicitly benefiting some at the expense of others. Publicly, they argued that different producer groups all shared the same basic interests and that developmental policies like canal building or low corporation taxes aided everyone alike. Where proposals for government action seemed less demonstrably harmonious, Platt avoided them. Hence from 1895 to 1898 he and his party disapproved measures favored by labor, including a strengthened eight-hour law and an employers' liability act; rejected a graduated inheritance tax; and continued regulatory policies without significant enforcement. In these decisions, Platt typified nineteenth-century party leaders who disguised material conflicts within the society and declined to help some groups while hurting others.[12]

The large business interests that furnished the party's money at election time provided an exception. Drawn mostly from the transportation, utility, banking, and insurance companies that craved lax regulation and public privileges, the party's campaign fund created special relations between Republican leaders and the contributing corporations. Guarded from public view, their alliance gave certain classes of big business—alone among the state's economic groups—regular access to political representation.[13]

12. On the composition of the Republican electoral coalition, see McSeveney, *Politics of Depression*; and Albert C. E. Parker, "Empire Stalemate: Voting Behavior in New York State, 1860–1892," Ph.D., Washington University, 1975. For an example of the Republicans' rhetoric about the harmony of interests, see *Public Papers of Frank S. Black, Governor, 1897–1898* (Albany, 1898), p. 10.

13. Platt's correspondence concerning the Pennsylvania Railroad tunnel bill of 1902 provides one of the best examples of his assistance to business corporations on legislative matters; see his letters to and from A. J. Cassatt, J. P. Allds, S. Fred Nixon, T. E. Ellsworth, and B. B. Odell, Jr., during January, February, and March 1902, in the Platt Papers, Yale University Library. On campaign contributions see notes 6 and 25.

Platt's Republican party strategy had almost all the elements of success. Devoted to strengthening the machine upon which winning elections depended, his approach made the most of the basic partisan loyalties that characterized late nineteenth-century American voters. In secret alliance with the wealthiest economic groups, Platt avoided measures affecting the other, weaker interests. Geared to satisfy most of the people while capturing the spoils of office, his methods substantially shaped New York politics in the 1890s.

There were, however, two grave weaknesses in Platt's approach. Especially in the state's large cities, substantial numbers of educated, professional men felt increasing dissatisfaction with party bosses and machines and with the old party loyalties that traditionally sustained the machines. Most of these citizens had favored the Republican party in 1893 and 1894, and to maintain his majority Platt needed their support. Yet recognizing independents in a party coalition was not easy, and for the first three years after the Republicans came to power, Platt rarely did so. The second challenge to Platt's mastery of New York State politics came from a variety of demands on the government to adopt economic policies helping some groups while hurting others. Organized economic interests increasingly asked for government assistance, while unorganized citizens became more aroused than ever against uncontrolled transportation and utility companies. Over time, the weakening of party loyalties and the demands for divisive economic policies substantially reshaped the traditional patterns of New York State politics.

Identifying the urban independents and their motives is not easy. Some were merely disgruntled Republicans; others were disillusioned Cleveland Democrats now without a party; still others were genuine nonpartisans. Most numerous when they were most indistinguishable from one another—at nonpartisan municipal elections—the independents defy complete and accurate differentiation. Contemporaries often failed to distinguish the different antimachine groups. They used the terms "Mugwump," "independent," and "nonpartisan" somewhat interchangeably and left the historian little choice except to do so too.

What these groups shared was their growing conviction that partisanship was irrelevant to municipal government. A city was "simply a business corporation," they said, to which state and national politics had no application. At first inclined to demand only simple, economical government, the independents increasingly advocated tenement house reform, rapid transit facilities, parks, baths, clean streets, and the closer regulation of utility and transportation companies. Such expansion of city services enhanced the need for nonpartisan government. National party principles had nothing to do with street cleaning.[14]

In the 1890s independence remained largely confined to the cities of New York State. In the rural districts, without vigorous local governments performing diverse police and social service functions, the stimulus for nonpartisanship proved absent. As Theodore Roosevelt reminded Seth Low in 1900, "the country districts . . . have no sympathy with the anti-machine feeling of the independents in the big cities."[15]

An amendment to the New York State Constitution adopted in 1894 gave urban independents their big chance to influence state politics. Beginning in 1897 city offices were to be filled at off-year local elections untainted by party contests for the governorship or the presidency. All across the state the city independents prepared to compete for municipal offices in 1897. In New York, the Citizens' Union organized to try to elect the first mayor of the consolidated metropolis. In Albany, Rochester, Syracuse, and Buffalo independent citizens' groups also appeared. The results proved disastrous to the Republicans. In New York City, Seth Low, the mayoral candidate of the Citizens' Union, ran well ahead of the Republican nominee, though they both lost to Tammany's candidate, Robert A. Van Wyck. The Republicans also lost local elections in Albany, Rochester, Syracuse, and Buf-

14. The Citizens' Union, *The City for the People! Campaign Book of the Citizens' Union* (New York, 1897), p. 5; Council of Confederated Good Government Clubs, *An Address to the Citizens of New York* (New York, 1897), a flyer.

15. Roosevelt to Low, Aug. 3, 1900, in Elting E. Morison, ed., *The Letters of Theodore Roosevelt*, 8 vols. (Cambridge, Mass., 1951–54), 2.

falo. Statewide, the party barely controlled the legislature and met defeat for the highest state office contested in 1897, the Chief Judgeship of the Court of Appeals. Just one year after William McKinley had carried every large city in New York for the Republicans, the party had lost its statewide majority and been put out of power in every big city. Almost everyone recognized that the independents bore responsibility for the defeat.[16]

In response to the events of 1897, Platt's Republican organization made a series of concessions designed to win back the urban independents. Generally successful in the short run, those concessions slowly served to legitimize the practice of independence from political parties. To the historian in search of the origins of the weakened party loyalties characteristic of our own century, the New York State municipal elections of 1897 provide as important an event as any that may be found.

A new primary election statute adopted in 1898 represented the machine's first concession to the independents. "We want a fair, liberal, honest primary law," Governor Black told a fellow member of Platt's machine, "one against which no complaint can be made by a Mugwump or anybody else. . . . We can afford to be liberal in the matter, and those of us who are pretty strong partisans and sensible at the same time can perform a great service by yielding a little wherever necessary." Providing for rigid state regulation of primary elections, the new measure explicitly allowed party members to join nonpartisan municipal organizations.[17]

Of more importance that year, Platt brought about the nomination and election of Theodore Roosevelt as governor of New York. Roosevelt had always stood, in Mark Sullivan's phrase, "at the outer edge of party regularity." If he had never really broken

16. Low's campaign is covered in Gerald Kurland, *Seth Low: The Reformer in an Urban and Industrial Age* (New York, 1971). The upstate campaigns of 1897 must be traced through the newspapers for each city.

17. Black to Lemuel E. Quigg, Feb. 15, 1898, Quigg Papers, New-York Historical Society Library; Louis Sturcke, *Primary Election Legislation in the State of New York* (New York, 1898) provides a full explanation of the new primary law.

with the machine, he had never really been part of it either. At each point in his political career, Roosevelt had taken actions that regular Republicans found objectionable. While Platt disliked the thought of picking such a man for governor, he recognized that Roosevelt's freedom from the machine, in combination with his recent heroism at San Juan Hill, would make him a formidable gubernatorial nominee. Indeed, recently uncovered correspondence suggests that it was Roosevelt's independence, more than his heroism, that caused New Yorkers to want him for governor in 1898. As one correspondent told Platt, "Many Democrats and Mugwumps, (Independents as they are more politely termed) have said to me that they would vote for him." Roosevelt himself understood that the purpose of his candidacy was to restore the independents to the Republican coalition. "It is very important that we should get the idea firmly established," he wrote, "that the forces which were divided last year, are united this year."[18]

As governor in 1899 and 1900, Roosevelt achieved considerable success in keeping the independents in the Republican coalition. He consulted them frequently on policies and appointments; he put through specific measures they wanted, such as a new civil service law in 1899; and he persuaded regular Republicans to do what was necessary to keep up the alliance with urban independents. Platt expressed support for Roosevelt's course of action. "I expected you to have consideration of the views and wishes of our independent friends," Platt told the governor in May 1899, "and, indeed, wished you to take that course in the hope that you would succeed in uniting the party." In furtherance of that goal, Roosevelt carefully fashioned political rhetoric that combined support for the party with skepticism of the machine's claims. "It

18. Mark Sullivan, *Our Times, 1900–1925*, 6 vols. (New York, 1926), 1:78; Leroy H. Van Kirk to Platt, Sept. 17, 1898, Platt Papers; Roosevelt to Lemuel Quigg, Sept. 30, 1898, in Morison, ed., *Letters*, vol. 2. G. Wallace Chessman, *Governor Theodore Roosevelt: The Albany Apprenticeship, 1898–1900* (Cambridge, Mass., 1965), pp. 7–70, covers Roosevelt's nomination and election as governor.

is only through the party system that free governments are now successfully carried on," Roosevelt declared, "and yet . . . the usefulness of a party is strictly limited by its usefulness to the State."[19]

Over the next decade, the principle of independence that Roosevelt represented and Platt now recognized became a permanent feature in New York politics. The Republicans' absorption of Roosevelt and his rhetoric slowly legitimized skepticism of the machine. By 1901, when Seth Low again ran for mayor of New York City—this time with the support of Platt's organization, as well as the Citizens' Union—some staunchly Republican upstate weeklies welcomed their party's alliance with the independents and rejoiced in Low's resulting victory. Four years later, many weeklies took satisfied note of the havoc that independents were wreaking on the traditional party organizations in New York City's municipal elections. Slowly, independence spread beyond the cities and into the country. In 1906 when Charles Evans Hughes was elected governor, while the rest of the Republican slate went down to defeat, ticket-splitting had become as common a practice in rural counties as in urban counties. In all parts of the state that year there were uncommonly large discrepancies between the votes for different candidates of the same party. Numerous upstate county electorates registered conspicuously smaller Republican votes for Congress and assembly than for governor. Ticket-splitting afterwards remained an established phenomenon in the state, as a significant minority of voters learned to pick and choose their candidates in defiance of habitual party loyalties. The regular parties scarcely collapsed, but by 1910 what had been a minority viewpoint in the mid-1890s was the conventional wisdom in New York: bossed party machines deserved to be beaten, not supported.[20]

19. Platt to Roosevelt, May 6, 1899, Platt Papers; *Public Papers . . . 1899*, pp. 248–49.
20. For the upstate response in 1905, see *St. Lawrence Plaindealer*, Nov. 15, 1905; *Norwich Sun*, Nov. 18, 1905; *Fredonia Censor*, Nov. 8, 1905.

Economic developments provided a second source of challenges to traditional party politics as practiced by Platt. While observers from the 1890s to the present have considered industrialization as ultimately responsible for the enlargement of governmental tasks in the late nineteenth and early twentieth century, the pathways from socioeconomic development to public policy change were long and twisted. In New York at least two such routes may be observed: the organization of economic interests to demand government assistance and the intensification of public reaction against irresponsible transportation and utility corporations. Especially in the years following the depression of the mid-1890s, these developments slowly weakened the dominant Republican party's ability to forestall divisive economic policies.

Beginning in the late 1890s, economic groups that had never before significantly pressured state government began competing for influence with the habitually organized mercantile and industrial interests. Labor organizations cooperated in lobbying through the Workingmen's Federation, while real estate interests, taxpayers' associations, and even farmers all found new vehicles for voicing their demands on government. As a consequence, the party in power found itself under more pressure than ever before to meet the needs of conflicting interest groups.[21]

One sign of the increasing competition between organized economic interests for influence over the state government is provided by correspondence in the records of the New York Central Railroad Company. Letters from the company's lawyers to its own lobbyists in Albany, as well as to legislators, disclose revealing changes in the railroad's relations with the state government. In the mid-1890s the correspondence suggests how confidently the New York Central handled legislative matters. Writing about one measure, the company's general counsel told a senator in April 1895, "We are interested in this bill and would

21. On labor organizations see Irwin Yellowitz, *Labor and the Progressive Movement in New York State, 1897–1916* (Ithaca, 1965); and Howard L. Hurwitz, *Theodore Roosevelt and Labor in New York State, 1880–1900* (New York, 1943).

like to have it pushed through and become a law before May 20th." On another matter the senator was asked to "please see that . . . [the bill] is not progressed until you hear from me further." Within the next decade the company became far less secure in its legislative relations. Writing to the company's lobbyist in 1901, the general counsel of the New York Central discussed one measure "introduced . . . in behalf of some labor organization . . . [which] does not meet our views at all." On another matter a few years later the lobbyist was requested to "quietly ascertain what force it is that is pushing the bill and what prospect there is of its passing in the form in which it now is." By 1904 big business interests were evidently not alone in organizing to influence the state government of New York.[22]

The arrogance of municipal transportation and utility corporations also stimulated demands for new state economic policies. Overcapitalized and under-regulated, street railroads and power companies typically acquired perpetual franchises, merged with one another, and charged as much as the traffic would bear. By the late 1890s city residents across the state were calling for higher taxes and shorter franchises for the companies, or, as an alternative, municipal ownership of public service corporations.[23]

Governor Theodore Roosevelt fashioned one answer for the divisive economic policy problems that troubled the ruling Republican party: the simple acknowledgment of economic diversity. "We must recognize," he said, "the fact that, aside from their general interest as citizens, special groups of citizens have special interests." Rather than pretend—as nineteenth-century politicians typically had—that all classes shared the same wants and needs and benefited equally from government promotion of eco-

22. Corporate Records of the New York Central Railroad Company, Syracuse University Library. The four letters quoted here are: Ira A. Place to Joseph Mullin, April 13, 1895, and April 10, 1895; Charles C. Paulding to William P. Rudd, Feb. 27, 1901; and Ira A. Place to William P. Rudd, Feb. 24, 1904.

23. For a classic analysis expressing outrage against public utility and transportation corporations, see Gustavus Myers, "History of Public Franchises in New York City," *Municipal Affairs* 4 (March 1900), 71–206.

nomic development, Roosevelt admitted their differences, consulted them, and accorded them respect. Such an approach did
not in itself prevent discontent, but it at least established lines of
contact between government officials and interest-group leaders.
While Roosevelt's recognition of group differences significantly
anticipated twentieth-century policy patterns, his early application of the method required his own considerable charisma.
Roosevelt's successor as governor, Benjamin B. Odell, Jr., did not
carry the new practice forward, and, indeed, Odell made a rhetorical specialty of denying group differences on material questions.
As party politicians always had, Odell found it difficult to acknowledge real divisions in the electorate or to cope with the
divisive demands that an industrial society placed on government.[24]

In 1905 the legislative life insurance investigation brought to a
climax the forces for economic policy change in New York State.
A crisis for the Republican party, the inquiry discredited many of
its key leaders. One by one they took the witness stand and bared
their financial involvement with the once-trusted life insurance
companies. United States Senator Chauncey M. Depew admitted
receiving a substantial annual retainer from the Equitable, and
his testimony failed to shake suspicions that the fees mainly
purchased political influence. Party chairman and former governor Benjamin B. Odell, Jr., also had his reputation scarred by the
inquiry. Finally, Thomas Collier Platt, now virtually out of
party power but still in the Senate, took the witness stand and
described receiving tens of thousands of dollars in cash from the
largest companies at election time and then afterwards protecting
their interests. Platt's brief testimony, studded though it was with
an old man's vagueness and repetition, provided the investiga-

---

24. *The Works of Theodore Roosevelt: Memorial Edition*, 24 vols. (New York,
1923–26), 16: 460; for an illustration of Odell's claim that different groups shared
the same interests, see *Public Papers of Benjamin B. Odell, Jr., Governor for 1902*
(Albany, 1907), p. 367.

tion's clearest portrait of the process by which big business bought influence in the state government.[25]

Across the state the perception that business interests systematically corrupted democratic government created a sensation and led to new understandings of the relationship between the political and economic systems. "The wrath of thousands of private citizens whose voices are never heard in public is at white heat over the disclosures," declared a Republican daily paper in Rochester. "Civic virtue and civic pride are passing through the greatest and most dangerous crisis in the history of the republic," warned a Democratic weekly in Cortland.[26]

The insurance investigation and its aftermath changed New York State politics. Corporate campaign contributions were outlawed, and lobbying was regulated. The state assembly got a thorough housecleaning from its new young speaker, James W. Wadsworth, Jr. William Randolph Hearst nearly became mayor of New York City on a platform of municipal ownership. And, of most importance, in 1906 the investigating committee's chief counsel, Charles Evans Hughes, won election as governor of New York and brought with him to Albany a commitment to new methods of making economic policy.[27]

As governor, Hughes championed the tactic of taking complex and controversial economic questions out of party politics and making the decisions according to impartial standards. In prac-

25. Robert F. Wesser, *Charles Evans Hughes: Politics and Reform in New York, 1905–1910* (Ithaca, 1967) and Morton Keller, *The Life Insurance Enterprise, 1885–1910: A Study in the Limits of Corporate Power* (Cambridge, Mass., 1963) splendidly place the life insurance investigation in its political and economic setting. For the testimony by Depew, Odell, and Platt, see *Testimony Taken Before the Joint Committee of the Senate and Assembly of the State of New York to Investigate and Examine into the Business and Affairs of Life Insurance Companies Doing Business in the State of New York*, 10 vols. (Albany, 1905–6), pp. 3167–3205, 3143–60, 3385–97.

26. Rochester *Democrat and Chronicle*, Oct. 18, 1905; *Cortland Democrat*, Oct. 27, 1905.

27. Wesser, *Charles Evans Hughes*, describes these events.

tice this meant transferring authority from the legislature to administrative agencies, of which the most important were the new Public Service Commissions created to regulate transportation and utility companies. During his four years as governor Hughes relied increasingly on administrative boards in a wide range of areas, and he repeatedly pointed to the advantages of efficiency and accountability which such an approach offered. Above all, he believed, administration provided a way of resolving economic conflict over government policies, for "once [the tasks of government are] created and defined," Hughes said, "there is little room for disagreement as to the manner in which they should be performed."[28]

Along with Governor Roosevelt's practice of recognizing diverse interest groups, Hughes's reliance on administration completed a significant transformation in policymaking during the Progressive era in New York. The acknowledgment of group conflicts and the provision for their resolution according to systematic procedures together established a real departure from nineteenth-century methods of making economic policy. It should not be assumed that the new methods harmed the regulated interests. Hughes had predicted that regulation would benefit business and bring about "friendly cooperation" between corporations and the government. The available evidence suggests that Hughes was correct.[29]

By 1910 the political system in New York State had become something quite different from what it was under Platt in the 1890s. Party loyalty and voter participation had declined, while the government's increased attention to economic matters had given rise to new methods of policymaking. Interest-group or-

28. Jacob Gould Schurman, ed., *Addresses and Papers of Charles Evans Hughes* (New York, 1908), p. 277.

29. Schurman, ed., *Addresses*, p. 137. See Bruce W. Dearstyne, "Regulation in the Progressive Era: The New York Public Service Commission," *New York History* 58 (July 1977), 331–47, for an excellent account of how the railroad companies opposed the creation of the Public Service Commissions but later found their conservative policies highly satisfactory.

ganizations now commanded much of the confidence parties once enjoyed, while administrative agencies replaced the legislature as the locus of some of the most divisive decisions.

It was not a coincidence that the government expanded its intervention in the economy at the same time that many citizens lost the habit of voting straight party tickets every year. Indeed the concurrence of the two developments, as well as their capacity to reinforce each other, represented an entirely logical state of affairs. The loss of confidence in party organizations naturally diminished the power of party leaders to thwart economic policies they opposed. By the same token, the rising demand for policies that the parties resisted further weakened the parties. The joint progress of these two developments effectively shaped twentieth-century political conditions in New York, and in the nation as well.

While the present essay has so far said nothing of a progressive movement, the political innovations described here bear close comparison to movements usually labeled "progressive." In response to a variety of pressures on politics-as-usual, particularly in the aftermath of two pronounced crises, the leaders of the dominant Republican party took steps to reform nominating procedures, recognize independency from the machine, regulate big business corporations, and replace political methods of decision-making by expert administrative techniques. These reforms were the work of Republican leaders trying to keep their party in power. As such, they were designed less to transform the political system than to maintain as much as possible of its character through carefully chosen concessions and reforms. To be sure, Republican leaders differed in their degrees of loyalty to existing political practices and in their openness to change. In these respects, Roosevelt and Hughes unquestionably were more "progressive" than Platt and Odell. Still, all four leaders shared the search for political innovations to preserve the party by meeting the crises at hand.

To focus on the party leaders who acquiesced in a series of political reforms is, of course, to tell only half the story. Throughout the period, and especially in crisis times, there were men and women—who may as well be called "progressives"—voicing the demands and issuing the challenges that growing cities and growing industries brought to bear against the existing system of politics. There were urban independents and, later, those in the countryside who copied the independents' appeals. There were consumers complaining about transportation and utility companies. There were representatives from every sector of the economy asking for government help or for the cessation of government policies that hurt. But even as they responded to these voices, the party leaders scarcely abandoned political power to the diverse "progressive" forces. Quite the contrary was the case. Each Republican leader of the period actively fashioned strategies for enabling the party to retain power amidst the challenges it faced. Those strategies resulted in measures we label "progressive" reforms, but their origins and meaning must be sought as much in the exigencies of party politics as in a progressive movement.

Nevertheless, the careful study of the transformation of New York State politics discloses a good deal about progressivism. Both political crises recounted here called forth responses that closely resemble the progressive movement as historians have characterized it. At the time of the municipal elections of 1897, political initiative came from reformers like those described by Richard Hofstadter and George E. Mowry: urban, educated, and professional men whose rhetoric was moralistic and whose aims were restorative rather than revolutionary. Reluctant to expand government drastically, they sought modest measures to weaken corrupt bosses and adjust material conflicts.[30] Theodore Roosevelt was their ideal politician.

Less than a decade later, a second crisis changed the character of the progressive movement in New York. While their anti-boss and anti-business rhetoric retained traditional elements, the re-

---

30. Richard Hofstadter, *The Age of Reform: From Bryan to F. D. R.* (New York, 1955), chapters 4–6; George E. Mowry, *The California Progressives* (Berkeley, 1951), chapter 4; Mowry, *The Era of Theodore Roosevelt and the Birth of Modern America, 1900–1912* (New York, 1958), chapter 5.

formers to whom initiative had now passed demanded more extensive changes in government. The measures they proposed were not unlike those that Samuel P. Hays and Robert H. Wiebe have described: expert, administrative solutions to systematize and rationalize the social and economic order.[31] Hughes's approach to economic policymaking encompassed what these reformers had in mind.

Each political crisis provided occasion for the expression of ideals and the formulation of measures that historians have identified with progressivism. The usual approach to the study of the movement is to begin with the reformers and ask who they were and what they wanted. An alternative approach, suggested here, is to start with the political system, ask how it changed, and concentrate on the moments of turmoil when it changed the most. At such times, and in their aftermaths, "progressive" reforms emerged from the interacting efforts of those in power to stay there and those with grievances against existing politics to have them met.

The year 1910 provides a convenient stopping point for the present essay because it was then that the Republicans fell from power in New York, and the Democrats took on the continuing task of adjusting the political system to new social and economic circumstances. Indeed, 1911 saw what might be termed a third political crisis of the Progressive era in New York: the Triangle Shirtwaist Company fire. In its aftermath, the Democratic-controlled state legislature appointed the Factory Investigating Commission which over the next five years stimulated an avalanche of legislation concerning labor and social welfare, subjects generally ignored before 1910. These new policies marked yet more departure from nineteenth-century political practices.[32]

31. Samuel P. Hays, *Conservation and the Gospel of Efficiency* (Cambridge, Mass., 1959); Robert H. Wiebe, *The Search for Order, 1877–1920* (New York, 1967).

32. J. Joseph Huthmacher, "Charles Evans Hughes and Charles Francis Murphy: The Metamorphosis of Progressivism," *New York History* 46 (Jan. 1965), especially pp. 31–33.

The political changes experienced in New York at the beginning of the twentieth century should not, of course, be exaggerated. While parties lost their hegemony over economic policymaking and ceased to have the loyalty of so many citizens, they retained a strong voice whenever the state government pursued its traditional policy of distributing resources to promote economic growth, and they continued to dominate the electoral process itself. Despite the coming of state control over primary elections, the traditional structures of party organization persisted, and in the year-in-and-year-out choice of candidates for public office the party machines continued to reign supreme. Some of the sharpest political tactics from the nineteenth century still persist. What Republican governor in twentieth-century New York has not tried, as Platt did, to use the state government to enlarge his party's share of downstate power and patronage?

Nonetheless, from 1890 to 1910, urbanization and industrialization took a substantial toll on nineteenth-century political practices. The traditional system of politics met a succession of crises and emerged transformed. Government undertook fresh and vigorous policies on economic questions, while voters weakened in their partisan attachments and went to the polls less often than before. In the long run, these patterns originated in the challenges that growing cities and growing industries posed to politics-as-usual. In the short run, they were the work of men like Roosevelt and Hughes, whom we call progressives.

9

The Discovery That Business Corrupts Politics: A Reappraisal of the Origins of Progressivism

Almost any history textbook that covers the Progressive era and was written at least twenty years ago tells how early twentieth-century Americans discovered that big business interests were corrupting politics in quest of special privileges and how an outraged people acted to reform the perceived evils. Commonly, the narrative offers ample anecdotal evidence to support this tale of scandal and reform. The autobiographies of leading progressives—including Theodore Roosevelt, Robert M. La Follette, William Allen White, Frederic C. Howe, and Lincoln Steffens, among others—are frequently cited, because all of them recounted the purported awakening of their authors to the corrupt politico-business alliance.[1] Muckraking journalism, not only by Steffens but also by David Graham Phillips, Charles E. Russell, Ray Stannard Baker, and numerous others, is often drawn upon

---

1. Although it is a common autobiographical convention to recount one's growth from ignorance to knowledge, it is nonetheless striking that so many progressive autobiographies should identify the same point of ignorance and trace a similar path to knowledge. See Roosevelt, *An Autobiography* (New York, 1913), 85–86, 186, 297–300, 306, 321–23; La Follette, *La Follette's Autobiography: A Personal Narrative of Political Experiences* (Madison, Wis., 1960), 3–97; White, *The Autobiography of William Allen White* (New York, 1946), 149–50, 160–61, 177–79, 192–93, 215–16, 232–34, 325–26, 345, 351, 364, 428–29, 439–40, 465; Howe, *The Confessions of a Reformer* (New York, 1925), 70–72, 100–12; and Steffens, *The Autobiography of Lincoln Steffens* (New York, 1931), 357–627.

too, along with evidence that the magazines for which they wrote achieved unprecedented circulation. Political speeches, party platforms, and newspaper editorials by the hundreds are also offered to buttress the contention that Americans of the early 1900s discovered the prevalence of illicit business influence in politics and demanded its removal. But all of this evidence would probably fail to persuade historians today that the old textbook scenario for progressivism is correct.

And for good reason. Every prominent interpretation of the progressive movement now encourages us not to take the outcry against politico-business corruption too seriously. Some historians have seen progressivism as dichotomous: alongside the individualist, anti-business strain of reform stood an equally vocal, and ultimately more successful, school that accepted industrial growth and sought even closer cooperation between business and government.[2] Other recent interpreters have described progressivism as a pluralistic movement of diverse groups, including businessmen, who came together when their interests coincided and worked separately when they did not.[3] Still other historians have seen businessmen themselves as the key progressives, whose methods and techniques were copied by other reformers.[4] Whichever view of the movement they have favored, historians have increasingly recognized the Progressive era as the age when Americans

2. Richard Hofstadter, *The Age of Reform: From Bryan to F.D.R.* (New York, 1955), 133; George E. Mowry, *The Era of Theodore Roosevelt, 1900–1912* (New York, 1958), 55–58; John Braeman, "Seven Progressives," *Business History Review*, 35 (1961): 581–92; and Sheldon Hackney, *Populism to Progressivism in Alabama* (Princeton, 1969), xii–xiii, 329–30.

3. John D. Buenker, "The Progressive Era: A Search for a Synthesis," *Mid-America*, 51 (1969): 175–93; David P. Thelen, "Social Tensions and the Origins of Progressivism," *Journal of American History* [hereafter, *JAH*], 56 (1969): 323–41; and Peter G. Filene, "An Obituary for 'The Progressive Movement,'" *American Quarterly*, 22 (1970): 20–34.

4. Robert H. Wiebe, *Businessmen and Reform: A Study of the Progressive Movement* (Cambridge, Mass., 1962); Gabriel Kolko, *The Triumph of Conservatism: A Reinterpretation of American History, 1900–1916* (New York, 1963); and Samuel P. Hays, "The Politics of Reform in Municipal Government in the Progressive Era," *Pacific Northwest Quarterly*, 55 (1964): 157–69.

accommodated, rather than tried to escape, large-scale business organizations and their methods.[5] More often than not, the achievement of what used to be called reform now appears to have benefited big business interests. If our aim is to grasp the results and meaning of progressivism, the evidence in the typical textbook seems to lead in the wrong direction.

The currently dominant "organizational" interpretation of the progressive movement has particularly little room for such evidence. Led by Samuel P. Hays and Robert H. Wiebe, a number of scholars have located the progressive impulse in the drive of newly formed business and professional groups to achieve their goals through organization and expertise. In a related study, Louis Galambos has described the progressive outcry against the trusts as merely a phase in the nation's growing acceptance of large corporations, and, with Hays and Wiebe, he has suggested that the rhetorical attack on business came to very little. The distinctive achievement of this interpretation lies in its account of how in the early twentieth century the United States became an organized, bureaucratic society whose model institution was the large corporation. Where reformers of the 1880s and 1890s had sought to resist the forces of industrialism, or at least to prevent their penetration of the local community, the progressives of the early 1900s accepted an industrial society and concentrated their efforts on controlling, ordering, and improving it. No interpretation of the era based on ideological evidence of a battle between the "people" and the "interests" can capture the enormous complexity of the adjustments to industrialism worked out by different social groups. Hays and Wiebe have succeeded better than any previous historians in describing and characterizing those adjustments and placing them in the context of large social and

5. Samuel P. Hays, *The Response to Industrialism, 1885–1914* (Chicago, 1957); Robert H. Wiebe, *The Search for Order, 1877–1920* (New York, 1967); Louis Galambos, *The Public Image of Big Business in America, 1880–1940: A Quantitative Study in Social Change* (Baltimore, 1975); William L. O'Neill, *The Progressive Years: America Comes of Age* (New York, 1975); and David P. Thelen, *Robert M. La Follette and the Insurgent Spirit* (Boston, 1976).

economic changes. In this light the progressives' claims to have discovered and opposed the corruption of politics by business seem to become a curiosity of the era, not a clue to its meaning, a diversion to the serious historian exploring the organizational achievements that constituted true progressivism, a suitable subject for old textbooks.[6]

Despite its great strengths, however, the organizational model neglects too much.[7] Missing is the progressives' moral intensity, as well as their surprise and animation upon discovering political and social evils. Missing, too, are their own explanations of what they felt and what they were doing. And absent, above all, is

6. Louis Galambos provided a sympathetic introduction to the work of the "organizational" school; see his "The Emerging Organizational Synthesis in Modern American History," *Business History Review*, 44 (1970): 279–90. For another effort to place the work of these historians in perspective, see Robert H. Wiebe, "The Progressive Years, 1900–1917," in William H. Cartwright and Richard L. Watson, Jr., eds., *The Reinterpretation of American History and Culture* (Washington, 1973), 425–42. In addition to the works by Wiebe, Hays, and Galambos, already cited, several other studies by Hays also rank among the most important products of the organizational school: Samuel P. Hays, *Conservation and the Gospel of Efficiency: The Progressive Conservation Movement, 1890–1920* (Cambridge, Mass., 1959), "Political Parties and the Community-Society Continuum," in William Nisbet Chambers and Walter Dean Burnham, eds., *The American Party Systems: Stages of Political Development* (New York, 1967), 152–81, and "The New Organizational Society," in Jerry Israel, ed., *Building the Organizational Society: Essays on Associational Activities in Modern America* (New York, 1972), 1–15. Although Wiebe and Hays share the same broad interpretation of the period, their works make quite distinctive contributions, and there are certain matters on which they have disagreed. Some of Wiebe's most important insights concern the complex relationships between business and reform, while Hays has demonstrated particular originality on the subjects of urban politics and political parties. Concerning the middle classes, they have differing views: Wiebe has included the middle classes among the "organizers," while Hays has emphasized their persistent individualism. Compare Wiebe, *The Search for Order, 1877–1920*, chap. 5, and Hays, *The Response to Industrialism, 1885–1914*, chap. 4.

7. For related comments on the organizational model's shortcomings, see William G. Anderson, "Progressivism: An Historiographical Essay," *History Teacher*, 6 (1973): 427–52; David M. Kennedy, "Overview: The Progressive Era," *Historian*, 37 (1975): 453–68; O'Neill, *The Progressive Years*, x, 45; and Morton Keller, *Affairs of State: Public Life in Late Nineteenth Century America* (Cambridge, Mass., 1977), 285–87.

a description, much less an analysis, of the particular political circumstances from which progressivism emerged in the first years of the twentieth century. In place of these vivid actualities, the organizational historians offer a vague account of what motivated the reformers who advocated bureaucratic solutions and an exaggerated estimation of their capacity to predict and control events. Actually, progressive reform was not characterized by remarkable rationality or foresight; nor were the "organizers" always at the forefront of the movement. Often the results the progressives achieved were unexpected and ironical; and, along the way, crucial roles were sometimes played by people and ideas that, in the end, met defeat.

The perception that privileged businesses corrupted politics was one such ultimately unsuccessful idea of particular short-run instrumentality. Especially in the cities and states, around the middle of the first decade of the twentieth century, the discovery of such corruption precipitated crises that led to the most significant political changes of the time. When the crises had passed, the results for political participation and public policy were roughly those that the organizational interpretation predicts, but the way these changes came about is far from adequately described by that thesis. The pages that follow here sketch an account of political change in the early twentieth century and show how the discovery of politico-business corruption played this central, transforming role—though not with quite the same results that the old textbooks describe.

Admittedly, to interpret progressivism on the basis of its political and governmental side is a more risky endeavor than it once was. Indeed, a major thrust of contemporary scholarship has been to subordinate the Progressive era's political achievements to the larger social and economic changes associated with what Wiebe has called "the process of America's modernization."[8] From such a perspective, "developments in politics" become, as John C. Burnham has observed, "mere epiphenomena of more basic

8. Wiebe, "The Progressive Years, 1900–1917," 429.

forces and changes."[9] But what if political behavior fails to fit trends that the rest of society seems to be experiencing? What conclusions are to be drawn, for instance, from the observation that American political rhetoric was preoccupied with attacking corporations at precisely the moment in the early twentieth century when such businesses were becoming ascendant in economic and social life? One approach simply ignores the anomalous behavior or, at most, considers it spurious or deceptive. Another answer lies in the notions that American politics is fundamentally discontinuous with the rest of national life and that, as several political scientists have suggested, it has always retained a "premodern" character.[10] A better solution, however, rests upon a close study of the ways in which apparently anachronistic political events and the ideas they inspired became essential catalysts for "modernizing" developments. Studied in this manner, politics has more to tell us about progressivism than contemporary wisdom generally admits.

Shortly after 1900, American politics and government experienced a decisive and rather rapid transformation that affected both the patterns of popular political involvement and the nature and functions of government itself. To be sure, the changes were not revolutionary, but, considering how relatively undevelopmental the political system of the United States has been, they are of considerable historical importance. The basic features of this political transformation can be easily described, but its causes and significance are somewhat more difficult to grasp.

9. John D. Buenker, John C. Burnham, and Robert M. Crunden, *Progressivism* (Cambridge, Mass., 1977), 4. For some disagreements among these three authors about how central politics was to progressivism, see *ibid.*, 107-29.

10. Samuel P. Huntington, *Political Order in Changing Societies* (New Haven, 1968), 93-139; Walter Dean Burnham, *Critical Elections and the Mainsprings of American Politics* (New York, 1970), 175-93; and J. G. A. Pocock, *The Machiavellian Moment: Florentine Political Thought and the Atlantic Republican Tradition* (Princeton, 1975), 549.

One important category of change involved the manner and methods of popular participation in politics. For most of the nineteenth century, high rates of partisan voting—based on complex sectional, cultural, and communal influences—formed the American people's main means of political expression and involvement. Only in exceptional circumstances did most individuals or groups rely on nonelectoral methods of influencing the government. Indeed, almost no such means existed within the normal bounds of politics. After 1900, this structure of political participation changed. Voter turnout fell, and, even among those electors who remained active, pure and simple partisanship became less pervasive. At approximately the same time, interest-group organizations of all sorts successfully forged permanent, nonelectoral means of influencing the government and its agencies. Only recently have historians begun to explore with care what caused these changes in the patterns of political participation and to delineate the redistribution of power that they entailed.[11]

American governance, too, went through a fundamental transition in the early 1900s. Wiebe has accurately described it as the emergence of "a government broadly and continuously involved in society's operations."[12] Both the institutions of government and the content of policy reflected the change. Where the legislature had been the dominant branch of government at every level,

---

11. I have elsewhere cited many of the sources on which these generalizations are based; see my "The Party Period and Public Policy: An Exploratory Hypothesis," *JAH*, 66 (1979): 279–98. On the decline in turnout and the increase in ticket-splitting, see Walter Dean Burnham, "The Changing Shape of the American Political Universe," *American Political Science Review* [hereafter, *APSR*], 59 (1965): 7–28. On the rise of interest-group organizations, see Hays, "Political Parties and the Community-Society Continuum." For two studies that make significant contributions to an understanding of how the political changes of the early twentieth century altered the power relationships among groups, see J. Morgan Kousser, *The Shaping of Southern Politics: Suffrage Restriction and the Establishment of the One-Party South, 1880–1910* (New Haven, 1974); and Carl V. Harris, *Political Power in Birmingham, 1871–1921* (Knoxville, 1977).

12. Wiebe, *The Search for Order, 1877–1920,* 160.

lawmakers now saw their power curtailed by an enlarged executive and, even more, by the creation of an essentially new branch of government composed of administrative boards and agencies. Where nineteenth-century policy had generally focused on distinct groups and locales (most characteristically through the distribution of resources and privileges to enterprising individuals and corporations), the government now began to take explicit account of clashing interests and to assume the responsibility for mitigating their conflicts through regulation, administration, and planning. In 1900, government did very little in the way of recognizing and adjusting group differences. Fifteen years later, innumerable policies committed officials to that formal purpose and provided the bureaucratic structures for achieving it.[13]

Most political historians consider these changes to be the products of long-term social and economic developments. Accordingly, they have devoted much of their attention to tracing the interconnecting paths leading from industrialization, urbanization, and immigration to the political and governmental responses. Some of the general trends have been firmly documented in scholarship: the organization of functional groups whose needs the established political parties could not meet; the creation of new demands for government policies to make life bearable in crowded cities, where huge industries were located; and the determination of certain cultural and economic groups to curtail the political power of people they considered threatening. All of these developments, along with others, occurred over a period of decades—now speeded, now slowed by depression, migration, prosperity, fortune, and the talents of individual men and women.

13. McCormick, "The Party Period and Public Policy"; Robert A. Lively, "The American System: A Review Article," *Business History Review*, 29 (1955): 81–96; James Willard Hurst, *Law and the Conditions of Freedom in the Nineteenth-Century United States* (Madison, Wis., 1956); Theodore J. Lowi, "American Business, Public Policy, Case-Studies, and Political Theory," *World Politics*, 16 (1964): 677–715; and Wiebe, *The Search for Order, 1877–1920*, 159–95.

Yet, given the long-term forces involved, it is notable how suddenly the main elements of the new political order went into place. The first fifteen years of the twentieth century witnessed most of the changes; more precisely, the brief period from 1904 to 1908 saw a remarkably compressed political transformation. During these years the regulatory revolution peaked; new and powerful agencies of government came into being everywhere.[14] At the same time, voter turnout declined, ticket-splitting increased, and organized social, economic, and reform-minded groups began to exercise power more systematically than ever before.[15] An understanding of how the new polity crystallized so rapidly can be obtained by exploring, first, the latent threat to the old system represented by fears of "corruption"; then, the pressures for political change that had built up by about 1904; and, finally, the way in which the old fears abruptly took on new meaning and inspired a resolution of the crisis.

Long before 1900—indeed, since before the Revolution—Americans had been aware that governmental promotion of private interests, which became the dominant form of nineteenth-century economic policy, carried with it risks of corruption. From the English opposition of Walpole's day, colonists in America had absorbed the theory that commercial development threatened republican government in two ways: (1) by spreading greed, ex-

14. James Willard Hurst, *Law and Social Order in the United States* (Ithaca, 1977), 33, 36, and *Law and the Conditions of Freedom*, 71–108; and Grover G. Huebner, "Five Years of Railroad Regulation by the States," *Annals of the American Academy of Political and Social Science*, 32 (1908): 138–56. For a further account of these governmental changes, see pages 345–46, 350–56, below.

15. Burnham, "The Changing Shape of the American Political Universe," and *Critical Elections and the Mainsprings of American Politics*, 71–90, 115; and Jerrold G. Rusk, "The Effect of the Australian Ballot Reform on Split-Ticket Voting, 1876–1908," *APSR*, 64 (1970): 1220–38. For a contemporary effort to estimate and assess split-ticket voting, see Philip Loring Allen, "Ballot Laws and Their Workings," *Political Science Quarterly*, 21 (1906): 38–58.

travagance, and luxury among the people; and (2) by encouraging a designing ministry to conspire with monied interests for the purpose of overwhelming the independence of the legislature. Neither theme ever entirely disappeared from American politics, although each was significantly revised as time passed. For Jeffersonians in the 1790s, as Lance Banning has demonstrated, both understandings remained substantially intact. In their belief, Alexander Hamilton's program of public aid to commercial enterprises would inevitably make an agrarian people less virtuous and would also create a phalanx of privileged interests—including bank directors, speculators, and stock-jobbers—pledged to support the administration faction that had nurtured them. Even after classical republican thought waned and the structure of government-business relations changed, these eighteenth-century fears that corruption inevitably flowed from government-assisted commercial development continued to echo in American politics.[16]

For much of the nineteenth century, as Fred Somkin has shown, thoughtful citizens remained ambivalent about economic abundance, because they feared its potential to corrupt them and their government. "Over and over again," Somkin stated, "Americans called attention to the danger which prosperity posed for the safety of free institutions and for the maintenance of republicanism."[17] In the 1830s the Democratic party's official ideology began to give voice to these fears. Using language similar to that of Walpole's and Hamilton's critics, Andrew Jackson decried

16. Banning, *The Jeffersonian Persuasion: Evolution of a Party Ideology* (Ithaca, 1978); J. G. A. Pocock, "Virtue and Commerce in the Eighteenth Century," *Journal of Interdisciplinary History*, 3 (1972): 119–34, and *The Machiavellian Moment*, 506–52; Gordon S. Wood, *The Creation of the American Republic, 1776–1787* (Chapel Hill, 1969), 32–33, 52, 64–65, 107–14, 400–403, 416–21; Morton Keller, "Corruption in America : Continuity and Change," in Abraham S. Eisenstadt et al., eds., *Before Watergate: Problems of Corruption in American Society* (New York, 1979), 7–19; and Edwin G. Burrows, "Albert Gallatin and the Problem of Corruption in the Federalist Era," *ibid.*, 51–67.

17. Somkin, *Unquiet Eagle: Memory and Desire in the Idea of American Freedom, 1815–1860* (Ithaca, 1967), 24.

"special privileges" from government as dangerous to liberty and demanded their abolition. Much of his wrath was directed against the Second Bank of the United States. That "monster," he said, was "a vast electioneering engine"; it has "already attempted to subject the government to its will." The Bank clearly raised the question of "whether the people of the United States are to govern . . . or whether the power and money of a great corporation are to be secretly exerted to influence their judgment and control their decisions." In a different context Jackson made the point with simple clarity: "Money," he said, "is power." Yet Jackson's anti-bank rhetoric also carried a new understanding of politico-business corruption, different from that of the eighteenth century. For the danger that Jackson apprehended came not from a corrupt ministry, whose tool the monied interests were, but from privileged monsters, acting independently from public authorities and presenting a danger not only to the government but also to the welfare of other social and economic groups ("the farmers, mechanics, and laborers") whose interests conflicted with theirs. Jackson's remedy was to scale down governmental undertakings, on the grounds that public privileges led to both corruption and inequality.[18]

Despite the prestige that Jackson lent to the attack on privilege, it was not a predominant fear for Americans in the nine-

18. [Jackson] *Annual Messages, Veto Messages, Protests, &c. of Andrew Jackson, President of the United States* (Baltimore, 1835), 162, 165, 179, 197, 244. Numerous studies document the Democratic party's use of the accusation that privileged business was corrupting politics: Lee Benson, *The Concept of Jacksonian Democracy: New York as a Test Case* (Princeton, 1961), 52–56, 96–97, 236; William G. Shade, *Banks or No Banks: The Money Issue in Western Politics, 1832–1865* (Detroit, 1972), 56–59; Marvin Meyers, *The Jacksonian Persuasion: Politics and Belief* (Stanford, 1957), 23–24, 30, 157–58, 196, 198; and Edward K. Spann, *Ideals and Politics: New York Intellectuals and Liberal Democracy, 1820–1880* (Albany, N.Y., 1972), 60, 68–78, 105–6. President Martin Van Buren's special message to Congress proposing the subtreasury system in 1837 contained accusations against the Bank similar to those Jackson had made, except that Van Buren expressed them more in "pure," eighteenth-century republican language; James D. Richardson, ed., *A Compilation of the Messages and Papers of the Presidents, 1789–1897*, 10 vols. (Washington, 1896–99), 3: 324–46.

teenth century. So many forms of thought and avarice disguised the dangers Jackson saw. First of all, Americans were far from agreed that governmental assistance for some groups hurt the rest, as he proclaimed. Both the "commonwealth" notion of a harmonious community and its successor, the Whig-Republican concept of interlocking producer interests, suggested that economic benefits from government would be shared throughout society. Even when differences emerged over who should get what, an abundance of land and resources disguised the conflicts, while the inherent divisibility of public benefits encouraged their widespread distribution. Especially at the state and local levels, Democrats, as well as Whigs and Republicans, freely succumbed to the nearly universal desire for government aid. Not to have done so would have been as remarkable as to have withheld patronage from deserving partisans.[19] Nor, in the second place, was it evident to most nineteenth-century Americans that private interests represented a threat to the commonweal. While their eighteenth-century republican heritage warned them of the danger to free government from a designing ministry that manipulated monied interests, classical economics denied that there was a comparable danger to the public from private enterprises that were independent of the government. Indeed, the public-private distinction tended to be blurred for nineteenth-century Americans, and not until it came into focus did new threats of

19. McCormick, "The Party Period and Public Policy," 286–88. On the "commonwealth" ideal, see Oscar Handlin and Mary Flug Handlin, *Commonwealth: A Study of the Role of Government in the American Economy: Massachusetts, 1774–1861* (New York, 1947); and Louis Hartz, *Economic Policy and Democratic Thought: Pennsylvania, 1776–1860* (Cambridge, Mass., 1948). For a classic expression of the Whig concept of interlocking producer interests, see Calvin Colton, ed., *The Works of Henry Clay, Comprising His Life, Correspondence, and Speeches,* 5 (New York, 1897): 437–86; and, for a later Republican expression of the same point of view, see Benjamin Harrison, *Speeches of Benjamin Harrison, Twenty-third President of the United States* (New York, 1892), 62, 72, 157, 167, 181, 197. For a discussion of the Republican ideology and economic policy, see Eric Foner, *Free Soil, Free Labor, Free Men: The Ideology of the Republican Party before the Civil War* (New York, 1970), 18–23.

politico-business corruption seem as real as the old ones had in the 1700s.[20]

As time passed, Jackson's Democratic party proved to be a weak vehicle for the insight that privileged businesses corrupted politics and government. The party's platforms, which in the 1840s had declared a national bank "dangerous to our republican institutions," afterwards dropped such rhetoric. The party of Stephen A. Douglas, Samuel J. Tilden, and Grover Cleveland all but abandoned serious criticism of politico-business corruption. Cleveland's annual message of 1887, which he devoted wholly to the tariff issue, stands as the Gilded Age's equivalent to Jackson's Bank veto. But, unlike Jackson, Cleveland made his case entirely on economic grounds and did not suggest that the protected interests corrupted government. Nor did William Jennings Bryan pay much attention to the theme in 1896. Unlike his Populist supporters who charged that public officials had "basely surrendered . . . to corporate monopolies," the Democrat Bryan made only fleeting mention of the political influence of big corporations or the danger to liberty from privileged businesses.[21]

From outside the political mainstream, the danger was more visible. Workingmen's parties, Mugwumps, Greenbackers, Prohibitionists, and Populists all voiced their own versions of the accusation that business corrupted politics and government. The Greenbackers charged that the major parties were tools of the

---

20. Lively, "The American System," 94; Carter Goodrich, "The Revulsion against Internal Improvements," *Journal of Economic History*, 10 (1950): 169; and Hays, *The Response to Industrialism, 1885–1914*, 39–40. On the reluctance of state legislatures to prohibit their members from mixing public and private business, see Ari Hoogenboom, "Did Gilded Age Scandals Bring Reform?" in Eisenstadt et al., *Before Watergate*, 127–31.

21. Compare the Democratic platforms of 1840–52 with those for the rest of the century; see Donald Bruce Johnson and Kirk H. Porter, eds., *National Party Platforms, 1840–1972* (Urbana, 1973); for the People's party platform of 1896, see *ibid.*, 104. For Cleveland's message of 1887, see Richardson, *Messages and Papers of the Presidents, 1789–1897*, 8: 580–91; and, for a compilation of Bryan's speeches of 1896, see his *The First Battle: A Story of the Campaign of 1896* (Chicago, 1896).

monopolies; the Prohibitionists believed that the liquor corporations endangered free institutions; and the Populists powerfully
indicted both the Democrats and Republicans for truckling to the
interests "to secure corruption funds from the millionaires." In
Progress and Poverty (1879), Henry George asked, "Is there not
growing up among us a class who have all the power . . . ? We
have simple citizens who control thousands of miles of railroad,
millions of acres of land, the means of livelihood of great
numbers of men; who name the governors of sovereign states as
they name their clerks, choose senators as they choose attorneys,
and whose will is as supreme with legislatures as that of a French
king sitting in a bed of justice."[22] But these were the voices of
dissenters and frail minorities. Their accusations of corruption
posed a latent challenge to an economic policy based on distributing privileges to private interests, but for most of the nineteenth century their warnings were not widely accepted or even
listened to by the political majority.

The late 1860s and early and mid-1870s, however, offer an
apparent exception. These were the years when the Crédit Mobilier and other scandals—local and national—aroused a furor
against politico-business corruption. "Perhaps the offense most
discredited by the exposures," according to C. Vann Woodward,
"was the corrupting of politicians to secure government subsidies and grants to big corporations—particularly railroads."
For several years, in consequence, there was a widespread revulsion against a policy of bestowing public privileges and benefits
on private companies. Editorializing in 1873 on the Crédit Mobilier scandal, E. L. Godkin of the *Nation* declared, "The remedy is

---

22. Johnson and Porter, *National Party Platforms, 1840–1972*, 90; and George,
*Progess and Poverty—An Inquiry into the Cause of Industrial Depressions and of
Increase of Want with Increase of Wealth: The Remedy* (New York, 1880), 481.
For examples of other late nineteenth-century dissenters who recognized the
corruption of politics and government by business interests, see H. R. Chamber-
lain, *The Farmers' Alliance: What It Aims To Accomplish* (New York, 1891), 12,
37–38; and Henry Demarest Lloyd, *Wealth against Commonwealth* (New York,
1894), 369–404.

simple. The Government must get out of the 'protective' business and the 'subsidy' business and the 'improvement' and the 'development' business. It must let trade, and commerce, and manufactures, and steamboats, and railroads, and telegraphs alone. It cannot touch them without breeding corruption." Yet even in the mid-1870s, by Woodward's own account, it was possible for railroad and other promoters, especially in the South and Midwest, to organize local meetings that rekindled the fervor for subsidies in town after town. The fear of corruption that Godkin voiced simply was not compelling enough to override the demand for policies of unchecked promotion.[23]

Even the nineteenth century's most brilliant and sustained analysis of business and politics—that provided by the Adams brothers, Charles Francis, Jr. and Henry, in their *Chapters of Erie* (1871)—failed to portray the danger convincingly. Recounting the classic Gilded Age roguery of Jay Gould and Jim Fisk, including their corruption of courts and legislatures and their influence on the president himself, the Adamses warned that, as Henry put it, "the day is at hand when corporations . . . having created a system of quiet but irresistible corruption—will ultimately succeed in directing government itself." But the Adams brothers presented Gould and Fisk as so fantastic that readers could not believe that ordinary businessmen could accomplish such feats. Rather than describing a process of politico-business corruption, the Adamses gave only the dramatic particulars of it. Words like "astounding," "unique," and "extraordinary" marked their account. Writing of the effort by Gould and Fisk to corner the market on gold in 1869, Henry said, "Even the

---

23. Woodward, *Reunion and Reaction: The Compromise of 1877 and the End of Reconstruction* (Boston, 1951), 65; and Godkin, "The Moral of the Crédit Mobilier Scandal," *Nation*, 16 (1873): 68. Also see Allan Nevins, *The Emergence of Modern America, 1865–1878* (New York, 1927), 178–202; and John G. Sproat, *"The Best Men": Liberal Reformers in the Gilded Age* (New York, 1968), 72–73. For the ebb and flow of public aid to private enterprise in this era, see Keller, *Affairs of State,* 162–96. For other expressions of Godkin's opinion, see the *Nation*, 16 (1873): 328–29, and 24 (1877): 82–83.

most dramatic of modern authors, even Balzac himself, . . . or Alexandre Dumas, with all his extravagance of imagination, never have reached a conception bolder or more melodramatic than this, nor have they ever ventured to conceive a plot so enormous, or a catastrophe so original." Far from supporting the Adamses' thesis, such descriptions must have undermined it by raising doubts that what Gould and Fisk did could be widely or systematically repeated.[24]

Expressed by third parties and by elite spokesmen like Godkin and the Adamses, the fear that business corrupted politics exerted only minor influence in the late nineteenth century. When they recognized corruption, ordinary people seem to have blamed "bad" politicians, like James G. Blaine, and to have considered the businessmen guiltless. Even when Americans saw that corruption involved the use of money, they showed more interest in how the money was spent—for example, to bribe voters—than in where it came from. Wanting governmental assistance for their enterprises, but only sporadically scrutinizing its political implications, most people probably failed to perceive what the Adamses saw.[25] Nor did they, until social and industrial developments created deep dissatisfaction with the existing policy process. Then, the discovery that privileged businesses corrupted politics played a vital, if short-lived, role in facilitating the momentous transition from the nineteenth-century polity to the one Americans fashioned at the beginning of the twentieth century.

By the 1890s, large-scale industrialization was creating the felt need for new government policies in two distinct but related ways. The first process, which Hays and Wiebe have described so

24. Adams and Adams, *Chapters of Erie* (reprint ed., Ithaca, 1956), 136, 107. Originally published as articles during the late 1860s and early 1870s, these essays were first issued in book form in 1871 under the title *Chapters of Erie and Other Essays* (Boston).

25. For the vivid expression of a similar point, see Wiebe, *The Search for Order, 1877–1920*, 28.

well, was the increasing organization of diverse producer groups, conscious of their own identities and special needs. Each demanded specific public protections for its own endeavors and questioned the allocation of benefits to others. The second development was less tangible: the unorganized public's dawning sense of vulnerability, unease, and anger in the face of economic changes wrought by big corporations. Sometimes, the people's inchoate feelings focused on the ill-understood "trusts"; at other times, their negative emotions found more specific, local targets in street-railway or electric-power companies. Older interpretations of progressivism gave too much weight to the second of these developments; recently, only a few historians have sufficiently recognized it.[26]

Together, these processes created a political crisis by making people conscious of uncomfortable truths that earlier nineteenth-century conditions had obscured: that society's diverse producer groups did not exist in harmony or share equally in government benefits, and that private interests posed a danger to the public's interests. The crisis brought on by the recognition of these two problems extended approximately from the onset of depression in 1893 until 1908 and passed through three distinct phases: (1) the years of realignment, 1893–96; (2) the years of experimentation and uncertainty, 1897–1904; and (3) the years of discovery and resolution, 1905–08. When the crisis was over, the American political system was different in important respects from what it had been before.

During the first phase, the depression and the alleged radicalism of the Populists preoccupied politics and led to a decisive change in the national balance of party power. Willingly or unwillingly, many former voters now ceased to participate in

---

26. Hays, *The Response to Industrialism, 1885–1914;* and Wiebe, *The Search for Order, 1877–1920.* On the fear and anger of the unorganized, see Hofstadter, *The Age of Reform,* 213–69: Irwin Unger and Debi Unger, *The Vulnerable Years: The United States, 1896–1917* (Hinsdale, Ill., 1977), 102–8; and David P. Thelen, *The New Citizenship: Origins of Progressivism in Wisconsin, 1885–1900* (Columbia, Mo., 1972).

politics, while others from almost every social group in the North and Midwest shifted their allegiance to the Republicans. As a result, that party established a national majority that endured until the 1930s. Yet, given how decisive the realignment of the 1890s was, it is striking how quickly the particular issues of 1896—tariff protection and free silver—faded and how little of long-standing importance the realignment resolved.[27] To be sure, the defeat of Bryan and the destruction of Populism established who would not have control of the process of accommodating the nation to industrial realities, but the election of 1896 did much less in determining who would be in charge or what the solutions would be.

In the aftermath of realignment, a subtler form of crisis took hold—although several happy circumstances partially hid it, both from people then and from historians since. The war with Spain boosted national pride and self-confidence; economic prosperity returned after the depression; and the Republican party with its new majority gave the appearance of having doctrines that were relevant to industrial problems. Soon, President Theodore Roosevelt's activism and appeal helped foster an impression of political command over the economy. However disguised, the crisis nonetheless was real, and, in the years after 1896, many voices quietly questioned whether traditional politics and government could resolve interest-group conflicts or allay the sense of vulnerability that ordinary people felt.

Central to the issue were the dual problems of how powerful

27. The three most important studies of the electoral realignment of the 1890s are Paul Kleppner, *The Cross of Culture: A Social Analysis of Midwestern Politics, 1850-1900* (New York, 1970); Richard Jensen, *The Winning of the Midwest: Social and Political Conflict, 1888-1896* (Chicago, 1971); and Samuel T. McSeveney, *The Politics of Depression: Political Behavior in the Northeast, 1893-1896* (New York, 1972). A number of studies associate the realignment with subsequent changes in government policy: Walter Dean Burnham et al., "Partisan Realignment: A Systemic Perspective," in Joel H. Silbey et al., eds., *The History of American Electoral Behavior* (Princeton, 1978), 45–77; and David W. Brady, "Critical Elections, Congressional Parties, and Clusters of Policy Changes," *British Journal of Political Science*, 8 (1978): 79–99.

government should be and whether it ought to acknowledge and adjust group differences. Industrialism and its consequences seemed to demand strong public policies based on a recognition of social conflict. At the very least, privileged corporations had to be restrained, weaker elements in the community protected, and regular means established for newer interest groups to participate in government. But the will, the energy, and the imagination to bring about these changes seemed missing. Deeply felt ideological beliefs help explain this paralysis. The historic American commitment, on the one hand, to weak government, local autonomy, and the preservation of individual liberties—reflected in the doctrines of the Democratic party—presented a strong barrier to any significant expansion of governmental authority. The ingrained resistance, on the other hand, to having the government acknowledge that the country's producing interests were not harmonious—voiced in the doctrines of the Republican party—presented an equally strong obstacle to the recognition and adjustment of group differences.[28]

Weighted down by their doctrines as well as by an unwillingness to alienate elements of their heterogeneous coalitions, both parties floundered in attempting to deal with these problems. The Democrats were merely more conspicuous in failing than were the Republicans. Blatantly divided into two wings, neither of which succeeded in coming to grips with the new issues, the Democrats blazoned their perplexity by nominating Bryan for president for a second time in 1900, abandoning him for the conservative Alton B. Parker in 1904, and then returning to the Great Commoner (who was having trouble deciding whether to stand for nationalizing the railroads) in 1908. The Republicans, for their part, were only a little less contradictory in moving from McKinley to Roosevelt to Taft. Roosevelt, moreover, for all of the excitement he brought to the presidency in 1901, veered wildly in

28. For a discussion of the major parties' ideological beliefs, see Robert Kelley, "Ideology and Political Culture from Jefferson to Nixon," *American Historical Review*, 82 (1977): 531–62. And, for a brilliant account of the resistance to change, see Keller, *Affairs of State*.

his approach to the problems of big business during his first term—from "publicity" to trust-busting to jawboning to conspiring with the House of Morgan.[29]

While the national leaders wavered and confidence in the parties waned, a good deal of experimenting went on in the cities and states—much of it haphazard and unsuccessful. Every large city found it difficult to obtain cheap and efficient utilities, equitable taxes, and the variety of public services required by an expanding, hetereogeneous population. A few, notably Detroit and later Cleveland and New York, made adjustments during the last years of the nineteenth and the first years of the twentieth century that other cities later copied: the adoption of restrictions on utility and transportation franchises, the imposition of new taxes on intangible personalty, and the inauguration of innovative municipal services. But most cities were less successful in aligning governance with industrialism. Utility regulation was a particularly difficult problem. Franchise "grabs" agreed to by city councilmen came under increasing attack, but the chaotic competition between divergent theories of regulation (home rule versus state supervision versus municipal ownership) caused the continuance of poor public policy.[30] In the states, too, the late 1890s and early 1900s were years of experimentation with various

29. On the Democratic party's doctrinal floundering in these years, see J. Rogers Hollingsworth, *The Whirligig of Politics: The Democracy of Cleveland and Bryan* (New York, 1963). For the Republican side of the story, see Nathaniel W. Stephenson, *Nelson W. Aldrich: A Leader in American Politics* (New York, 1930); and John M. Blum, *The Republican Roosevelt* (Cambridge, Mass., 1954). Roosevelt's doctrinal uncertainties can be traced in his annual messages as president; see Hermann Hagedorn, ed., *The Works of Theodore Roosevelt, Memorial Edition*, 17 (New York, 1925): 93–641. For a recent treatment of these matters, see Lewis L. Gould, *Reform and Regulation: American Politics, 1900–1916* (New York, 1978).

30. Melvin G. Holli, *Reform in Detroit: Hazen S. Pingree and Urban Politics* (New York, 1969); Martin J. Schiesl, *The Politics of Efficiency: Municipal Administration and Reform in America, 1880–1920* (Berkeley and Los Angeles, 1977); Mowry, *The Era of Theodore Roosevelt, 1900–1912*, 59–67; Thelen, *The New Citizenship*, 130–201; and David Nord, "The Experts versus the Experts: Conflicting Philosophies of Municipal Utility Regulation in the Progressive Era," *Wisconsin Magazine of History*, 58 (1975): 219–36.

methods of regulation and administration. What Gerald D. Nash has found for California seems to have been true elsewhere as well: the state's railroad commission "floundered" in the late nineteenth century due to ignorance, inexperience, and a lack of both manpower and money. These were, Nash says, times of "trial and error." Antitrust policy also illuminates the uncertainty that was characteristic of the period before about 1905. By the turn of the century, two-thirds of the states had already passed antitrust laws, but in the great majority the provisions for enforcement were negligible. Some states simply preferred encouraging business to restraining it; others felt that the laxity of neighboring states and of the federal government made antitrust action futile; still others saw their enforcement policies frustrated by court decisions and administrative weaknesses. The result was unsuccessful policy—and a consequent failure to relieve the crisis that large-scale industrialization presented to nineteenth-century politics and government.[31]

In September 1899, that failure was searchingly probed at a conference on trusts held under the auspices of the Chicago Civic Federation. Attended by a broad spectrum of the country's political figures and economic thinkers, the meeting's four days of debates and speeches amply expressed the agitation, the uncertainty, and the discouragement engendered by the nation's search for solutions to the problems caused by large business combinations. In exploring whether and to what extent the government should regulate corporations and how to adjust social-group differences, the speakers addressed basic questions about the nineteenth-century American polity.[32] Following the conference, the

---

31. Nash, "The California Railroad Commission, 1876–1911," *Southern California Quarterly,* 44 (1962): 293, 303; Harry L. Purdy et al., *Corporate Concentration and Public Policy* (2d ed., New York, 1950), 317–22; Hans B. Thorelli, *The Federal Antitrust Policy: Origination of an American Tradition* (Baltimore, 1955), 155–56, 265, 352–55, 607; and William Letwin, *Law and Economic Policy in America: The Evolution of the Sherman Antitrust Act* (New York, 1965), 182–247.

32. Civic Federation of Chicago, *Chicago Conference on Trusts* (Chicago, 1900).

search for answers continued unabated, for there was little consensus and considerable resistance to change. In the years immediately following, pressure to do *something* mounted. And roughly by the middle of the next decade, many of the elements were in place for a blaze of political innovation. The spark that finally served to ignite them was a series of disclosures reawakening and refashioning the old fear that privileged business corrupted politics and government.

The evidence concerning these disclosures is familiar to students of progressivism, but its meaning has not been fully explored. The period 1904–08 comprised the muckraking years, not only in national magazines but also in local newspapers and legislative halls across the country. During 1905 and 1906 in particular, a remarkable number of cities and states experienced wrenching moments of discovery that led directly to significant political changes. Usually, a scandal, an investigation, an intraparty battle, or a particularly divisive election campaign exposed an illicit alliance of politics and business and made corruption apparent to the community, affecting party rhetoric, popular expectations, electoral behavior, and government policies.[33]

Just before it exploded in city and state affairs, business corruption of politics had already emerged as a leading theme of the new magazine journalism created by the muckrakers. Their primary contribution was to give a national audience the first systematic accounts of how modern American society operated. In so doing, journalists like Steffens, Baker, Russell, and Phillips created insights and pioneered ways of describing social and political relationships that crucially affected how people saw things in their home towns and states. Since so many of the

33. For other analyses that indicate the importance of the year 1906 in state politics around the country, see Richard M. Abrams, *Conservatism in a Progressive Era: Massachusetts Politics, 1900–1912* (Cambridge, Mass., 1964), 131; and Dewey W. Grantham, Jr., "The Progressive Era and the Reform Tradition," *Mid-America*, 46 (1964), 233–35.

muckrakers' articles identified the widespread tendency for privilege-seeking businessmen to bribe legislators, conspire with party leaders, and control nominations, an awareness of such corruption soon entered local politics. Indeed, many of the muckraking articles concerned particular locales—including Steffens's early series on the cities (1902-03); his subsequent exposures of Missouri, Illinois, Wisconsin, Rhode Island, New Jersey, and Ohio (1904-05); Rudolph Blankenburg's articles on Pennsylvania (1905); and C. P. Connolly's treatment of Montana (1906). All of these accounts featured descriptions of politico-business corruption, as did many of the contemporaneous exposures of individual industries, such as oil, railroads, and meat-packing. Almost immediately after this literature began to flourish, citizens across the country discovered local examples of the same corrupt behavior that Steffens and the others had described elsewhere.[34]

In New York, the occasion was the 1905 legislative investigation of the life insurance industry. One by one, insurance executives and Republican politicians took the witness stand and were compelled to bare the details of their corrupt relations. The companies received legislative protection, and the Republicans got bribes and campaign funds. In California, the graft trials of San Francisco city officials, beginning in 1906, threw light on the illicit cooperation between businessmen and public officials.

34. The fullest treatment of the muckrakers is still Louis Filler's *The Muckrakers*, a new and enlarged edition of his *Crusaders for American Liberalism* (University Park, Pa., 1976). Filler's chronology provides a convenient list of the major muckraking articles; *ibid.*, 417-24. Steffens's initial series on the cities was published as *The Shame of the Cities* (New York, 1904). His subsequent articles on the states appeared in *McClure's Magazine* between April 1904 and July 1905; these essays were later published as *The Struggle for Self-Government* (New York, 1906). Blankenburg's articles on Pennsylvania appeared in *The Arena* between January and June 1905; Connolly's "The Story of Montana" was published in *McClure's Magazine* between August and December 1906. Other major magazine articles probing politico-business corruption include "The Confessions of a Commercial Senator," *World's Work*, April–May 1905; Charles Edward Russell, "The Greatest Trust in the World" [the meat-packing industry], *Everybody's Magazine*, 1905; and David Graham Phillips, "The Treason of the Senate," *Cosmopolitan Magazine*, 1906.

Boss Abraham Ruef had delivered special privileges to public utility corporations in return for fees, of which he kept some and used the rest to bribe members of the city's Board of Supervisors. San Francisco's awakening revitalized reform elsewhere in California, and the next year insurgent Republicans formally organized to combat their party's alliance with the Southern Pacific Railroad. In Vermont, the railroad commissioners charged the 1906 legislature with yielding "supinely to the unfortunate influence of railroad representatives." Then the legislature investigated and found that the commissioners themselves were corrupt![35]

Other states, in all parts of the country, experienced their own versions of these events during 1905 and 1906. In South Dakota, as in a number of midwestern states, hostility to railroad influence in politics—by means of free passes and a statewide network of paid henchmen—was the issue around which insurgent Republicans coalesced against the regular machine. Some of those who joined the opposition did so purely from expediency; but their charges of corruption excited the popular imagination, and they captured the state in 1906 with pledges of electoral reform and business regulation. Further west Denver's major utilities, including the Denver Tramway Company and the Denver Gas and Electric Company, applied for new franchises in 1906, and these applications went before the voters at the spring elections. When the franchises all narrowly carried, opponents of the companies produced evidence that the Democratic and Republican parties had obtained fraudulent votes for the utilities. The case made its way through the courts during the next several months, and, although they ultimately lost, Colorado's nascent progres-

35. Robert F. Wesser, *Charles Evans Hughes: Politics and Reform in New York, 1905–1910* (Ithaca, 1967), 18–69; Richard L. McCormick, *From Realignment to Reform: Political Change in New York State, 1893–1910* (Ithaca, 1981), chap. 7; George E. Mowry, *The California Progressives* (Berkeley and Los Angeles, 1951), 23–85; Spencer C. Olin, Jr., *California's Prodigal Sons: Hiram Johnson and the Progressives, 1911–1917* (Berkeley and Los Angeles, 1968), 1–19; Winston Allen Flint, *The Progressive Movement in Vermont* (Washington, 1941), 42–51; and the *Tenth Biennial Report of the Board of Railroad Commissioners of the State of Vermont* (Bradford, Vt., 1906), 25.

sives derived an immense boost from the well-publicized judicial battle. As a result, the focus of reform shifted to the state. Dissidents in the Republican party organized to demand direct primary nominations and a judiciary untainted by corporate influence. These questions dominated Colorado's three-way gubernatorial election that fall.[36]

To the south, in Alabama, Georgia, and Mississippi, similar accusations of politico-business corruption were heard that same year, only in a different regional accent. In Alabama, Braxton Bragg Comer rode the issue from his position on the state's railroad commission to the governorship. His "main theme," according to Sheldon Hackney, "was that the railroads had for years deprived the people of Alabama of their right to rule their own state and that the time had come to free the people from alien and arbitrary rule." Mississippi voters heard similar rhetoric from Governor James K. Vardaman in his unsuccessful campaign against John Sharp Williams for a seat in the U. S. Senate. Georgia's Tom Watson conjured up some inane but effective imagery to illustrate how Vardaman's opponent would serve the business interests: "If the Hon. John Sharp Williams should win out in the fight with Governor Vardaman, the corporations would have just one more doodle-bug in the United States Senate. Every time that a Railroad lobbyist stopped over the hole and called 'Doodle, Doodle, Doodle'—soft and slow—the sand at the little end of the funnel would be seen to stir, and then the little head of J. Sharp would pop up." In Watson's own state, Hoke Smith trumpeted the issue, too, in 1905 and 1906.[37]

36. Herbert S. Schell, *History of South Dakota* (Lincoln, Neb., 1961), 258-61; Fred Greenbaum, "The Colorado Progressives in 1906," *Arizona and the West*, 7 (1965): 21-32; and Carl Abbott, *Colorado: A History of the Centennial State* (Boulder, 1976), 203-6.

37. Hackney, *Populism to Progressivism in Alabama*, 257; Watson's *Weekly Jeffersonian*, July 25, 1907, as quoted in William F. Holmes, *The White Chief: James Kimble Vardaman* (Baton Rouge, 1970), 184; Dewey W. Grantham, Jr., *Hoke Smith and the Politics of the New South* (Baton Rouge, 1958), 131-46; and C. Vann Woodward, *Origins of the New South, 1877-1913* (Baton Rouge, 1951), 369-95.

New Hampshire, Rhode Island, New Jersey, Pennsylvania, Ohio, Indiana, North Dakota, Nebraska, Texas, and Montana, among other states, also had their muckraking moments during these same years. Although the details varied from place to place, there were three basic routes by which the issue of politico-business corruption entered state politics. In some states, including New York, Colorado, and California, a legislative investigation or judicial proceeding captured attention by uncovering a fresh scandal or by unexpectedly focusing public attention on a recognized political sore. Elsewhere, as in New Hampshire, South Dakota, and Kansas, a factional battle in the dominant Republican party inspired dissidents to drag their opponents' misdeeds into public view; in several southern states, the Democrats divided in similar fashion, and each side told tales of the other's corruption by business interests. Finally, city politics often became a vehicle for spreading the issue of a politico-business alliance to the state. Philadelphia, Jersey City, Cincinnati, Denver, and San Francisco all played the role of inspiring state reform movements based on this issue. Some states took more than one of these three routes; and the politicians and reformers in a few states simply echoed what their counterparts elsewhere were saying without having any outstanding local stimulus for doing so. This pattern is, of course, not perfect. In Wisconsin and Oregon, the discovery of politico-business corruption came earlier than 1905–06; in Virginia its arrival engendered almost no popular excitement, while it scarcely got to Massachusetts at all.[38]

38. Geoffrey Blodgett, "Winston Churchill: The Novelist as Reformer," *New England Quarterly*, 47 (1974): 495–517; Thomas Agan, "The New Hampshire Progressives: Who and What Were They?" *Historical New Hampshire*, 34 (1979): 32–53; Charles Carroll, *Rhode Island: Three Centuries of Democracy*, 2 (New York, 1932): 676–78; Erwin L. Levine, *Theodore Francis Green: The Rhode Island Years, 1906–36* (Providence, 1963), 1–19; Arthur S. Link, *Wilson: The Road to the White House* (Princeton, 1947), 133–40; Ransom E. Noble, Jr., *New Jersey Progressivism before Wilson* (Princeton, 1946), 24–81; Eugene M. Tobin, "The Progressive as Politician: Jersey City, 1896–1907," *New Jersey History*, 91 (1973): 5–23; Lloyd M. Abernethy, "Insurgency in Philadelphia, 1905," *Pennsylvania Magazine of History and Biography*, 87 (1963): 3–20; Hoyt Landon Warner,

An anonymous Kansan, whose state became aware of business domination of its politics and government in 1905 and 1906, later gave a description of the discovery that also illuminates what happened elsewhere. When he first entered politics in the 1890s, the Kansan recalled, "three great railroad systems governed" the state. "This was a matter of common knowledge, but nobody objected or was in any way outraged by it." Then "an awakening began" during Roosevelt's first term as president, due to his "hammering on the square deal" and to a growing resentment of discriminatory railroad rates. Finally, after the railroads succeeded in using their political influence to block rate reform, "it began to dawn upon me," the Kansan reported, "that the railway contributions to campaign funds were part of the general game. . . . I saw they were in politics so that they could run things as they pleased." He and his fellow citizens had "really been converted," he declared. "We have got our eyes open now. . . . We have seen that the old sort of politics was used to promote all sorts of private ends, and we have got the idea now that the new politics can be used to promote the general welfare."[39]

State party platforms provide further evidence of the awakening to politico-business corruption. In Iowa, to take a midwest-

---

Progressivism in Ohio, 1897–1917 (Columbus, 1964), 143–210; Clifton J. Phillips, *Indiana in Transition: The Emergence of an Industrial Commonwealth, 1880–1920* (Indianapolis, 1968), 93–100; Charles N. Glaab, "The Failure of North Dakota Progressivism," *Mid-America*, 39 (1957): 195–209; James C. Olson, *History of Nebraska* (Lincoln, Neb., 1955), 250–53; Alwyn Barr, *Reconstruction to Reform: Texas Politics, 1876–1906* (Austin, 1971), 229–42; Michael P. Malone and Richard B. Roeder, *Montana: A History of Two Centuries* (Seattle, 1976), 196–99; Robert S. Maxwell, *La Follette and the Rise of the Progressives in Wisconsin* (Madison, Wis., 1956); Herbert F. Margulies, *The Decline of the Progressive Movement in Wisconsin, 1890–1920* (Madison, Wis., 1968); Raymond H. Pulley, *Old Virginia Restored: An Interpretation of the Progressive Impulse, 1870–1930* (Charlottesville, 1968); and Abrams, *Conservatism in a Progressive Era.*

39. "How I Was Converted—Politically: By a Kansas Progressive Republican," *Outlook*, 96 (1910): 857–59. Also see Robert Sherman La Forte, *Leaders of Reform: Progressive Republicans in Kansas, 1900–1916* (Lawrence, Kansas, 1974), 13–88.

ern state, charges of corporation influence in politics were almost entirely confined to the minor parties during the years from 1900 to 1904. Prohibitionists believed that the liquor industry brought political corruption, while Socialists felt that the powers of government belonged to the capitalists. For their part, the Democrats and Republicans saw little of this—until 1906, when both major parties gushed in opposition to what the Republicans now called "the denomination of corporate influences in public affairs." The Democrats agreed: "We favor the complete elimination of railway and other public service corporations from the politics of the state." In Missouri, a different but parallel pattern emerges from the platforms. There, what had been a subordinate theme of the Democratic party (and minor parties) in 1900 and 1902 became of central importance to both parties in 1904 and 1906. The Democrats now called "the eradication of bribery" the "paramount issue" in the state and declared opposition to campaign contributions "by great corporations and by those interested in special industries enjoying special privileges under the law." In New Hampshire, where nothing had been said of politico-business corruption in 1900 and 1904, both major parties wrote platforms in 1906 that attacked the issuance of free transportation passes and the prevalence of corrupt legislative lobbies. Party platforms in other states also suggest how suddenly major-party politicians discovered that business corrupted politics.[40]

40. *The Iowa Official Register for the Years 1907–1908* (Des Moines, 1907), 389, 393; *Official Manual of the State of Missouri for the Years 1905–1906* (Jefferson City, Mo., 1905), 254; and *Official Manual of the State of Missouri for the Years 1907–1908* (Jefferson City, Mo., 1907), 365. Also see State of New Hampshire, *Manual for the General Court, 1907* (Concord, N.H., 1907), 611–63. State party platforms for the early 1900s are surprisingly hard to locate. For some states, particularly in the Northeast and Midwest, the platforms were printed in the annual legislative manuals and blue books, but otherwise they must be found in newspapers. Of the ten states—Iowa, Missouri, New Hampshire, New York, New Jersey, Indiana, Pennsylvania, Illinois, Wisconsin, and South Dakota—for which I was able to survey the party platforms of 1900–1910 fairly completely (using the manuals, supplemented when necessary by newspapers), only two fail to support the generalization given here: Wisconsin, where an awareness of

The annual messages of the state governors from 1902 to 1908 point to the same pattern. In the first three years, the chief executives almost never mentioned the influence of business in politics. Albert Cummins of Iowa was exceptional; as early as 1902 he declared, "Corporations have, and ought to have, many privileges, but among them is not the privilege to sit in political conventions or occupy seats in legislative chambers." Then in 1905, governors across the Midwest suddenly let loose denunciations of corporate bribery, lobbying, campaign contributions, and free passes. Nebraska's John H. Mickey was typical in attacking "the onslaught of private and corporation lobbyists who seek to accomplish pernicious ends by the exercise of undue influence." Missouri's Joseph W. Folk advised that "all franchises, rights and privileges secured by bribery should be declared null and void." By 1906, 1907, and 1908, such observations and recommendations were common to the governors of every region. In 1907 alone, no less than nineteen state executives called for the regulation of lobbying, while a similar number advised the abolition of free passes.[41]

What is the meaning of this awakening to something that Americans had, in a sense, known about all along? Should we accept the originality of the "discovery" that monied interests endangered free government or lay stress instead on the familiar elements the charge contained? It had, after all, been a part of

---

politico-business corruption was demonstrated in the platforms of 1900 and 1902 as well as those of later years; and New Jersey, where the Democrats used the issue sparingly in 1901 and 1904, while the Republicans almost completely ignored it throughout the decade.

41. New York State Library, *Digest of Governors' Messages* (Albany, N. Y., 1903–09). This annual document, published for the years 1902–08, classifies the contents of the governors' messages by subject and permits easy comparison among them. For Mickey's and Folk's denunciations, see New York State Library, *Digest of Governors' Messages, 1905*, classifications 99 (legislative lobbying), 96 (legislative bribery).

American political thought since the eighteenth century and had been powerfully repeated, in one form or another, by major and minor figures throughout the nineteenth century. According to Richard Hofstadter, "there was nothing new in the awareness of these things."[42] In fact, however, there was much that was new. First, many of the details of politico-business corruption had never been publicly revealed before. No one had ever probed the subject as thoroughly as journalists and legislative investigators were now doing, and, moreover, some of the practices they uncovered had only recently come into being. Large-scale corporation campaign contributions, for instance, were a product of the 1880s and 1890s. Highly organized legislative lobbying operations by competing interest groups represented an even more recent development. In his systematic study of American legislative practices, published in 1907, Paul S. Reinsch devoted a lengthy chapter to describing how business interests had developed a new and "far more efficient system of dealing with legislatures than [the old methods of] haphazard corruption."[43]

Even more startling than the new practices themselves was the fresh meaning they acquired from the nationwide character of the patterns that were now disclosed. The point is not simply that more people than ever before became aware of politico-business corruption but that the perception of such a national pattern itself created new political understandings. Lincoln Steffens's autobiography is brilliant on this point. As Steffens acknowledged, much of the corruption he observed in his series on the "shame" of the cities had already come to light locally before he reported it to a national audience. What he did was take the facts in city after city, apply imagination to their transcription, and form a new truth by showing the same process at work

42. Hofstadter, *The Age of Reform*, 185.

43. Reinsch, *American Legislatures and Legislative Methods* (New York, 1907), 231. On the history of party campaign funds, see James K. Pollock, Jr., *Party Campaign Funds* (New York, 1926); Earl R. Sikes, *State and Federal Corrupt-Practices Legislation* (Durham, N.C., 1928); and Louise Overacker, *Money in Elections* (New York, 1932).

everywhere. Here was a solution to the problem the Adams brothers had encountered in writing *Chapters of Erie*: how to report shocking corruption without making it seem too astounding to be representative. The solution was breadth of coverage. Instead of looking at only two businessmen, study dozens; explore city after city and state after state and report the facts to a people who were vaguely aware of corruption in their own home towns but had never before seen that a single process was at work across the country.[44] This concept of a "process" of corruption was central to the new understanding. Uncovered through systematic journalistic research and probing legislative investigations, corruption was now seen to be the result of concrete historical developments. It could not just be dismissed as the product of misbehavior by "bad" men (although that kind of rhetoric continued too) but had to be regarded as an outcome of identifiable economic and political forces. In particular, corruption resulted from an outmoded policy of indiscriminate distribution, which could not safely withstand an onslaught of demands from private corporations that were larger than the government itself.[45]

Thus in its systematic character, as well as in its particular details, the corruption that Americans discovered in 1905 and 1906 was different from the kind their eighteenth- and nineteenth-century forebears had known. Compared with the eighteenth-century republican understanding, the progressive con-

---

44. Steffens later commented insightfully on his own (and, by implication, the country's) process of "discovery" during these years; see his *Autobiography*, 357–627. Also see his *Shame of the Cities*, 3–26; and Filler, *The Muckrakers*, 257–59.

45. Around 1905 a social-science literature emerged that attempted to explain the process of corruption and to suggest suitable remedies. In addition to Reinsch's *American Legislatures and Legislative Methods*, see Frederic C. Howe, *The City: The Hope of Democracy* (New York, 1905), and *Privilege and Democracy in America* (New York, 1910); and Robert C. Brooks, *Corruption in American Politics and Life* (New York, 1910). Several less scholarly works also analyze the cause of politico-business corruption; see, for example, George W. Berge, *The Free Pass Bribery System* (Lincoln, Neb., 1905); Philip Loring Allen, *America's Awakening: The Triumph of Righteousness in High Places* (New York, 1906); and William Allen White, *The Old Order Changeth: A View of American Democracy* (New York, 1910).

cept of corruption regarded the monied interests not as tools of a designing administration but as independent agents. If any branch of government was in alliance with them, it was probably the legislature. In a curious way, however, the old republican view that commerce inherently threatened the people's virtue still persisted, now informed by a new understanding of the actual process at work. Compared with Andrew Jackson, the progressives saw big corporations not as monsters but as products of social and industrial development. And their activist remedies differed entirely from his negativistic ones. But, like Jackson, those who now discovered corruption grasped that private interests could conflict with the public interest and that government benefits for some groups often hurt others. The recognition of these two things—both painfully at odds with the nineteenth century's conventional wisdom—had been at the root of the floundering over principles of political economy in the 1890s and early 1900s. Now, rather suddenly, the discovery that business corrupts politics suggested concrete answers to a people who were ready for new policies but had been uncertain how to get them or what exactly they should be.

Enacted in a burst of legislative activity immediately following the awakening of 1905 and 1906, the new policies brought to an end the paralysis that had gripped the polity and constituted a decisive break with nineteenth-century patterns of governance. Many states passed laws explicitly designed to curtail illicit business influence in politics. These included measures regulating legislative lobbying, prohibiting corporate campaign contributions, and outlawing the acceptance of free transportation passes by public officials. In 1903 and 1904, there had been almost no legislation on these three subjects; during 1905 and 1906, several states acted on each question; and, by 1907 and 1908, ten states passed lobbying laws, nineteen took steps to prevent corporate contributions, and fourteen acted on the question of passes (see Table 1). If these laws failed to wipe out corporation influence in politics, they at least curtailed important means through which businesses had exercised political power in the late nineteenth

Table 1   Selected Categories of State Legislation, 1903–08

Type of Legislation	1903–04	1905–06	1907–08	1903–08
Regulation of Lobbying	0	2	10	12
Prohibition of Corporate Campaign Contributions	0	3	19	22
Regulation or Prohibition of Free Railroad Passes for Public Officials	4	6	14	24
Mandatory Direct Primary	4	9	18	31
Regulation of Railroad Corporations by Commission	5	8	28	41
TOTALS	13	28	89	130

Note: Figures represent the number of states that passed legislation in the given category
     during the specified years.

Source: New York State Library, *Index of Legislation* (Albany, N.Y., 1904–09).

and early twentieth century. To be sure, other means were soon found, but the flood of state lawmaking on these subjects, together with the corresponding attention they received from the federal government in these same years, shows how prevalent was the determination to abolish existing forms of politico-business corruption.[46]

Closely associated with these three measures were two more important categories of legislation, often considered to represent the essence of progressivism in the states: mandatory direct primary laws and measures establishing or strengthening the regulation of utility and transportation corporations by commission. These types of legislation, too, reached a peak in the years just after 1905–06, when so many states had experienced a crisis dis-

46. The figures in this paragraph (and in the accompanying table) are based on an analysis of the yearly summaries of state legislation reported in New York State Library, *Index of Legislation* (Albany, N.Y., 1904–09). The laws included here are drawn from among those classified in categories 99 (lobbying), 154 (corporate campaign contributions), 1237 (free passes), 160 (direct nominations), and 1267, 1286 (transportation regulation). The legislative years are paired because so many state legislatures met only biennially, usually in the odd-numbered years; no state is counted more than once in any one category in any pair of years. The *Index of Legislation* should be used in conjunction with the accompanying annual *Review of Legislation* (Albany, N. Y., 1904–09).

closing the extent of politico-business corruption. Like the laws concerning lobbying, contributions, and passes, primary and regulatory measures were brought forth amidst intense public concern with business influence in politics and were presented by their advocates as remedies for that problem. Both types of laws had been talked about for years, but the disclosures of 1905–06 provided the catalyst for their enactment.

Even before 1905, the direct primary had already been adopted in some states. In Wisconsin, where it was approved in 1904, Robert M. La Follette had campaigned for direct nominations since the late 1890s on the grounds that they would "emancipate the legislature from all subserviency to the corporations." In his well-known speech, "The Menace of the Machine" (1897), La Follette explicitly offered the direct primary as "the remedy" for corporate control of politics. Now, after the awakening of 1905–06, that same argument inspired many states that had failed to act before to adopt mandatory direct primary laws (see Table 1). In New York, Charles Evans Hughes, who was elected governor in 1906 because of his role as chief counsel in the previous year's life insurance investigation, argued that the direct primary would curtail the power of the special interests. "Those interests," he declared, "are ever at work stealthily and persistently endeavoring to pervert the government to the service of their own ends. All that is worst in our public life finds its readiest means of access to power through the control of the nominating machinery of parties." In other states, too, in the years after 1905–06, the direct primary was urged and approved for the same reasons that La Follette and Hughes advanced it.[47]

47. Ellen Torelle, comp., *The Political Philosophy of Robert M. La Follette* (Madison, Wis., 1920), 28; and Hughes, *Public Papers of Charles E. Hughes, Governor, 1909* (Albany, 1910), 37. Also see Maxwell, *La Follette and the Rise of the Progressives*, 13, 27–35, 48–50, 53–54, 74; Allen Fraser Lovejoy, *La Follette and the Establishment of the Direct Primary in Wisconsin, 1890–1904* (New Haven, 1941); Wesser, *Charles Evans Hughes*, 250–301; Direct Primaries Association of the State of New York, *Direct Primary Nominations: Why Voters Demand Them. Why Bosses Oppose Them* (New York, 1909); Ralph Simpson Boots, *The Direct Primary in New Jersey* (New York, 1917), 59–70; Grantham, *Hoke Smith*

The creation of effective regulatory boards—progressivism's most distinctive governmental achievement—also followed upon the discovery of politico-business corruption. From 1905 to 1907 alone, fifteen new state railroad commissions were established, and at least as many existing boards were strengthened. Most of the new commissions were "strong" ones, having rate-setting powers and a wide range of administrative authority to supervise service, safety, and finance. In the years to come, many of them extended their jurisdiction to other public utilities, including gas, electricity, telephones, and telegraphs. Direct legislative supervision of business corporations was also significantly expanded in these years. Life insurance companies—whose corruption of the New York State government Hughes had dramatically disclosed—provide one example. "In 1907," as a result of Hughes's investigation and several others conducted in imitation of it, Morton Keller has reported, "forty-two state legislatures met; thirty considered life insurance legislation; twenty-nine passed laws. . . . By 1908 . . . [the basic] lines of twentieth century life insurance supervision were set, and thereafter only minor adjustments occurred." The federal regulatory machinery, too, was greatly strengthened at this time, most notably by the railroad, meat inspection, and food and drug acts of 1906.[48]

The adoption of these measures marked the moment of transition from a structure of economic policy based largely on the allocation of resources and benefits to one in which regulation and administration played permanent and significant roles. Not confined for long to the transportation, utility, and insurance

---

and the Politics of the New South, 158, 162, 172–73, 178, 193; Schell, *History of South Dakota*, 260; Olin, *California's Prodigal Sons*, 13; and Charles Edward Merriam and Louise Overacker, *Primary Elections* (Chicago, 1928), 4–7, 60–66.

48. Huebner, "Five Years of Railroad Regulation by the States"; Robert Emmett Ireton, "The Legislatures and the Railroads," *Review of Reviews*, 36 (1907): 217–20; and Keller, *The Life Insurance Enterprise, 1885–1910: A Study in the Limits of Corporate Power* (Cambridge, Mass., 1963), 257, 259. The manner in which the states copied each other's legislation in this period is a subject deserving of study; for a suggestive approach, see Jack L. Walker, "The Diffusion of Innovations among the American States," *APSR*, 63 (1969): 880–99.

companies that formed its most immediate objects, regulatory policies soon were extended to other industries as well. Sometimes the legislative branch took responsibility for the ongoing tasks of supervision and administration, but more commonly they became the duty of independent boards and commissions, staffed by experts and entrusted with significant powers of oversight and enforcement. Certainly, regulation was not previously unknown, nor did promoting commerce and industry now cease to be a governmental purpose. But the middle years of the first decade of the twentieth century unmistakably mark a turning point—that point when the direction shifted, when the weight of opinion changed, when the forces of localism and opposition to governmental authority that had sustained the distribution of privileges but opposed regulation and administration now lost the upper hand to the forces of centralization, bureaucratization, and government actions to recognize and adjust group differences. Besides economic regulation, other governmental policy areas, including health, education, taxation, correction, and the control of natural resources, increasingly came under the jurisdiction of independent boards and commissions. The establishment of these agencies and the expansion of their duties meant that American governance in the twentieth century was significantly different from what it had been in the nineteenth.[49]

The developments of 1905–08 also changed the nature of political participation in the United States. Parties emerged from the years of turmoil altered and, on balance, less important vehicles of popular expression than they had been. The disclosures of politico-business wrongdoing disgraced the regular party organizations, and many voters showed their loss of faith by staying at home on election day or by casting split tickets. These trends had been in progress before 1905–06—encouraged by new election laws as well as by the crisis of confidence in traditional politics

49. Among the best accounts of this transformation in policy are Herbert Croly, *Marcus Alonzo Hanna: His Life and Work* (New York, 1912), 465–79; Hurst, *Law and the Conditions of Freedom*, 71–108; and Wiebe, *The Search for Order, 1877–1920*, 164–95.

and government—but in several ways the discovery of corruption strengthened them. Some reigning party organizations were toppled by the disclosures, and the insurgents who came to power lacked the old bosses' experience and inclination when it came to rallying the electorate. The legal prohibition of corporate campaign contributions now meant, moreover, that less money was available for pre-election entertainment, transportation to the polls, and bribes.[50]

While the party organizations were thus weakened, they were also more firmly embedded in the legal machinery of elections than ever before. In many states the direct primary completed a series of new election laws (beginning with the Australian ballot in the late 1880s and early 1890s) that gave the parties official status as nominating bodies, regulated their practices, and converted them into durable, official bureaucracies. Less popular now but also more respectable, the party organizations surrendered to state regulation and relinquished much of their ability to

50. The causes of the decline in party voting have been the subject of considerable debate and disagreement among political scientists and historians in recent years. Walter Dean Burnham began the controversy when he first described the early twentieth-century changes in voting behavior and explained them by suggesting that an antipartisan industrial elite had captured the political system after the realignment of the 1890s; "Changing Shape of the American Political Universe." Jerrold G. Rusk and Philip E. Converse responded by contending that legal-institutional factors could better account for the behavioral changes that Burnham had observed; Rusk, "The Effect of the Australian Ballot Reform on Split Ticket Voting"; and Converse, "Change in the American Electorate," in Angus Campbell and Philip E. Converse, eds., *The Human Meaning of Social Change* (New York, 1972), 263–337. All three political scientists carried the debate forward—and all withdrew a bit from their original positions—in the September 1974 issue of the *American Political Science Review*. At present, the weight of developing evidence seems to indicate that, while new election laws alone cannot explain the voters' changed behavior, Burnham's notion of an elite takeover after 1896 is also inadequate to account for what happened; McCormick, *From Realignment to Reform*, chap. 9. What I am suggesting here is that the shock given to party politics by the awakening of 1905–06 played an important part in solidifying the new tendencies toward lower rates of voter participation and higher levels of ticket-splitting. On the relative scarcity of campaign funds in the election of 1908, see Pollock, *Party Campaign Funds*, 37, 66–67; Overacker, *Money in Elections*, 234–38; and Brooks, *Corruption in American Politics and Life*, 234–35.

express community opinion in return for legal guarantees that they alone would be permanently certified to place nominees on the official ballot.[51]

Interest organizations took over much of the parties' old job of articulating popular demands and pressing them upon the government. More exclusive and single-minded than parties, the new organizations became regular elements of the polity. Their right to represent their members before the government's new boards and agencies received implicit recognition, and, indeed, the commissions in some cases became captives of the groups they were supposed to regulate. The result was a fairly drastic transformation of the rules of political participation: who could compete, the kinds of resources required, and the rewards of participation all changed. These developments were not brand new in the first years of the twentieth century, but, like the contemporaneous changes in government policy, they derived impressive, decisive confirmation from the political upheaval that occurred between 1905 and 1908.

Political and governmental changes thus followed upon the discovery that business corrupts politics. And Americans of the day explicitly linked the two developments: the reforms adopted in 1907–08 were to remedy the ills uncovered in 1905–06. But these chronological and rhetorical connections between discovery and reform do not fully explain the relationship between them. Why, having paid relatively little heed to similar charges before, did people now take such strong actions in response to the disclosures? Why, moreover, did the perception of wrongdoing precipitate the particular pattern of responses that it did—namely, the triumph of bureaucracy and organization? Of most importance,

---

51. Peter H. Argersinger, "'A Place on the Ballot': Fusion Politics and Antifusion Laws," *American Historical Review*, 85 (1980): 287–306; Merriam and Overacker, *Primary Elections*; and William Mills Ivins, *On the Electoral System of the State of New York* (Albany, 1906).

what distinctive effects did the discovery of corruption have upon the final outcome of the crisis?

By 1905 a political explosion of some sort was likely, due to the accumulated frustrations people felt about the government's failure to deal with the problems of industrialization. So combustible were the elements present that another spark besides the discovery of politico-business corruption might well have ignited them. But the recognition of such corruption was an especially effective torch. Upon close analysis, its ignition of the volatile political mass is unsurprising. The accusations made in 1905–06 were serious, widespread, and full of damaging information; they explained the actual corrupt process behind a danger that Americans had historically worried about, if not always responded to with vigor; they linked in dark scandal the two main villains— party bosses and big businessmen—already on the American scene; they inherently discredited the existing structure of economic policy based on the distribution of privileges; and they dramatically suggested the necessity for new kinds of politics and government. That businessmen systematically corrupted politics was incendiary knowledge; given the circumstances of 1905, it could hardly have failed to set off an explosion.

The organizational results that followed, however, seem less inevitable. There were, after all, several other known ways of curtailing corruption besides expert regulation and administration. For one, there was the continued reliance on direct legislative action against the corruption of politics by businessmen. The lobbying, anti-free pass, and campaign-contribution measures of 1907–08 exemplified this approach. So did the extension of legislative controls over the offending corporations. Such measures were familiar, but obviously they were considered inadequate to the crisis at hand. A second approach, favored by Edward Alsworth Ross and later by Woodrow Wilson, was to hold business leaders personally responsible for their "sins" and to punish them accordingly. There were a few attempts to bring individuals to justice, but, because of the inadequacy of the criminal statutes, the skill of high-priced lawyers, and the public's lack of appetite for personal vendettas, few sinners were jailed. Finally, there were proposals for large structural solutions changing the political and economic environment so that the old corrupt practices became impossible. Some men, like Frederic C. Howe, still advocated the single tax and the abolition of all privileges granted by government.[52] Many more believed in the municipal ownership of public utilities. Hundreds of thousands (to judge from election returns) favored socialist solutions, but most Americans did not. In their response to politico-business corruption, they went beyond existing legislative remedies and avoided the temptation to personalize all the blame, but they fell short of wanting socialism, short even of accepting the single tax.

Regulation and administration represented a fourth available approach. Well before the discoveries of 1905–06, groups who stood to benefit from governmental control of utility and transportation corporations had placed strong regulatory proposals on the political agendas of the states and the nation. In other policy areas, the proponents of an administrative approach had not advanced that far prior to 1905–06, but theirs was a large and growing movement, supported—as recent historians have shown—by many different groups for varied, often contradictory, reasons.[53] The popular awakening to corruption increased the opportunity of these groups to obtain enactment of their measures. Where their proposals met the particular political needs of 1905–08, they succeeded most quickly. Regulation by commis-

52. Ross, *Sin and Society: An Analysis of Latter-Day Iniquity* (Boston, 1907); John M. Blum, *Woodrow Wilson and the Politics of Morality* (Boston, 1956); John B. Roberts, "The Real Cause of Municipal Corruption," in Clinton Rogers Woodruff, ed., *Proceedings of the New York Conference for Good City Government*, National Municipal League publication (Philadelphia, 1905), 148–53; and Howe, *Privilege and Democracy in America*.

53. For an astute analysis of which groups favored and which groups opposed federal railroad legislation, see Richard H. K. Vietor, "Businessmen and the Political Economy: The Railroad Rate Controversy of 1905," *JAH*, 64 (1977): 47–66; and, for an excellent survey of the literature on regulation, see Thomas K. McCraw, "Regulation in America: A Review Article," *Business History Review*, 49 (1975): 159–83. The best account of the emergence of administrative ideas is, of course, Wiebe, *The Search for Order, 1877–1920*, 133–95.

sions seemed to be an effective way to halt corruption by transferring the responsibility for business-government relations from
party bosses and legislators to impartial experts. That approach
also possessed the additional political advantages of appearing
sane and moderate, of meeting consumer demands for government protection, and, above all, of being sufficiently malleable
that a diversity of groups could be induced to anticipate favorable
results from the new policies.[54]

In consequence, the passions of 1905–06 added support to an
existing movement toward regulation and administration, enormously speeded it up, shaped the timing and form of its victory,
and probably made the organizational revolution more complete—certainly more sudden—than it otherwise would have
been. These accomplishments alone must make the discovery of
corruption pivotal in any adequate interpretation of progressivism. But the awakening did more than hurry along a movement
that already possessed formidable political strength and would
probably have triumphed eventually even without the events of
1905–06. By pushing the political process toward so quick a
resolution of the long-standing crisis over industrialism, the
passions of those years caused the outcome to be more conservative than it otherwise might have been. This is the ultimate irony
of the discovery that business corrupts politics.

Muckraking accounts of politico-business evils suggest one
reason for the discovery's conservative impact. Full of facts and
revelations, these writings were also dangerously devoid of effective solutions. Charles E. Russell's *Lawless Wealth* (1908)—
the title itself epitomizes the perceptions of 1905–06—illustrates
the flaw. Published orginally in *Everybody's Magazine* under
the accusatory title, "Where Did You Get It, Gentlemen?," the
book recounts numerous instances of riches obtained through the
corruption of politics but, in its closing pages, merely suggests

---

54. On the adaptability of administrative government, see Otis L. Graham,
Jr., *The Great Campaigns: Reform and War in America, 1900-1928* (Englewood
Cliffs, N.J., 1971), 50-51; and Wiebe, *The Search for Order, 1877-1920*, 222-23,
302.

that citizens recognize the evils and be determined to stop them. This reliance on trying to change how people felt (to "shame" them, in Steffens's phrase) was characteristic of muckraking and of the exposures of 1905–06. One can admire the muckrakers' reporting, can even accept David P. Thelen's judgment that their writing "contained at least as deep a moral revulsion toward capitalism and profit as did more orthodox forms of Marxism," yet can still feel that their proposed remedy was superficial. Because the perception of politico-business corruption carried no far-reaching solutions of its own or genuine economic grievances, but only a desire to clean up politics and government, the passions of 1905–06 were easily diverted to the support of other people's remedies, especially administrative answers. Had the muckrakers and their local imitators penetrated more deeply into the way that business operated and its real relationship to government, popular emotions might not have been so readily mobilized in support of regulatory and administrative agencies that business interests could often dominate. At the very least, there might have been a more determined effort to prevent the supervised corporations themselves from shaping the details of regulatory legislation. Thus, for all of their radical implications, the passions of 1905–06 dulled the capacity of ordinary people to get reforms in their own interest.[55]

The circumstances in which the discovery of corruption became a political force also assist in explaining its conservatism. The passions of 1905–06 were primarily expressed in state, rather than local or national, politics. Indeed, those passions often served to shift the focus of reform from the cities to the state capitals. There—in Albany, or Madison, or Sacramento—the remedies were worked out in relative isolation from the local, insurgent forces that had in many cases originally called attention to the evils. Usually the policy consequences were more

---

55. Russell, *Lawless Wealth: The Origin of Some Great American Fortunes* (New York, 1908), 30–35, 52–55, 274–79; and Thelen, "Lincoln Steffens and the Muckrakers: A Review Essay," *Wisconsin Magazine of History,* 58 (1975): 316.

favorable to large business interests than local solutions would have been. State utility boards, for example, which had always been considered more conservative in their policies than comparable local commissions, now took the regulatory power away from cities and foreclosed experimentation with such alternatives as municipal ownership or popularly chosen regulatory boards. In gaining a statewide hearing for reform, the accusations of politico-business corruption actually increased the likelihood that conservative solutions would be adopted.[56]

Considering the intensity of the feelings aroused in 1905 and 1906 and the catalytic political role they played, the awakened opposition to corruption was surprisingly short-lived. As early as 1907 and 1908, the years of the most significant state legislative responses to the discovery, the messages of the governors began to exhibit a more stylized, less passionate way of describing politico-business wrongdoing. Now the governors emphasized remedies rather than abuses, and most seemed confident that the remedies would work. Criticism of business influence in government continued to be a staple of political rhetoric throughout the Progressive era, but it ceased to have the intensity it did in 1905–06. In place of the burning attack on corruption, politicians offered advanced progressive programs, including further regulation and election-law reforms.[57] The deep concern with business corruption of politics and government thus waned. It had stirred people to consciousness of wrongdoing, crystallized their discontent with existing policies, and pointed toward concrete solutions for the ills of industrialism. But it had not sustained the more radical, anti-business possibilities suggested by the discoveries of 1905–06.

Indeed, the passions of those years probably weakened the

56. Nord, "The Experts versus the Experts"; and Thelen, *Robert M. La-Follette and the Insurgent Spirit*, 50–51.

57. New York State Library, *Digest of Governors' Messages, 1907, 1908.* In a number of states where politico-business corruption had been an issue in the party platforms around 1906, the platforms were silent on the subject by 1910.

insurgent, democratic qualities of the ensuing political transformation and strengthened its bureaucratic aspects. This result was ironical, but its causes were not conspiratorial. They lay instead in the tendency—shared by the muckrakers and their audience— to accept remedies unequal to the problems at hand and in political circumstances that isolated insurgents from decision-making. Once the changes in policy were under way after 1906, those organized groups whose interests were most directly affected entered the fray, jockeyed for position, and heavily shaped the outcomes. We do not yet know enough about how this happened, but studies such as Stanley P. Caine's examination of railroad regulation in Wisconsin suggest how difficult it was to translate popular concern on an "issue" into the details of a law.[58] It is hardly surprising that, as regulation and administration became accepted public functions, the affected interests exerted much more influence on policy than did those who cared most passionately about restoring clean government.

But the failure to pursue anti-business policies does not mean the outcry against corruption was either insincere or irrelevant. Quite the contrary. It was sufficiently genuine and widespread to dominate the nation's public life in 1905 and 1906 and to play a decisive part in bringing about the transformation of American politics and government. Political changes do not, of course, embrace everything that is meant by progressivism. Nor was the discovery that business corrupts politics the only catalytic agent

58. Caine, *The Myth of a Progressive Reform: Railroad Regulation in Wisconsin, 1903–1910* (Madison, Wis., 1970), 70. Also see Mansel G. Blackford, *The Politics of Business in California, 1890–1920* (Columbus, Ohio, 1977); Bruce W. Dearstyne, "Regulation in the Progressive Era: The New York Public Service Commission," *New York History*, 58 (1977): 331–47; and McCraw, "Regulation in America." These and other studies cast considerable doubt on the applicability at the state level of Gabriel Kolko's interpretation of regulatory legislation; for that position, see his *The Triumph of Conservatism*. Commonly, the affected interests opposed state regulation until its passage became inevitable, at which point they entered the contest in order to influence the details of the law. Businessmen often had considerable, but not complete, success in helping shape such legislation, and they frequently found it beneficial in practice.

at work; certainly the rise of consumer discontent with utility and transportation corporations and the vigorous impetus toward new policies given by Theodore Roosevelt during his second term as president played complementary roles. But the awakening to corruption—as it was newly understood—provided an essential dynamic, pushing the states and the nation toward what many of its leading men and women considered progressive reform.

The organizational thesis sheds much light on the values and methods of those who succeeded in dominating the new types of politics and government but very little on the political circumstances in which they came forward. Robert H. Wiebe, in particular, has downplayed key aspects of the political context, including the outcry against corruption. Local uprisings against the alliance of bosses and businessmen, Wiebe has stated, "lay outside the mainstream of progressivism"; measures instituting the direct primary and curtailing the political influence of business were "old-fashioned reform."[59] Yet those local crusades, by spreading the dynamic perception that business corrupts politics, created a popular demand for the regulatory and administrative measures that Wiebe has claimed are characteristic of true progressivism; and those "old-fashioned" laws were enacted amidst the same political furor that produced the stunningly rapid bureaucratic triumph whose significance for twentieth-century America Wiebe has explained so convincingly. What the organizational thesis mainly lacks is the sense that political action is open-ended and unpredictable. Consequences are often unexpected, outcomes surprising when matched against origins. While it is misleading, as Samuel P. Hays has said, to interpret progressivism solely on the basis of its anti-business ideology, it is equally misleading to fail to appreciate that reform gained decisive initial strength from ideas and feelings that were not able to sustain the movement in the end.[60] The farsighted organizers

59. Wiebe, *The Search for Order, 1877–1920*, 172, 180.
60. Hays, "The Politics of Reform in Municipal Government."

Index

Southern politics (*continued*)
  during the colonial era, 147
  during the nineteenth century, 105–8, 175, 203
  during the New Deal era, 183, 184
  during the Progressive era, 176–77, 223, 335
  See also the entries for individual southern states
Spanish-American War, 328
Spencerian determinism, 256
Split-ticket voting, 201, 222, 274, 290–91, 301, 319, 346
Spoils system
  See Patronage appointments
State constitutions, 151–52, 216
States' Rights ("Dixiecrat") party, 184
Statistics (science of), 271
Steffens, Lincoln, 311, 332, 333, 340–41, 352
Sterilization of the mentally defective, 282
Stevens, Thaddeus, 161
Stickney, Albert, 230–40, 242–59
Strong, William, 45
Suffrage requirements, 17, 158, 179, 223
Suggestions on Government (Moffett), 231–32
Sullivan, Mark, 299
Sunday observance, 39, 43, 45–46, 47, 48, 54, 56, 159
Sundquist, James L., 72
Swierenga, Robert P., 34, 44
Syracuse, 298

Taft, William H., 329
Tammany Hall, 45–46, 173, 298
Tariff issue, 37, 57, 58, 74, 82, 165, 173, 204, 208, 210, 215–16, 239, 328
Temperance issue
  See Liquor issue; Prohibition party
Tennessee, 161, 169
Texas, 336
Thelen, David P., 263, 352

"Theory of Critical Elections, A" (Key), 65–67, 77–78
Third parties, 8, 109, 136–37, 162–63, 171, 174–75, 179, 230, 326
  See also the entries for particular third parties
Third party system, 162, 200
Thompson, E. P., 98, 108
Thurmond, J. Strom, 184
Tilden, Samuel J., 323
Transportation Revolution, 120–21, 122, 128, 129, 158
Triangle Shirtwaist Company fire, 309
True Republic, A (Stickney), 231, 236, 239, 244
Truman, Harry S., 184
Tuberculosis, 280
Turner, Frederick Jackson, 8
Tweed, William Marcy, 173
Tweed Ring, 232
Two-partyism, 162

Unemployment, 187
Union party, 168
United States Congress, 72, 79, 156, 199, 301
United States Constitution, 151, 153–55
United States senators, 272
Urban party machines, 173, 184

Van Buren, Martin, 161, 162, 238
Van Wyck, Robert A., 298
Vardaman, James K., 335
Venereal disease, 280
Vermont, 104, 182, 334
Vietnam War, 186, 187, 188
Virginia, 104, 147, 149, 169, 336
Virginia dynasty, 161
Voter turnout
  during the colonial era, 149
  during the contemporary era, 186, 188
  during the early 1900s, 7, 21, 177, 179, 222–23, 274, 277, 290, 306, 310, 317, 319, 346–48